Sisterhood Questioned?

'Christine Bolt's elegantly conceived and crisply argued *Sisterhood Questioned?* is an outstanding contribution to women's history. Bolt confronts the fissures in the feminist movements in Britain and the United States and offers some informed conclusions about why, when, and even if sisterhood was questioned. The result is must reading.'

Jean H. Baker, *Goucher College*

Sisterhood Questioned? assesses the nature and impact of divisions in the twentieth-century American and British women's movements.

Until 1920, feminists had been united in the struggle for suffrage, and the sisterhood of women had been taken for granted. But after the end of the First World War, differences within and between the feminist movements became increasingly apparent, especially in the areas of race, class and internationalism.

In this lucidly written study, Christine Bolt sheds new light on these differences, which flourished in an era of political reaction, economic insecurity, polarising nationalism and resurgent anti-feminism. The author reveals how the conflicts were seized upon and publicised by contemporaries, and how the activists themselves were forced to confront the increasingly complex tensions. In particular, the American and British women's movements grew further apart as British women became more conscious of American money, expectation of influence and opposition to the existence of Britain's empire.

Drawing on a wide range of sources, the author demonstrates that women in the twentieth century continued to co-operate despite these divisions, and that feminist movements remained active right up to as well as beyond the reformist 1960s.

This readable and informative survey, including both new research and synthesis, provides the first close comparison of race, class and internationalism in the British and American women's movements during this period. It is invaluable reading for all those with an interest in American history, British history or Women's Studies.

Christine Bolt is Emeritus Professor of American History at the University of Kent. Her books include *The Anti-Slavery Movement and Reconstruction* (1969), *Victorian Attitudes to Race* (1971), *American Indian Policy and American Reform* (1987) and *The Women's Movements in the United States and Britain, from the 1790s to the 1920s* (1993).

Sisterhood Questioned?

Race, class and internationalism in the American and British women's movements, *c.* 1880s–1970s

Christine Bolt

Routledge
Taylor & Francis Group
LONDON AND NEW YORK

To Ian

First published 2004 by Routledge
11 New Fetter Lane, London EC4P 4EE

Simultaneously published in the USA and Canada by Routledge
29 West 35th Street, New York, NY 10001

Routledge is an imprint of the Taylor & Francis Group

Typeset in Galliard by The Running Head Limited, Cambridge
Printed and bound in Great Britain by MPG Books Ltd, Bodmin

British Library Cataloguing in Publication Data
A catalogue record for this book is available from the British Library

Library of Congress Cataloging in Publication Data
Bolt, Christine.
Sisterhood questioned?: race, class, and internationalism in the American and British women's movements, c.1880s–1970s / Christine Bolt.
p. cm.
Includes bibliographical references and index.
1. Feminism—United States. 2. Feminism—Great Britain. 3. Race.
4. Social classes. 5. Internationalism. I. Title.
HQ1426.B6837 2004
305.42 '0941—dc22 2003021055

ISBN 0-415-15852-4 (hbk)
ISBN 0-415-15853-2 (pbk)

Contents

Acknowledgements

I have incurred many debts in the course of writing this book, and it is a pleasure to acknowledge them.

Parts of the typescript were commented on, to my very great benefit, by Elizabeth Clapp, June Hannam, Rhodri Jeffreys-Jones, Pat Thane, and the late Robert Wiebe. Jean Baker read the whole book, and I am for ever in her debt.

Librarians and archivists, as always, made research enjoyable, especially at The Arthur and Elizabeth Schlesinger Library on the History of Women in America, Radcliffe Institute for Advanced Study; The Library of Congress; The Swarthmore College Peace Collection; The Women's Library, London Metropolitan University; The British Library of Political and Economic Science, London School of Economics; The British Library; and the Templeman Library, University of Kent – particular thanks being due to Angela Faunch and Anna Miller.

I had the privilege of a term's research leave from Kent, where my colleagues, David Turley and George Conyne, helped to make such leave possible and took an encouraging interest in the women's movement. The then Executive Officer of American Studies, Yvonne Latham, typed the opening chapters of the book with great efficiency, and Jackie Waller, the Executive Officer for History, handled queries with her usual dispatch.

I learned much from audiences at talks I gave on the main themes of *Sisterhood Questioned?* at the Modern History Faculty, Oxford; Anglia Polytechnic University; The Minda De Gunzburg Center for European Studies at Harvard University; London Guildhall University; and the Rockefeller Foundation's Study and Conference Center at Bellagio, Lake Como, Italy.

I am grateful to have received generous funding from the British Academy, and for a stimulating month-long residency at Bellagio in the early stage of the project.

My editor at Routledge, Victoria Peters, has been a constant source of encouragement and helpful suggestions.

Many thanks go to those who advised me on copyright and/or granted permissions at: The Schlesinger Library (Nancy Cott and Ellen Shea); The Library of Congress (Frederick Bauman); The Swarthmore College Peace Collection (Wendy Chmielewski); The Women's Library (Antonia Byatt and Maxine Willett); The British Library of Political and Economic Science (Sue Donnelly); The British Broadcasting Corporation (Vicky Mitchell); and to Carolyn H. Kim

(Charlotte Sheedy Literary Agency) for the Pauli Murray Papers; Shirley Tabata Ponomareff for The League of Women Voters Records; Joyce Kornbluh, the Labor Studies Center, University of Michigan Institute of Labor and Industrial Relations, for the Twentieth-Century Trade Union Women oral history project; Rosalie Huzzard for The Women's International League for Peace and Freedom Papers at the London School of Economics; and the Lord Methuen for the Courtney Collection. I should also like to thank the publishers, Ashgate, for permission to reproduce material from my contribution (chapter 10) to the collection of essays, *Anglo-American Attitudes: From Revolution to Partnership*, edited by Fred M. Leventhal and Roland Quinault (2000). Every effort has been made to trace copyright holders, but if any have been inadvertently overlooked, the publisher will be pleased to make the necessary arrangements at the first opportunity.

C. B.

Abbreviations

Libraries

LC	The Library of Congress
LSE	The British Library of Political and Economic Science, London School of Economics
SL	The Arthur and Elizabeth Schlesinger Library on the History of Women in America
SPC	The Swarthmore Peace Collection
WL	The Women's Library

Others

AAUW	American Association of University Women
AFC	America First Committee
AFL	American Federation of Labor
AFM	America First Movement
ALAWF	American League Against War and Fascism
ASWPL	Association of Southern Women for the Prevention of Lynching
ATS	Auxiliary Territorial Services
AUAM	American Union Against Militarism
BCL	British Commonwealth League
BFBPW	British Federation of Business and Professional Women
BPW	National Federation of Business and Professional Women's Clubs
BUF	British Union of Fascists
CCI	Comintern Communist International
CCCW	Committee on the Cause and Cure of War
CCWO	Consultative Committee of Women's Organisations
CIC	Commission on Inter Racial Cooperation of the Methodist Episcopal Church South
CIO	Congress of Industrial Organisations
CLUW	Coalition of Labor Union Women
EEOC	Equal Employment Opportunity Commission
ELFS	East London Federation of Suffragettes

ERA	Equal Rights Amendment
ERI	Equal Rights International
FEPC	Fair Employment Practices Commission
FLSA	Fair Labor Standards Act
GFWC	General Federation of Women's Clubs
ICW	International Council of Women
ICWDR	International Council of Women of the Darker Races
ICWG	International Co-operative Women's Guild
ICWPP	International Committee of Women for Permanent Peace
ICWW	International Congress of Working Women
IFTU	International Federation of Trade Unions
IFWW	International Federation of Working Women
ILO	International Labour Office
ILP	Independent Labour Party
IWSA	International Woman Suffrage Alliance
LSI	Labour and Socialist International
LWV	League of Women Voters
NAACP	National Association for the Advancement of Colored People
NACW	National Association of Colored Women
NAWSA	National American Woman Suffrage Association
NCJW	National Council of Jewish Women
NCNW	National Council of Negro Women
NCSW	National Commission on the Status of Women
NFWW	National Federation of Women Workers
NOW	National Organisation of Women
NRA	National Recovery Administration
NUSEC	National Union of Societies for Equal Citizenship
NUWM	National Unemployed Workers Movement
NUWSS	National Union of Women's Suffrage Societies
NWP	National Woman's Party
ODI	Open Door International
PPU	Peace Pledge Union
SDA	Sex Discrimination Act
SCHW	Southern Conference for Human Welfare
SEIU	Service Employees Industrial Union
SPG	Six Point Group
SSA	Social Security Act
TUC	Trades Union Congress
UNIA	Universal Negro Improvement Association
WAC	Women's Army Corps
WCG	Women's Co-operative Guild
WCTU	Woman's Christian Temperance Union
WIL	Women's International League
WILPF	Women's International League for Peace and Freedom
WJCC	Women's Joint Congressional Committee

WLL	Women's Labour League
WPC	Women's Peace Crusade
WPP	Women's Peace Party
WSPU	Women's Social and Political Union
WTUL	Women's Trade Union League
WVS	Women's Voluntary Service for Civil Defence
WWCTU	World Women's Christian Temperance Union
WWP	World Women's Party
WYWCA	World Young Women's Christian Association
YWCA	Young Women's Christian Association

1 Introduction

> Feminists love to call each other sisters but there ain't hardly nobody you dislike as much as your sister if you don't like her.
>
> Black lawyer and activist, Florynce Kennedy, 1988

> ... trashing your sisters is a serious bad habit ...
>
> Trade union activist, Catherine Conroy, on National Organisation of Women infighting, 1970s[1]

With the onset of second wave feminism[2] in the 1960s and 1970s, activists realised that the sisterhood of women could not be taken for granted, as it largely had been by their feminist predecessors in the nineteenth and earlier twentieth centuries. They realised that those predecessors – mainly white and western – had falsely assumed that they could speak and set the agenda for all women. In doing so, the early feminists may have hoped to rally women's support and inflate the power of feminism, but they also largely ignored the experiences of women in the colonial and postcolonial world, slighted the interests of women of colour in the west, and failed to locate and appreciate women's movements in their local contexts. In telling the story of their own activism in the later twentieth century, once neglected or patronised women demolished 'the notion of a universal female experience', while trying not to destroy faith in the global dimension and significance of feminism.[3]

This heated debate did not develop in the first stages of feminism, when diverse activists ostensibly achieved a high degree of unity in two main ways. First, they created an appealing as well as powerful women's culture, based on a veneration for the maternal qualities said to be universally displayed by women in child rearing, home making and social reform. And second, feminists' distinctive national agendas were linked by their drive for the vote, which, it was hoped, would be the key to progress of all kinds. The American and British women's movements seemed especially well attuned, emerging at about the same time, exchanging personnel and ideas, and working closely together in an established Anglo-American reform nexus.[4]

After the First World War, with the suffrage struggle no longer uniting them and maternalism coming under popular and academic challenge, American and British feminists were obliged to confront well established but previously masked differences within and between their movements, notably over race, class and internationalism. And they had to do so in a world that, far from embracing visions of progress, was instead afflicted by political reaction, economic insecurity, polarising nationalism and resurgent anti-feminism.

My purpose in the chapters that follow has been broadly to examine the significance of divisions within the women's movements of the United States and Britain. More specifically, while acknowledging the achievements of feminists working in the organisations of race, class and internationalism, I have looked at their difficulties and considered how far they were related to their own disputes. Race and class both clearly defined women as importantly as gender, and equally clearly disturbed and shaped the development of feminism; yet their impact was very different in the two countries, and class and racial responses to feminism have won very different judgements from contemporaries and historians alike. Female internationalism has been less controversial in the past and among scholars, but securing a united feminist voice in this quickly established area of interest also proved difficult. All three divisions were the creation of male society before women activists responded to them, and all three were more profound than the divisions among women who worked within their constraints.

I have also attempted, throughout, to show how the power shift in the Anglo-American relationship affected the Anglo-American reformer relationship, as British women became more than ever conscious of American money, expectation of influence and opposition to the existence of Britain's empire. In addition, I have tried to establish when and how, in the twentieth century, the activism of American feminists came to overshadow that of their British counterparts.

Women reformers certainly produced a rich array of disputes and divisions. But did it matter that two interwar British feminists fought 'like . . . tom cats' over proposals to merge their organisations, while a contemporary observer thought that seeking amalgamations between different groups of women activists was like expecting Serbs and Croats to get along?[5] Did it matter that proponents and opponents of protective industrial legislation for women sustained a long battle on both sides of the Atlantic, and that two of its prominent American warriors, Alice Paul and Doris Stevens, eventually became estranged, with Stevens deploring Paul's domineering style and preoccupation with an 'intra-mural fight for power and control'?[6] Did it matter if union women thought feminist leaders were selfish individuals and 'very snobbish'?[7]

Well, yes, of course it did, for all sorts of reasons; and after studying many different kinds of protest movement for many years, it seems to me that these are the most obvious ones. Unless quarrels are the healthy means of clarifying complicated issues, they take up time which could be spent more profitably. The longer they continue, the more likely they are to block intellectual and programmatic growth, and damage vulnerable elements within activist ranks. The disputes generated by social movements are, in addition, wonderfully helpful to their opponents, ever ready to denounce dissidents as unbalanced and peculiar individuals. Since it is so often claimed that women cannot work with other women – or, indeed, in groups at all – any feminist tendency towards divisions can be presented as an innate weakness of the weaker sex. Finally, activists' differences matter because they can inhibit the development of those national or movement-wide organisations that most effectively mobilise their supporters and help them to promote their case to a wider public.

While the divisions that are my concern all had their roots in the nineteenth century (see chapter 2), they were strengthened beyond eradication in the years from 1914 to 1945, which are accordingly given the largest share of my text. The race factor emerged early in the American movement, many of whose activists turned from agitating against black slavery to protesting the slavery of sex. Abolitionism and its aftermath quickly revealed the difficulties in the way of racial co-operation among reformers, and these were intensified from the end of the nineteenth century as the campaign for women's suffrage became caught up in the South's system of racial segregation and disenfranchisement of black men. Race again assumed vital importance for white American women when a new phase of feminism began in the 1960s. And at that point the vehement challenge posed by women of colour to feminism's universalist claims can only fully be understood in the context of their frequently problematical roles within American race and feminist organisations from the 1830s onwards. In tracing these difficulties, I have looked at black and white women's sense of mission towards other members of their respective races at home and abroad; have assessed black women's involvement with white women in politics and reform; and have detailed the need of black women to rely on their own domestic and international associations, on their own emphases within feminism, and on their sometimes prickly collaboration with black men and the growing civil rights movement. The similar problems encountered by other American women of colour – not least in seeking reformer coalitions – are also examined.

Since by the 1830s slavery had become a distant (if still important) issue to British women, and since the non-white population of Britain was small before the 1950s, race questions lacked the continuing centrality for British feminists that they had for their American sisters. None the less, the British interest in race was intense, there was a long black presence in Britain, and British feminism was more strongly shaped than its American equivalent by imperial crises and opportunities until the second half of the twentieth century. Then, with the end of the British Empire, increased Commonwealth immigration to Britain, the creation of the United Nations and its encouragement of international conferences on women, white British feminists were obliged to defend their ideas and programme against criticisms made by non-western women, and by British women of colour who owed much to the example of black American activists.

For British women, class rather than race influenced the first collective response to the wrongs of their sex, appearing in the discussions of utopian socialism during the 1820s. And though the claims of socialism did not effectively compete with feminism for the loyalty of discontented women until after the First

World War, its pull was growing from the 1890s, as Britain's global industrial dominance came under threat and the working-class movement gained ground. By that time, American feminists were more class conscious than they had been in the pre-Civil War period, for American class divisions had deepened under the impact of increasing immigration and ill regulated economic growth. However, *anxiety* about class did not drive the leading American feminists, who continued to believe that labour women[8] could organise separately from labour men, in the United States and internationally; and who continued to contrast Britain's inhibiting class system with their own more fluid society. They had a point, but on neither side of the Atlantic did labour women receive the degree of censure for their deficiencies and divisions that white middle-class feminists – affluent, elitist and influential – received for theirs. And on each side of the Atlantic, labour women, like women of colour, generally had the prudence to avoid public criticisms of their men. In assessing the British and American labour movements' inability to maximise their influence with working women, attention is paid to what the political Left, unions and international bodies offered to women, particularly with regard to work issues, birth control and welfare provision.

The theme of internationalism has been selected because the involvement of American and British women in the internationalising of feminism was great from the first, partly since this was an area in which they had some scope to take the initiative, rather than having to respond to a deeply entrenched feature of the social structure such as race or class. But like those two issues, internationalism proved taxing and divisive. Rivalry quickly erupted between Britain and the United States for the leadership of international organisations, there were disagreements over goals and tactics, and the forces of nationalism proved stubbornly resilient. Moreover, if feminists sensibly used traditional arguments about female qualities to justify a new visibility in world affairs, their aspirations still proved unwelcome to politicians because foreign policy was an overwhelmingly male dominated area. And even on matters to do with peace, where women as mothers might have been thought to have the best chance of establishing their instinctive and legitimate concern, feminists themselves were at odds.

What emerges is the continuity of women's difficulties. Adversely affected by two world wars and the Great Depression of the 1930s, the American and British feminist movements never enjoyed the support that women's numbers encouraged them to hope for, and frustration frequently brought personal quarrels and organisational schisms. But the movements also demonstrated women's agency, and continued to produce co-operative groups and exceptional individuals who could rise above the divisions which feminists both inherited and made.

For all the racial tensions that affected women's activism, Florynce Kennedy conceded that 'Some of my favorite people are white . . . It was the feminist community that got me visible. Most blacks don't or didn't know who I am.'[9] For all the sectarianism that afflicts mature social movements, America's Florence Luscomb managed to support suffragism, peace advocacy, civil liberties, organised labour and a range of social reforms, and was described at 89 years of age as 'the very model of a modern revolutionary' by *Time* magazine.[10] In Britain, the feminist, journalist, investigator and lecturer, Monica Whately, showed a similar intellectual breadth and zest for campaigning. She was remembered as a 'very vivid person' who 'belonged to every organisation that was going', and 'Any case which sought justice and freedom for the oppressed found in her a staunch supporter with courage and integrity'.[11] For all their differences over the leadership of interwar internationalism, the American suffragist Carrie Chapman Catt and her British counterpart Margery Corbett Ashby sustained public civility, mutual respect and a long co-operation. American women worked in the British women's movement, Britons visited the American lecture circuit with frequency and relish, and labour women in Britain and the United States managed warm personal contacts as well as strong disagreements about organisation.

Overall, despite the resentments and problems that race, class and internationalism provoked, they allowed for the emergence of pluralistic feminist movements which fulfilled the needs of two mature and diverse countries without deterring activists from making their crucial claims to sisterhood.[12]

2 The setting, 1880s–1914

The Anglo-American connection

If tackling reform issues at home was difficult enough, labouring in an international movement was enough to try the patience of a saint, and reformers are seldom saintly. Emily Greene Balch, an American academic and activist who worked at Geneva in the 1920s as the head of the Women's International League for Peace and Freedom, was a thoroughly cosmopolitan woman, regularly visiting English and continental friends and with no illusions about her world. She once mused, 'If Europeans seem to Americans to find it difficult to believe, too difficult to act, Americans seem to Europeans too naive, impulsive and idealistic, not to say sentimental, exaggerated, unstable, puzzling, incalculable. We are more or less aware of this.' The American journalist and activist, Hazel Hunkins-Hallinan, who lived in London and worked for the British feminist movement for decades, was similarly struck by the differences between Britain and the United States, believing that one could as well compare 'a single continuous piece of one material with a crazy quilt'.[1] But neither Balch nor Hunkins-Hallinan despaired of trans-Atlantic co-operative efforts, and nor did their contemporaries.

While my focus is on the forces that eventually put a strain on British and American feminists, on their distinctiveness and on the cultural contrasts between their respective countries, it is vital to grasp that these reformers first emerged out of a sympathetic Anglo-American environment. Until the 1850s, the British and American economies complemented each other, with the United States exchanging its raw materials for capital, labour, technology and manufactured goods from Britain.[2] There were similarly close links between political radicals and humanitarian reformers, whose letters, articles and visits were fostered by evangelical revivalism and religious nonconformity, a belief in human perfectibility, an admiration for republicanism, and a determination to advance their modernising ideas both at home and abroad.[3]

However, the Anglo-American relationship was always both testing and variable. Reformers in the two countries sometimes behaved like competitors rather than collaborators in doing good. Activists in Britain were not immune from the cultural condescension towards the United States that comforted many of their countrymen after the loss of the colonies; whereas for their part, American reformers frequently reacted by searching restlessly for their country's defining imagination and cultural independence.[4] And although by the late nineteenth century each nation had industrialised and democratised, the United States was then less economically dependent on Britain and more concerned with its vast internal market, while the Americans' general commitment to limited government contrasted sharply with the often paternalistic interventionism favoured by British politicians. None the less, awareness of the social costs and political dangers attendant on rapid economic change produced a fresh wave of reform from the 1890s, bringing British and American social critics and activists together again, reaffirming their belief in progress, and according a new prominence to women and women's concerns. At the same time, the anxieties produced by the Spanish–American war and Boer War led the two powers into a novel celebration of their diplomatic and racial closeness.[5]

The connection between individual British and American reformers was buttressed by an interlocking network of reforming families, sects and areas, mostly urban and, in the case of the United States, northeastern. It involved single issue crusaders as well as more numerous veterans of linked good causes. They were able to learn from each other's ideas, social experiments, company, tactics and organisation, but inevitably they were aware of national sensitivities about praising foreign ideas and agitators, and conscious that their possibilities for action were dictated primarily by proudly proclaimed national traditions, institutions and developments. Co-operating British and American reformers consequently produced contrasting social movements.

Some of these structural determinants were common to the nineteenth and twentieth centuries alike. Important on the British side were the monarchy and class system, a clearly defined establishment, strong and ideological political parties, parliamentary sovereignty, a relatively homogeneous population, awareness of space limitations and insularity. Crucial influences in the United States were republicanism, federalism, a racially and ethnically diverse people and linked cosmopolitanism, the separation of church and state, entrenched agrarian sentiment, and an unwillingness openly to concede the importance of class, notwithstanding marked distinctions based on social status and wealth.

Other differences emerged or were especially significant in the twentieth century. Accordingly, the American and British Left pulled apart once the United States became the world's dominant capitalist power. Conversely, enthusiasm for America grew among conservative Britons who formerly had been its critics. Moral and religious crusades were pursued by various groups in the United States which were disenchanted with the secularisation of society, and they found no strict equivalent in Britain. More elaborate links were forged between British and Commonwealth reformers, and America's mounting hostility to the continuation of the British Empire put a strain on trans-Atlantic relations. So too did the republic's oscillation between isolation and global assertiveness. Hence as the twentieth century wore on, the old Anglo-American connection was slowly replaced by a still more exasperating, shifting but undeniable lattice of bonds, to the formation of which America's growing cultural vitality and Britain's declining power were central.[6]

Race

The domestic consequences of race thinking

If the relations between progressive Britons and Americans altered under the impact of political and economic transformation, the racial prejudices entertained in the two countries were consistently similar and unfailingly strong. Initially shaped by English insularity, they quickly hardened into colour consciousness as a result of colonial encounters, crises and opportunities.[7] By the nineteenth century, Britain and the United States had also felt the impact of new pronouncements on race by European theorisers: notably the identification of the world's principal races, the allocation to them of distinguishing physical and mental characteristics, and the subsequent elaboration of such classifications by ethnologists and anthropologists. Commentators on each side of the Atlantic were convinced of the superiority of the English-speaking (or Anglo-Saxon) race, and accepted Romanticism's transformation of the Enlightenment's rational and noble savage into the unruly child of nature – a creature blessed with sensibility but marred by unpropitious circumstances and unruly passions. They enthusiastically used Charles Darwin's doctrine of evolution to strengthen belief in a hierarchy of races which placed the technologically advanced races at the top, while stressing human differences, racial competition and the inevitable destruction of the weakest. And by the 1880s and 1890s, pioneering genetic studies appeared to offer additional proof that physical differences were immutable, rather than modified by environmental change.[8]

Well into the twentieth century, all these views were dignified by the support they received from authority figures of every kind. They were accepted by the press, imaginative writers, politicians and the general public in Britain and the United States because they fed national vanity, buttressed imperialist assertions, dignified class and racial discrimination, and could be directed at non-whites and whites alike, as witness the slurs against eastern and southern European immigrants in America, and against Irish and eastern European Jewish settlers in Britain.[9]

Where do feminists fit into this evolving race thinking? The first answer is – not as its devisors and chief intellectual exponents. Race prejudice and racism clearly precede the rise of feminism and the emergence of considerable numbers of women writers. They were then perpetuated by political and scientific organisations that were dominated by men. But just as feminists had been influenced by the ideologies of the Enlightenment, liberalism and domesticity, so they were affected by contemporary racial arguments, and affected according to race and class.

Individuals who favour the total reformation of society are always in a minority, and being on the receiving end of discrimination does not necessarily lead to largeness of spirit. It may just as easily foster the desire to belong – to be at one, wherever possible, with the ideas of the dominant and discriminatory group. Accordingly, white women in the American South, reflecting the world view of their race and seeking white allies, generally failed to reach out to black women, despite their common experience of an increasingly tension-riven, paternalistic household economy.[10] White female abolitionists in Britain and America also supported prevailing views of black people when they portrayed them as needing control and representation by others. This shared outlook manifested itself differently in the two countries. In the case of Britain, the small numbers of resident and visiting black women abolitionists during the nineteenth century rendered them interesting and useful to white humanitarians, rather than threatening to accepted social divisions. Hence, if expected to be grateful and preferably biddable, they were not subject to flagrant racial discrimination.[11] In the United States, by contrast, rapport between black and white feminist-abolitionists, though not unknown, was inhibited before the Civil War by their social distance and customary confinement to separate antislavery auxiliaries, as well as by the women's rights conventions' indifference and occasional hostility towards women of colour.[12] But on both sides of the Atlantic, white women's antislavery rhetoric had damaging longterm consequences for women of colour: deflecting attention away from chattel slavery to the slavery of sex; objectifying and generalising about female slaves; and thus ensuring that, once emancipated, they would not be regarded as the equals of white women, whether they lived in the American South or the British Empire.[13]

After 1865, good relations between black and white women in America were further strained by the willingness of Republicans and many abolitionists to see the vote extended to free black men without conceding the case for female enfranchisement. This decision must be understood in the context of the duration and importance of the antislavery agitation, the relative weakness of the women's movement, and the belief of politicians that they would be able to control the fairly small black vote. Unhappily, it divided white feminist-abolitionists, and the first casualty was the wartime Equal Rights Association, through which they had worked with a handful of black women for racial and sexual emancipation. The end result was the use of racist arguments for the suffrage by impatient white elitists like Elizabeth Cady Stanton, the disgusted repudiation of them by many former allies, and the establishment of two separate national women's suffrage associations in 1869. Their creation formally severed the feminist–abolitionist connection forged over thirty years earlier; and while forcing the women organisers to rely on themselves, it boded ill for future black–white female solidarity.[14] By the First World War black women were obliged to mobilise separately from whites, in their own clubs, temperance and suffrage societies; a development which was frequently condemned by black campaigners and which would prove deeply damaging to feminism's reputation in the later twentieth century.[15]

It seems likely that some white feminists unconsciously accepted the segregation of the races: after all, it had been institutionalised throughout America as early as the first half of the nineteenth century. Nevertheless, some southern feminists deliberately accepted it, exploiting the 'negro problem' and reassuring white men of their region that votes for white women would ensure the maintenance of white supremacy and improve 'the quality of the electorate'. Equally clearly, prominent northern feminists tolerated separatism as a necessary evil which, once *de jure* segregation was adopted by the South in the 1890s, could not be challenged without alienating more numerous white supporters and delaying the growth of feminism in the part of the United States where its exponents and a proposed women's suffrage amendment to the Constitution were most vilified. And as we shall see (in chapter 5), white American women's subordination of black women's interests during the suffrage agitation made it sadly predictable that, once enfranchised, African American women would find it difficult to register and cast their votes, particularly in southern states where black men were already discouraged from going to the polls. Of course white feminists commonly showed scant concern for the citizenship rights of Native American, Chinese American and Mexican American women, albeit the women of these groups were primarily turned towards their own communities until the interwar years of the twentieth century. Nor could the early American feminists' frequent displays of nativism and anti-Semitism do other than distance them from immigrant and Jewish women. However, the alternating neglect and manipulation of black women actively seeking the suffrage was a failure of a different magnitude.[16]

White prejudices did not, however, prevent black American women from establishing their own local reform associations. Such associations, though they would have benefited from a share in white women's superior financial resources, gave black feminists the opportunity to produce independent leaders and to focus collectively on improving educational opportunities, child rearing, home management, health care, and the moral security of young women. Black women also endeavoured to shape feminist ideology to their own circumstances and priorities. They thereby avoided the divisive white debate about how far to accept or rebut men's identification of women with physical weakness and domesticity. Work outside the home was accepted as a necessity, the strength of black women was taken for granted, and they were sustained by the conviction that black men were similarly disadvantaged. Moreover, since by the twentieth century they sought to advance their cause through the major, male-led organisations of their race, as well as through their own associations, black feminists steered clear of the accusation that they were fomenting a sex war: a *canard* that often distracted their white counterparts. Indeed, black men did not initially oppose women's participation in reform, as white men had done. But naturally there is a crucial difference between freely chosen autonomy and the separation resulting, in part, from white women's discrimination.[17]

The most prominent exponents of American black feminism displayed a profound sense of mission towards working-class members of their race, seeking 'to help those less fortunate than ourselves': 'the masses of our women, by whom, whether we will it or not, the world will always judge the womanhood of the race'. If relations between leaders and followers were frequently close in black groups, this was to a certain extent because there was less disparity of means between them than was found in white organisations; social exclusiveness was certainly not unknown among black club women. Black campaigners, like white, commonly adopted a 'respectable' and cultivated style of operation. And in bodies like the National Association of Colored Women (NACW, 1896), which had attracted 15,000 members in 31 states by 1904, they sought 'harmony of action and cooperation among all women in raising to the highest plane, home, moral and civil life'.[18]

On each side of the Atlantic it was, none the less, white women who placed the greatest emphasis upon an elitist female mission, pursuing it in the clubs, charity organisation societies, consumer, social purity and temperance associations, settlement houses, urban and missionary groups that made up their reform network. These bodies were attractive both to non-feminists and to reformist feminists (variously described by historians as social, maternalist and welfare feminists), and they will therefore be considered in this study. Through them, and notwithstanding their diverse outlooks, white women found an opportunity for self-assertion and for improving the position of their sex. At a time when middle-class birthrates were falling, white middle-class women were proud to minister to the unfortunate and prolific elements in society; and were often ready to proclaim themselves the mothers of the allegedly superior white race. Entering into contemporary debates about racial and social purity, the meaning of progress and civilisation, the legitimacy of empire, and the essence of nationality, Social Darwinism and Anglo-Saxonism, they used such debates to signal their respectability, confirm their social status and legitimise their reform activities.[19]

In the course of these activities and debates, white British feminists – unlike their American sisters – were not driven to discriminatory behaviour by fear of close contacts with a substantial non-white population. In fact, though anti-slavery sentiments had been eroded by the 1860s, a strain of anti-imperialism sustained the British commitment to the brotherhood of man,[20] and could still ensure that persons of colour visiting Britain obtained a fair hearing. One such was the black American journalist, political activist and campaigner against lynching, Ida B. Wells, though her British hosts might simply have enjoyed showing themselves more liberal than public opinion in the United States. As Sir Edward Russell mused, when introducing Wells, 'We had our own faults, but it had never been one of these to hold our tongues about the inequities of other people'.[21] However, imperialism did provide a major outlet for the racial pride of British women, who proclaimed their distinctive female mission to help the native women of the British Empire.

Race and women's overseas mission

By the late nineteenth century, both American and British women had established themselves overseas as missionaries, though American women obviously had less inducement to look abroad for missionary opportunities than their British sisters. The United States had no national 'surplus' of adult unmarried women – a phenomenon anxiously observed from the late 1840s in Britain – and activists saw themselves as facing many challenges in a vast continent from Native Americans, African Americans and increasingly diverse immigrants. But even in the conservative South, where charity was often felt to begin at home, missionary efforts were thought to be at once respectable and important; and after 1880 foreign missions were increasingly and effectively promoted throughout the nation, with predictable emphasis being placed on parts of the world which were economically and strategically significant for the United States.[22]

If the hardships associated with overseas missionary work were a deterrent to the faint hearted, these enterprises might seem romantic and flattered women's sense of importance. Naturally the religious imperative was strongly urged. In the words of the pioneering Mississippi feminist, Nellie Nugent Somerville, the 'question with us is not will the heathen be saved without the gospel but will we be saved if we do not extend it'. Furthermore, it was stressed that missionary labour required from church women 'more faith to carry it on and more patience in waiting for results than any other', since entrenched ways were not easily changed and the attitudes of local communities had to be considered. Just the same, pride could be taken in 'the intelligence[,] business ability and extreme piety' of women in the missionary field, and it was gratifying to be told that 'the salvation of the women and children of heathen lands depends largely upon our faithfulness to this charge'.[23] Since at the outset the churches had been unwilling either to send out unmarried female missionaries or to bless separate female mission societies, American women's success in producing both, and in making their foreign mission movement the most important female endeavour in the United States before the First World War, with over three million dues-paying members, is certainly noteworthy.[24]

Equally certain is the complicated impact of the American women's missionary endeavours. On the one hand, some material benefits were received by the missionised people. With the passage of time, more women who had been trained as teachers, nurses and doctors went to the mission fields, where they could offer practical assistance specifically aimed at women and children. The female evangelists also gained. As transmitters of white culture generally, rather than simply of white religion, they demonstrated that women reformers could rise above the practical and smallscale measures that were meant to be their hallmark; and, as professionals, they avoided the charge of impractical moralising so frequently levied against missionaries.[25]

On the other hand, American missionary women did not overtly advance the cause of women's rights in the United States, for only a few of them were avowed feminists.[26] The organisational independence of women's missions did not lead women in the field to abandon traditional female values. And they, like other Americans, appear to have espoused race thinking and to have regarded the expansion of their exemplary nation – 'the vestibule of heaven', as one female missionary put it – as being distinct from colonialism. The African American evangelist, Amanda Berry Smith, recalled that when a Methodist Episcopal colleague went to 'Africa to help my people by establishing missions and schools', she 'felt it was my duty to do all I could to help'. An opponent of racism, she nevertheless reported that the 'poor women of Africa', like 'those of India', where she had previously worked, 'had a hard time' at the hands of man. She apparently did not see her condemnation of African and Indian mores as being akin to the resented and patronising pronouncements of European imperialists, and of white reformers on African American culture in the late nineteenth century. Women missionaries, if more muted in their imperialism than men, generally perceived no peril in emphasising their social distance from their converts, relished the authority they exercised over them, and hence offset the good they might have done when they opposed masculine acts of aggression overseas.[27]

The strength of the female foreign mission movement encouraged three initially domestic organisations to seek an outlet beyond America. By 1904, the Lake Mohonk Conference of Friends of the Indian (1883), a powerful pressure group which involved women, had extended its interest from Native Americans to 'other dependent peoples'.[28] The Woman's Christian Temperance Union (WCTU, 1874) launched a world Union in 1883. And in 1895 the Young Women's Christian Association (YWCA, 1858) followed suit. The WWCTU, as Ian Tyrell has shown, operated in many countries by relying on a small Anglo-American elite of women, international conventions, national affiliates, and a range of round-the-world missionaries, resident missionaries and organisers. It campaigned for the spread of Christianity, temperance, the eradication of opium trafficking, peace and social purity. But its leaders' conviction of the redeeming power of the Anglo-Saxon race ultimately tied the union to the progress of American and British imperialism, and alienated the good opinion of local people, as did its middle-class composition and assumptions. The WYWCA – employing eight hundred American women 'teachers, administrators, and social workers' who 'served overseas in over thirty countries' between 1895 and 1970 – did rather better. Nancy Boyd has established that the Association's emissaries enjoyed considerable independence from male influence, and were bold in maintaining that women should be accepted as social leaders, and in claiming that if Americans abroad were passing on 'the worst of our civilization', then women were challenged by that very fact to convey the best. Yet, like their WWCTU sisters, they were unable to repudiate the class system overseas that provided them with servants and considerable deference.[29]

For British missionary women, there were many of the same practical problems and pitfalls. Women were drawn to the field, declared the *English Woman's Review* in 1872, because it suited their self-image and provided 'a life of honorable and profitable activity . . . and . . . the means of [doing] incalculable good to hundreds of other women'.[30] Like men, women missionaries encountered real hardships and met resistance from both indigenous peoples and colonial governments. In addition, their contributions were frequently subsumed within those of their husbands or, if they were single, questioned altogether. As J. N. Murdock warned at the 1888 London Missionary Conference, 'Women's work in the foreign field must be careful to recognise the headship of man in ordering the affairs of the Kingdom of God'.[31]

British female evangelists did not have to debate the basic legitimacy of empire, and they had a wider foreign field than their American counterparts in which to operate, as the British Empire reached its zenith at the end of the nineteenth century. But they too led the missionary advocacy of social change for women; and while their attempts to force change might benefit women, not least by attracting the attention of local reformers, they might encourage the imposition of inappropriate western customs on the women who were being proselytised.[32] Moreover, the suspicions aroused overseas by their ideas were easily transferred to the arguments of western feminists, who displayed a comparable determination to 'emancipate' native women and began to attract attention from the intellectuals and activists of non-western countries in the later nineteenth century.[33]

The British feminists who learned about these missionary struggles could only be strengthened in their own sense of moral and racial superiority; and that consciousness, as Antoinette Burton has demonstrated in the context of India, contributed significantly to the 'domestic culture of imperialism'.[34] A positive connection with imperialism could of course be useful to suffragists, since votes for women were opposed by anti-feminists like Britain's Sir Almroth Wright as unacceptable to any 'virile and imperial race', and as liable to destroy faith in the empire among colonies that were especially paternalistic in tradition and outlook.[35] Unfortunately, feminists who responded by embracing imperialism tended to propagate generalised images of backward and oppressed 'Oriental' womanhood, and Burton has emphasised the dangers for British feminism in the assumption that a supposedly superior elite among women could speak for the less privileged and fortunate.[36] In particular, the desire to emancipate women could easily become a desire to control them, as was revealed in the battle over regulating prostitutes for the Indian army, waged between colonial officials and differing groups of social purists during the second half of the nineteenth century.[37] In the same period, the interest of British and Indian men in 'uplifting' Indian women displays a similar conflict between the wish to inspire and the determination to force reform. Yet we should not underestimate what British feminists actually *did*, for and in collaboration with Indian women. Western women's claims to be the superior sex were part of an opportunistic and empowering strategy, adopted at a time when all manner of pundits proclaimed their position to be the most advanced in the world, and believed that the position of women was the test of any society's general emancipation. It was a strategy with high risks and class overtones, but with some educational, welfare and organisational benefits for their overseas sisters, as well as gratification for themselves.[38]

Internationalism

Its attractions for women

Women interested in collaborating with other women beyond national boundaries had a variety of organisations to choose from by the early twentieth century, and Americans had generally taken the initiative in their creation. This was certainly true of the WWCTU and the WYWCA, even though Britain's Josephine Butler had made social purity a transnational campaign in 1875 when she established the British, Continental and General Federation for the Abolition of Government Regulation of Prostitution.[39] By the 1880s it was apparent that the women's movement was international in fact and spirit, and an International Council of Women (ICW, 1888) was launched at a meeting of the Americans' National American Woman Suffrage Association (socialist internationalism is considered below on pp. 25, 29–34, and 113–21).

The founding meeting of the ICW brought together women from the United States, Europe, Canada and India for discussions on political and legal conditions, education and employment, temperance and social purity, philanthropy and organisation. It was followed at intervals by other international conferences and from the 1890s drew upon the work of national women's councils. However, the ICW's desire to maximise its membership resulted in caution on the controversial issue of votes for women, driving bolder spirits to set up the International Woman Suffrage Alliance (IWSA) at Berlin in 1904. The alliance's aim was 'to secure the enfranchisement of the women of all nations, and to unite the friends of woman suffrage throughout the world in organised cooperation and fraternal helpfulness'.[40] While it recognised the importance of forming branches globally and tapping into the entwined forces of nationalism and feminism in countries like Egypt, China and India, IWSA was dominated by Americans. It was headed until 1923 by their suffrage leader, Carrie Chapman Catt, who took pleasure in her close control of the alliance.[41] Matters did not indefinitely remain so satisfactory, as we shall see (in chapter 4).

There are many reasons for such feminist cosmopolitanism. Whatever cynical enemies may have thought of their enthusiasms, the nineteenth-century reform communities out of which feminists came rightly recognised that the miseries produced by slavery, war, intemperance, economic upheavals, and the denial of citizenship to subordinate groups, took no account of national boundaries and demanded action internationally. And these reformer views eventually had some impact, for, as Christina Phelps has noted, 'The half century beginning with 1856, a period of congresses and conferences, witnessed the rise of international administrative law. Although the principle of nationality was unquestionably in the ascendant, national states were indirectly and inexorably drawn into the movement for cooperation.'[42] Women's international activity thus emerged in a favourable climate and was a useful antidote to the sentimental middle-class depiction of woman dwelling in the private sphere, sheltered from the turbulence of the masculine, public world. When, in cautious stages, women were admitted to local government franchises during the nineteenth century, the domestic focus of such politics left the female image largely unchanged. Without the challenge of the internationalists, foreign relations might logically have continued to be presented as the preserve of men; and even with that challenge, women only slowly obtained (low level) employment in the American foreign service in the last quarter of the nineteenth century, and were excluded from it in Britain until the 1940s.[43]

In each country, Jewish women were notably international in outlook; seeking to help the uprooted victims of conflict or discrimination and at the same time to demonstrate that they played no part in the alleged global conspiracy of Jews, so persistently dwelt upon in anti-Semitic propaganda. By 1912, an International Council of Jewish Women had been formed, with the United States sustaining the most important affiliate.[44] For women of colour, the expense of internationalism and its domination by white women were serious deterrents. They none the less travelled to Europe when they could in search of greater acceptance, as well as education, training and employment. They also argued, in educator Anna Cooper's words, that 'women's cause is one and universal', seizing the opportunity of urging their case at such gatherings as Chicago's 1893 World Fair; slowly developing a trans-national outlook in their own organisations; and, exceptionally, joining the international bodies run by whites.[45]

American women, irrespective of religion or race, were driven by the idealism which had been an integral part of their country's founding ideology and which still envisaged the United States setting an example to the rest of the world, and so surmounting its geographical, diplomatic and military isolation. Martha Banta has shown how, by the 1890s, 'the sense of national pride increasingly found expression in internationalist terms', with women being projected as the morally superior symbols of the nation, their roles including fastidious or spiritual upholder of liberty, and mother of the world. Furthermore, many American women who felt ambivalent towards Britain because of the old colonial connection, or resented Britons' class and national arrogance, had no difficulty about links with continental European countries. The American IWSA activist, Anna Shaw, for instance, formed a devoted friendship with her Dutch co-worker, Aletta Jacobs, as did the normally cool Carrie Catt, who regarded Jacobs as 'a truly wonderful and great woman'. Catt's friendship with another Dutch IWSA comrade, Rosa Manus, was warmer still, evoking the mother–daughter relationship.[46] The current of rivalry that always enlivened Anglo-American links, though present in American–European connections, was never so marked.

Nothwithstanding the national differences that periodically threatened to wreck international organisations, British and American women found in them useful information; a standard of comparison; diversion from local troubles; stimulating travel, company and conference venues; and confirmation of their belief that female subjection and sisterhood alike were universal. In the first years of their existence, these transnational associations reflected rather than challenged the dominance of British and American feminism by white middle-class women. And they contented themselves with prudent tactics, focusing on high profile meetings, resolutions, fact gathering, publications, correspondence and self-education. While seeking to advance the cause of suffragism internationally, women activists also concerned themselves with the events overseas that claimed men's interest, taking part in the ongoing debate about imperialism, not least as it manifested itself during the Spanish–American War of 1898 and the Boer War of 1899.

Women and war

These two wars were waged against the background of *fin de siècle* anxieties which had produced both new reform programmes and more reactionary efforts to redefine and reassert middle-class manliness and to equate it with civilisation. In response, feminists like the American author and lecturer, Charlotte Perkins Gilman, flatly condemned primitive masculinity for its combination of 'combat, egotism, and desire'.[47] They argued that women, by contrast, as homemakers, mothers and protectors of the vulnerable, had a special interest in international co-operation, agencies and arbitration as a means of averting the slaughter of young men in war. This interest had been pursued through the societies of the closely connected British and American peace movements, and strengthened by contacts with the peace women of continental Europe. Since the first half of the nineteenth century, Quaker women on each side of the Atlantic had been particularly active in promoting peace activities. In Britain, 1874 saw the creation of a Women's Peace and Arbitration Auxiliary of the London Peace Society (1816). And in the United States, where by the later part of the century women were at least as prominent as men in peace societies, the ICW meeting of 1899 led to the formation of an International Standing Committee on Peace and International Arbitration. Additional stimulation was given to female pacifism in the United States by the peace and foreign relations sections of elaborately departmentalised bodies like the WCTU and NACW, and by the foundation of the American School Peace League (1908) by Fannie Fern Andrews. The exclamation of the American clubwoman and suffragist, Julia Ward Howe, after the Franco-Prussian War, summed up the feelings of many of her co-campaigners: 'If women of the world unite, blood will no longer flow'.[48] But the world was no more a larger home in need of motherly management than women were united in its service. Indeed, the more women felt the need to take an interest in the broad spread of foreign affairs, the more likely they were to differ; the *Woman's Journal* rightly reported during the Spanish–American War of 1898 that 'As usual, it is "many women, many minds"'.[49]

Historians have been slow to detail female perspectives on the Spanish–American War. This may be partly because the conflict over Cuba has been overshadowed by the First World War, leading suffragist Mary Peck to reminisce that it resembled a kind of 'martial Arcadia'.[50] Another reason is the common assumption of American and British historians as well as contemporaries that the ideology and events of foreign affairs were masculine: that it was an area where women were at best invisible. At their worst, when they went out to the colonies, women have been taxed by scholars with opposing the easy 'copulation and concubinage' that had initially flourished there, and so contributing to deteriorating race relations. A very different, though still critical, picture has recently come from social historians writing in the former colonies, and from women historians seeking to establish the complex interactions of gender, race, class and nationality in the imperial context, and to assess the impact of women commentators on colonialism. Yet Edward Crapol, Joan Hoff-Wilson, Rhodri Jeffreys-Jones, Carol

Miller and Leila Rupp remain rare among historians in giving women's foreign policy interests serious attention.[51]

Accordingly the external affairs we normally learn about in late nineteenth-century America concern male imperial strategists, big navy advocates, expansionist politicians, businessmen and clerics, with women making a brief entry only in the context of Anglo-Saxonism. While Anglo-Saxons were commonly defined as masculine and associated with self-assertion, 'physical interests and material possessions', it was conceded that their confidence had affected even middle-aged matrons 'without activity in the higher areas of reflection'. Women were also acknowledged to be treated exceptionally in Anglo-Saxon communities; but their reforming zeal was a mixed blessing, because 'not a few of the philanthropic paroxysms that seize at intervals upon England and the United States are of a very sickly sort'.[52] The promotion of friendship between Britain and the United States, as the leading Anglo-Saxon races, has unsurprisingly been projected as an exclusively masculine business.[53] And women have been similarly ignored in accounts of anti-imperialism, the standard American history not mentioning them except to say that the New England Anti-Imperialist League was clearly declining once it indicated, at its fourth annual meeting, that 'the presence of ladies is especially desired'.[54]

None the less, contemporary American women's anxieties about the war with Spain can be gleaned from a variety of sources, including the WCTU, women's clubs, the National Council of Women, the National American Woman Suffrage Association (NAWSA, 1890), the American Peace Society, the Universal Peace Union and the Anti-Imperial League. On the one hand, the uncompromising view was expressed that peace should be maintained and that America should 'inspire in other nations the courage to practice it'.[55] On the other hand, there was support for the judgement that a peaceful settlement with Cuba was impossible: Spanish inhumanity on the island, not least towards women and children, justified intervention by the United States to help 'a weaker neighbor whose wrongs had troubled us these many years'.[56] The feminist ideologue, Elizabeth Cady Stanton, described herself as 'strongly in favor of this new departure in American foreign policy'.[57] Displays of patriotism were in order because the United States was fighting 'The first disinterested war on earth. We elevate the standard of the political world', and accordingly women should show 'Tears, love, and honor, . . . for all our gallant boys on sea and land who fling their generous lives into this glorious protest!'[58]

But jingoists could not charm away the feeling among some American women that one evil had led to another, and that the war in the Philippines was selfishly motivated: 'unmistakable evidence', declared suffragist Caroline Severance, 'of the decadence of patriotism'. In addition to the inevitable battlefield horrors, imperialist conflict had stimulated liquor abuse and prostitution; and, complained the feminist-pacifist Lucia Ames Mead, it had committed the country to territorial and economic aggrandisement, 'race hatred and civic corruption'. Aware that this was so, the feminist leader Susan B. Anthony chided her friend Mrs Stanton that she should be using her tireless pen to denounce 'every Nabob

– man or woman – who does injustice to a human being – for the crime! of color or sex'.[59]

Such diversity of opinion was to be found even in the columns of the leading suffrage periodical, the *Woman's Journal*, making it plain that the foreign policy differences that bedevilled men bedevilled feminists too. Just the same, the hostilities were an opportunity for activists as well as an outrage. They were able to use them to indict masculine civilisation: Congress, after all, was 'practically unanimous for war' in 1898. Conditions among the troops enabled women to highlight social purity issues, and the conflict also allowed them to raise the franchise question.[60] In Anthony's words, 'if the women of our nation had been counted among the constituencies of every State Legislature and of the Congress of the United States, the butchery of the Spanish–American War would never have been perpetrated'.[61] Suffragists went on accurately to predict that when Cuba was free, Cuban patriots would 'not think of women's freedom';[62] and to complain that women in America's new colonies were being excluded from the vote despite being 'better fitted' for it 'in every way' than their menfolk.[63]

Yet the end-of-century imperial debate did not provide women with a sustained area of focus, because the United States quickly reverted to a more usual, lower key foreign policy. Women's interest in domestic affairs remained paramount.[64] Politicians felt no need to heed them, either over avoiding or concluding the Spanish war, and women in the areas won from Spain did not get the vote. It is scarcely surprising that many female activists saw the crisis as another chance for serving, since in 'every war through which our nation has passed on to victory, the effort, the sacrifices and the prayers of women have been efficient aids to the attainment of such victories'.[65] For Jewish American women, the war offered 'an unusual opportunity . . . to controvert such accusations as have in the past been cast against their loyalty'. While 'deprecating that the nations have not passed beyond the stage where war is possible', the National Council of Jewish Women (NCJW) was therefore 'ready to serve in whatever way it may be called upon', which meant 'putting aside all personal bias and acting only as loyal citizens'. Appropriately, one clear benefit to come out of the conflict, in acknowledgement of the importance of women's caring role, was the establishment by Congress of the Army Nurse Corps in 1901 and the Navy Nurse Corps in 1908.[66]

Despite the educational activities of peace campaigners like Lucia Mead, it proved easier to raise probing questions about foreign policy at a time of crisis and new departures than to show how the female public could be re-educated, the activism of its members maintained, and politicians persuaded to take much notice of a group which lacked both votes and a voice in the foreign policy establishment. Another military conflict – the First World War – would be necessary for American women's sense of injustice and opportunity to be comparably aroused,[67] and with more lasting consequences. Meanwhile, the cause of international peace reclaimed the energies of the numerous women who had hoped, briefly, to exert a substantial influence on the nation's leaders.

British women were even more concerned than their American sisters about the case for and against empire. It is therefore understandable that they produced a number of well-connected commentators on colonial matters, among them the confident and complicated explorer of West Africa, Mary Kingsley; the Middle Eastern adventurer and political adviser, Gertrude Bell; and the Colonial Editor of *The Times* during the 1890s, Flora Shaw, who was proud that she had 'helped to rouse the British public to a sense of Imperial responsibility and Imperial greatness'.[68] Furthermore, British suffragists were able to identify with the white dominions, where women's rights were advanced – indeed, after the enfranchisement of New Zealand and Australian women between 1893 and 1902, more advanced than in the mother country. American women had no exact overseas inspiration, though they could take heart from the extension of voting rights in their frontier territories and states. But in the British dominions and American west alike, political conditions were fluid and the suffrage was granted to women as scarce civilisers rather than as bold agitators.[69]

The attitudes of British women to empire were also shaped by party political loyalties in a way in which American women's were not, since American parties were less programmatic and more loosely organised and neglectful of women supporters (outside the suffrage states) until the twentieth century. Thus, for example, many Conservative women took a keen interest in foreign affairs – and particularly empire – in order to assist their men, because political entertaining was a legitimate and enjoyable form of assertion, and because they might find themselves posted overseas: as witness Lady Ripon's confession in 1880 that 'What I most feared and dreaded has happened. India has been offered and now doctors are deciding our fate'.[70] For such political wives, overt pronouncements on policy were a risk, unless they coincided with the official standpoint. Hence Mary Endicott Chamberlain, wife of the Secretary for the Colonies, felt it safe to write in the pro-British *North American Review* in 1900 that the Anglo-Saxon 'bore "the responsibility for the civilization and welfare of the vast populations which turn to the English-speaking world for protection and good government"'.[71] Yet it was more useful for strong opinions to be urged in letters or on social occasions, and Jennie, Lady Randolph Churchill was just one of a number of women who was very accomplished at making political contacts and getting her views across in the interest of her family.

However, even the American Jennie Churchill could not turn the Anglo-American rapprochement of 1895–1904 into a development with the same significance for women as for men. Naturally, she stayed in close touch with Americans in Britain,[72] seeking on occasion to interpret the one to the other, and launching a quarterly called the *Anglo-Saxon Review* which was designed to use her contacts on both sides of the Atlantic. The journal none the less avoided politics for the most part, and Jennie was adamant that it should not vulgarly promote the motto that 'blood is thicker than water'.[73] Just the same, she did manage to organise the sending of an American hospital ship to care for the wounded in South Africa during the Boer War, a suitably caring and ostensibly apolitical gesture by an intensely political woman.[74]

Another difference between British and American women at the time of the

Boer War was the growth of the Left in Britain, and its continuing weakness in the United States (despite the advent of the Populist Party). Although British party political differences over empire would – like the Left – become stronger in the twentieth century, there were at least some additional voices raised against imperialism from this source, with the social investigator and eventual suffragist, Beatrice Webb, proving outspokenly critical of hysterical jingoism and sordid economic manoeuvres in South Africa. Unfortunately, as Porter and Howe have observed, the Fabians tended to support empire because it existed and in the hope of furthering their domestic programme by bartering 'their support over the South African war to the highest bidder'.[75]

A final important contrast between British and American women and their circumstances was the distinctive importance for Britons of emigration to the colonies. While American women were exhorted to take part in the westward movement – in the settlement of their country's internal colonies – this process did not create an equivalent colonial mentality, and we have already noted that there was no 'surplus' woman problem to cope with in the United States. The Female Middle Class Emigration Society was founded in Britain in 1862, and during the next twenty-three years it helped over three hundred women to settle in the colonies, besides provoking a full discussion of the purpose and ways of promoting female emigration. Eventually seven similar societies appeared, including the successful and enduring Women's Migration and Overseas Appointments Society; and in 1900 the Imperial Order of the Daughters of the Empire was launched in Canada, soon spawning a network of branches whose members devoted themselves to 'patriotism, loyalty and service', and whose enterprise funded, among other things, the dispatching of a hospital ship to South Africa during the Boer War.

The 20,000 or so women assisted by these associations between them constituted only a fraction of the women who went to the colonies, and they revealed the obvious class and racial prejudices of the organisers, who included some of the early feminists.[76] Accordingly if opportunities were publicised in Canada, Australia and South Africa, it was felt that 'The other Colonies, as regards a better class of women, offer but few openings or advantages'. Moreover, a white girl in those 'other colonies', before there were many whites in an area, was 'lifted far above the position she should occupy simply because she was white, and consequently became less useful to her mistress'.[77] There was also jealousy that servants were valued over the 'ladies' and 'educated women' who could succeed abroad if only they were given a start.[78] None the less, the emigration societies and journals are a striking testament to the strength of the imperial vision among Victorian and Edwardian women; and especially to what Julia Bush has described as their imperious maternalism, which was supposed to secure the imperial race and complement the role of male imperialists.[79]

The South African war did not minimise such differences between British and American women. The American public inclined to the Boer side and was therefore at odds with the United States government which, out of gratitude for backing in 1898, influenced by American missionaries in South Africa, and considering its longterm economic and political interests, supported the British. With its aversion to standing armies, American public opinion could not sympathise with what the feminist author Rebecca West called Britons' sentimental support for their army of poor men who, driven to enlist, 'put the coloured illustrations in the book of our lives and lightened the drab black and white of the text'. But opinion on both sides of the Atlantic was keenly engaged as well as divided over the war; and understandably so, given the complex considerations leading to and thrown up by the conflict. The suffragist Lady Frances Balfour was unusual, in 1900, in pronouncing herself to be straightforwardly 'Insulated, isolated, and insolent with regard to "foreign devils"'.[80]

These complexities are epitomised in the writing and lecturing of the feminist Olive Schreiner, whose 1883 novel, *The Story of an African Farm*, had made a huge impact on British and American women. Schreiner did not give race relations a central place in that narrative, and her subsequent writings, up to the outbreak of war, were driven by a desire to depict the Boers as an uncomplicated and defenceless people, and to offer a critical analysis of Britain's imperial policy – somehow without paying much attention to race. Only when the war was over did she 'espouse the cause of the Africans'.[81]

In the end, the imperial outlook of British women – like that of Schreiner herself – was moulded by their social circumstances: by family, religion, race, class and political allegiance. Hence the conflict drew out to South Africa some women who were intent on serving their country in a traditional humanitarian fashion; some who were bent on grabbing a share of the excitement that accompanies great contests; and some who were deeply dismayed by the doubts that the Boer War was raising about British competence and motives. Their divisions of opinion are well illustrated by the correspondence of the suffragists Kate and Leonard Courtney, in connection with the South Africa Conciliation Committee. Thus while fellow feminist Priscilla Bright McLaren declared 'that Satan is in great form everywhere', Boer sympathiser Dorothy Bradby specifically deplored the sight of 'our England rolling about bellowing and waving drunken flags because we have committed one of the worst crimes in history; and most of those who *know* it is a crime urging us to make the best of it now it is done'. Such differences of outlook were also recorded in the contemporary press, notwithstanding attempts to present the war in simple terms as a conflict between the primitive Boers and the civilised British, who were determined to end misrule and do right by the Africans.[82] Affected by the scepticism about this presentation, once the war dragged on, even the imperialist Jennie Churchill feared the alienating effect of a British triumph achieved 'mainly by brute force', and an editorial in her *Anglo-Saxon Review* expressed dismay about the British search 'not for victory but for conquest'.[83] And for thoughtful women, the conduct of the concentration camps set up by the British for the dependents of Boer soldiers was as worrying as the military conduct of the war.

To an imperialist such as the feminist writer and reformer Millicent Fawcett, who regarded the struggle as one on 'behalf of the English and other "Uitlanders" in the Transvaal who were denied the rights of citizenship in the Boer republic', explaining Britain's case to doubters was essential.[84] She managed to do this via the Women's Liberal Unionist Association, sending publications to the United States as well as to continental European countries. As a government supporter, Fawcett was biased, but her partiality for her sex was not a dominating factor in the report on the camps she produced in 1902, with the aid of a special investigatory commission. In it, Boer women were disparaged and black women slighted. Yet male incompetence and cruelty were efficiently exposed and Fawcett's report still commands interest. Along the way, she found a keen ally in the prominent social purist and feminist, Josephine Butler. When the war came, as a staunch patriot Butler allowed love of country to overcome her earlier criticism of Britain's South African policies. She, like Fawcett, sympathised with the Uitlander demand for representation; and she compared it with women's demand for the vote.[85] Her additional wish was to speak out for the 'native races', whom she saw as enslaved by the Boers and entitled to a suitably subordinate liberty within the British Empire. Her preoccupation, shared by sympathetic contemporaries, was with African men.[86]

Fawcett's chief female critic on the subject of the camps was another feminist reformer, the independent and outspoken Emily Hobhouse. Her preliminary account of their conditions had needled the government into setting up Fawcett's commission, but she never made the influential impact that her knowledge of the camps led her to seek, and her reporting on the camp women is problematical. Although Hobhouse rightly pointed out that Fawcett's feminism did not prevent her from disparaging the Boer women, she herself, in avoiding this fault, ignored black women and subscribed to conventional notions about the threat of 'Kaffir' men. Hobhouse's marginalisation clearly owed much to the nature of her findings, since the government was embarrassed by the camp controversy at a time when the British prided themselves on their protection of the weak and the position of their women. And, after all, she had found the usefulness she craved, while receiving some tributes. When she died in 1926, her ashes were interred in the Women's Memorial in Bloemfontein and the South African Prime Minister, Jan Smuts, remembered her as a 'heaven-sent messenger' to his people. None the less, Hobhouse's treatment by Britain is a salutary warning that in the international arena, though frequently wishing to rise above political partisanship, women have often secured more advantages by showing their willingness to work the political system like men.[87]

Class

Having fought for the liberties once enjoyed by Englishmen, and having rejected the aristocratic order prevalent throughout Europe in the late eighteenth century, for much of the next century many Americans were uneasy about embracing the class and political divisions encouraged by industrial capitalism. Equality of opportunity, vast resources, limited government, the benign working of the market and a diverse, fluid population would, it was believed, render such divisions superfluous. Conversely, as Britain recovered from the loss of the

American empire, adjusted to the early onset of industrialisation, and faced pressure for political democratisation, it displayed a marked desire to retain and strengthen class differences. Class organisations and movements consequently offered more promising outlets to British women than to their American sisters, though they developed in both countries. These took the form of trade unions, socialist groups and leftwing parties; cross-class feminist associations; and middle-class women's societies focused on the problems of the poor.

Of the three types, the middle-class organisations were the most problematical and the most powerful. Flattering to their instigators, approved by men and offering no threat to the status quo, their missionary rhetoric and invasion of privacy offended the recipients of assistance. Moreover, they confirmed the class gulf between women that was signalled by the reliance of middle-class reformers on working-class servants. But they did provide poor women with information, material assistance, educational and recreational opportunities, and access to political clout which sometimes resulted in valuable welfare legislation.[88]

The cross-class alliances had the most to recommend them. Suffrage campaigns in the United States and Britain fell into this category by the early twentieth century. Equally important were the British Women's Co-operative Guild (WCG, 1883) and the Women's Trade Union Leagues (WTUL), the latter originating as the Women's Protective and Provident League in 1874 in Britain, and reaching America in 1903. Such bodies gave organisational opportunities to working-class women, put pressure on existing trade unions which were reluctant to admit them, and forced women from very different backgrounds – notably Jewish and Christian activists – to collaborate and confront their prejudices about each other. Undoubtedly, however, they were undermined by prosperous women's expectation that they would lead, by the resulting resentment of working-class women, and by the opposition of working-class men to bourgeois societies which encroached upon the time and loyalties of their women. By the First World War, the cross-class groups were going against the tendency of British women to mobilise separately according to class, and the WTUL did not survive the additional polarisation of women caused by the war. In the United States, where class divisions, though growing, were still less marked and intractable, the league survived for another two decades; and white bourgeois American women were clearly more willing to step across the inconclusively debated class barrier than across the bitterly contentious colour bar.[89]

All this might lead one to suppose that trade unions and the Left generally would have provided working-class women with their natural collective outlets. Yet much stood in the way, and such women found 'that they must constantly look after their own interests'. Although we now know how important women were to industrialisation, until the later nineteenth century, American and British women in the paid workforce were few in number, unevenly distributed geographically, and concentrated in low wage, high turnover, so-called women's jobs. Employers welcomed them as cheap labour with little basis for collective consciousness or combination. Expected to leave paid work on marriage or pregnancy, and to juggle domestic and workplace responsibilities, women were regarded with suspicion by insecure male workers. Since only a minority of the latter were unionised by the First World War, and they were themselves exploited under capitalism, it is not surprising that they feared women workers' competition, neglect of the home and supposed indifference to organisation. The remedy, men commonly believed, was a 'family wage' paid to male breadwinners and sufficient for the support of a family. In the national affairs of unions and socialist groups alike, the reliance placed on evening meetings, public debate, personal mobility and direct action disadvantaged women, as did society's emphasis on male power as the norm. Yet just as the world of women's work was more complex than a focus on paid employment would lead us to believe, so – as Kathryn Gleadle puts it – the 'community remained a focal point' for women's action at the 'local and familial level'.[90]

Partisans frequently presented women with a stark choice between the claims of feminism and those of socialism; but here too is complexity, for both had much to offer. The women's movement was broadly respectable and female led, devised an elaborate programme, and pursued it pragmatically. In an era when women were defined by their selflessness and dependence, it was innovative in stressing women's right to choice and autonomy, and their related right to work equally for themselves and the greater good. It was innovative, too, in its recognition of the powerful impact of internalised social conditioning on sex roles. Socialism drew supporters by giving priority to the needs of an array of disadvantaged elements in society. Its theorists were generally better known than those of feminism. And through its recognition of the shaping and transforming importance of material and political forces, socialism also analysed the larger context of desired changes in a way that feminism sometimes failed to do.[91]

What is more, the two movements ostensibly had much in common, so that one can appreciate the belief of socialist ideologue August Bebel that they could, although 'marching separately, strike jointly'.[92] Devising similar programmes for women, both developed in response to economic change, deploring the existing power structure and women's exploitation. Both argued that the conditions experienced by women, far from being at their peak in western countries, had been better in earlier, pre-industrial times. Both stressed the role of the family in female subordination, while recognising the importance of women's maternal role. Both were led by internationally minded activists, with socialists forming their first international organisation, the Communist League, in 1848; and thereafter – working through the First (1864) and Second (1889) Internationals – finding it as hard as feminists did to agree on contentious issues and to throw off the bonds of nationalism. Both were better at indicting than altering prevailing conditions, not least because of ideological deficiencies and divisions. Both paid too little attention to transforming entrenched attitudes and had a weakness for mechanical approaches, feminists tending to see liberation coming with the granting of equality before the law, socialists tending to link it with women's involvement in social production and the assumption of household duties by the state.[93] Furthermore, both were guilty of tunnel vision, with white feminists being ready to define the oppression of women of colour as a race matter, and male socialists representing female and race problems as part of a larger class dilemma. Both were inclined to moderate tactics in Britain and the United States: countries which permitted considerable political freedom responded to pressures for change, and relied comparatively little on state force to crush dissent. Both, though bold in outlook for their times, were fearful of censure from within their own circles. And though both were inclined to generalise about class and race as if they were fixed entities, they were actually obliged to grapple with their complex and shifting realities.[94]

Despite these similarities and their intermittent contacts over suffragism, welfare issues and internationalism, middle-class and working-class women generally went separate ways, made uneasy by residence, work, organisational and cultural differences; by competition for scarce resources; and by the willingness of most feminists simply to reform the existing social system. Such gradualism was anathema to radical European socialists like Germany's Clara Zetkin, who worked to destroy the old order and often saw feminists as the class enemy. Zetkin's position found support in Britain where, it was declared, working-class women knew that 'the practical question is the question of class antagonism'.[95] When feminists in the American section of the First International demanded equal consideration for feminist and working-class concerns, they met a frosty reception from its organisers; as a result, American female socialists likewise came to accept that the 'emancipation of labor is a social problem, a problem concerning the whole human race and embracing both sexes'. The feminist campaign was believed to be a second order struggle because the 'emancipation of women will be accomplished with the emancipation of men, and the so-called women's rights question will be solved with the labor question'.[96]

Another area of contention between feminists and socialists was the overall significance of women's suffrage and the terms on which it might be sought, with many feminists accepting and many socialists rejecting compromise measures which required property or other qualifications from voters. Legislation protecting women in the workplace had also become a divisive issue between British feminists and labour women by the end of the nineteenth century, though feminists themselves disagreed over it, and socialist women did so initially, before moving into line with the thinking of their male colleagues. In the United States, where protective labour legislation for women had been legitimised by the Supreme Court in *Muller* v. *Oregon* in 1908, the issue continued to be troublesome, but primarily among feminists rather than between feminists and socialists.[97] However, the most important practical obstacle to collaboration was awkward timing: when organised feminism emerged during the 1840s and 1850s, the structures of a democratic utopian socialism fairly sympathetic towards women had collapsed,[98] and the organisations of a class based labour movement had not yet come into place. They would do so from the 1870s, but only slowly acknowledged women's special needs. Hence when labour in Britain, at the end of the century, recognised the need to break with New Liberalism and form an independent Labour Party to represent its class and reforming interests, the pressure to act came from men who expected loyalty from the women of their class but who for the most part lacked any obvious feminist orientation.[99]

All in all, feminists had no alternative but to proceed as they did in terms of class: that is, attempting cross-class ventures but – starting in Britain – often going their own way in the face of socialist hostility. As the British suffragist Ray Strachey diplomatically conceded, feminists and labour women each 'approved of the aims of the other, and shared the same ultimate ideal'; but 'their paths towards it diverged'.[100] In the chapters that follow, we shall see how this divergence increased between the two world wars; assess what the consequences were; and consider how in matters concerning race and internationalism, American and British women were comparably divided by their circumstances and actions.

3 The impact of the First World War

The significance of the First World War has been fiercely debated and understandably so. It is natural to suppose that a conflict which lasted so much longer than was expected, required so many novel expedients, and cost so much in blood, effort and treasure, left a profound mark upon the peoples who fought it. Yet as Penny Summerfield has pointed out, there is a tendency to generalise about the impact of wars on women that would be unthinkable with regard to men, whose diversity is taken for granted.[1] It is, moreover, difficult to establish how far such conflicts simply accelerate trends already under way. And it is equally hard to determine how far people traumatised by forcible wartime changes either exaggerate their significance or seek the comfort of traditional ways in post-war years.

In terms of the overall impact of the First World War, judgements on the British experience range from Arthur Marwick's influential view that 'the first total war in history' was a crucial agent of social change, to the essays edited by Constantine, Kirby and Rose, which see continuity rather than permanent transformation in most areas of life. American historians of the war have similarly diverse emphases, but on the whole its disruptive and disillusioning power is emphasised.[2] As far as British and American women are concerned, the case for continuity in conditions seems the stronger. Anti-feminist ideas were not destroyed by the conflict. Economic and political equality remained elusive. And feminist attempts to reshape family politics in the interests of women rather than male breadwinners encountered predictable hostility from a range of groups. However in the areas of internationalism, class and race, the impact of the First World War on the British and American women's movements was disruptive and largely unhelpful, not least because it underlined the growing differences between the two movements and the diversity of their constituents, only partially concealed by a shared interest in the suffrage.

War disrupts internationalism

The clearest casualty of the war was the confident internationalism of the nineteenth and early twentieth centuries: a confidence that had been displayed by bourgeois and socialist women alike. Peace societies formed in that period collapsed,[3] and according to Sylvia Pankhurst, the British socialist leader of the East London Federation of Suffragettes (ELFS), 'Internationalism seemed vanquished; its most prominent sponsors turned war-mongers.' Pankhurst exaggerated, but her wretchedness is understandable. Although her own family had stood together against the Boer War, in 1914 Emmeline and Christabel had abandoned militant suffragism and committed their Women's Social and Political Union (WSPU, 1903) to supporting the war effort. Suffragettes were thus among the many Britons for whom 'Patriotism flamed high; the best and worst of it; service and sacrifice, love of excitement, desire for advertisement, fear and prejudice'.[4]

In America, Sylvia Pankhurst felt, for a long time 'the War was remote as events in a history book; its naked cruelties were not realised.'[5] President Wilson's 1914 proclamation of neutrality had suited a people glad to avoid entangling alliances: a people who were conscious of an exceptional destiny, made easy by their geographical security, and highly critical of this particular European conflict. But once America was involved, in 1917, the war was promoted at home by a zealous Committee on Public Information. Unfortunately, in rallying the public the committee fostered extreme intolerance of disloyalty, whenever and however it was deemed to appear. Those who continued to advocate a restrained patriotism or, worse, internationalism on pre-war lines, could find themselves vulnerable to abuse, intimidation and even imprisonment.

Of course civil liberties were badly eroded in both Britain and the United States during the conflict, while propagandists on each side of the Atlantic unblushingly equated the Allied cause with the assertion of righteousness and the defence of civilisation. None the less, the abrupt switch of the United States from aloofness to a harsh bellicosity created domestic friction out of proportion to the human or material sacrifices it had to make in wartime.

As nationalist sentiments intensified, the international socialist component of the women's movement struggled to survive. But the damage was made worse because of the existing organisational and ideological problems that beset British and American socialists, at home and in their overseas dealings. These may be summarised as follows. The Second International never extended practical help to the socialist parties of connected countries; but its congresses brought women socialists together, and it eventually devised a programme for women's emancipation and issued directives on the subject that were hard to ignore. Its first resolution in favour of women's suffrage was passed in 1900, and in 1907, when the International Socialist Women's Secretariat was formed, support for female enfranchisement was made a matter of principle. Having taken this step, the Second International ruled that votes for women should be pursued through party machinery rather than the women's movement, as part of a drive for 'the full democratisation of political franchise in general'.[6]

The International's injunction embarrassed female socialists on both sides of the Atlantic. Taking the United States first: on the one hand, and especially in the west, activists were reluctant to sever old ties with women's suffrage groups just when those groups were expanding their own operations and attempting to work with, rather than for, wage-earning women. On the other hand, once America's elite suffrage women attracted undue attention from the press and showed signs of wanting to dominate the newly galvanised suffrage campaign, left- and right-wing socialist theorists, particularly in New York, publicly divided over whether to adhere to Second International policy. The feminist–socialist collaboration in suffragism continued of necessity, but so too did the tensions, aggravated by other difficulties within and between the two groups over sexual emancipation, the unionisation of women, and the emphasis of radical feminists, from about 1910, on women's entitlement to political, economic and behavioural freedom. In addition, established socialist-feminist organisations were finding it daunting to promote gender consciousness among the 'new immigrant' women, whose mobilisation increasingly challenged social activists in the early twentieth century.[7]

Hence when war came, the Second International was unable to rally already divided American socialists in opposing the hostilities, while they in turn were anguished at the International's inability to do anything to stem the tide of nationalism that was sweeping through Europe, even though in 1907 it had committed itself to the opposition of war and to fomenting revolution through strikes and similar action in the event of hostilities. Of the ten socialist parties in the eight warring countries, only four refused to support their governments, for all the emphasis socialism placed on wars being the indefensible outcome of the economic imperatives of imperialistic capitalism.[8] Forced back on their own resources, some American women socialists, ironically in collaboration with bourgeois activists, did petition, arrange meetings and speak out individually against militarism, preparedness and their country's participation in the war, braving governmental repression and the shock of seeing their Women's National Committee, set up by the American party in 1908, abolished in 1915. Such domestic peace efforts – considered further below (pp. 45–6) – were paralleled in 1915 by an international anti-war conference of socialist women, held in Switzerland and drawing delegates from the United States and Britain. And although the limited attendance and the perceived need for secrecy were in poignant contrast with lofty pre-war hopes, at least the women were more willing than male colleagues to rise above nationalist claims.[9]

After the Bolshevik Revolution in 1917, international socialism again failed to unify its forces, with some followers continuing to endorse the war and others moving into the Communist movement, supporting the founding of the Communist International in 1919, severing ties with reformist socialism, and denigrating both its achievements and its collaboration with bourgeois feminism. While theoretically committed to women's rights and approving the creation by the American Communist Party (1919) of a National Women's Commission, the new International (ultimately known as Comintern) treated them as 'an oppressed sector of the working class' and denied them the independent voice they had enjoyed under socialism. Furthermore Communist expansionism provoked virulent attacks by super-patriots in the United States. Although the Bolshevik Revolution was initially acclaimed by the British Left, British women socialists were, like their American sisters, subsequently divided by the creation of a national Communist Party under the direction of Comintern.[10]

The connection of British feminists with socialist internationalism was – like that of American activists – complicated by the Second International's determination to see socialist suffragists work through socialist parties: a stance that caused Mrs Fawcett to sniff that she had 'little confidence in the professions of political parties concerning woman suffrage'. Women's international activities were reported on usefully in the bulletin of the Women's Labour League (WLL, 1906). But British socialist women active abroad, who were separated by their party allegiances, vied with each other for control of the female branch of socialist internationalism. And, points out Karen Hunt, whereas feminist internationalists stressed the solidarity of sex, their socialist counterparts emphasised 'the solidarity of the human race'. Yet in Britain as in America, collaboration between socialist and bourgeois women did take place. Thus, for example, Susan Pedersen has demonstrated how pre-war British socialists and feminists formed a 'tentative coalition' to push for innovative family policies which would 'reconcile women's claims to personal rights and economic independence with the health and well-being of children'.[11] And female socialists from the Independent Labour Party (ILP, 1893) supported organised suffragism in various capacities and on various terms.[12]

However, official relations with the Second International were damaged and disrupted when sections of the British Left backed their country's war effort. As they did in the United States, unionists mostly endorsed the involvement, and they were joined by the bulk of the Fabian Society (1884) and the Labour Party (1906), which moved from denouncing 'the policy which has produced the War' to joining in the government's military drive and providing two members of the war cabinet. Even the Independent Labour Party contained individuals who approved the Labour Party line, albeit the most prominent ILP spokesmen continued in the pacifist camp. Labour women's organisations were divided too, with the WLL supporting and the WCG and ELFS opposing the war. If, in such trying circumstances, good will between individual socialist and feminist activists continued to manifest itself and the British labour movement was not reduced to impotence, this was no thanks to the vigour of the international leadership.[13]

In fairness, it must be said that little scope existed for achieving a different outcome. Had Clara Zetkin been challenged on the International by an equally strong ideologue who did not share her aversion to bourgeois feminists, much agonising and friction between women socialists and feminists might have been avoided; yet no such challenger appeared. While the International was not prepared for the war, or for its duration, then neither were most people. And the best pro-peace organisation in the world would have been hard pressed to retain its unity in the face of the obloquy encountered by the war's leftwing opponents, including Zetkin, and the opportunities for war service presented to its supporters. The quarrels that shook international suffragism as the conflict developed are a further indication that the dilemmas of international socialism were only partly self-inflicted.

Wartime internationalism

As Ann Wiltsher has pointed out, while the forty years before 1914 had seen the formation in Europe of 'over 400 religious, cultural, professional, humanitarian and political international organisations', once war broke out 'not one of these international groups attempted to retain contacts'.[14] Many IWSA women wanted to avoid this paralysis, and the pressure of their hopes was felt first in Britain, because of its early entry into the war and the location of IWSA headquarters in London. On both sides of the Atlantic, however, what activists could do was shaped by the progress of the war, the disruption of normal communications, and the extraordinary determination of small groups of continental European women, who suffered the war's worst privations, to keep internationalism alive.[15]

British activism

Women's international endeavours evolved after 1914 by a wearisome process of trial and error, if always in the hope of combining argument and action. Whereas politicians hesitated over how to halt the carnage, the women were aware that 'every delay makes more difficult the beginning of negotiations, more nations become involved, and the situation becomes more complicated'.[16] IWSA therefore hastily devised a manifesto which was sent to the British Foreign Secretary and the European ambassadors in the capital, calling on the European powers to 'leave untried no method of conciliation or arbitration for arranging international differences which may help to avert deluging half the civilized world in blood'.[17] The manifesto was followed by a well publicised Women's Peace Meeting in London. Gaining support from a broad spectrum of British women's organisations and revealing their frustration at female votelessness during such a crisis, the meeting also recorded their sense that, however much they deplored war, women would be expected to 'offer their services to their country'.[18] But while the leaders of the two main suffrage societies – the militant WSPU and the National Union of Women's Suffrage Societies (NUWSS, 1897) fronted by Millicent Fawcett – promptly committed themselves to do just that, each society contained women who were unhappy with the official line.

For these dissidents, it was important to keep communications open between internationalists and, as European links were weakened, to rally opposition to the war in the idealistic and still uninvolved United States. Accordingly the British suffragette Emmeline Pethick Lawrence, when speaking out for women's suffrage in the United States during 1914–15, simultaneously attempted to stir up American peace campaigners; and the English social worker, educator and suffragist, Mary Sheepshanks, who ran the IWSA office, made sure that its wide ranging journal, *Jus Suffragii*, continued to appear. But the restraint required in providing even-handed reporting of the war quickly took its toll, and in May 1915 Sheepshanks was complaining that coverage was 'getting very monotonous . . . By this time women of every nation have said their say about the war, and it is getting more and more difficult to get suitable material as we have to bar out every criticism of the combatants.'[19] The chief difficulty arose, however, when a sizeable group of NUWSS women pushed for participation in an international congress due to be held at The Hague in 1915: a congress which the cautious management of IWSA had declined to mount.

Before 1914, members of the NUWSS group had been convinced that a new international order built on 'the solidarity of human interests' was replacing the old order riven by national and racial divisions. If fear, aggression and old-fashioned masculinity had dashed their hopes and once again propelled the world into war, it was necessary to re-educate public opinion in the short and long term about the need for change. In the process, it was vital to highlight the connection between the male oppression of war and the male oppression of women; vital to establish the possibility of making a just peace and a post-war regime in which threatening disputes between nations would be submitted to arbitration and international law. The public promotion of these aims within the suffrage movement was vigorously contested by Mrs Fawcett, who, as president of the NUWSS and a fervent patriot, opposed any arguments or actions that would expose women's differences, jeopardise the prospects of suffragism, or hinder Britain's fight for victory and a world dominated by its 'progressive democracy'. In her judgement, the Union had no mandate to work on international lines to promote the right sort of peace settlement after the war', and 'it would hardly be possible to bring together the women of the belligerent countries without violent outbursts of anger and mutual recriminations'. Thus persuaded, she dismissed the fury her stance provoked among more pacific colleagues as largely 'due to nerves and overwork'.[20]

On this occasion, Mrs Fawcett was neither just nor candid. After the NUWSS council and executive meetings of February and March 1915, at which international matters came to a head and the Union decided against representation at the impending Hague conference, all the officers (except the president and treasurer) and over half the executive resigned. The only internationalist not to do so was the Scottish lawyer Chrystal Macmillan, who was out of the country. Through their letters of resignation, the executive members made it plain that they were not interested in a 'superficial unity' attained by inaction, or in the undemocratic 'sinking of the principles of the minority'. Rather they believed in a broadly based alliance which would go beyond relief work, 'uphold the ideal of moral force in human affairs', and so discredit militancy not just in suffragism but also 'on the vast scale involved in a European war'.[21]

From the point of view of the NUWSS's respectable image and ability to promote suffragism when the opportunity arose in wartime, it was as well that Mrs Fawcett's avoidance of peace endeavours prevailed. It is impossible to determine how far the views of the seceders were shared by the NUWSS members at large, but there is some evidence that support eventually rallied behind the nationalist stance, despite initial resentment of the ban on sending delegates to The Hague. Mrs Fawcett and her faithful lieutenant, Ray Strachey, were naturally delighted with the outcome and able to tell the official story of these events to their advantage.[22] For the defeated NUWSS internationalists, there was little in which they could take comfort, either as suffragists or as members of the similarly diverse larger peace movement, whose supporters ranged from pacifists who believed all war was wrong to more numerous individuals of what Ceadel has called the 'pacificist' outlook, who accepted limited force to avert war, believed war was sometimes necessary, and looked to international co-operation and institutions to avert hostilities.[23]

The dispute over the Hague Congress illustrates the danger of associating feminism with another controversial movement, however integral a part of feminism peace efforts seemed to women who thought that their maternal sensibilities gave them a unique mandate to oppose militarism.[24] An additional danger under these circumstances lay in the belief of some internationalists that they had to choose between pacificism and feminism. And if they chose pacificism for the duration of the war, straining or severing old feminist ties, there was a risk that they would remain focused on peace and international work at the expense of their domestic concerns, once the conflict was over. This was certainly the case with the committed Christian and public speaker Maude Royden; the teacher and writer Helena Swanwick; and the trenchant Mary Sheepshanks.[25]

A lesser group of peace women might have bowed before political defeat and heightened nationalism. But women like Chrystal Macmillan, Maude Royden, Helena Swanwick, the suffrage organisers Catherine Marshall, Margaret Ashton and Alice Clark (later an academic historian), and the administrator and reformer Kathleen Courtney, did not give up easily.[26] After all, Marshall, Macmillan and Courtney had been active in planning the Hague gathering. Their faith was justified when, in trying to get there, they were joined by a host of other prominent British activists, including key labour women. What followed was a mixture of farce and high achievement.

Although Macmillan and Courtney speedily made the trip from Britain, and Pethick Lawrence travelled to the Netherlands direct from her American speaking tour, the British government refused passports to the remaining delegates, who were then caught by its closure of the North Sea to shipping. Waiting fruitlessly at Tilbury in the hope of a government change of heart and a last minute steamer, the women were predictably hailed by the press as misguided and ridiculous 'peacettes'. Similar abuse was heaped on the internationalists who did manage to attend the Hague Congress, where the British representatives made up for their tiny numbers by playing a valuable role in its debates, and by helping to draw up a peace plan similar to that contained in President Wilson's later Fourteen Points. They also participated in the missions sent by the congress to lobby heads of state in both neutral and belligerent countries for a continuous mediating conference of neutrals. The women's aims included democratic peace negotiations; an end to secret treaties; the establishment of democratic conduct of foreign affairs; economic collaboration; universal disarmament; and the arbitration of future disputes by a permanent international organisation.[27]

If the male power brokers visited declined to call a mediating conference for fear of being unsuccessful, or of appearing unduly influenced by women operating outside their customary sphere, they none the less thought it worth seeing the envoys. The calculating American President complimented the women on 'by far the best formulation which up to the moment has been put out by anybody',[28] and they were generally offered, in the maxim of the Foreign Office, all assistance short of help. British women thereafter worked actively in Amsterdam on a new venture – the International Committee of Women for Permanent Peace (ICWPP). The committee employed Macmillan as its secretary and from 1919 became, on Marshall's suggestion, a permanent body called the Women's International League for Peace and Freedom (WILPF), based at Geneva. It arose out of the Hague Congress and by the end of 1915 counted ten European countries as members, in addition to Britain and the United States.[29]

According to Ceadel, the Women's International League (WIL), Britain's section of the ICWPP, was 'doctrinally too confused ever to become important'; and while he does not spell out how importance is to be measured, influence on government is implied.[30] His judgement is unjust, since from its inception WIL clearly aimed at publicising the decisions made at The Hague and reconvening at the close of the war to influence the peacemaking process. It clearly believed that 'the only guarantees of a lasting peace are the satisfaction of the peoples and the establishment of a League of Nations, making disarmament possible'.[31] To these ends, WIL formed some fifty branches, held meetings throughout Britain, produced literature, lobbied, and co-operated with like-minded organisations, including the prominent Union of Democratic Control. Along the way, its supporters endured surveillance, harassment and isolation.[32] Fairer criticisms of WIL might be that it recruited only a small number of largely middle-class women (3,687 in 1918),[33] and was too cautious in its approach.

Meetings of the WIL executive, on which the ex-NUWSS executive members were strongly represented, seemed interminable to Sylvia Pankhurst, and its avoidance of notable radicals irked her. Despite its brave opposition to conscription, her complaint that WIL 'carried no fiery cross' could not be rebutted. Yet she had to concede that it 'tried, in a quiet way, sincerely, if at times haltingly, to understand the causes of war, and to advance the causes of Peace by negotiation, and the enfranchisement of women'.[34] Furthermore, its feminist purpose alone would have ruled out extreme tactics, because British suffragists hoped that the WSPU's abandonment of militancy in 1914 would help them when the next extension of the vote was debated. WIL's strength in Wales, Scotland and the provinces might have reduced the time it could spend on metropolitan activities. But the British reform tradition has always depended on centres of influence outside London, and since there was less opposition to pacificism in those regions than in the south, it would have been foolish to neglect them. Nor did WIL members overlook practical assistance to the victims of war, undertaking international relief work on behalf of refugees and internees.[35]

Even the common association of female peace efforts with earnest and atypical middle-class women is not entirely fair. Despite disagreements among themselves, some socialist women protested against the war and conscription; condemned the linked forces of militarism and imperialism; and engaged in relief efforts. The WIL executive included such key labour activists as Margaret

Bondfield and Ethel Snowden. And the successful Women's Peace Crusade (WPC), launched in 1916, was an initiative of working-class women that secured the backing of WIL and other women's organisations. Helena Swanwick, for one, was pleased to report that, in addition to her WIL duties, she was 'stomping the country again quite a lot for the . . . WPC'.[36]

Through a series of meetings and demonstrations, the WPC tapped women's growing resentment of wartime conditions and collected signatures for a petition demanding a negotiated peace. The Crusade drew in ex-members of the WSPU who were repelled by the bellicose patriotism of Emmeline and Christabel Pankhurst, and active socialists who were encouraged by the Russian Revolution and unwilling either to be stranded by the collapse of the Second International, or to be upstaged by middle-class peace protests. Among them was Helen Crawford, a veteran of the campaign to stop rent profiteering in Glasgow and a woman well able to apply WSPU techniques to the campaign while avoiding suffragette extremes. In Glasgow, as in many towns and cities throughout Britain, the peace crusaders benefited from a warm relationship with the ILP and the WCG. For their part, by working with the WPC, Guild women and members of the WIL were able to add practical peace work to their conference resolutions denouncing the war and urging a negotiated peace.[37]

At the end of hostilities, British women had shown that peace was a woman's issue. They had demonstrated that they could campaign for peace and internationalism in wartime as well as peacetime, and with self-sacrificing passion as well as caution. Their wide-ranging efforts had not been nullified by the ideological disputes that affected feminism, socialism and the peace movement. Cheryl Law has shown that notwithstanding their diverse attitudes to the war, British suffragists managed to collaborate in putting pressure on the government for the vote: staging demonstrations, sending protest letters to the Prime Minister, and forming a consultative body which kept in touch with the parliamentary committee set up to 'discuss the many aspects of electoral and franchise reform' being considered by 1917. The women of WIL had brought a practical humanitarianism to peace endeavours that won applause from the pacifist philosopher Bertrand Russell, who was dissatisfied with the negative and 'idealistic theorising' of many other peace societies.[38] WIL also shared the commitment of WILPF as a whole to seek women's emancipation in the context of a broad process of change which would address the rights of labour and colonised peoples: aims which the critical Sylvia Pankhurst herself entertained. And British women peace campaigners had seen the need to stay in touch with wartime opinion and activists in the United States, not least to offset the visits there of Emmeline and Christabel Pankhurst, who were determined to dissipate American neutralism and stir up sympathy for the Allies.[39]

American campaigners

Unlike their British sisters, American women did not experience the pressure to action exerted by immediate national involvement in the First World War. They therefore had a little longer to consider their responses, within the powerful if unprepared American peace coalition,[40] before patriots rallied behind their country's war effort. Prominent in their pre-war national peace movement, American women had also benefited from the strengthening of their already elaborate network of associations by the Progressive reform upsurge of the early twentieth century. They were thus well equipped to make their voices heard both through established women's organisations and through the new peace groups which sprang up after 1915 in the United States.

As in Britain, women were obliged to look to their own resources because of the differences among the national peace societies, notably about how far to avoid peace activism and concentrate on 'what might be done in the realm of international reorganization and international law after the war'.[41] But American women had the advantage of being able to create a feminist peace organisation – the Woman's Peace Party (WPP, 1915) – without initially threatening suffragism. This was because the basic American division between militant and moderate suffragists had already occurred with the formal 1914 separation from the long established NAWSA of the inventive Congressional Union, headed by the Quaker social reformer Alice Paul, and known after 1916 as the National Woman's Party (NWP). Moreover, since they had taken the lead in internationalising feminism, American feminist pacifists were also in a good position to lead women's drive for acceptance in international politics: a campaign which had been stalled in their own country since the Spanish–American War.

American women were not content to ruminate about the conflict in a leisurely fashion. Mounting a large and novel protest parade of women in New York City in August 1914, they drew in female activists not formerly associated with the peace movement. Their arguments were more familiar, focusing on the claim that women were – as mothers, home builders and reformers – peculiarly disadvantaged by the costs and distractions of the wars men made; and on the assertion that women were – as selfless carers, workers, cross-cultural community builders and opponents of every kind of violence – especially suited to participate in the peacemaking process.[42] Furthermore, a conservative racial element underpinned the basic maternalist emphasis. Accordingly the minister, academic and reformer, Anna Garlin Spencer, protested against the war

> in the name of race culture and social welfare. Unless national ethics can be made to conform to high personal ethics, the diseases of our civilization will destroy its life. To breed from the unfit because the fit have been destroyed in war is to insure national degeneracy. To spend money needed for education, child protection, public health, and all social uses on armaments is to invite national disaster. To deliberately prepare for wholesale scientific human slaughter is worse than savagery. To dedicate youth to the trade of war is to cheat future generations of their birthright.[43]

A few months after the parade, and following careful debate, the WPP came into being, to give expression to these ideas. It was also in part a response to the

American tours of Emmeline Pethick Lawrence and the Hungarian feminist Rosika Schwimmer, as well as owing something to the pride of women like Garlin Spencer, who objected to the 'necessity of foreign women being used to awake American women to their duty'.[44] If IWSA had ceased to give a lead after 1914, and European women were waiting for a sign from the Americans,[45] then they would give that sign independently through the WPP. The party sent a large delegation to the Hague Congress, headed by the internationally respected settlement house leader, Jane Addams, who chaired the gathering in the Netherlands. The delegates reflected the party's support by young and old activists, conservatives and socialists, elite and working-class women. Going to the meeting with detailed plans for a mediated peace and a new diplomacy after it was secured, they played the key role in formulating the Hague resolutions; and Addams, despite misgivings that she might end up looking absurd, led one of the delegations to European capitals and was politely received by Woodrow Wilson.

Again in 1915, the WPP backed the proposal endorsed by the legislature of Wisconsin and made by a University of Wisconsin instructor, Julia Grace Wales, for a continuous mediating panel of experts. This was to be drawn from the neutral countries and authorised to submit peace proposals to the belligerents until an agreement could be reached. For the next two years the party also kept fruitless pressure on President Wilson to call a conference of neutrals, hoping that he was sincere in his reiterated commitment to neutrality and peace. With equal futility in the face of an increasingly hostile Congress, press and sectors of the business community involved in war production, WPP women opposed the domestic military build-up underway from late 1915 in the name of 'preparedness'. And they endorsed the unofficial conference to pursue the 'Wisconsin plan' that took place from December 1915 to the summer of 1916, with the backing of the maverick American manufacturer, Henry Ford.

After the conference, the 'peace ship' that conveyed an ill-assorted group of optimists to Europe attracted more attention than their deliberations once there, which were poorly managed both by Ford and by the mercurial Rosika Schwimmer. Although a Neutral Conference for Continuous Mediation was created at Stockholm, the relations between conference members were less than pacific and the press was willing to give the venture coverage, but only to ridicule all concerned. Nor was the reputation of WPP women improved with President Wilson by their brave criticism of American imperialism in Asia and in Latin America, even if public opinion rallied somewhat behind their resistance to his desire to occupy northern Mexico in the course of America's entanglement in the Mexican revolution. Nothing daunted, the WPP had by 1917 become the 'first secular peace organization' to establish a 'lobbying headquarters in Washington, DC, for the purpose of establishing ongoing relations with legislators in an attempt to influence policy'.[46]

While some feminist pacifists had thus set up an organisation of their own, and turned away from male peace associations that had 'as little use for women and their points of view' as the militarists, a number of women reformers moved with comparable deliberation but in collaboration with male colleagues to found a peace society that would reflect their distinctive outlook. Involving themselves first in the American League to Limit Armament (1914) and then in the Anti-Militarism and Anti-Preparedness Committees (1915), by 1916 they were backing the American Union Against Militarism (AUAM, 1914). Its president was Lillian Wald, a prominent public health expert and settlement house worker who also supported the WPP. Its supporters were largely veteran reformers of political bent who feared the damaging impact of war on 'social conditions and social programs'. Among them were Jane Addams; the crusading head of the National Consumers' League, Florence Kelley; the Chicago settlement house activist, Mary McDowell; the WTUL campaigner, Elizabeth Glendower Evans; the Harvard professor and expert on public health issues, Dr Alice Hamilton; and the Wellesley academic and experienced public servant, Emily Balch.[47]

The Union agitated against preparedness and conscription, advocating a mediating peace conference and new international machinery to avert future wars: nothing, it believed, should distract 'from preparation for that world peace which it might be our country's privilege to initiate at the end of the war'.[48] Making itself heard through meetings, a Washington lobbyist and the effective distribution of peace literature, the AUAM was based in the cities. It shared the WPP's opposition to imperialistic ventures, being most active against American intervention in Mexico; and from 1917 the Union was devoting increasing attention to defending the civil liberties of opponents of the war. Moreover as Doris Daniels has shown, Wald tirelessly reminded President Wilson of his reform constituency, 'assaulting him with her presence and by letter on the issues of conscription, submarine warfare, armed neutrality, a league of nations and civil rights for conscientious objectors'.[49]

For all the American peace groups, the entry into the war of the United States in 1917 posed a second immense challenge, whereas their British counterparts had faced only one, in 1914. Under the pressure of rethinking their policies, both the WPP and the AUAM fractured. In the WPP, the main divide was between women who continued to make opposing militarism and declining war work their priority, and suffragists who argued that their cause was nearing victory and would benefit by women's service to their country in the conventional ways. Neither the moderate nor the militant branch of American suffragism felt obliged to stop campaigning because their country was fighting a war, and the division between suffragists affected the peace rather than the suffrage societies. As a result, the situation in 1917 did not duplicate that which had confronted British women activists in 1914–15, and it was less alienating for old feminist comrades. Nor was there the symmetry in American suffragist attitudes that existed in Britain, where many militant suffragettes easily adapted themselves to supporting the militantly patriotic tactics expected on the home front during wartime. It was militant American suffragists in the NWP who for the most part supported radical peace activities but rejected the call to war work, even after 1917, and sought instead to advance suffragism by holding the party in power responsible for inaction in the national Congress, and by resorting to such shock tactics as the picketing of the White House and the publicising of the trials of women imprisoned for their protests.[50]

However Mrs Carrie Chapman Catt, the leader of the NAWSA moderates, did strongly resemble Mrs Fawcett at the head of the NUWSS, although Fawcett was much more determined than Catt to restrain the expression of pacifist sentiments in IWSA and *Jus Suffragii.* While Catt had supported the 1914 peace parade and the creation of the WPP, she remained wary of combining one reform movement with another and, as American suffrage activities intensified, she was determined to put domestic feminism before pacifism and internationalism.[51] Like Fawcett, Mrs Catt wrongly feared that the 1915 Hague Congress would end in damaging disarray;[52] and like Fawcett, she was not deflected from her purpose by clashes with more radical colleagues – specifically the WPP's New York branch, which included all manner of militants. Catt emphasised that 'but for the suffrage movement in Great Britain, the massing of women for war service would not have been possible';[53] and she and her moderate suffragist allies believed that showing American women's indispensability as war workers – rather than as the mothers and reformers they were once proud to be – would bring them the reward of the vote.[54]

Woodrow Wilson's second administration was pledged to pass only war measures, and by publicising women's war service NAWSA leaders hoped that female suffrage would be acted upon as such a measure instead of being dismissed as either a threat or an irrelevance. But they, like the moderate peace women, overestimated their influence with the president. Mrs Catt and her colleagues appealed to him in a variety of ways: arguing that enfranchised women would no longer be distracted from war work by the suffrage campaign; that a country engaged in a fight for democracy should not deny it at home; and that women voters would be grateful to those who enfranchised them. Wilson's response was disappointing: he moved only slowly to endorse the suffrage amendment and to exhort pivotal politicians to do so. As Jeffreys-Jones reminds us, the suffrage amendment was not enacted until after peace was secured, and the president may have been as much influenced by the sufferings of militant suffragists as by the entreaties of the Catt supporters. Jeffreys-Jones further suggests that the Catt strategy left women in disarray, just when Wilson needed all the domestic support he could get for the post-war settlement and the League of Nations.[55] Of course it is impossible to prove that female unity would have helped to secure so controversial a package, or that the women who proved themselves to be only 'peacetime pacifists' lost all credibility – pacific Americans of both sexes were torn between consistency and conventional patriotism. What cannot be disputed is that the differences between women activists, which were aggravated by the war and the climax of suffragism, persisted in the post-war years.

'Social radicalism' also caused difficulties in the peace coalition,[56] and these had equally significant repercussions for post-war internationalism. The personification of this radical tendency was the leader of the New York branch of the WPP, Crystal Eastman: journalist, attorney, socialist, feminist, pacifist, internationalist and general lifeforce. Eastman was criticised for her 'flamboyant political methods and unconventional life-style . . . throughout the war',[57] yet her charm and zest allowed her to make friends across the spectrum of peace groups, and though a radical she was fully aware of the balancing value of moderate campaigners. Even so, she could not build durable bridges to WPP conservatives or prevent social workers dismayed by the radicalisation of the AUAM from departing to take up respectable war service positions.[58] The only comfort was that neither organisation collapsed under the strain. The WPP ultimately became the American section of WILPF, while the AUAM laid the foundations for the American Civil Liberties Union and the Foreign Policy Association. Other radical spirits found some hope in the short lived People's Council (1917–18).

The council was modelled on those set up in revolutionary Russia, and reached out to radical, labour and farmer groups. Its determination to work for social justice as well as peace attracted some prominent feminist pacifists, including Emily Balch, Mary Ware Dennett, Rebecca Shelly, Fola LaFollette, Lella Secor and Elizabeth Freeman, whose interests encompassed suffrage, labour rights, the anti-lynching campaign and birth control. But Alonso has established that these women soon found their exclusively feminist interests being subordinated to those of socialism and peace. If the council's backing for an early peace conference answerable to the people was inspiring, its support for the 'democratization of political life' did not stress *women's* struggle for democratic freedoms. Activists accustomed to working through separate feminist associations not surprisingly went back to them; and they were lucky to have this option because the council began to run into trouble almost as soon as it was formed. Organised labour opposed it, women radicals still gave greater offence than men, and male socialists continued to be suspicious about working with bourgeois reformers.[59]

By the end of the war, cosmopolitan American peace women had helped to give a radical and feminist flavour to a peace movement once characterised, Marchand maintains, by 'genteel reform, self-interested business philanthropy, and conservative legalism'.[60] Although these activists, like men, had differed about the best course to follow both before and after 1917, they had brought a new confidence to women's old indictment of militarism; and, if unable to influence President Wilson's course as a neutral, they had reinforced his sense of the importance of a just peace. In a country which had always attached great importance to an educated citizenry, it was fitting that women should build on their accepted role as teachers and place more emphasis than men on educating the public about peace and internationalism.[61] Hence the veteran peace publicist Lucia Mead lectured and developed policy statements for the WPP,[62] while Fannie Fern Andrews was representative of the campaigners who accepted the need to 'assist the nation in winning the war for permanent peace'. Accordingly she adjusted the programme of her American Peace School League (1908) so that she could co-operate with the United States Commissioner for Education in educational war work, especially the promotion of the League of Nations.[63] American feminist pacifists were also forced to accept that there were limits to American exceptionalism. For having initially escaped the hostility encountered by their British sisters in a nation at war, they were exposed to more extreme manifestations of patriotism once America had entered the conflict. As a result, women like

Catt, Addams and Wald, who had stepped back from radical pacifism to protect their diverse reform interests, were ironically forced to defend their reputations against conservative attacks well into the 1920s (see chapter 4).[64]

Making peace

After the 1915 Hague Congress and until the end of the war, women in the United States and Britain had perforce to concentrate on domestic peace activities. But the ICWPP was committed to convening an international conference of women to coincide with the official peace conference. In fact this was not held until May 1919, in neutral Zurich, the victors having chosen to meet from January that year in Paris, a venue unacceptable to many women. The published peace terms reached women delegates as their Swiss meeting began. A majority of the ICWPP's national sections were represented in Switzerland, with the United States raising the largest delegation and Britain coming close behind (both countries sent over twenty members).[65] As had been the case at The Hague, the meeting was remarkable for the sublimation of national resentments and the ability to reach resolutions by way of discussion and compromise. It was enlivened by the presence of many committed feminists and socialists, and by the contributions of many seasoned campaigners, including the Montana suffrage leader Jeannette Rankin, who had increased her fame as the first woman member of Congress by becoming one of the fifty members who voted against America's entry to the war.[66] Jane Addams again presided.

Agreeing to push the Paris peacemakers for the lifting of the Allied food blockade proved easier than framing a view about the legitimacy of violence in national revolutions. Still more contentious was the peace settlement itself. Here the delegates came together by accepting the League of Nations. But they had reservations about the Covenant terms – notably its failure to guarantee 'self-determination in all territorial adjustments; free and equal access to raw materials; . . . [and] reduction of [the] armaments of all member-states'. And they damned the harsh treatment of Germany. The women presciently warned that it would 'create all over Europe discords and animosities which can only lead to future wars'. Their conference was the first international body to condemn the peace.[67] The Feminist Committee of the conference drew up a Women's Charter which asserted the 'supreme international importance' of the status of women, and laid down their entitlement to 'suffrage; property rights; maternity and guardianship rights; equal educational opportunities; equal pay; and "adequate economic provision for the service of motherhood"'.[68]

The British and American delegations found they had much in common during the Zurich conference. They did not share continental women's preoccupation with revolutionary change, and each delegation contained women who condemned the entire peace treaty.[69] Hence when the ICWPP was replaced by WILPF, a genuinely international body which allowed for sectional and individual representation on its executive committee,[70] the British had no difficulty in accepting the election of Addams as its president and Balch as its international secretary. The secretaryship was a lifeline for the fearless Balch, who heard at Zurich that Wellesley had dismissed her because 'she had been employed to teach economics not pacifism'.[71] Britain's Helena Swanwick became one of the two vice-presidents, the other – in a healing move – being Lida Gustava Heymann of Germany.

So much had been expected of America and its president, whose Fourteen Points so resembled those of the peace women, that Wilson remained in 1919 the chief target of their Zurich resolutions. And at least he acknowledged them, unlike the other Big Four negotiators.[72] Internationalists would continue to look for a lead from the United States after 1919, but its world role proved increasingly disappointing to them and placed a new strain on the relations between American and British feminists, as we shall see (in chapter 4).

The experiences of WILPF women at Zurich resembled those of the IWSA and ICW activists who, prompted by their French representatives, mounted a Conference of Women Delegates in Paris to try to influence the peacemaking process. In one clear respect they did better than the WILPF group, managing to establish women's eligibility for office in the League of Nations. Yet since women had actively pressed for such a league during the war, and the conflict had led to their enfranchisement in twenty countries, this was only a moderate concession. The optimistic American Fannie Fern Andrews managed to rejoice that women had been 'invited to present their Resolutions to one of the Standing Committees of the Peace Conference' and had encouraged 'some of the great humanitarian and educational efforts now being put forward on a world scale'; but the British representatives were dissatisfied with both the official conference and their own, which lacked the size and emotion of the Zurich assembly. Moreover, leaving aside the League, the women's conference failed to secure representation 'on the various international bodies which were being established'.[73] The meeting did provide an early taste of the time consuming and frustrating labour involved in seeking to sustain the role in international affairs that had been opened to women by the war.

Class and race in wartime

The war did not dismantle the barriers of class and race that separated British and American women, any more than it had united them against militarism. If women's groups proved keen to co-operate, the distinctive circumstances and histories of elite women, working-class women and women of colour pulled against the superficial levelling tendencies inherent in any great national crisis. Many poorer women, often struggling to survive and driven as individuals to grasp whatever came their way, were unaffected by the radicalism of feminist pacifists. Furthermore, despite the novel links they forged with proliferating government agencies in the areas of work, welfare and reform, poorer women largely operated through their customary organisational channels and encountered familiar irritants as middle-class activists attempted to give them help and guidance.

In Britain, women frequently experienced desperate hardship once their men went away to fight; or, as in the case of some quarter of a million individuals, once the 'suspension of trade and the closing down of luxury production' had cost them their own jobs. When by 1915 men's departure and the wartime economy had created new openings for women, they faced hostility from male unionists. Believing women's true place to be in the home, and fearing the loss of hard-won benefits enjoyed by skilled and trained workers, such unionists argued that women should only be allowed to take men's jobs – whether fully or in a simplified form – while the conflict lasted. Where women worked as full replacements for men, union leaders stressed that the newcomers should not be blacklegs but should be paid at the male rate. Although the government and employers accepted the unions' defensive demands, they were hard to implement for the 1,590,000 women added to the industrial labour force between 1914 and 1918, because both the practice of paying women less than men, and the habit of regarding them as by definition unskilled, were so deeply entrenched. Some women did, none the less, enjoy a better income and the challenge of holding down formerly masculine jobs.

A similar situation eventually developed in the United States, where approximately one million women were recruited to the industrial workforce between 1917 and 1918, and where their employment was also assisted by the wartime reduction of immigration. White women found themselves able to choose from a wider range of jobs, both civilian and military, while some black women were admitted to white collar occupations and skilled factory work that had once been closed to them. But as in Britain, employers, unions and government alike condoned the exploitation of women workers, with protective legislation being relaxed or suspended when it suited. And at the end of the war, women on each side of the Atlantic were discharged, excluded from skilled jobs, and forced to go back to traditional occupations or the home.[74]

Against this background of opportunity and hope, suffering and disappointment, American and British women workers were not content merely to be the victims of circumstance. The numbers of unionised women had, after all, risen sharply in the years before the First World War. Women's patterns of employment were already changing, and they had participated in the intense strike activity of the early twentieth century. More black American women than men had then moved from the South to the North in search of a better life, while labour women in both countries had sought the vote with an enthusiasm and militancy they had not generally displayed during the nineteenth century. As one British WCG woman put it, 'I joined the Suffrage, because having had such a hard . . . life myself, I thought I would do all I could to relieve the sufferings of others. I took great interest in all women's organisations.'[75] Undaunted by the war's elevation of everything masculine, such women – and their middle-class female allies – were energetic in publicising and seeking redress for wartime difficulties.

In Britain, Mary MacArthur, the secretary of the WTUL and of the National Federation of Women Workers (NFWW), transferred her formidable skills to the Central Committee for Women's Training and Employment, helping women to obtain work and using the NFWW and the Labour Supply Committee to check on women's working conditions and to speak out against low wages and other injustices. Women factory inspectors supplied expertise to the same ends, and a more militant voice came from Sylvia Pankhurst who, through her ELFS, provided what community services she could to women in distress, all the while drawing attention to their hardships, supporting their self-help efforts, and chivvying slow moving officials – female as well as male – who had the power to change things. Not least by means of training workshops, the suffrage societies aided women thrown out of jobs at the beginning and end of the war, and in the intervening years they provided baby clinics, maternity centres and refreshment rooms. The NFWW, the WTUL, the WCG and the WLL combined in the Standing Joint Committee of Industrial Women's Organisations 'to ensure that working-class women had fair representation on all government committees of interest to them'. These bodies in turn co-operated with the War Emergency Workers' National Committee, a coalition of working women's groups; and when conventional pressure tactics failed, working women joined unions, and took part in workplace and rent strikes, demonstrations and marches. As a result of such group efforts, Graves reminds us, women ensured that the government consulted them about rent controls, job training, separation allowances for the families of men in the armed forces, food prices and rationing.[76]

In the United States, there was a comparable upsurge of lobbying and self-help activities. Having anticipated America's eventual involvement in the war, and with the endeavours of British feminists to act as a spur, American suffrage societies co-operated with other women's associations to give employment assistance to displaced women workers, and to mount Americanisation drives among immigrants that offered practical services as well as lectures about American history and culture.[77] The national WTUL combined war work with its normal activities. Accordingly it joined with various women's organisations to press for the creation of a permanent Women's Bureau in the Department of Labor (secured in 1920). In addition, it trained labour activists, sustained its drive for the eight hour day, and planned for the resumption of peacetime struggles.[78] White and black women moved restlessly in search of better jobs, joined unions, and participated in the strikes that erupted in the war-torn economy. And making the best of its reluctantly granted advisory role, the Women's Committee of the Council for National Defense fought to make women's voices heard in government circles and laboured (unsuccessfully) to co-ordinate female war work. Women's visibility at the national political level was further increased by the creation of a Women's Council, which drew information from the growing number of female social workers and labour reformers who were employed in federal government agencies, and who were anxious to use their new influence on behalf of wage-earning women.[79]

Yet if at one level these endeavours confirmed the strength and similarity of British and American female activism, with hindsight we can see that they also conceded and often encouraged the divisions among women in the two countries, while revealing the contrasts between the two women's movements.

Welfare provision for American women was not given any special national boost during the war, despite the fact that before 1914 female reformers had invoked their maternal feelings and duties to dominate the debate about welfare legislation and institutions. As a result of this dominance, they had secured a female controlled Children's Bureau (1912), which through its investigations and wide contacts informed women and the federal government about such questions as child labour and mortality. And they had contributed to the passage of protective labour laws for women, as well as to the enactment of widows' or mothers' pension laws (from 1906 at the state level, with nineteenth-century antecedents) before they were adopted in any other country.[80] The wartime neglect of women's welfare therefore needs explaining, and part of the explanation relates to the shorter involvement of the United States in the First World War, and to its already having introduced the mothers' pensions which the war necessitated. It is nevertheless a useful reminder that there were limits to the impact of maternalism, even in a country where its power was enhanced by the highly educated and organised female reform network, the relatively weak and decentralised nature of the polity and trade union movement, the frequent unresponsiveness of entrenched political parties, and the stubborn political and court opposition to social programmes that might erode the supposed independence of working men.[81]

American women's maternalism is in fact a complex phenomenon, and among its adherents were feminists and non-feminists, activists with limited vision and those who placed their objectives in the context of broad social reform. But maternalism is frequently seen as associating women with a matriarchal and genteel culture that writers and intellectuals were beginning to challenge, that the professionalisation of social work was already undermining, and that the disillusioning destruction of war would date.[82] Worse still, maternalism was divisive both in the way in which its claims were promoted and in the way in which they were implemented. A growing number of scholars have established that American maternal and infant health programmes were advanced by stressing their importance for 'race betterment' at a time of high immigration and racial tension. Although maternalists claimed that they were speaking for women regardless of race or country of origin, they often strengthened the prejudices of eugenicists and the assumption of elite white women that they had a right to direct and so uplift poorer women. As a result, black children and mothers, particularly in the South, were patronised and discriminated against in public health programmes and when they applied for pensions. The burden placed on the overstretched resources of black activists consequently increased. Moreover, women's pensions in the United States were designed to support children not mothers, so ignoring the larger maternalist assertions about mothers' crucial contribution to society.[83]

British women also pressed for a more generous endowment for motherhood, and were encouraged by the impressive funding and level of independence for women involved in the wartime separation allowances. They benefited from working within a somewhat more interventionist state than their American sisters, and, though willing to use the 'race betterment' arguments that had come naturally to them in the imperial context, they were less driven by notions of a racial crisis in urgent need of attention. None the less, middle-class British reformers similarly alienated applicants for assistance by an enthusiastic monitoring of their worthiness. And they too found that the men with whom they collaborated – for example in the civil service – had their own agenda and a keen interest in keeping expenditure down. Hence the war brought two key pieces of welfare legislation for British women only in the absence of men; and Pedersen has shown that the separation allowances, together with the subsequent dependents' benefits for unemployed men, did not reward women for the important service of motherhood but rather recognised the rights of male citizens temporarily unable to earn.

Before 1914, bourgeois and labour feminists had often differed over how to tackle women's vulnerability in marriage, the home and the paid workforce, and they continued to disagree during the war. However, in order to stay on terms with labour men and to obtain political action on behalf of their sex, British labour women tended to accept the men's approach to welfare provision. Their inclination to work with men of their class, encouraged by the wartime enhancement of the political power of the Left, would be determinedly cultivated by labour men once the conflict was over. This said, British class complexities must ever be borne in mind. As June Hannam has stressed, the labour and socialist movements included middle-class as well as working-class women, and such women both divided among themselves and disagreed with male colleagues over welfare provision.

The British welfare focus, more than that of the United States, was ostensibly on adults not children, but the results for women were mixed. Take the administration of separation allowances. Because this work was eventually assumed by the state, the vetting of soldiers' wives by female social workers was ended; and with its demise, a serious blow might have been struck at the alienating notion that working-class women were irresponsible and in need of supervision. Yet the shift of control over separation allowances from the voluntary to the public sector, which in the long run could only weaken middle-class women's traditional reform work, meant the alteration but not the abandonment of surveillance. Furthermore, in practical terms children *were* significant beneficiaries of British wartime welfare, which built in large part on the earlier efforts of women's organisations and local government. The culmination here, Thane points out, was the Maternity and Child Welfare Act of 1918, enabling local authorities to set up maternity and child welfare committees which would receive 'a central government subsidy for a range of activities'. By contrast, newer female proposals for mothers' pensions were rejected as too expensive. The fact that such pensions were an American initiative could not work to their advantage, any more than the American example in reforming married women's property laws had galvanised cautious British legislators in the nineteenth century.[84]

Class, racial and political differences also persisted among American and British suffragists. Before the war, bourgeois campaigners on both sides of the

Atlantic had attempted to broaden support for women's enfranchisement and to associate it more firmly with the democratic tendencies in society.[85] But class divisions manifested themselves again at the end of the conflict when the National Woman's Party in America declined to embrace a wide-ranging social reform agenda, and the WSPU's national leadership in Britain accepted the government's age and property qualification for the female franchise. The lives of socialist women were, in addition, complicated not only by their need to work out their relationship with the Labour Party but also by the differences that developed between Labour Party members and supporters of the Communist Party of Great Britain, and by the hostility of many bourgeois feminists towards both (see chapter 6 for more on party political issues).[86]

Margaret Bondfield proudly stated, at the 1919 convention of the American WTUL, that working women were not going back to what they had been before the war, and that organisation and internationalism would take them forward.[87] However, their suffrage experiences had not inclined many of them towards further campaigning with bourgeois women. Not surprisingly, therefore, British labour women preferred to co-operate with their American counterparts when working for a labour women's peace conference at the end of hostilities. The International Congress of Working Women was finally held in Washington, DC, from October to November 1919. Intended to build on the wartime feeling in a number of countries that the peace treaty should attempt to regulate labour standards and conditions internationally, the congress concentrated on the needs and responsibilities of women workers, using the familiar claim that 'Women are the builders of the race. To us is entrusted the protection of life.' Unhappily, the British delegation fundamentally disagreed with other representatives at the congress about how widely the assembly should cast its net for members, and labour internationalism would only get harder in the years that followed (see chapter 6).[88]

As far as race is concerned, while the war provoked black American suffragists to greater militancy and increased white suffragist appreciation of their importance, it did not bring black and white suffrage organisations together. Consequently, women of colour were obliged to rely largely on themselves as they began the post-war struggle to register and cast their votes (see chapter 5).[89]

Finally, tactical and timing matters underlined Anglo-American differences. Suffrage militancy spread from Britain to the United States, and among the leading American suffragists who took 'fire from the English torch' were Alice Paul, Lucy Burns, Doris Stevens, Harriot Stanton Blatch, Mary Beard and Florence Luscomb. But the import was, as imports usually are, a mixed blessing. It was especially difficult for the majority of American suffragists to accept that militants in Britain, with its slow movement towards democracy, were leading the political arm of the women's movement and attracting the attention of feminists throughout the world. Many American activists disliked extreme militancy and doubted whether it was needed in their country, where some women already voted and the male population was alleged to be more enlightened than in Britain. Mrs Fawcett's relations with Mrs Catt were also sometimes difficult, as we have seen, and the British need to continue their agitation for universal suffrage after 1918 widened the gulf between the two countries.[90]

Conclusions

The opportunities and dilemmas facing American and British female advocates of peace, internationalism and reform between 1914 and 1919 had proved particularly testing. On a positive note, they had refused simply to settle for the relief work which, as Helena Swanwick grumbled, 'except for a few leaders and organisers, requires only jog-trot feminine capacities and has no permanent effect on policy'.[91] Women of all classes had agitated together and separately against militarism and for a better post-war world. American women, working in a more promising setting than their British sisters and without substantially disrupting suffragism, were especially inventive and adventurously feminist in the pursuit of peace and internationalism. The women's wartime gains – like those of their male allies – were mainly in terms of publicity and organisation. But female energies were institutionalised by the conflict, as they had not been by the Spanish–American War and the Boer War, and so continued on a firmer footing in the 1920s.

On the other hand, male and female peace activists were sometimes at odds in a movement men still expected to lead. They achieved no political breakthrough and could not, Maude Royden admitted, make pacifism appeal to the general public as a 'glorious romance'. Instead it seemed 'a dull, drab, sordid, selfish thing' to all too many patriots. Their failure might not have mattered if women had built upon this drab image by taking a frankly hard-nosed interest in the economic aspects of foreign policy. Unfortunately, until the interwar years, they usually failed to do so.[92] Conservative women were alarmed by the radical image of peace campaigning, though in fact it recruited women of every kind, and the adventurous cross-class alliances it forged survived no longer than the hostilities. Meanwhile, a larger body of British and American women, including feminists anxious to make use of their organisational skills, took up a huge range of war work. They found in it usefulness, stimulation, gender solidarity and an outlet for the special feminine qualities which they claimed as determinedly as peace advocates did. For Jewish and African American women, the respectability of war work ultimately added to its appeal, but black club women recognised that even here they needed to 'work quietly, yet effectively, not with the flare of trumpets, but with quiet determination to make our work count'. It is worth remembering that women from all backgrounds secured this relief work in the face of the initially patronising incredulity of male officials.[93] And they did so without neglecting efforts for improved maternal welfare in Britain, and for female suffrage in both countries.

In addition, and significantly for the future, the different experience of war by the United States and Britain had raised questions about the Anglo-American relationship: questions that affected women and after 1919 increasingly influenced their behaviour towards each other (see chapter 4). The novelist, social reformer and anti-suffragist, Mrs Humphrey Ward, might have responded enthusiastically to Theodore Roosevelt's request at the end of 1915 that she use her pen to influence American public opinion in England's favour,[94] but the self-conscious friendship which had united Britons and Americans since the 1890s was coming under strain. According to Rebecca West, it was impossible to exaggerate the degree to which Britons, in 1900, had 'believed in the innocence of the United States . . . (unless we were in the British Foreign Office in which case we feared that Washington might try to steal our Empire from us)'.[95] Yet in order to maintain its unprecedented wartime commitments, Britain was driven to seek financial help from the United States and, although neither its need for loans nor the consequences of borrowing were as grave as they would be by the Second World War, some British observers were uneasy. Perhaps the United States was not innocent but selfishly isolated and economically alarming. Perhaps it would soon be in Britain's place. Perhaps the Foreign Office was right. Even such dedicated American peace women as Anna Garlin Spencer and Jane Addams had, like President Wilson, shown a strong desire to follow an American path to peace and internationalism.[96]

None the less, the British and American suffrage, welfare and peace campaigns trained enormous numbers of women who, at the war's end, renewed old struggles and took up new ones, sustained by friendship and idealism as well as tested by their own disagreements.

4 Feminist internationalism and nationalism between the wars

Are women free enough to need no further help from an international organization?

Quotation from article in *The Woman Citizen*, 15 May 1920[1]

The answer to this question, posed at the 1920 conference of the International Women's Suffrage Alliance, was delivered in the negative by the leading feminists of the United States and Britain, just as it had been in the years from the 1880s to the First World War. The vice-president of the National Woman's Party, Doris Stevens, spoke for many women when she declared that 'Since the subjection of women is world-wide, we feel that this subjection can be removed finally and permanently only through international co-operation'.[2] And the post-war world at first seemed encouraging to internationalism. Despite the undermining upheavals of war, Leila Rupp has noted that some 500 international associations were still operating in 1920.[3]

The organisations focused on in this chapter are those dominated by white, middle-class activists: namely the International Woman Suffrage Alliance (renamed the International Alliance of Women for Suffrage and Equal Citizenship in 1926 and hereafter referred to as the Alliance); the Women's International League for Peace and Freedom; the Inter-American Commission; and the Committee on the Cause and Cure of War. The endeavours of the International Council of Women of the Darker Races, the International Federation of Working Women and the International Co-operative Women's Guild will be considered in chapters 5 and 6, in the context of wider discussions of race and class issues. Given their significance for race and internationalism alike, imperial issues have been considered in the context of both themes in chapters 4 and 5.

Major difficulties none the less faced internationalists in general, and British and American women in particular. First, the debate about the nature and wisdom of the connection between pacifism and feminism, which had erupted during the First World War, continued intermittently throughout the interwar years and became especially troubling in the late 1930s. In the second place, women internationalists were confronted by an array of daunting problems connected with economic insecurity, assertive nationalism and, by the 1930s, a

'"Back to the Kitchen" movement which is gaining momentum in every country'.[4] Third, with female enfranchisement having been granted by many countries at the end of the First World War, campaigners were no longer widely united across national barriers by a desire to end their shared votelessness. And finally, the domestic and international circumstances of Britain and the United States increasingly diverged.

In America, activists were affected by a period of economic expansion and political reaction for much of the 1920s, succeeded in the following decade by a peculiarly severe depression and a political response to it that showed the dynamism of a reunited and liberalised Democratic Party. Following the American rejection of League of Nations membership, they were also faced with isolationist pressures which mounted with the collapse of the international economy and the growing conviction, in some quarters, that the United States had entered the First World War as a result of unworthy economic pressures. In Britain, by contrast, the post-war years were economically difficult for women from the outset and, while British membership of the League gave them one advantage in internationalism, the strength of political conservatism between the wars worked against feminists who had traditionally looked for encouragement to a more interventionist liberalism or socialism.

An additional strain for campaigners on both sides of the Atlantic came from the marked chill that affected Anglo-American relations after 1918. The First World War had already demonstrated to Britain its disturbing need for financial aid from the United States. The years that followed produced further tensions between the two countries as America, sustaining its own young empire but still hostile to European colonialism, emerged 'as [Britain's] . . . competitor on a global scale', and the British struggled to reassert their imperial power, ineffectually in the 1920s but with some success after America 'retreated into economic isolationism' in the 1930s.[5]

Under these trying world and national conditions, British and American feminist internationalists understandably devoted much time to their own distinctive policy concerns. Activists in America, for instance, as Rhodri Jeffreys-Jones has shown, drew on a stronger tradition of organised female consumerism than existed in Britain, asserting their power as consumers in the prosperous 1920s and bringing pressure to bear on government for tariff reductions. They likewise displayed a growing interest in Latin American women, regarding their overtures as in no way imperialistic; and they rallied to an opportunity not straightforwardly presented to British women of backing the treaty designed to outlaw war that became known as the Kellogg-Briand Pact (1928). In the following decade, they played a leading part in agitating for an inquiry into 'the munitions industry's influence on foreign policy'. And between 1939 and 1941 they were obliged to respond to an 'America First', militant and largely female branch of pacifism which did not have an equivalent in Britain. Among British activists, though there was in the 1920s some opposition to war profiteering comparable to that which peaked in the United States in the 1930s, the focus of attention was primarily on the activities of the Geneva-centred League of Nations, on female emancipation in the various parts of the empire, and on the relative merits of pacifism and anti-Fascism.[6]

These contrasting policy priorities in turn sometimes soured personal relations between the two countries' feminist leaders, and certainly strengthened their awareness of differences in national style. Differences in British and American mores and sensibilities had, of course, always been evident to Anglo-American feminists. But their pride in national aspirations and achievements had been less obtrusive and had consequently grated less in the early days of the organised women's movement, when America and Britain were growing closer together politically, economically and diplomatically.

This chapter will first consider the impact on the Anglo-American feminist connection of contrasting national styles. It will then assess the importance to that connection of activists' growing differences over the issue of protective legislation for women. A discussion of American and British feminists' foreign policy preoccupations will point up how they were divided by their geographical focus and attitudes to empire, despite their shared interest in promoting women's rights abroad. And an account of British and American peace efforts will reveal the greater confidence, organisational strength and policy range of American campaigners. By looking at the last three questions in some detail, it will also be possible to indicate the intra-feminist divisions that existed in each country, and to do justice to the achievements as well as the failures of Anglo-American internationalism.

National style and leadership tensions

Of necessity, differences in national style are hard to pin down: hard to distinguish from merely individual prejudices that do not deserve serious consideration. But in the case of America and Britain, they are none the less real – fascinating and exasperating travellers, diplomats and all who had reason to reach out across the Atlantic. We have noted (above, p. 6) that Emily Balch saw Britons and Americans as possessing very different characteristics, and it was commonly thought that these resulted in a British style which favoured understatement, formality and compromise, reverence for party political and class ties, respect for authority and established institutions, and acceptance of the validity of secret diplomacy and traditional alliances. By contrast, the American style prized open diplomacy, social fluidity, informality, extreme individualism, and the celebration of religious conviction, material success and national exceptionalism.

Clearly such generalised perceptions of difference did not prevent individual American and British activists from co-operating. Reformers in the two countries had competed in doing good since the nineteenth century, and their tradition of accepting observers and collaborators from overseas still continued. Thus, for instance, Elizabeth Robins, Hazel Hunkins-Hallinan, Betty Gram and Crystal Eastman were able to work in the British movement after the war, and Ray Strachey, the half-American historian of that movement and biographer of Millicent Fawcett, was an ardent Anglophile. She once confided to Fawcett that 'I often think to myself with a real pang of pleasure that I have married an Englishman and have English children'; she added, 'I've always thought it was one of the solidly good things in the world. Englishness, I mean, and the characteristics of it.' The American-born British MP Nancy Astor modelled her Consultative Committee of Women's Organisations on the Women's Joint Consultative Committee that she had observed during her trip to the United States in 1922. And other British feminists made similarly successful American visits, notably Margery Corbett Ashby, president of the Alliance from 1923 to 1946, who toured the United States in 1925, 1934 and 1937.[7]

As an internationalist and a publicly diplomatic woman, Corbett Ashby said of her 1925 trip, 'I have made up my mind to consider the real reason of my coming is the interest in studying the Americans at home and trying to understand their attitude towards world affairs & not to bother over much about my "uplift" of them but to complete my own education.' After all, she met old friends and made new ones, and the veteran suffragist Harriot Stanton Blatch even 'offered to raise money for . . . [the Alliance] in the States', so that Corbett Ashby 'Nearly wept with gratitude'. However, if she admitted that Americans seemed 'more like us than I had imagined', her superiority complex and sense of Englishness were intensified by the compliments she received about English law and education; by being assured that no American woman could make such 'well constructed & expressed' speeches; and by the American public's sceptical approach to the League of Nations.[8]

A similar awareness of national differences is evident in the dealings of American and British feminists who collaborated productively in the British women's movement. Thus if Nancy Astor's brilliance and confidence were appreciated by Mrs Ashby, the Englishwoman felt that Astor needed a mentor (Ray Strachey obliged) 'because she was an American and had no respect for parliamentary discipline or good manners'.[9] Like Astor, the American journalist Hazel Hunkins-Hallinan had settled in Britain and she achieved the unique distinction of heading for many years a national feminist organisation – the egalitarian Six Point Group (SPG, 1921) – without having climbed to office, as Astor had, 'through marriage to an English title!' She, like Astor, benefited by being taken in hand by a local activist: in her case Teresa Billington-Greig, who was, Hunkins-Hallinan recalled, a 'wonderfully strong, determined person, and absolutely sure she was right'. But that combative quality did not lead to trouble because Billington-Greig knew 'the Six Point Group wouldn't be Americanised by me', a process opposed by British feminists as well as British conservatives. Furthermore, Hunkins-Hallinan believed that 'being a foreigner has its advantages sometimes', because it allowed her to apply the perspectives of two countries to British issues. It also let her rise 'above the petty factions' that existed 'between all the British feminist groups': 'I didn't have a part of them: no part in their past history'. For this reason, she modestly believed that she was 'more useful in my position than an English woman of even more talents would have been'.[10]

On the other hand, Hunkins-Hallinan was friendly with Crystal Eastman throughout the radical activist's post-war stay in London, and the two women, besides finding paid jobs hard to secure, had 'a shared antipathy to certain British ways'.[11] One of these was the strong 'instinct for compromise' among the English which, Eastman thought, led to 'unnatural' and 'unworkable' attempts to keep ideologically and practically opposed feminists together during the 1920s, when a 'complete realignment' of feminist forces had taken place in the United States. However, there is something to be said for the cautious British style if the matter of protective legislation for women is considered (see below, pp. 56–60). This was the chief issue that divided interwar feminists on each side of the Atlantic, and when British Labour Party women and middle-class feminists debated it in provocative class terms, nobody gained.[12]

The attempt to build a permanent international organisation of working women, following the 1919 International Congress of Working Women, was also bedevilled by personal and principled disagreements between British and American activists. At the policy level, they differed about the wisdom of mobilising separately from working men. And at the personality level, as Jacoby has pointed out, Margaret Dreier Robins, the head of America's national WTUL, was a forceful character who clashed fiercely with Marion Phillips, the secretary of the British Standing Joint Committee of Industrial Organizations, one of the bodies through which her countrywomen were represented internationally (see chapter 6).[13]

In both these cases, British and American feminists alike were convinced that their customary ways of speaking and doing were best, and they acted upon this conviction. During the nineteenth century, British activists had congratulated themselves on their decorum and pragmatism, while Americans had laid claim to boldness and idealism. By the twentieth century, their perceptions had not greatly changed, but feminist awareness of national differences had increased in direct proportion to the growth of American power. Not surprisingly, the British disliked losing ground and the Americans were less willing than they had been to tolerate British pretensions. Accordingly Emily Balch confided to Jane Addams, 'I do think the British are difficult', and regretted their tendency to react 'with a sledge hammer', which was the British 'way of being frank'. A similarly exasperated Carrie Catt wrote to an American reformer in 1925 that suffragists in Britain shared 'the characteristics of their country and are a little resentful toward the United States when it takes the lead in anything. For many years matters in the Alliance moved along with great smoothness; but this was during the time when I held every rein in my own hands and raised the money for its maintenance. After I was elected President of the NAWSA [in 1915] and was obliged to allow many of the details to be turned over to officials in Great Britain, I lost some of the control, naturally, which I had very strictly held before, and with the loss of control there came a bolder manifestation of resentment toward this country because the Alliance was so completely dependent upon us for support.'

Catt went on to recall a meeting when 'the very statesmanlike and splendid president of the suffrage movement in England' alienated the last American treasurer of the Alliance by at once opening 'the subject of money', and saying that 'you rich Americans cannot dictate the policy of the Alliance with the threat of giving or not giving funds for its support'. Catt was unamused, noting that 'Had it not been for this country the Alliance could not have lived to this day.' Moreover, Catt alleged that when Corbett Ashby visited America in 1925, 'in the backside of her mind was the intention of getting in touch with a great many people who she thought had in some way not been properly informed about the Alliance. I think the English suffragists were very suspicious of me. I think they thought somehow I was restraining Americans from giving to the Alliance.'[14] When such feelings were aggravated by differences over issues, the prospects for maintaining a truly harmonious relationship between American and British feminists were further diminished.

Divisive policy issues

Protective legislation and egalitarian feminism

Of all the issues that undermined goodwill between the two countries' campaigners, the most trying and intractable was industrial or protective legislation for women. Forcing this particular issue were a cadre of determined radicals from the National Woman's Party of the United States, who set about exporting their opposition to protective legislation. They carried their case to Geneva, and to the national and international associations of women: and they began with Britain. In 1925, Crystal Eastman celebrated the creation in London of a British advisory group to the NWP: 'the first national group of what is bound to become a world-wide Equal Rights Committee', formed to 'guard the rights of women and watch over their real interests in all international agreements, treaties and "conventions," and to advocate and proceed with the full program of Equal Rights for men and women throughout civilisation.' The eight-strong advisory group was described by Eastman as 'a practical bit of co-operation between British and American feminists', and Elizabeth Robins, the American actress, writer, and former suffragette, long based in Britain, was one of its members.[15] Its formation opened a battle whose salvoes exploded sporadically until the Second World War.

The debate over protective legislation had disturbed British feminists and labour women alike before it had surfaced in the United States, because Britain's prior experience of industrialisation had politicised the issue as early as the 1840s. But the British were not polarised at home by any equivalent of America's Equal Rights Amendment (ERA) – proposed by the NWP in 1923 and allegedly threatening the Progressive era's hard-won protective laws for women. It took deteriorating economic conditions and the NWP shock troops on the international scene to reanimate the question among British feminists at home and abroad, and to make permanent the rift between British labour women in favour of protection and middle-class feminists who stressed the importance of freedom.

Having given warning of its international ambitions in 1925, the NWP in 1926 applied to affiliate to the Alliance. It hoped through the organisation to prevent 'further passage or ratification' of international 'protective labor conventions for women employed at night or in such hazardous work as the mines and the lead paint industry, for [party activists] . . . feared the precedent which would be set if women were excluded from any employment opportunities.'[16] The NWP's membership bid was turned down by the Alliance at its 1926 Paris conference; but the decision at once divided feminist internationalists outside America.

In Britain, sympathy for the NWP stance was concentrated in the National Union of Societies for Equal Citizenship (NUSEC, 1919), in the Women's Freedom League (1907), and in the SPG: a group whose leaders included the energetic suffragist, journalist and businesswoman, Lady Margaret Rhondda.[17] The SPG in fact withdrew its own application for Alliance membership, as a gesture of solidarity with the NWP, and the Alliance was further weakened by losing a number of egalitarian European organisations. Moreover, some alienated British women subsequently joined the Open Door International (ODI, 1929) and the Equal Rights International (ERI, 1931) in their fight for equal rights. That fight principally encompassed three forms of action. It involved pushing for the Equal Rights Treaty, first envisaged by Rhondda in 1926, and formally proposed in 1928 as the international counterpart to America's Equal Rights Amendment. It meant backing the Equal Nationality Treaty, urged after 1930 as a means of securing independent citizenship rights for married women. And it entailed pressing the League of Nations to uphold women's equality and live up to the promise of Article VII of its Covenant that 'All positions under or in connection with the League, including the Secretariat, shall be open to men and women.'[18]

The 1926 NWP application to the Alliance also strained relations between the principal American and British feminist internationalists, though the diplomatic Corbett Ashby did her best to stay on terms with everyone concerned in the quarrel. She met and reassured Belle Sherwin, the president of the League of Women Voters (LWV, 1920), the American group most opposed to the NWP and in 1926 the representative of the United States on the Alliance. She responded in a measured fashion when Mrs Catt warned her about the NWP, though she denied firmly NWP allegations that the Alliance had approached it as a potential member and for money. She, like Catt, could clearly see that the Alliance had 'grown to its present prestige and prosperity' by 'the avoidance of national disputes in our international body'. Alice Paul, the NWP's intrepid leader, disingenuously declared that her group just wanted to 'offer aid to those who are working in the international woman movement'. But her allegations about the Alliance had given offence and Corbett Ashby additionally felt that NWP opposition to the 'policy and political action' of the LWV was a good reason for retaining the status quo. So, clearly, did the admissions committee. Thereafter, Corbett Ashby hoped that 'unofficial co-operation' between the Alliance and the excluded NWP would 'still be possible': as it turned out, a pious hope.[19]

To its British allies, as well as to its own members, the NWP's willingness to act made it admirable, whereas groups such as the Alliance allegedly were 'neither built nor intended for swift, continuous and effective action'. For these supporters, the bold activism of NWP leaders on equal rights issues provided a refreshing contrast to the 'mole like qualities' often displayed by less confident campaigners. It was, Lady Rhondda assured Stevens, 'absolutely clear that the torch of the militants which has been handed from one side to another of the Atlantic time & again during the last century is now in the hands of the Woman's Party & I would follow you if I were the only woman in Europe to do it. But I should not be the only woman'.

Rhondda, like NWP members, was convinced that most women internationalists were social reformers 'interested in a dozen things besides equality; the majority of them do not even place equality first on the list'. Unfortunately for those of her egalitarian persuasion, these reformers were similarly fond of getting their own way, and in 1928 Rhondda admitted that 'the prejudice against the National Woman's Party has not at all died down since Paris but rather increased (naturally enough since the Corbett Ashby crowd were faced with the alternatives of either blackening the name of the NWP or allowing their own action to be shown up as pretty muddy – and naturally if rather meanly they chose the former alternative)'. Under these circumstances, Rhondda felt that only a trip to England by Paul and Stevens, bearing 'a constructive programme', could improve matters. The drive for international equal rights legislation being their show, they were 'bound to lead it'.[20]

The differences over equal rights between and among British and American feminists were aggravated by the fact that Stevens and, more particularly, Paul, had a considerable talent for generating feuds. Thus, for example, Paul condemned the British head of the ERI, Helen Archdale, as dilatory and 'unwilling for us (the Americans) to have anything to do' with her organisation: 'I do not know why – perhaps she was afraid we would do something extreme' and put it 'into difficulty. At all events we were treated as outsiders.' This was naturally irksome to the Americans, because 'We paid practically all of the expenses of the . . . [ERI] in Geneva, and in addition gave them a donation of £200'. What made matters worse was the inability of Archdale, in her turn, to understand Paul's point of view; and so when she confided to an American correspondent in 1934 that 'The distressing breach between the NWP and the ERI wants all the glueing we can give it', she genuinely seemed at a loss to know how the rupture had come about. In fact, as Miller has pointed out, some ERI women modified their original position on the Equal Rights Treaty, having come to believe that it was not practical politics: Paul and her followers did not make this shift.[21]

The tetchiness of Stevens and Paul may have been compounded by their frustration over the geographical and hence ideological distance of American feminists from the headquarters of international endeavour at Geneva. Alice Paul frankly urged a British collaborator in the 1930s to get women to act 'without our having to work from this hemisphere as we are so far away'. She was convinced that 'Our greatest difficulty in doing anything [in Geneva] . . . lay of course in the fact that we were outside of the League.' This outsider status predictably provoked animosity: even the polite Corbett Ashby, when in America trying to raise money, chided her hosts about staying out of the League of Nations. It was, she reflected, 'a stage of development the States had to go through' – 'trying to get the good out of . . . [the League] without the responsibilities'; though she could not help adding that 'far too much fuss' was being made about Americans' aloofness, and 'that the League would go on quite well without them'. Aware of how the world's most powerful nation was regarded abroad, Carrie Catt felt obliged to warn an English ally that 'whatever you hear in Geneva about the United States or anybody in it is pretty sure to be a big, black lie'.

Even when the Americans acted positively and generously, they ran into exasperating difficulties with their British allies. We have already noted that Americans' money was vital in keeping international associations going, whether they operated in or outside Geneva. But while this might be conceded, it presented problems, with Americans frequently feeling that the generosity was not properly acknowledged, and women of other nations fearing that those who wielded the power of the purse might assume that they were entitled to assume the power of command – just as Mrs Catt had done. Hence one wealthy American internationalist, Alva Belmont, in 1929 confided to Paul that 'I do not believe that we will get any assistance at all from England. They take the position that they are friendly to us, but are very jealous of our power and will not in any way assist us to increase it.'[22]

What should be our verdict on these antipathies and disputes? On the one hand, there are a number of reasons why they can be regretted, and some of these have significance beyond the Anglo-American connection. Internationalism had been disrupted by the First World War; and despite its impressive recovery, Rhondda acknowledged as late as 1928 that 'International feminism is still a bit difficult to arouse interest in except in the already educated.'[23] Differences between reformers have usually been used against them, and even sympathetic observers were of the opinion that women should correct their tendency 'to be severe on each other'.[24] Unified groups have, by contrast, frequently gained respect – for instance the Anglo-Jewish community in the eyes of the Foreign Office during the First World War.[25] The loyalty that women felt for their respective organisations, and the tendency they displayed to exaggerate their own societies' virtues, only exacerbated differences over women's needs and how to realise them internationally. Consequently, such differences persisted throughout the 1930s, with Stevens then deploring that 'so much energy' was 'spent and still is, in wasteful controversy'.[26]

The NWP came in for especially strong criticism from contemporaries, and it did indeed alienate moderate American and British women by its singleminded advocacy of equal rights legislation, and its assumption that only NWP members were true feminists.[27] Of course the division between egalitarian and protectionist feminists originated in the domestic, not the international, politics of Britain and the United States. But given the extraordinary drive of women like Paul and Stevens, their determination to take the equal rights struggle abroad was profoundly significant.[28] For it both put a strain on Anglo-American feminist relations and precipitated 'a schism in the international women's movement', which, Becker has argued, weakened that movement's ability 'to resist the impact of the deepening worldwide depression and the rise of fascism'.[29]

On the other hand, although the differences between British and American feminists could be wearing and embarrassing, national action and international collaboration still continued. The British egalitarians were happy to recognise the lead given by their American counterparts, while the American equal rights advocates freely acknowledged the value of a vigorous woman like Rhondda. Moderate internationalists on either side of the Atlantic were similarly cordial towards each other. Furthermore, if Anglo-American tensions were particularly important during the interwar years, because of the two countries' leadership of international feminism, the divisions between European women activists were often just as great, notably over political ideology and the best way of responding to the deteriorating global situation. Given the severity of world problems and of male hostility towards women's involvement in foreign affairs, it is unwise to assume that unity among feminist internationalists would automatically have accorded them greater political influence. And whatever their problems, the internationalist women of the United States and Britain were not the sort of reformers who, as America's Jane Addams once said, travelled 'from the mire of self-pity straight to the barren hills of self-righteousness'.[30] They were generally intrepid doers. Accordingly, in turning to their efforts to forge links with Latin American and Commonwealth women, and to sustain disarmament, international institutions and peace, we must bear in mind that these efforts had very positive consequences, even as they underlined the frequently different preoccupations of British and American feminists.

The British Empire and Latin America

We have noted in chapter 2 that British and American feminists alike, if to lesser degrees, were shaped by and helped to shape debates over the possession of colonies, with the prospect of service abroad and 'uplifting' native women proving at once highly appealing to white activists and subtly corrosive of the feminist ideal of universal sisterhood. What has been called 'feminist orientalism' or 'imperial feminism' used the alleged cruelty and backwardness of 'the East' with regard to women to justify the leadership of international feminism by white western females. In the process, white western men were reminded of the civilised behaviour towards woman that was meant to be one of the distinguishing features of their masculinity.[31] Women of colour, living in the formal and informal empires of Britain and the United States, developed increasingly pointed and embarrassing responses to such reasoning. Yet in assessing them, it is necessary to recognise that some western feminists, especially in WILPF, *did* attempt to live up to their claim to work for 'social, political and economic justice' for all, 'without distinction of sex, race, class or creed'.[32]

For British activists, the future of India and its women was of special significance, and had been since the emergence of organised feminism, as a number of scholars have pointed out.[33] From the 1860s, the educational reformer Mary Carpenter had encouraged fund raising to improve Indian women's education and health care, initially by sending out British women to provide both, but eventually by training Indian women to assume the work. Equally famously, Josephine Butler had campaigned against India's army operated brothels, where prostitutes were subjected to medical examinations similar to those which had enraged Butler when the British government sustained the Contagious Diseases Acts (1869–86) in selected British towns frequented by the military. Just as they assumed that they knew what was best for poor women at home, activists like Carpenter and Butler assumed they could legitimately speak for Indian women, no matter how limited their personal experience of India actually was. Like most reformers, they also naively underestimated the resilience of ancient customs that they wished to overthrow. But these female pioneers do seem to have been genuinely interested in a part of the world that, Said reminds us, had long been a source of projection, fantasy, yearning and ambition to male travellers, artists, philosophers and politicians. And as the twentieth century developed, British women were involved in the foundation of India's first national feminist organisations: the Women's Indian Association (1917), the National Council of Women in India (1925), and the All Indian Women's Conference (1927, incorporating the Women's Indian Association from the 1920s).

Of course British activists continued to be censorious of Indian practices, so that if their old preoccupation with female seclusion in the *zenana* had moderated by the 1920s, their outrage over child marriage, female infanticide, women's health, widows' rights and the practice of *sati* had not. In 1927 this outrage was given release and notoriety with the publication of a book entitled *Mother India* by the American journalist, Katherine Mayo. Her blunt attack on Hindu practices strengthened the arguments of British imperialists against Indian self-rule and precipitated angry Indian denunciations of Britain and the United States. But Mayo's work won the enthusiastic endorsement of Margery Corbett Ashby, whose interest in India had been sparked at an early age by her father's visit to the sub-continent. A similarly keen concern was shown by the distinguished suffragist, reformer and eventual independent MP (1929–49), Eleanor Rathbone.

When Rathbone campaigned for the enforcement of existing laws regulating the age of matrimony and for the raising of the marriage age, she annoyed British India officials ever suspicious of outside interference in their affairs and determined to 'keep off the woman question'. Rathbone's investigations and interventions also irked male and female reformers in India itself, despite the tactful comments she made in her book on child marriage: namely that Indian women would use their 'noble qualities of heart and brain' to protest at evil; that reform would help the Indian agitation for independence; that the women's movement had 'always been widely internationalised'; and that 'reformers everywhere learn from each other'. She was not helped by her initial association with Mayo – who, as one British feminist was obliged to concede, would have 'been better advised, and really far cleverer if she had succeeded in making a more impartial exposé' of the Indian customs she disliked, however much the treatment of women in India, China and Japan 'makes one's blood boil'.[34] We must recognise, none the less, that this is not the whole story.

In the first place, the views of nineteenth-century British feminists on female subordination in India were not simply ethnocentric: they were, after all, strictly in line with those of reformist Indian men. While it would have been inspiring to move beyond the men, reformers frequently try to go with the national grain. In depicting Indian women as 'pacific recipients' of their efforts, and in denouncing '*purdah*, child marriage, denial of divorce or remarriage, the oppressed condition of widows, ignorance and lack of property rights', the early feminists took account of that grain.[35] And even as male Indian reformers added to their thinking about women in the twentieth century, so did western feminists. Their new objects of concern then became Indian independence and Indian women's *political* emancipation.

These causes were investigated in India by individual British women like Ellen Wilkinson, Monica Whately, Agatha Harrison and Margaret Cousins, whose reception there was far warmer than that of earlier visitors. In Britain, such individuals were reinforced by Rathbone and a few other political women, notably Lady Astor, as well as by various women's groups – including the British section of WILPF, which 'kept India in the forefront of . . . [its] full and varied programme', and which will be the focus of my discussion of Indian issues in this chapter (see chapter 5, pp. 87–8, for further comments on British women and India). In addressing the political rights of Indian women, WIL confirmed the liberalising thrust of a female internationalism which recognised, as the *Englishwoman's Review* had in 1871, that ignorance of India usually led to indifference, and should be dispelled.[36] Female internationalism likewise acknowledged that only by showing 'extreme consideration' for each other's national aspirations and priorities could collaborating organisations ensure the success of international endeavours.[37]

At the end of the First World War, the WIL council urged the government to avoid sex based limitations on the suffrage in India, and to grant its women 'equal political and educational status with men, so that the principle of equal human rights, so slowly recognised in our own country, may be adopted immediately in our East Empire'. The government was exhorted to grant self-determination to India without delay, 'not only on the grounds of justice and right' but also for an economic reason – namely that the policy of repression necessitated 'huge forces, both naval and military', which imposed an 'intolerable financial burden on this country'. WIL subsequently called on the government to allow the nomination and election of Indian women as legislators, and to ensure their representation at the interwar Round Table conferences on the Indian constitution, because they would be 'essential in the constructive work of Constitution building'. Making it clear in 1933 that it fully supported the political demands of the Indian women's associations, WIL urged the British government to do so too. However, the authorities rejected Indian women's call for full adult suffrage, forcing their British allies to press for the best compromise measure that could be secured. From generally pragmatic British feminists, who had themselves been obliged to accept the suffrage in two stages, this political realism was understandable.

Indian women who could be consulted in Britain – among them Mrs Rama Rau and Mrs Nehru – were sought out with interest, though WIL was 'careful not to compromise its own position' by associating itself with British party politics or with policy proposals on India made by other women's groups. It none the less worked during the 1930s with an advisory council of British women's organisations: a body intended to promote among these groups an 'interest in and knowledge of Indian affairs . . . and to provide for co-operation between organised women in both countries and the women delegates to the Round Table Conferences'. Expressions of thanks came in from Indian women leaders, who particularly appreciated backing on the suffrage question and the 'educational work throughout' Britain carried out by their friends, not least via WIL's monthly news sheet. They also solicited British assistance in 'securing the representation of Indian women on International Committees in Geneva', and invited to their conferences a number of experienced British feminists who were willing to 'listen and learn' – including Emmeline Pethick-Lawrence, Margery Corbett Ashby and Agatha Harrison. It really did seem that 'in due course relations between Indian and British women became completely natural'.

Notwithstanding Britain's largely hostile response to the disorders accompanying the Indian independence struggle, WIL leaders were prepared to denounce the bombing by British forces of Indian civilians and to condemn British treatment of arrested Indian nationalists. Indeed, Harrison believed she could draw strength from her earlier feminist experiences; for since 'many of us had experienced this kind of thing on a smaller scale during the suffrage days', it seemed plausible 'that we could help now in protesting against arrest with violence'. And by the outbreak of the Second World War, Harrison was arguing on behalf of WIL women that Britain must make it clear to India that it would move to independence 'immediately on cessation of war, and that in a transitional period the present form of the Central Government shall be replaced by a government responsible to the public'. Given British equivocation on the subject, she thought it was no wonder that 'Hitler had challenged the British government to prove her sincerity by recognising India as a free nation'.

Does this all suggest the existence of an ably asserted feminist influence on Indian politics, both in India and in Britain? The answer has to be – only up to a point. With the arrival in feminist circles of truly well informed activists on Indian matters like Eleanor Rathbone and Agatha Harrison, the days of the alienating armchair adviser were over. Yet many challenges remained. In 1932, Harrison reported that Miss Rathbone 'was finding it difficult to interest other women MPs in Indian problems', and the MPs' caution was understandable. British civil servants, unused to women taking a sustained interest in foreign affairs and struggling to control Indian pressures for change, were positively hostile to feminist interventions in the run up to the 1935 India Bill. Hence despite feminist lobbying, the suffrage granted to Indian women was more restricted than Indian activists had hoped, and was conferred according to qualifications that they would not have chosen. While there was wisdom in WIL's determination to work with British politicians rather than simply abandon itself to radical protest, such prudence could not hope to be popular with the women's organisations in India. But without the combined efforts of Indian and British women, the India Bill might have been considerably worse; and these efforts contributed both to the growing momentum of Indian nationalism and to the slow and painful British movement towards granting Indian independence.[38]

In making their efforts for Indian freedom, British women also had to take American attitudes into account. The instinctive hostility of the United States towards British colonialism had both positive and negative consequences. On the positive side, it helped to reinforce the determination of WIL women to maintain their pro-independence stance on India, and at least women in the American section of the League were aware that American censure of Britain could be unfair. As an American friend of Emily Balch remarked in 1931, 'the most anti-imperialist government England has ever had, and the most sympathetic Viceroy India has ever had' received no credit and much abuse in some sectors of the American press; prompting Balch to reply that the Indian drive for independence involved 'complexities and uncertainties which Britain has no right to overlook'.[39] On the other hand, the American criticism of British policy towards India did not develop until after the First World War, a delay which had alienated Indian activists; while any such criticism only served to increase the frostiness of British officials, about which Eleanor Rathbone complained with understandable venom.[40]

Similarly problematical were the attitudes of some Indian women towards western feminism. If women's organisations in Britain, the United States and India alike could see the value of transnational collaboration, there remained a significant undercurrent of Indian hostility towards any presumption that British women could 'speak for the women of India', and towards the ideology that was thought to dominate the British and American feminist movements. As one Indian woman nationalist and poet visiting the United States put it in 1929, 'I do not like what you call feminism. We have none of it in India, and I hope we will not have it. Your women, you will pardon my frankness, seem to be suffering from a bad inferiority complex. Your highest ideal seems to be man, and what he does.'[41]

India was the greatest but by no means the only part of British feminists' engagement with the wider world. We have noted in chapter 2 how female emigration to the colonies encouraged women's interest in the 'white' Dominions and in Africa, and that the Boer War fostered both imperialist and anti-imperialist sentiments among women. During the interwar years, WIL women made it clear that their condemnation of British rule was not confined to India, but ranged from Ireland to Egypt, from Africa to Hong Kong.

A Native Races Committee was set up to focus WIL's interest in minorities, and the Committee was allegedly effective in keeping it in touch with the 'increasing number of people' working 'to stop the unjust exploitation of African peoples'. The loss of land involved in the 'European "invasion" of Africa', and the passing round of colonies at the end of wars, were especially deplored. Conversely, the system of mandates created after the First World War was urged upon the government as an appropriate way of administering all British colonies, because it involved the notion of trusteeship for races 'not yet able to stand alone'. An extension of democratic rights in the colonies was likewise strongly recommended: these rights to include a greater measure of adult suffrage; compulsory, free, universal education; freedom of speech, press and organisation; entitlement to trade union and peasant organisation; and basic social and welfare legislation.

A few feminists also expressed their outrage over South Africa's oppression of black women, the exploitation of prostitutes in Malayan and Kenyan brothels, child slavery (*mui tsai*) in Hong Kong, and female circumcision in Kenya. Egalitarian feminists did their best to rally British and Commonwealth women behind the Equal Nationality Treaty. And the British Commonwealth League (BCL, from 1925 to the Second World War), set up to foster women's groups in Commonwealth countries, provided another important forum for the raising of imperial questions, as well as for the discussion of the experiences of women of colour and the challenging of discrimination in individual cases (see chapter 5, pp. 83–5, for a fuller account of the BCL).

Unfortunately, by the interwar years earnest British expressions of concern about colonial problems could give as much offence as blunter manifestations of imperial thinking. The BCL might carefully declare its focus to be on 'women of the less forward races', but this term sounded to non-Europeans uncomfortably like provoking nineteenth-century references to 'backward' peoples in need of uplift. While social purists continued their efforts after the First World War, in an era of greater sexual freedom the movement increasingly came to be associated with an outmoded matriarchalism, so that campaigns against prostitution lost their old inspirational power, in the colonies as elsewhere. An issue like female circumcision easily provoked male and female embarrassment in parliament, making the outspokenness on this subject of Eleanor Rathbone and the Duchess of Atholl impressive but ineffective. The fact that Atholl was the leading interwar antifeminist MP was a factor, too. When Helen Archdale wrote to congratulate her on a speech condemning female initiation ceremonies in Africa, and attempted to enlist her backing for the Equal Rights Treaty so as 'to expose and to remove' such evils, Atholl declined to give it, believing the treaty to be unenforceable. She favoured, instead, 'promoting all forms of work for the relief and raising of these women', and accordingly formed her own Committee for the Protection of Coloured Women in the Colonies, which helped to publicise the problems affecting women and to pressure the government for action. Atholl's approach put her on a par with such elite contemporaries as Joan, The Hon. Lady Grigg, who – as Susan Williams observes – worked hard to improve maternal conditions for Kenyan women, but without posing any threat to the racial hierarchy in what her husband persisted in calling 'dark Africa'.

If it was hard to arouse the interest of women MPs in India, it was still harder to move them on Africa, which during the interwar period, unlike India, lacked an independence movement of growing potency. And as Delia Jarrett-Macauley has observed, the BCL revealed as much as it resolved tensions between women of colour and white women. The pressure of WIL women did contribute to the inclusion of a woman on the League of Nations Mandates Commission, thereby giving them not only the opportunity to defend the interests of women and children in the territories, but also the scope to consider 'big financial and military questions'. Similarly, WIL women did effectively defend the work of the Commission, and did join the efforts to balance the interests of Jewish and Arab women affected by Britain's Palestine Mandate. Yet British feminist endeavours here, even more than over India, were constrained by a deteriorating international situation and by their own cultural conditioning.[42]

For many American women during the 1920s and 1930s, opposition to imperialism was an article of faith. Before female enfranchisement in 1920, American suffragists felt they should be 'in the van of every progressive movement', and were mortified by the degree to which the United States lagged behind other nations, repudiating its Constitution, principles and history in its denial of votes to women. After 1920, they relied on information about the progress of women outside the United States to prevent themselves from becoming 'complacent about their own limited gains'.[43] But given the immense power of the United States in the post-war world, such cosmopolitanism did not ensure easy relations either with the women leaders of Latin America, or with those in the areas which came into America's orbit following its brief involvement with formal imperialism: that is Hawaii, Puerto Rico, the Philippines and Cuba.

None the less, American feminists took a keen interest in the attempts of women in these countries to obtain the suffrage and egalitarian legislation. They praised the eagerness and enthusiasm for civic duties of Hawaiian women, after they secured the vote in 1920,[44] and the NWP sent supporters to the women's suffrage campaigns that developed from the 1920s in Cuba, Puerto Rico and the Philippines. In its fight to achieve equality legislation, the party was also involved with Hawaii, Puerto Rico and the Philippines.[45]

In addition, soon after the First World War American feminists turned their attention to strengthening existing links with Latin American activists. Free from her national suffrage responsibilities and wealthy enough to travel extensively, Carrie Catt reflected in 1923 that she had 'become a real fan for Pan Americanism'; but she was prepared to admit that the movement might not work out. The women of the two continents were seriously separated by language, but Catt saw graver obstacles to co-operation, deploring in Latin America the sort of laws that had prevailed in the United States fifty years earlier; the pronounced sexual exploitation of women; and the loss of caste experienced by women who worked for money. She noted, too, that organisation among women was 'exceedingly backward' and that Latin American women 'have not yet learned how to conduct collective discussions or deliberative meetings'. Yet Catt concluded that it was 'desperately important' for Pan-Americanism to succeed, if the problems of Europe were not to be repeated in the western hemisphere. Accordingly she recommended that North American women proceed conservatively in appealing to their Latin American sisters, playing down sexual, labour and political questions and concentrating initially on education, civil rights (omitting divorce), the care of children and (in general terms) peace.[46] Catt had already convinced herself that the 'women from the Latin countries seemed particularly keen about having America retain the presidency and assume a dominating position in the International Alliance';[47] but affected by British assertiveness once Mrs Ashby headed the Alliance, Catt had to look elsewhere to find ways of exerting American feminist influence south of the border.

The Pan-American Conferences of the 1920s and 1930s, and the Inter-American Commission of Women which sprang from them, presented the ideal opportunity. Mrs Catt took the initiative in trying to increase collaboration between North and Latin American women, and her 'self-sacrificing, generous and inspired leadership' was duly acknowledged. But as she grew more preoccupied with her National Committee on the Cause and Cure of War (CCCW, 1925), the opportunity was increasingly seized by Doris Stevens of the NWP.[48] In publicly appealing to the women of Latin America, Stevens stressed the 'growing solidarity among the women of the Americas'; and, when urging the adoption of the Equal Rights Treaty at the Pan American Conference of 1928, she declared 'It is fitting that the American Continent should be the first union of republics to be asked for an equal rights treaty. The demand for women's rights was born on this continent . . . It is not in our traditions to be laggards of liberty. The impulse to gather together our power and push on more rapidly is strong in us.'[49] Stevens was therefore gratified that she was able to rally the governments of Cuba, Ecuador, Paraguay and Uruguay behind the Equal Rights Treaty at the seventh Pan American Conference in 1933, as well as gaining Latin American support for the Equal Nationality Treaty and the Inter-American Commission of Women, which had conceived of both treaties. She was predictably chagrined when follow-up successes proved elusive, and when, from 1933 to the end of the decade, American social feminists from the League of Women Voters appeared at the Pan American Conferences to oppose such egalitarian measures.[50]

The involvement of Doris Stevens and Alice Paul in Latin America showed how constructive they could be outside the broils of European internationalists. In reflecting on the initial breakthrough in Latin America for equal rights, Stevens rejoiced that for the first time in known history, women appointed by government had met to propose a world law to improve the position of women.[51] She proclaimed her conviction that 'The world is our forum; we do not believe in dividing hemispheres any more than we believe in dividing sexes. What are hemispheres? What are continents? What are states? Nothing more in the last analysis than communities of men and women.'[52] The successful launch of the Inter-American Commission of Women, under Stevens's leadership, was greeted with delight by Paul, who thought it must be wonderful 'to work with the support of twenty-one governments back of one'; and Stevens was even moved to exclaim that 'I love the Spanish Americans. Their vitality makes northern peoples seem cool[,] pastoral and slow-geared.'[53]

Hemispheric collaboration between women also brought gains independent of the equality treaties. Generally it helped to challenge North American assumptions that their neighbours were 'somewhat belated, especially in their legislation relating to women'.[54] At the same time, it generated a number of welcome Latin American expressions of appreciation for North American interest and help. In 1925, for instance, women from the United States section of WILPF were invited by the Haitian section to investigate island conditions following the 1915 American occupation. Their subsequent report and pressure on the United States government may have influenced its decision to withdraw American troops.[55] And in 1930, Nicaraguan women – encouraged by American feminists' opposition to the occupation of their country by the United States – looked for assistance from American women in their suffrage struggle.[56] Such invitations made it clear that a number of Latin American activists were willing to acknowledge North American women's lead and inspiration in the international feminist movement.[57]

However, inter-American relations were seldom plain sailing. Being grateful is hard, and not everyone affected by the Inter-American Commission managed it.[58] Thus Cuba's Dr Ofelia Dominguez admitted publicly at the time of the 1930 Pan-American Conference, 'I sincerely admire the qualities of the American people; I believe in many respects the life of that people is worthy of imitation, but I cannot endure without indignation the submissive attitude we adopt in the face of their impositions.' Dominguez felt that Stevens, though admirable, was affected 'by the strongly and deeply rooted prejudices in the minds of her people'; and knew how to 'make use of smiles of cordial superiority if no idea is brought out which would conflict with her convictions. When this occurs then the spirit of her race speaks through her lips and in a polite expression and an ample smile there follows the imperious gesture and arbitrary imposition.'[59]

While Stevens was very positive about her Latin American work, her dominating personality clearly provided ammunition for her enemies and eventually undermined her effectiveness. But if she privately admitted that 'the Latin Americans were unmanageable',[60] she faced difficulties that would have hindered anyone. Stevens had to supervise the responses and correspondence of the Inter-American Commission, and raise 'every penny for its work, in addition to directing the research of the laws concerning women in the 21 Americas'. She admitted that the egalitarian feminist agenda would take time to achieve, since Latin America was 'a hot-bed of sentiment' in favour of discriminatory regulations. In the countries where equal rights had made progress – Uruguay, Paraguay, Ecuador and Cuba – there were encouraging conditions not present throughout Latin America: 'All four of them were in the midst of civil rebellion, foreign war/or economic collapse, and all four have highly conscious feminist movements . . . women, in common with other groups of inferior status, advance in the proportion that chaos comes upon those who govern us.' The Hispanic press could prove disappointing in its coverage of the Commission's campaign. And though Stevens's husband was convinced that, 'more than anyone else she has brought about a provable change in Latin American relationships', in 1939 one correspondent confided to her that 'Most people actually are entirely ignorant even of the existence of the Commission'.[61] Women activists had been right when in 1925 they predicted that Latin American women would have to 'blaze their own trail and find their own emancipation';[62] and Francesca Miller has now traced the course of their activities.[63]

Yet despite the constant acknowledgements by the feminist internationalists of the United States and Britain that they must respect national sensibilities, the activists of both countries continued to give offence by their assumptions that they could reach out and inspire feminists in other parts of the world. Alienated by expressions of British and American pride within the language of internationalism, non-western women increasingly turned to their own nationalist movements for encouragement, only to find that they had exchanged one set of irritants for another.

Thus, for example, in the Indian independence struggle, Gandhi may have seen women as 'conscious subjects who had a definite social role to fulfil as active self-conscious agents of social change'; he may have needed and used the support of the female half of the Indian population. By their passive resistance to British authority and their endurance of brutal acts of suppression, Indian women exposed the hypocrisy of Britons who claimed to be in India partly to protect them against their benighted menfolk. But when independence drew near, 'Gandhi grew apprehensive of an imminent clash of interests between man and woman. He feared that woman, enthused with her newly acquired voting rights and legal status . . . [might] decide to have a say in the political deliberations of the nation. As if to coax and cajole women out of such a course of action, Gandhi said: "And you, sisters, what would you do by going to Parliament? Do you aspire after the collectorships, commissionerships or even the Viceroyalty?"' Similarly testing encounters with the twists and turns in national liberation movements were endured by feminists in countries as diverse as Ireland and Poland, France and Norway, Germany and Italy, China and Algeria.[64]

War and peace

More vexatious than matters to do with mission and imperialism, though initially less divisive of British and American feminists than protective and equal rights legislation, were the issues of peace and war. During the First World War, as we have seen, feminists on each side of the Atlantic had helped to radicalise the peace movement and to strengthen claims long made that peace was a woman's issue. Yet there was no easy way forward when peace finally came.

As had been the case with the Equal Rights Treaty and Equal Nationality Treaty, the fact that the United States was outside the League of Nations and seeking to clarify its world role sometimes inhibited American feminists. In a different way, British activists were constrained by their country's involvement in the League, and determination both to reassert its diplomatic influence and to recover its economic power. Furthermore, as the importance of suffragism diminished and the threats to peace multiplied in the post-war world, some feminists were drawn away from the changing women's movement to a pacifism which, in the United States, might encourage isolationism rather than internationalism. The interwar years would also in time confirm what the Spanish–American, Boer and First World Wars had made abundantly plain: namely that not all women were opposed to war. On the contrary, the feminist historian Mary Beard maintained, 'Women have regarded it as natural and often revelled in it'. Unsurprisingly, therefore, 'Peace societies flower in times of safety and fade in times of crisis'.[65] But as a contributor to *The Woman Citizen* pointed out in 1930, women who enthused about 'valor and guns and the honor of the family' were destined to learn that 'the first thing any country destroys, when it goes to war, is itself'.[66]

Building on its pre-1914 significance and American isolationism, strengthened by lengthy debates and activism during the First World War, and able to sustain an ambitious educational programme and a wide range of objectives, the female peace movement was stronger in the United States than in Britain, and in addition to maintaining their own section of WILPF, the Women's Peace Society, the Women's Peace Union and various specialist peace committees, American women supported the CCCW. This body was designed by Carrie Catt to offer the independent women's groups mobilised within it a means of co-operation and self-education, a balanced view of 'their citizenship duties', and an 'exceptional opportunity to help create a sane and responsible public'. Mrs Catt, who headed the CCCW until 1932, worked from the belief that associating her organisation with radical and pacifist societies would not be helpful, in the wake of the post-war political reaction. But while the delegates composing the Committee were admitted to be 'more or less conservative', she felt that there was 'nothing conservative about the program.'

Rejecting Beard's outlook, Catt argued that 'in *all* nations' practically 'all women are more or less interested in the general question of Peace'. Nevertheless, she conceded that 'Few have a definite program in mind as to how to attain it'. The CCCW came to their aid, seeking to inform the public opinion that was vital in a democracy like the United States, and so to prevent congress from neglecting 'liberal policies in international affairs' because it 'has not been convinced they have had popular backing'. Vital to this strategy were the regular CCCW conferences, reading courses, and discussion groups known as marathon round tables. These round tables acted as community educators, stimulated the local press to run helpful articles, interviewed senators and congressmen about their attitudes towards pending legislation, and publicised group decisions when disclosure was deemed helpful.[67]

The CCCW was also able to develop a clear set of goals at the national level, and to keep pace with world crises and opportunities as they arose. Thus in the hope of fostering international collaboration, its activists – along with organisations like the LWV and WILPF – sought to rally American support for the Permanent Court of International Justice, created under the aegis of the League of Nations in 1920; worked for the adoption of the 1928 Kellogg-Briand Pact outlawing war 'as an instrument of national policy'; and endorsed the efforts of the post-war disarmament conferences. The Committee pressed for a review of the machinery and funding of American foreign policy making, and for the creation of an international police force. It urged a more just treatment of China, and approved financial and economic measures against treaty-breaking countries, notably Japan. And backing was given to reciprocal trade treaties and the cultivation of inter-American solidarity, as well as to the safeguarding of civil liberties at home and assistance for overseas victims of persecution, migrations and war.

As the international situation deteriorated in the 1930s, the CCCW advocated amending America's Neutrality Acts (1935–7) to prevent the aiding of aggressive nations. Moreover, Committee members were well aware of Europeans' bitterness that America's interwar position gave it great power without commensurate responsibilities, and they were therefore at pains to argue both that the 'United States has never stood aloof', and that they were trying to educate 'our general public to an appreciation of the fact that in the future the United States must take some responsibility for helping with a world organization'. Finally, in the spirit of nineteenth-century reformers, Committee activists urged women to use their power as 'the world-shoppers' and 'refuse quietly to buy *any imports* from a nation engaged in or threatening war . . . This is direct and passive resistance. It would have a tremendous effect if it came from a body of women in all nations. No country, party or man would be endangered by this personal refusal.'[68]

It is difficult to judge the record of the CCCW. Nevertheless, both gains and disappointments may be noted. The group managed to stay together, when the omens did not look good; and by 1935, Alonso records, its 'eleven cooperating organisations represented a combined membership of over five million women throughout the country'. Carrie Catt made a strong effort to demonstrate that the 'peace people are not quarrelling – they are merely working on different programs'. She, like her pragmatic counterparts in Britain, accepted that women campaigners, in their dealings with politicians, needed to present a united front, even though 'all men are never invited in one mass to state their views'.[69] The CCCW could claim to have sounded public opinion more effectively than male politicians, who for most of their time made themselves answerable simply to governments.[70] And its endeavours were a further indication of the growth of female internationalism, as well as a confirmation that women's interest in foreign affairs, scarcely recognised in the nineteenth century, was a serious feature of the twentieth. Governments were aware that women leaders in this area were worthy of consultation, and activists were cheered by the knowledge that 'Great causes reach fruition slowly. This was the case with suffrage and it has been so with peace.'[71]

Unfortunately, a coalition of national women's organisations, each cautious about committing its members, was always in danger of becoming a talking shop. Sometimes the CCCW was just that. If its envoys were listened to, it must be acknowledged that *all* the major women's associations and other specialist women's peace groups worked for peace and internationalism after the First World War. Credit for women's higher visibility in world politics must be shared, especially in the area of naval disarmament, where women's pressures were significant from 1921, before the Committee was formed.[72] Most of what the CCCW campaigned for failed to come about; though if female consumer power did not, as hoped, unite women against war, Jeffreys-Jones has established that it helped them to educate those who eventually 'made America a more open trading country'. Women were thus able to leave 'their daughters the legacy of an economic approach to foreign policy'.[73] Given these disappointments, and in view of the denunciations American pacifists had to endure, we should at the very least admire their courage and persistence. We should likewise applaud their common sense in concentrating on moulding public opinion, when – in the 1920s at least – their party political leverage was small and their influence within the government was nil.[74] The reward for these qualities did not come until after the Second World War. But it did then come: in the form of American membership in the United Nations.

The major organisational alternative to the CCCW, for American peace women, was WILPF. Yet the range of issues it tackled and the radicalism of its politics made it a very different association. The secretary of the League from 1924, the Indiana settlement house and war relief worker, Dorothy Detzer, became the best known woman lobbyist of the interwar years: a woman who, more vigorously than Catt, stressed the differences between male and female approaches to foreign policy, while at the same time making it clear that 'Any war of the sexes is distasteful to me'. If Detzer was at one with Catt in urging that enlightened and mobilised public opinion 'could be the single most powerful factor in American life', she proved to be a more energetic grass roots organiser and a more passionate campaigner than Catt was by the interwar years. Consequently, Detzer helped to push WILPF's American membership up from 2,000 members in 9 branches in 1921, to 13,000 in 120 branches by 1937. She was also far more determined than Catt to seek allies across the class and race divide, pointing out the folly as well as immorality of racism in a world where non-whites outnumbered whites by three to one.[75]

It is therefore not surprising that NACW's Mary Church Terrell was a longterm supporter of WILPF, and urged other women of colour to join. For despite its elite leadership, the League was trying 'to end war and remove friction between the races at one and the same time'. It needed no convincing of Terrell's argument that 'Any group whose population and wealth are small and whose advantages are few, when compared with others, will suffer more from war than the more highly favoured.' And Terrell's belief in the importance of determined educational programmes to achieve reform might alone have made the League her natural home.[76]

During the 1920s and 1930s, the American section of WILPF was involved in an impressive array of activities. It was associated with imaginative lobbying for disarmament and with the unsuccessful pressure for a constitutional amendment to outlaw war. It took part in the unsuccessful campaign for American membership of the World Court and in the effective fight for ratification of the Kellogg-Briand Pact. On behalf of America's 'moral integrity', it protested at the economic exploitation of Liberia, and it participated in the successful agitation for United States withdrawal from Haiti and Nicaragua. It joined in the futile demands for action to restrain Japanese aggression against China. It urged the Senate to investigate the power of the United States munitions industry, with Detzer playing a vital part in pressurising politicians and arranging meetings and petitions. And it supported successful but fateful efforts for a ban on the American export of arms to nations at war.

The American League, like the CCCW, was plainly interested in the economic aspects of foreign policy, as well as in an internationalism that would keep the United States out of war and on good terms with its Latin American neighbours. Like the CCCW, the American League concerned itself with national and international matters, and it was alleged that its international concerns exceeded those of any other WILPF section, just as its commitment to pacifism was unusually intense. After 1935, Alonso has noted, the American League's main problem was to reconcile women who saw economic sanctions as a means of averting war with those who advocated strict neutrality, because they thought sanctions helped to foster war. As was the case in the CCCW, a serious attempt was made to focus on what united the membership – notably opposition to totalitarianism, commitment to the strengthening of American democracy, determination to help refugees and conscientious objectors, and support for world organisation. But if the national leadership ultimately agreed to support neutrality, differences continued among America's WILPF members according to their ideological inclination or the degree to which they were affected by threatening developments in Europe, and in particular the persecution of the Jews.[77]

The British section of WILPF stayed in close touch with its American counterpart, and despite their radical beginnings, both associations had to make good the loss of leftwing socialist members: in the United States driven out because of the Red Scare; and in Britain the victims of WIL's efforts to disarm its Labour Party critics, who feared the Left and did not believe that feminism, socialism and pacifism could be united in a feminist organisation. Whatever irritations Americans may have felt about British differences with continental activists, League women in the United States and Britain wanted to co-operate and avoid squabbles over such divisive matters as economic sanctions. While assorted Anglo-American antipathies flourished between the wars, pacifist feminists in the two countries found that they were able to make common cause at Geneva, when demonstrating for disarmament, on peace missions, and in opposing imperialism. The British, like their American sisters, organised educational meetings; and if the role of public opinion was not stressed as much in Britain as it was in the more self-consciously democratic United States, WIL activists helped to raise awareness about the preoccupations of British foreign policy.

Yet on the whole they had a narrower focus than their American sisters which, given the comparatively limited overall strength of the British women's peace movement, was wise. Taking advantage of Britain's membership of the League of Nations, WILPF's Geneva headquarters, and the vigour of the British League of Nations Union (1918), their practical focus was more international than national. Accordingly, they were most strikingly involved in organising the 1926 Peace Pilgrimage, which mobilised women from all over the country in marches to London, where they urged the government to support international arbitration and disarmament; in collecting some quarter of a million petitions to the Geneva Disarmament Conference (1932); and in backing the 1934–5 peace ballot and people's mandate to government, which together secured millions of responses from the public endorsing League of Nations principles and internationalism. Nevertheless, it was the British – with the fierce sense of national mission and identity they displayed even in feminist internationalism – who in 1934 played a stubbornly prominent role in WILPF debates about the power that should be exercised over the national sections by the League's international executive committee.[78]

Conclusions

By the mid-1930s, middle-class internationalists had established themselves as respected lobbyists. Their appeals to moral force and attention to educating public opinion were not sufficient – even in two stable and democratic countries like Britain and the United States – to counter the destructive forces of nationalism; but they were worthy of respect. Moreover, women such as Addams and Catt, Balch and Royden, Stevens and Swanwick, were obliged seriously to consider how the respective claims of nationalism and internationalism could be balanced: and especially how the dangerous political promotion of nationalist sentiment might be challenged. For they accurately recognised, in Carrie Catt's words, that history had invariably been the story of the effort by nations (and races) to impose on one another.[79]

Yet the interwar years also exposed the limitations of internationalism. In the first place, American and British activists were often regarded as self-interested and privileged by their continental European counterparts. On each side of the Atlantic, albeit in different ways, they were distanced from the European women who had suffered most during the First World War and on whom the shadows heralding the Second World War would soon settle. On each side of the Atlantic, activists defending internationalism failed to advance on the justification for female involvement devised at the end of the nineteenth century: namely that women's role as mothers and educators empowered them to protest against militarism; male sexual and domestic violence against women was not highlighted between the wars.[80] On each side of the Atlantic, some campaigners found it hard always to act upon their own high principles. They did indeed recognise that they lived 'in a world economy in which each nation must either cooperate or be cooperated against';[81] and they similarly acknowledged the necessity of rising above race and class prejudices. But on each side of the Atlantic, most middle-class white activists were unable to make common cause with working-class and non-white internationalists (see chapters 5 and 6).

On each side of the Atlantic, bourgeois campaigners included far from saintly women for whom Geneva – despite its importance as home to the League of

Nations – was not an uplifting mecca but an expensive 'anti-feminist center' with a 'beastly' climate and few cultural amenities;[82] women like Margaret Rhondda, whose internationalism was not diplomatic and all-encompassing, and who confessed that 'the laws against women in some small South American Republic don't make me see *properly* red . . . I just have a general feeling that a tidal wave would probably do that part of the world good'.[83] Finally, while British and American women shared a number of deficiencies, their struggles often served to demonstrate the growing strength of their separate identities.

American campaigners, if less confident in their nationalism than Britons, were confident enough to take their disruptive brand of egalitarianism abroad. Aware that their wealth underpinned many international endeavours, they resented British jealousy and accusations, whether veiled or vocal, that Americans wanted too much influence for their money. American and British feminist internationalists alike interested themselves in the women of countries closely connected to their own: but they did not usually work together in the same parts of the world. Even when activists from both sides of the Atlantic did come together – in WILPF and while lobbying at Geneva – America's aloofness from the League of Nations presented them with an embarrassing obstacle to full co-operation. Although American feminists had long been accustomed to relying more on their own organisations than on parties and government, the same cannot be said of the British, who generally aimed for insider status. They enjoyed this at Geneva, where the Americans remained outsiders: a situation from which no one benefited, given the hostility of most international diplomats to the women's agenda. Divergence between American and British activists is still more apparent in matters to do with race, the theme of the next chapter.

5 Feminism and race, 1920s–1930s

As the previous chapter has shown, while post-war internationalism predominantly involved white American and British women in shared enterprises, the connection also revealed their growing differences of circumstance and outlook. These differences were apparent in the international endeavours affecting women of colour, which are considered in the first part of this chapter. But for most women, the domestic agenda of feminism was more pressing than internationalism, and the political and reform aspects of this agenda in Britain and the United States, together with their racial significance, are the focus of the remainder of the chapter.

Although race was not the key issue for British feminists that it was for their American sisters between the wars, the thinking of activists in both countries was influenced by the well established organisational and social separation between non-whites and whites, which stemmed from contrasting attitudes to race as well as unequal access to power. For women of colour, race and gender problems were seldom separable. For men of colour, women's interests were usually collapsed under the umbrella of race. And for white women, race commonly assumed salience in the context of debates about their responsibilities towards the less fortunate and as preservers of racial peace. Despite the efforts made in the United States and Britain to reformulate feminist ideology after the First World War, it proved impossible to break through these entrenched ways of thinking to a vigorous inter-racialism that could also accommodate gender, to the benefit of non-white and white women alike.

Internationalism and women of colour

For women of colour, coming together as internationalists during the interwar years was more difficult than for the already organised middle-class and working-class white activists discussed in chapters 4 and 6. In the first place, nothing had happened by the end of the First World War to challenge the financial and organisational domination of this branch of feminism by prosperous activists who assumed that they had the right to guide less fortunate women and countries. Equally, nothing had happened to make socialist internationalism an obvious alternative for poorer women, since its exponents, committed to class analysis and action, still had difficulty in regarding race and gender as other than secondary considerations – and dangerously diversionary ones at that.[1]

None the less, the internationalist network did produce some race women, of whom the best known American was Mary Church Terrell. Having travelled and studied in France, Italy, Switzerland and Germany, and having acquired wide experience and high visibility as an educator, club woman and reformer, Terrell was well placed to make her mark abroad. Her extensive education made her privileged, her personality was commanding, and she was able to pass for white, with all the temptations and tensions that involved. Moreover, Terrell's unusually strong determination to keep her high profile in both black and white reform circles is shown by the years she spent from 1915 to 1921 on the white dominated national executive of WPP/WILPF, and by the ability she demonstrated in moving from the concerns of feminism's suffrage era to the struggles of the difficult post-war years. White internationalists knew they could rely on her to make a good impression, and were therefore willing to help with the expensive travel arrangements that largely determined who participated in their meetings.

For her part, when invited to Berlin in 1904 as an American representative at the annual assembly of the International Council of Women, Terrell welcomed the opportunity of 'presenting the facts creditable to colored women of the United States', and was proud of her ability to address the conference audience in German, unlike most of the American and English delegates. She even took in good part the eager German enquiries about when 'die Negerin' would come: the pale-skinned Terrell not being plausible as such to women who evidently surmised that 'die Negerin' would have 'rings in her nose as well as her ears, that she would both look and act entirely differently from other women and that she would probably be "coonjining" or "cakewalking" about the streets'. Accepting both her curiosity value and her responsibility as the sole black representative at the Berlin assembly, Terrell rejoiced that the Europeans she met were 'without exception . . . genuinely interested in the colored people of the United States, sympathised with them, regretted the obstacles interposed by race prejudice and hoped they would gloriously surmount them in the end'.[2]

After the First World War, Terrell continued her role as occasional ambassador for the United States, attending international WILPF's 1919 founding conference in Zurich, where she was – as she had been in Berlin – the only voice for women of colour, there being 'not a single delegate from Japan, China, India or from any other country whose inhabitants were not white'. Her performance prompted 'many invitations to speak in various parts of Europe', and Terrell reported that the conference was 'as interesting, as illuminating and as gratifying an experience as it falls to the lot of the average woman to enjoy.'[3]

A few other prominent African American activists made their way to the American gatherings of WILPF, and to meetings held further afield by internationalists. Notable among these pioneers were the club women and social reformers Hattie Q. Brown, Sallie Wyatt Stewart, Delilah L. Beasley, Addie W. Dickerson, Mary B. Talbert, Charlotte Atwood, Mary F. Waring, Addie W. Hunton and Mary McLeod Bethune. They clearly saw advantages in internationalism: acquiring a broader vision, in the case of Bethune; creating 'a different attitude' towards women of colour among foreigners, in the case of Stewart; and, in every case, meeting prominent people who might be useful to the women's cause.[4]

Moreover, all these black internationalists were able to capitalise on the sympathetic treatment they received abroad to shame Americans at home. And several of them exploited their position to challenge specific instances of domestic white prejudice and discrimination. Accordingly, the historian and journalist Delilah Beasley used her professional skills and prominence in international groups to rebut white fears about the consequences of creating an international house at the University of California at Berkeley, and to mount a wide ranging 'defence of her race'.[5] In the same way Terrell, aware that racial and gender injustices were often linked, successfully protested against WILPF women's proposed 1921 petition supporting the withdrawal from German territory of African soldiers who were serving among the occupying forces and were allegedly guilty of assaulting local women.

On this subject, WILPF activists in the United States and Britain alike showed an unusual obtuseness. Although one can see why they would object to white Europeans' use of African and Asian troops as 'cannon fodder' outside their own countries, on the ground that it was a stumbling block 'in the path of friendship and mutual respect' between the races, the interest of WILPF leaders in securing European women against 'outrage from such troops' understandably incensed Terrell.[6] While denouncing violence towards her sex, she suggested that Carrie Catt had already investigated and refuted the charges against black troops, and that they were 'committing no more assaults upon the German women than the German men committed upon the French women or than any race of soldiers would probably commit upon women in occupied territory'. Despite her anger, Terrell was glad not to have to resign over the matter, feeling that it was 'an education' for her to mix with the WILPF campaigners: to venture 'out of the "Ghetto" in Washington and . . . mingle occasionally with the dominant race'. Her courage as a force against segregation in the capital and against race barriers between women was acknowledged by the southern white reformer Virginia Durr.[7] But after the black troops incident, although she retained her interest in promoting world peace, Mrs Terrell's involvement in internationalism lessened; and white activists' willingness to condone the segregation of black visitors to the 1925 quinquennial of the International Council of Women could only remind her that black women faced 'huge obstacles' in a country where 'the colours of the inferiority and superiority struggle' were more intense than they were in Europe.[8]

These obstacles were particularly evident in the case of Amy Jacques Garvey, the leader of the women's division of her husband Marcus Garvey's Universal Negro Improvement Association (UNIA, 1916), the editor of UNIA's newspaper, *Negro World*, and a determined advocate of equal opportunities for black women within and beyond UNIA. As Rosalyn Terborg-Penn has pointed out, Mrs Garvey was ahead of her time in urging the mass of black women to take the lead in fighting for sexual and racial liberation at home and abroad. Most race and female leaders were still middle class, speaking to the middle class. Amy Jacques Garvey also had the advantage and disadvantage of belonging to two countries. Thus her Jamaican origins gave her an understanding of the global dimension of racial injustice and women's struggles, which she duly publicised in the woman's page of *Negro World*. Yet her role as Garvey's 'surrogate when he was away from New York', and her involvement in his American faction fights, made it likely that Jacques Garvey would return home if UNIA ever ran into serious trouble in the United States – as it had by the late 1920s. Amy Ashwood, Garvey's first wife and fellow Jamaican, who worked with him in UNIA before and during their marriage, was more successful in forging an independent political existence, not least in the interwar Pan African congresses and the International African Friends of Abyssinia (1935), formed to protest at Italy's invasion of its old enemy, Abyssinia. But she relied for a base on her London nightclub and restaurant, rather than on any race organisation, notwithstanding the efforts of some Garvey women to challenge male authority within the movement.[9]

Whatever the difficulties encountered by such pioneer black internationalists, Harriet Alonso and Carrie Foster have established that the American WILPF did not abandon its hopes of recruiting women of colour. They were, of course, partly valued as potential workers for a cause that needed all the supporters it could get. The League therefore undertook a membership drive that included 'contacts with black churches and schools, the distribution of peace literature among black young women, and helping to plan "peace pageants" in black community centers'. But, along the way, the race concerns of African Americans were seriously considered and promoted. Abbie Hunton was an energetic initiator of programmes for inter-racial co-operation at the local level, and other WILPF women worked with black organisations, invited black speakers to their meetings, and objected to discrimination in schools and accommodation, in immigration regulations and the granting of citizenship. Additionally, and applauded by its British counterpart, WILPF campaigned vigorously for national anti-lynching legislation. Black women were represented on the team that investigated conditions in American occupied Haiti for WILPF during 1926. And they also served 'on its national, state, and local boards'.

However, WILPF's limited number of black activists meant that at the highest level of policy and lobbying the League's objectives were pursued by white women like Dorothy Detzer, sometimes in collaboration with such male led race organisations as the National Association for the Advancement of Colored People (NAACP). Their combined efforts may have nudged the federal government's policy towards Africa 'in a less imperialistic direction' than it otherwise would have taken, but they made little impact on domestic discrimination against African Americans. And apparently some WILPF members, while paying lip service to equality, had 'very little feeling for minority groups'.[10]

In Britain, the outstanding feminist internationalist of colour between the wars was the poet, playwright and advocate of social reform, Una Marson, who moved to Britain from Jamaica in the 1930s, and whose biography has recently been written by Delia Jarrett-Macauley. The African feminist educator Adelaide Casely Hayford, though a woman of comparable restlessness and distinction, preferred to leave Sierra Leone for the United States, rather than Britain, when she wanted to make her way, to raise money for her school, to keep in touch with Pan Africanism, or to give 'the American Negro a new vision of Africa and her people'.

Once in Britain, Marson quickly joined London's League of Coloured Peoples (1933), run by fellow Jamaican, Dr Harold Moody. Like her African American counterparts, she combined feminism with opposition to racism. Like them, she urged the need for improved education and training for members of her race, and the importance of service to the race by its elite. Like them, she addressed many women's associations, including the Alliance and the British Commonwealth League, eagerly grasping the opportunity to speak as well as write against injustice. And like them, Marson was delighted when her efforts resulted in travel and the development of overseas contacts.[11]

Hence she recalled that her 1935 visit to Budapest for the Alliance's twelfth annual congress, where she represented the Women's Social Service Club of Jamaica, was 'the most exciting time of my life'.[12] Race relations had by then progressed from the days when Terrell had been the solitary woman of colour at such meetings, and women's groups from India, Persia, Syria and Palestine took up Alliance membership in 1935. Nevertheless, Margery Corbett Ashby noted that Marson was the 'first delegate from Jamaica and the first woman of African race – Negro'.[13] Using the occasion to press for change to benefit race women in Jamaica, Africa and Britain, Marson was confident that feminists could and would co-operate internationally to move that change along. The presence at the Alliance congress of non-western activists no doubt encouraged some of her audience to share Marson's basic optimism about the global reach of feminism, while her view that African women were 'the little sisters' of feminism, appealing for help to their 'big sisters', was a judgement that any of the white internationalists could have expressed.[14]

Although she prayed to 'God to keep my soul from hating' racists, Marson – like Terrell – could temper her strong feelings with public diplomacy. This quality duly contributed to her being asked by the League of Nations secretary in 1935 to serve for a month as an observer at the League's Geneva headquarters.[15] During Marson's period in Switzerland, an international crisis was boiling up over Italy's threat to the independence of Abyssinia, and having followed the crisis avidly and made contact with the Abyssinian delegation in Geneva, Marson was well placed to secure work with the Abyssinian legation on her return to London.

Internationalism, in this instance, led to an opportunity for individual direct action not always afforded by its emphasis on education, attending meetings and petitioning others to do things. However, as an underpaid and overtaxed secretary to the legation of a country which the League of Nations proved unable to assist, Marson found her appointment disillusioning as well as exhilarating. Most of all, she, like other black British activists, was hurt that 'English politicians . . . failed to defend the victim of fascist aggression', and dismayed that their country's major role in the League brought no dividends for Abyssinia. Given Britain's post-war defence of empire and its own willingness to acquire Abyssinia at the Versailles peace settlement, had that proved possible, such tolerance of Italian imperialism was always on the cards.

Criticism of American neutrality during the Italo-Ethiopian war by assorted anti-colonial African Americans, female and radical groups proved equally futile and disenchanting, inclining many of their members to isolationism and Anglophobia.[16] Yet Britain probably remained Marson's best base away from Jamaica. At any rate, the unenviable position of most West Indian women immigrants in the United States for a long time deterred Marson from seeking an alternative outlet for her many talents across the Atlantic. When she did live there during the 1950s, America's system of racial segregation and her own insecurities prevented her from making a success of the experience. And the timing of her stay meant that she could not draw sustenance from a strong African American feminist network, of the sort that evolved in the 1960s.[17]

When we ask whether the activities of black internationalists were, given their small numbers, important only to the individuals concerned, the answer must be no. Of course, in an area where black campaigners were in short supply, those who did exist might gain gratifying personal opportunities: but these were always more than personal. Contacts with white women were a crucial way of challenging the aloofness and antipathy of many white feminists towards their black counterparts. And the existence of black internationalists provided additional proof that African Americans had a 'talented tenth' to lead them, the need for which had long been urged by the black intellectual, 'theoretical feminist' and head of the NAACP, W. E. B. DuBois.[18]

On the negative side, black internationalists' scarcity limited what they could undertake, while their elite status curtailed the impact they could make outside their own circle. Moreover, Marson, above all, discovered that while looking abroad gave hope when domestic affairs seemed unpromising, it did nothing to counteract her loneliness, job insecurity and constant shortage of money. Whereas race women in the American WILPF not only knew each other through its meetings but were also sustained by their community based and nationally linked clubs, Marson had to seek support either in the white women's groups of a Britain which would 'never be her home',[19] or in 'black British and Jamaican organisations'. The latter were male dominated and tended to devote themselves to socialising, cultural activities and racial self-help, while seeking to inform and influence liberal white opinion. The League of Coloured Peoples is a good example of such bodies. Condemning imperialism, protesting racial discrimination at home and abroad, and valuing pride of race, the league recruited female members, some of whom (including Marson) served on its executive. But it did not make women a key concern, stressing instead the importance of recruiting student supporters.[20] Neither kind of association was entirely suited to Marson's needs.

For Marson, even more than for her white co-workers in Britain, internationalism brought an increased awareness of the racial and gender problems generated by imperialism. For their part, some American women of colour found domestic race problems and organisational challenges so daunting that they turned to Third World developments for solace.[21] But African American internationalists alienated by discrimination were able to form their own association: the International Council of Women of the Darker Races (ICWDR, 1920). This was obviously never an option in Britain. The nearest equivalent to the Americans' ICWDR was the British Commonwealth League; and between them the BCL and the ICWDR illustrate the contrasting course of race women on each side of the Atlantic – a course that their different population mix and histories dictated.

Unlike the LWV and CCCW in the United States, the ICWDR was formed in response to snubs black women received from fellow female activists.[22] However, like LWV and CCCW meetings, the Council's regular gatherings were constructive rather than angry, reflecting its leadership by middle-class veterans of the club movement: among them Mrs Terrell; Margaret Murray Washington, ICWDR's president and the widow of the conservative black educator and leader, Booker T. Washington; and the suffragist and educator Nannie Helen Burroughs. Rather like the LWV and CCCW, the Council emphasised the importance of educating its constituency, doing so through a network of local study groups. These groups had the important purpose of instructing African American children about their own history, and especially about their own prominent people. In addition, they focused on countries of specific concern to the United States, like Haiti, and on large regions of the world, such as Africa, China and India, where racial issues were of compelling interest.[23]

By encouraging 'racial and national pride as a precursor of self-determination' in the United States,[24] Council women were at once promoting the black nationalist philosophy which was growing in popularity in the African American community as a whole, and seeking added strength by identifying themselves with the struggles of 'darker races' abroad. They hoped to buttress women's claim that they were both nationalists and internationalists: that they were, in the words of activist Bernice Johnson Reagon, 'people builders, carriers of cultural traditions, key to the formation and continuance of culture'.[25] But though women's cultural influence had been accepted since the nineteenth century, we have already seen that society was less willing to recognise women as actors in foreign affairs. And so the black internationalists of the ICWDR were wise as well as realistic in avoiding overt support for nationalist campaigns outside the United States, no matter how striking the similarity between the caste system of South Africa and the southern states of America seemed to some Council members.[26] The organisation did not have the means to do much in this area and, even if the colour of its adherents might have made intervention in nationalist contests less risky than when it was undertaken by white feminists, the determination of Third World feminists to shape their own movements would have remained an insuperable obstacle to more than sisterly expressions of solidarity.

The BCL, by contrast, lasted longer and was less stretched and embattled than the ICWDR. After all, it was predominantly white in composition and enjoyed the backing of all the major women's groups in Britain, besides claiming representatives from the Commonwealth as a whole. The League's non-party, non-sectarian approach was old-fashioned, and its emphasis on 'pressing only for that equality which enables women to give of their best in service' evoked the reassuring rhetoric of nineteenth-century social feminism. Furthermore, its methods were sedate, consisting of organising conferences where 'problems common to women' within the British Commonwealth could be discussed; the general gathering and dissemination of information; and the holding of working lunches. Such prudence was sensible at a time when male officials and politicians consistently opposed the egalitarian aspects of female internationalism, and even male friends of the BCL were determined that women – underrepresented as they were in national governments – should not be granted 'a special position of advantage' on international bodies.

None the less, its safe image and broad support allowed the League to entertain several bold objectives. Foremost among these were its determination to make liberty 'go beyond the boundaries of sex and race'; its commitment to the 'political education' of women who were – or would hopefully soon become – full citizens; and its pledge to secure 'equality of liberties, status, and opportunities' between Commonwealth men and women. These objectives, the BCL stressed, required female enfranchisement and the co-ordination of marriage, maintenance and divorce laws throughout the Commonwealth.[27] In addition, they necessitated the presence of women representatives in the Colonial Office, on Commonwealth bodies, at Commonwealth conferences, and in Commonwealth delegations. Like other progressive women's organisations, the BCL also evinced a strong desire to promote peace and disarmament, and to ensure 'the full consideration of questions in which women take a special interest in the Assembly and the Council of the League of Nations'.[28]

However, aspects of the BCL's ideology and programme offset this liberal cosmopolitanism. While Indian women were acknowledged to be 'highly educated' and 'capable of doing their own work' – for example on behalf of the vote and against child marriage – white League speakers could still offend their sensibilities, and often became downright patronising about the members of 'less advanced' or 'less forward' races within the Commonwealth. BCL women, it was asserted, had a moral responsibility to help their sisters in these races by working for their education and to dispel ignorance about them, and by speaking out against 'casual relationships' between indigenous peoples and the 'wandering members of the British race, who may be without ties in a new country'. It was thought necessary to safeguard women in 'less advanced' races 'from the operations of custom or law which degrade them as human beings' – prostitution and child slavery being cases in point. Yet, as has been argued earlier (see above, pp. 62, 65–6), ameliorative proposals could provoke resentment in the countries under attack, even if local reformers had a comparable agenda. Moreover, though they were laudably anxious to promote the formation of women's groups within the Commonwealth, the League's leading members proved particularly keen to find opportunities for educated women: that is, for white women like themselves.

There was a final area of awkwardness. Unlike their visitors and members from overseas, most white BCL women were believers in the empire who supported the mandates system and felt they were making a point about their sex by studying imperial affairs. For as Lord Cecil expressed it at the League's founding conference, the days had gone when women were thought 'naturally and congenitally incapable' of understanding anything beyond 'the home – education – sanitary science'. Lady Astor was speaking to the converted at a BCL gathering in the late 1930s when she urged women of the empire to 'cling together': they must, she believed, keep their 'freedom in the Empire and keep the Empire together . . . because of civilization. The British Empire is the only League of Nations in the world to-day; it is very important.' Mrs Corbett Ashby was equally convinced that women should 'take their share in building up the work of the Empire'. For her this meant 'trying to solve such problems as the just and fair relationship of one race to another, of one culture to another'; and her approach drew tributes at BCL meetings from activists who felt that 'all questions of women's equality the world over were safe in her hands'.

But Mrs Corbett Ashby's patriotism also led her to use her platform at the League to deplore the tendency of many sensible women 'sitting at home' to be 'extraordinarily dumb' in expressing the interest and pride they felt in the empire. She wanted these silent patriots to raise their voices and offset the old-fashioned, patronising types whose imperial pronouncements were unhelpful.[29] To a black activist like Una Marson, the difference between the silently proud and the offensively superior imperialist might not always be apparent. Marson resented, as apologists for empire did not, the patronage meted out to women of colour in the Commonwealth and Britain alike. Her mentor Harold Moody protested at the 1932 BCL conference about the British 'reserve and obtuseness' that led to colour prejudice, and Marson herself made similar criticisms at League gatherings. It was only rarely that she met a white British feminist like Winifred Holtby, who promoted internationalism and shared both her interest in race and gender questions, and her growing belief 'that Africa mattered'.[30]

As Jarrett-Macauley and Barbara Bush have observed, South Africa had stirred Holtby's conscience during a visit she paid there in 1926: a visit which inspired her to provide financial backing for union activities in Cape Town, to expose the poor conditions of the black masses, and to denounce imperialism and white racism in her novel, *Mandoa, Mandoa*.[31] WIL women in Britain, operating through their Native Races Committee, were equally determined to address 'inter-racial matters', being 'convinced that many causes of war and unrest lie in the relations between races within a nation or Empire'.[32] Yet as Bush points out, even a progressive activist like Holtby failed to develop 'a coherent, theoretical analysis of colonial or racial oppression', and retained 'an emotional commitment to empire and the higher ideals of trusteeship'. In the same way, the female members of WIL and the BCL favoured the assimilation of black people into white society, being persuaded of 'native backwardness in mental and physical development', and of the benefits of European imperialism, including 'Christianity, western education, engineering achievements, modern medicine and surgery'.[33]

To make matters worse, the interwar years saw a determined British effort to justify and strengthen the empire, despite the 'number of concessions to nationalist movements' that had to be given after the First World War. Historians have shown that successive governments aimed to keep the colonies and make them pay, and to accommodate acquisitive powers such as Germany and Italy without provoking American anti-colonialism. Economically and strategically minded officials had little time for the moral and reformist goals of organisations like WIL. Imperial administrators did indeed proclaim the importance of imperial trusteeship. However, in the words of Cain and Hopkins, this concept was 'solid with respect to principle but flexible with regard to circumstance'. Hence, though principle demanded Britain's commitment to respecting native ways and ameliorating colonial grievances, in practice native rights were unlikely to be defended, except in regions that were unattractive to white settlers.

As far as African affairs were concerned, Bush has established that they were higher on the political agenda in the 1930s than in the 1920s, not least because of the growth of African nationalism; but for much of the interwar period the assumption was that 'British rule in Africa would endure into the distant future'. If Tropical Africa was important to Britain's balance of payments and to some interest groups, it accounted for 'not much over 3 per cent' of British exports when trade between the two countries peaked in 1938. The only nationalist voices in the region that were heeded were those of whites in Southern Rhodesia and Kenya: and they were heeded in order that they might be contained. Force, complex administrative structures, and 'the more subtle workings of cultural imperialism', were all necessary to the work of containment.[34] In South Africa, where white nationalism was more troubling than in Tropical Africa between the wars, Britain's main objective was to retain financial control. Although some local political advance was yielded, there was no wish to challenge white supremacy, or in any way to alter the position of the disenfranchised and economically exploited African population. For their part, the countries making up the empire were increasingly pursuing their divergent interests, with the Dominions seeking to be treated as Britain's equals and chafing at British determination to control imperial foreign policy.[35]

White feminist internationalists – like other internationalists working at a distance from their concerns – were mere noises far off in this imperial drama. Driven largely to ignore the centrifugal forces within the empire they admired, they were willing to acknowledge that public interest in African problems was frequently 'very limited', and that the BCL's dedicated efforts did not bring in as many members or make as much impact as had been hoped. Such activists even lacked strong African women's organisations with which they could co-operate. As Corbett Ashby recalled, for example, the Alliance 'did not touch Africa in the early days because it had no women's movement', and 'the initiative had to come from the country' that wished to be involved in Alliance operations. While noting that African women took part in community protests against oppressive colonial measures, Bush has stressed that they were generally denied formal education and that colonial authorities did business with a male elite. African women were thus effectively excluded from the 'entrée into modernity' which might have led to a higher profile in independence struggles and new forms of protest on their own account.[36]

Female African American and black British campaigners, usually hard up and faced with a dearth of female contact groups in Africa, could of course turn to the writings and international conferences of Pan Africanism to supplement their news of that part of the world. After all, the movement originated in North America before the First World War, and involved American and African activists during the interwar years of the twentieth century. Its labour, civil and human rights concerns complemented the domestic priorities of women of colour, and, as Langley has argued, its gatherings allowed promoters a stirring opportunity to assert their 'cultural values . . . [and] spiritual world-role'.

Some African women participated in Pan African operations: for example in the Women's Auxiliary Committee of the Gambian section of the 1926 National Congress of British West Africa; in the Gold Coast section of the West African Youth League; and in Sierra Leone's West African Civil Liberties and National Defence League. Pan African conferences also drew the attention of African American women, with Jessie Fauset, the literary editor of *The Crisis* (the journal of the NAACP), speaking about African women at the 1921 assembly; the NACW supporting the third congress, held in London in 1923; and black women's clubs and church associations involved in the meeting of 1927, for which Addie Hunton was 'a principal organizer'. In Britain, Una Marson came to Pan Africanism through her editorship of *The Keys*, the journal of the League of Coloured Peoples. She was then sustained in it by 'addressing African issues at conferences', and by forging 'good relationships with many [Pan African] student activists'.

Unfortunately, it was soon apparent that tensions existed between the African and American delegates to Pan African meetings, the Africans being determined to take the dominant role in Pan Africanism, and to devise their own political tactics, while the Americans felt that they should lead any global assertiveness by the coloured races. If the British Left sympathised with Pan African aims, at a time of growing labour and communist agitation the British government regarded its manifestations with suspicion, whether they were African or American led. And while its lobbying, lecturing and publishing efforts were varied and intrepid, interwar Pan Africanism failed to achieve any political power. By the 1930s its American, African and French endeavours had wound down, and the remaining West Indian and African agitators, who were concentrated in Britain, struggled to keep the cause going with protests against colonial injustices. Such campaigns were designed to rally the faithful and educate British public opinion, and they did so. But the effectiveness of this phase of Pan Africanism was seriously undermined by internal rifts among the black leaders and their white sympathisers, and its elite leadership continued to offer little either to black women or to the black masses. After a brief period of activity in the late 1920s and early 1930s, the international Communist movement proved no better able to give permanent sustenance to black aspirations (see below, chapter 6).[37]

In London, British feminists more often encountered Indian women activists than African women; and British activists were more likely to visit India than Africa. Because of India's early centrality to the British Empire, and its continuing economic importance between the wars, Indian pressures for independence were met with shifting British attempts at 'controlling and redirecting' them, rather than with resignation to the inevitable.[38] This attitude on the part of the British government and administrators meant that Indian nationalists, activist Indian women and sympathetic British feminists needed to tread carefully, and the necessity for caution inevitably put a strain on their complicated relationships.

None the less, British and Indian activists still managed to pursue a shared agenda for Indian women which highlighted education, social reforms, and the extension of the franchise (see chapter 4). In doing so, they tried to remain above party politics.[39] Such an approach seemed sensible in view of British politicians' broadly bi-partisan approach to India: an approach that allowed more scope for the Labour strain of anti-imperialism than diehard Tories led by Winston Churchill would have liked.[40] Some British women were also able to advance their reformist goals by living and campaigning in India, and by making radicalising contacts with prominent Indian nationalists. Kumari Jayawardena has interestingly reconstructed the lives of these women, among them the culturally sensitive feminists Margaret Cousins, Annie Besant, Margaret Noble and Madeleine Slade, who knew how to balance the priorities of women against those of Indian nationalism.[41]

Juggling their priorities was simply one of the difficulties that faced these and other foreign women in India. Indian nationalists and feminists not only resented any condemnation by outsiders of their national customs;[42] they were, in addition, wary of British individuals who took leadership roles that might have gone to local agitators. By the 1930s, women such as Cousins and Slade were well aware of the need to yield to home grown Indian women activists.[43] Indian feminists – like their counterparts throughout the non-western world – have objected to the strong emphasis that has been placed on the international impact of the western women's movement, stressing instead the importance to feminists of indigenous sources of inspiration. In India, it has been suggested, women had their own special power and respect, and found that their chief enemy was colonialism rather than man.[44] None the less, while Indian feminist women and nationalist men frequently claimed solidarity, women's claims were usually subordinated if they conflicted with those of nationalism.[45]

For British women, there were particular problems facing them at home. Those who took the Indian part, whether on women's rights or on constitutional reform, were likely to be regarded with suspicion when they organised money-raising tours in Britain, a suspicion only increased by their general association with radical politics and such unconventional faiths as theosophy. Nor did it help matters that Indian activists intent on raising world interest and collecting funds went on journeys to the United States as often as they did to London. Their American contacts were dismaying to British officials aware of the support for Indian nationalism that flourished among white and black anticolonialists, and determined to keep 'democratic republicanism' out of India. They were, in addition, an irritating reminder to British activists of the financial clout of the United States, and of its long rivalry with Britain in doing good in many parts of the world.[46]

However, the efforts of American and British internationalists between the wars did not prove strong enough to challenge the growing power of nationalism among non-western women. Although 'the idea of sisterhood . . . [and] the commonality of the human experience' worked against the concept of nation,[47] women in many countries supported the view of the cosmopolitan Indian revolutionary, Mrs K. R. Cama: 'I have nothing against American or English sisters', but 'to establish internationalism in the world there must be nations first'.[48] And neither in the United States nor in Britain did internationalism provide a base on which women of colour could be substantially recruited to the women's cause. For some working-class women, internationalism did provide this base, but the labour movement rather than the women's movement was the beneficiary (see below, chapter 6).

Domestic feminism and women of colour

Domestic feminism was still more problematical after the First World War, though its problems weighed most heavily on African American women, and disillusionment with its benefits was neither immediate nor universal. In fact, when women in Britain and the United States secured the vote at the end of the First World War, some energised feminists believed that they were at the beginning of an era of great promise. Whatever their differences about the necessity and consequences of involvement in the war, women's national organisations had seen the wisdom of undertaking war work, and in doing so had at times collaborated across the colour line. Individual women had discovered hope, adventure and better pay in new jobs which were military as well as civilian, abroad as well as at home. Women's wartime contributions were used by feminists and politicians alike to justify women's belated acceptance as full citizens, and in the immediate post-war years activists could take pleasure in women's initial courtship by politicians and in the passage of a remarkable range of legislation to benefit their sex. Additional sources of satisfaction were the larger female involvement in paid work, the expansion of birth control information and facilities, the availability of more labour saving goods, and the greater social freedom that was enjoyed by urban women.

Nevertheless, in both countries it also became apparent that feminists concerned with the domestic scene, like those involved in internationalism, had to struggle with a number of profoundly discouraging political, economic and cultural conditions, among them the uneven but inexorable decline of liberal reform at the national political level; the frequently destructive pressures of urban living; the economic stagnation of once vital industries and regions; renewed labour tensions; and the further development of a mass culture which ostensibly accorded women power but did so only within a traditional framework. Activists often found themselves entangled by old ideological and organisational dilemmas, and unable to agree on their responses to new social circumstances.[49] The remaining part of this chapter will look at the main difficulties facing women in politics and reform, and try to explain feminists' failure, in both areas, fundamentally to alter prevailing attitudes and arrangements regarding race. And the focus in this section is, perforce, on women of colour in America.

Politics

In the United States and Britain alike, suffragists were fully aware that, having obtained the vote, they needed to show that they would exercise it, and exercise it well. And whereas Britain's tiny minority of women of colour was not in a position to drive home this message, African American women were and did, having long recognised the disadvantage that black men's unique votelessness imposed upon them. Accordingly, black women had formed their own suffrage clubs and state suffrage societies, and exercised their votes in territories and states such as Wyoming, Colorado, New York and Illinois, which enfranchised women before the passage of the federal amendment in 1920.[50] Mrs Terrell spoke for many when she stated that because of the twin burdens of race and gender prejudice borne by black women, the vote 'means more to us than it does to any of our sisters in the other racial groups. Moreover it will be a terrible reflection on us, if we do not use our ballots to promote the welfare of our race.' In other words, female voting was no selfishly claimed right. Rather it was a means of using black women's special qualities and reform preoccupations to improve the overall sexual, educational and economic lot of their sex. Black male leaders of divergent views also had to be reassured that their considerable support for women's suffrage was not misplaced; that it was, in fact, destined to advance the race struggle against lynching, segregation and antimiscegenation laws in which members of both sexes were involved, but to which black men gave priority.[51]

Black women were further encumbered by the behaviour of many white women throughout the United States. In the South, comfortably off white suffragists had sought to empower themselves and advance the social reforms they advocated by presenting the vote as the privilege of qualified elites. As members of these elites, in a region dedicated to state rights, they were prepared to condone the disenfranchisement of supposedly unqualified black men, and to oppose black female suffrage lest it should undermine the South's system of racial segregation and white supremacy.[52] In the North, white female activists were keen to encourage southern suffragism without impaling themselves on the race and state rights questions, and hence we find the national organisers of NAWSA and NWP persistently rejecting black women's efforts to work with them in the last stages of the suffrage campaign and in the post-1920 drive to register women as voters. While they publicly claimed that black women's concerns were racial and not feminist in nature, this stance actually reflected the determination of NAWSA and NWP to avoid alienating influential southern conservatives just as they were attempting to rally their core membership, to secure white women's voting rights, and to adapt their programmes to the peacetime world. Although black feminists bombarded the NAACP with requests for aid, DuBois was a staunch friend of female enfranchisement, and the association's suffrage department responded with sympathetic publicity and pressure on Congress to act against states which limited women's suffrage, black men were no more able to secure signficant outsider assistance for the black female campaigners than the women themselves had been.[53]

Under these dispiriting circumstances, *The Woman Citizen* took comfort from the fact that southern politicians were allegedly 'afraid of the Negro woman vote', because 'the Negro women were so much more intelligent, progressive and ambitious than the men that they would not be able to intimidate them into silence'.[54] And confident black feminists had openly regretted the political corruption of some black men, seeing it as a factor in their eventual disenfranchisement. Such feminists certainly thought they could do better, and so were embarrassed when their efforts to register black women after 1920 were nullified by ruthless southern registrars already practised in excluding black men from the polls. Furthermore, while black women's assertions about their morality, intelligence and reform credentials may have impressed some politicians, white female activists and black male supporters, it cannot be pretended that the majority of white men welcomed the black women voters. At best, since they posed no physical threat to whites, as black men were said to do, they would not have to be controlled at the polls by white violence. At worst, they were allegedly part of the mass of ignorant and vicious individuals that racists convinced themselves would, if allowed, flock to vote.[55] In consequence, white suffragists felt obliged to reassure the anxious that it was 'the better educated' black women who voted, and without provoking 'a single adverse criticism'.[56]

Yet if their differences with whites made it difficult for African American women to vote, there were other inhibiting factors that had nothing to do with race and existed in the United States and Britain alike. Women's enfranchisement remained contentious: as Nolan and Daley observe, 'Most countries did not secure female suffrage before the 1940s. At least half the world lived in countries without female franchise in 1940.' Opponents were quick to point out that suffragism had mobilised only a minority of British and American women even by using conservative arguments for the vote and even during its impressive final decades; it was therefore highly unlikely that there would be a massive showing at the polls of newly enfranchised women, whatever their race. The turnout of American women at the 1920 presidential election was low, and, while it soon started to rise, women did not overtake men until 1964 (helped after 1945 because they outnumbered men in the population). British women seem to have made a similarly slow start as voters in the general election of 1918, when the overall turnout was less than 60 per cent; but Pat Thane's recent work shows that contemporaries later reported a good female presence at the polls. However, hard data about the male–female division in voting are as hard to come by for Britain as it is for the United States. And in both countries, the hostile attitudes of well connected anti-suffragists survived to inhibit timid female voters long after the abandonment of anti-suffrage organisation.[57]

Region and ethnicity also helped to determine female voting patterns in the United States. Thus women's involvement was commonly lower in the southern states and in conservative immigrant communities than in liberal northern states such as Rhode Island, which had enfranchised women before 1920.[58] None the less, race remained the chief obstacle to female voting in America, and especially in the South where, Jacqueline Jones reminds us, as late as 1952 some nine-tenths of black women had never voted.[59] Even in 1920, when interest in the vote was at its highest, intimidation at the registration stage meant that proportionately fewer black women than white were eligible to vote: for example by a ratio of one to eleven in Orleans parish, Louisiana.[60] A better black female voting record might have been secured had white feminists given practical support to the efforts of the Colored Women's Voters Leagues that black southern women formed to overcome the opposition they faced.[61] It was plainly fatuous to hope, as some did, that 'with a little patience, trust and vision the universal tie of motherhood and sisterhood can and will overcome the prejudice against them as voters'.[62] But it is equally plain that widespread compliance with the suffrage amendment required federal intervention, and that was simply not forthcoming in the 1920s. As Cott contends, 'in the few cities where they were not prevented by violence or by registrars', black women voted in 'about the same proportions as black men', in an era when male turnouts were declining. It was not, however, a parity they would be able to sustain in the face of male and white female indifference; and during the interwar years there was no 'rainbow alliance' of minorities that could improve matters for black women.

In the judgement of American feminist Anna Garlin Spencer, no 'union of all the different stocks' had been created in reform organisations, because the time for it was not yet ripe. Jewish women's internationalism and interest in female orientated reform was expressed through their own and white associations against a background of growing differences between the black and Jewish communities over economic and foreign policy issues. Other minorities – such as Native Americans, Hispanics and Asian Americans – were, for the most part, only beginning to involve themselves in mainstream politics, and were too separated by their distinctive settlement patterns, history and culture to ally with others in protesting at poverty and discrimination. Their major civil rights groups were also male dominated, like those of the African American community.

The NWP did take an interest in Chinese American women when it wanted their support for legislation granting equal nationality rights to women and men; but the party was not seriously sensitive to racial injustice. The situation was rather more promising among Native American women. The National Society of Indian Women supported a programme of racial self-help by the 1920s, and Indian female activists had developed extensive contacts with the General Federation of Women's Clubs (GFWC), the YWCA and the LWV. However, the white women involved often operated in the light of their own educational and welfare priorities, rather than adopting a more innovative and egalitarian approach. Prompted to 'take up the case of the Indian' by the GFWC and the white reformer John Collier, the LWV, for example, set about studying the 'Indian problem' in its usual fashion of 'starting at the bottom and proceeding slowly'. Small wonder that most of the Indian women in the first Indian branch of the LWV were in turn only 'politely interested' in relinquishing their alleged conservatism, and in learning how to use their votes. Matters had improved by the 1930s, as Indian women's right to vote and hold office was incorporated under the tribal constitutions adopted by the New Deal, and Indian women benefited from its programmes, if not from any thinking about them that was sensitive to their cultural traditions. And as Alison Bernstein has noted, a few Indian women leaders attained national prominence, notably by building on the contacts they had forged with white women activists, rather than by working through 'tribal politics or male mentors'. The drawback to such a strategy, she stresses, was that Indian women were naturally constrained by the treatment of their sex in white America.[63]

Racial solidarity would not have averted two other political developments which worked against American and British feminism at the national level: namely women's failure to vote as a bloc after 1920 and to found a viable women's political party, as politicians feared they might do. Feminist universalism, and the large claims some women had made about how they would transform politics, once enfranchised, may have encouraged politicians' anxieties about a female voting bloc; but they were groundless. Instead, long politicised women divided their votes between the full range of existing parties. Social feminism may have been driven by the unifying ideology of maternalism, but its cultural manifestations reflected female variety and equal rights feminism was an ever-present alternative. Moreover, in the last phase of suffragism, though preaching the significance of the vote for all women, feminists had increasingly recruited them into separate groups according to economic and other differences. There was no way in which this diversity of outlook and allegiance could have been reversed in the 1920s; it was not until the 1980s that social scientists began to see female bloc voting as a possibility, and even then 'their unity has been [deemed] more fortuitous than intentional'.[64]

The creation of a women's political party was equally problematical for feminists everywhere. In the United States, the NWP began as a militant organisation, prepared to accept coercive political tactics to secure the Nineteenth Amendment but lacking the wide-ranging appeal to voters necessary for mounting a challenge to the long established party system. Once the vote was secured, rather than avoiding a constricting organisation and ideology, and offering 'general and diffuse policy options' – as did the Democratic and Republican coalitions up to the Great Depression[65] – the NWP boxed itself in with an unbending equal rights ideology which ignored race. It then made matters worse by concentrating unduly on legal changes, and on lobbying established politicians at the expense of its initial campaign to get more women into political office. The NWP was undoubtedly brave and resilient. But it was a conventional pressure group, not a political party. Though priding itself on being an independent body which 'works for equal rights for men and women in all departments of life', and on being able to make politicians take notice in a way in which party political women could not, the NWP was eventually hampered by its small elite leadership, neglect of black and working-class women, and concentration in the northeastern states. In its preoccupation with one-issue politics, the NWP did resemble many American third parties and experienced the same fate: that is, an exaggerated reputation for radicalism, internal tensions, and influence in place of power – the sop frequently offered to women by anti-feminists.[66]

Another possible contender for the status of a women's party, in the view of the established American political parties, was the National League of Women Voters. Yet though enjoying a broader regional spread than the NWP, and accepting black women both as members of largely white state leagues and organised in separate state leagues, the LWV was even less inclined to keep up its early interventions in electoral politics. Commanding far fewer members than NAWSA, from which it was formed, the league none the less lobbied effectively for social feminist and constitutional reforms, carefully educating women for citizenship and generally avoiding political partisanship. However, like the NWP – and similarly influenced by pre-war ideas and leaders – the LWV subordinated race concerns to those of gender, rather than seeking a new relationship for the two in a new era. Few black women joined the league, one white activist suggested, because they did not want 'to vote at that time, not as they do now'. Had they expressed interest, she believed, 'we certainly would've done all we could'. Others may have thought the same, and a comparable caution was shown with regard to class. Hence, as Baxter and Lansing point out, the LWV missed whatever post-war opportunity existed to try to lead 'a political women's movement which could cut across class or political lines'.[67]

The truth was that American women were divided over the desirability of a new political party, with some believing it necessary because millions 'were not yet identified with the opinions and traditions of any political party', while others thought that women should try operating within the existing parties before taking an independent line – the independent vote having 'seldom played any other part than that of the fly on the wheel in the country's politics'. It was ruefully acknowledged, as the 1920s progressed, that American men were 'reconciled on the whole to women voters, but not to women in politics', and that the major parties' diversity and divisions inclined them towards stand-pat attitudes that alienated reformist women committed to the public interest.

In Britain, where women were also urged by feminists to 'get into politics and public life, for the sake of the general good' and 'to take their share in the work of humanity', there were comparable anxieties. Thus if female public figures were respected, women politicians were still few in number and handicapped by their sex: discouraged from standing for office by the cost of the undertaking and the frequently unwinnable seats they were offered; unlikely to win if opposed by a man; and denied their fair share of appointments if elected. Feminists in bodies like the Women's Freedom League saw the need for a campaign to galvanise the main parties and get more women into government, but they did not know how such a campaign was to be mounted.[68] They certainly did not see that a women's party would help them. As Pugh observes, activists not discouraged by the

Pankhursts' failure to form such a party in 1917–19 may have been deterred by knowledge of American difficulties in this area and by the greater strength of political loyalties among feminists in Britain, where during the 1920s even the weakened Liberals were active in putting forward women candidates for election as members of parliament, albeit to less effect than the Tories and Labour. Small wonder that most women politicians declined Lady Astor's invitation to be 'part of a feminist phalanx', fearing that it would be narrowing, alienate men, and create a gulf between the sexes 'far more difficult to bridge than the cleavage of party or "class"'. The Women's Citizens' Associations, which from 1917 spread throughout Britain, promoted 'a sense of citizenship in women', and encouraged their full enfranchisement and election to office. They were, as Law has demonstrated, a political force to be reckoned with; but they were an emphatically non-party organisation in the tradition of the LWV.[69]

Despite these obstacles and dilemmas, and despite the looser hold on their supporters exercised by political parties in the United States, particularly at the national level, neither British nor American women ignored partisan politics in the 1920s. For black women, that generally meant Republican politics. Throughout the decade, NACW women promoted political awareness, co-operating with the Republican National Committee, forming the backbone of the committee's Colored Women's Department, and founding the National League of Republican Colored Women (1924). Since the Women's Division of the Democratic Party neglected them, while the Republicans remained the dominant political party in the United States until the New Deal, the Republican leanings of black women are understandable. A case could also be made for consolidating any minority vote behind one party to make it worth cultivating by politicians. However, support for Republicans proved still more disappointing for black women than for black men, and their disillusionment turned them away from Republican politics to race campaigns. Although some black women did manage to vote after 1920, the disenfranchisement of black men persisted on a massive scale and the two sexes together did not have any numerical significance at the polls. African Americans comprised nearly 10 per cent of the country's population, but 'less than 5 per cent were even registered to vote' in the South in 1940, while those 'who resided elsewhere . . . constituted less than 3 per cent of the potential national electorate'. Moreover, the solidly loyal black minority vote was taken for granted instead of courted. Hence Harding, Coolidge and Hoover proved as ready as Presidents Roosevelt and Taft (1901–13) had been to condone injustice in patronage matters and to tolerate segregation, lynching, and unequal socio-economic conditions between the races.[70]

White women voters, by contrast, had the advantage of large numbers, and divided their votes between the existing parties. But the first gain for white and black women voters alike was just to be included in party political organisations. Thus in America, after enfranchisement, women were accorded greater representation on the National Committees of the Republicans and Democrats, and welcomed at the parties' national conventions. In Britain, they were drawn into the Conservative Party apparatus by the Women's Unionist Organisation, the

National Union's Central Council, the Advisory Committee of the Women's Division and a Women's Parliamentary Committee. As a rising political force fond of claiming the high moral ground, the Labour Party was anxious to secure the loyalty of labour women and therefore made them part of its post-war organisation by giving pre-war female sections representation on constituency party executive committees, by guaranteeing women seats on the National Executive Committee, and by creating a Women's Advisory Committee and a Chief Woman Officer (see chapter 6 on class and politics). The declining Liberal Party mostly contented itself with noting female demands through the Women's National Liberal Federation; it had little to propose at the national manifesto level by the late 1920s. Having received such formal recognition, women were expected to be grateful, to put party before gender issues, to content themselves with advisory and campaigning rather than policy making roles, to ignore both 'gallantry and condescension', and to continue to perform the supportive tasks with which they had been associated since the nineteenth century.[71]

Under these circumstances, it is hardly surprising that although white women in the United States pressed for and secured government offices at home and abroad during the 1920s, they remained in an inferior position to men, unduly reliant on wealth or family connections rather than political experience for preferment, and with some of the posts they gained fitting into 'a traditional notion of women's sphere, such as public welfare . . . and charities'. In the same period, there were usually only fifty female candidates a year for federal jobs, and while women served at every 'level of office in state and local government' – where competition from men was less and women's community connections could be brought to bear – by 1925 they held a mere 1.8 per cent of the 7,542 seats available in the forty-eight state legislatures, in addition to a handful of seats in the House of Representatives and the Senate. Black women had no presence in the national legislature and black men were in the same position until the 1928 election of Republican Oscar DePriest to the House of Representatives.[72] In Britain, women likewise did better in local government; but they secured only 15 per cent of elected local government offices and a still smaller number of posts at the national level – thirty-eight MPs from the 1920s to the 1945 general election, seventeen of them Conservatives, sixteen Labour and five Liberals.[73]

Disturbingly, a significant proportion of national legislative positions in both countries went to women elected to succeed husbands who had died in office, the belief apparently being that they would, acceptably to their constituencies, simply carry out the mandates imposed on their menfolk until a 'real' (that is, male) successor could be found through the normal political procedures. Women candidates were particularly likely to find themselves standing 'in order to break the ice' for others – as did the American reformers Florence Luscomb and Minnie Fisher Cunningham, and the English feminist Mrs Corbett Ashby: unsuccessfully in all three cases. Their claim that women in politics would 'raise its mental attitude and . . . improve its dignity', and that the time had come for campaigns 'based on issues and not mud slinging', clearly could not combat male and female fears that a vote for a woman was a wasted vote.[74]

Should we be dismayed about these meagre benefits for women? The answer must be yes, but not unduly surprised at them in the context of the 1920s. No group newly arrived in politics has made dramatic gains. The rules of the party game have to be learned, contacts in and outside legislatures made, committee appointments secured, and the reputation for soundness – for being 'one of us' – developed. Female politicians were not necessarily feminists, and were cautious about how they co-operated with each other. Moreover, the suspicion of parties that lingered among some women between the wars was unhelpful: they were too easily tempted, when the novelty of the vote had worn off and the political going got tough, to give up on party work and turn to their own associations. Yet just as unhelpful was the fact that the American and British two-party systems involved 'winner takes all' elections; more women office holders were produced in continental European countries which had proportional representation and multi-party systems. And such direct representatives mattered, as witness, not least, the impact of the black Republican, Oscar DePriest, elected in 1928 to Congress, where he 'immediately attracted national attention' and gained an audience for 'the role he played as spokesman for his race'.

The ability of women desiring political change to influence power brokers declined sharply once politicians believed they had the measure of the female impact on politics: that is by the late 1920s. Before this setback, however, activists using party contacts and two new lobbying bodies – the Women's Joint Congressional Committee (WJCC, 1920) in the United States and the Consultative Committee of Women's Organisations (CCWO, 1921) in Britain – campaigned hard to advance a new programme to help women and children.[75]

Reform

The WJCC and CCWO put campaigners in touch with each other, seeking to pool information, to prevent duplication of effort, and generally to co-ordinate women's political activities. Outlasting the decade, the WJCC enjoyed the support of ten major women's associations that claimed over 10,000,000 members. It came into being at the behest of the powerful but respectable LWV, and through its subcommittees chaired by forceful women it allowed its members to push measures with which they were particularly concerned.[76] But while the WJCC included the Council of Jewish Women, the National Association of Colored Women did not join it until 1924 and later withdrew, which was a pity in view of its endorsement of just the sort of social feminist goals to which the WJCC was committed. The committee's British counterpart, the CCWO, had the backing of forty-nine women's organisations, aimed to co-ordinate their political efforts and worked for parliamentary candidates sympathetic to women's issues. Tensions between its members had contributed to the committee's demise by 1928.[77] None the less, a wide range of women's groups in both countries collaborated to forward the agendas of feminism, and between them they enjoyed considerable success during the 1920s.

In the United States, additional funds were secured for the Women's Bureau and the Children's Bureau, which monitored the conditions of working women and children; and for the Sheppard-Towner Act (1921), which provided matching federal grants to states in order to ensure that pregnant women had access to help from 'public-health nurses, visiting nurses, consultation centers, child-care conferences, and literature distribution'. Activists also worked for equal nationality rights for women and men; for civil service reclassification legislation (1923), which established 'the principle of equal pay for equal work . . . in the public service'; for federal regulation of the food industry; for a federal women's prison (1924); for the 1924 (but eventually unratified) child labor amendment; and for compulsory school attendance in the District of Columbia. In addition, some states saw effective female pressures for action on the minimum wage, the eight hour day, workers' compensation, protective legislation, child labour, compulsory education and social purity.[78]

In Britain, women on local government bodies, and in the Women's Institutes, Townswomen's Guilds and other women's groups, continued to improve conditions and services for women, for children and for their communities, without overtly threatening the conventional division between the sexes. Nationally, women's gains included a law permitting them to be elected as members of parliament, and a Sex Disqualification (Removal) Act which ended 'all existing restrictions upon the admission of women into professions, occupations and civic positions including appointments as jurors and magistrates'. Measures were secured extending Scottish married women's property rights; allowing husbands and wives to inherit equally each other's property and the property of intestate children; and facilitating the recovery of sums payable under maintenance orders, from men living 'in other parts of the empire'. In addition, men and women achieved equal grounds for divorce, equal and extended grounds for separation, and equality with regard to the guardianship of infants. The maximum amount allowed to married women under separation orders was increased, as was the sum 'payable by a father for an illegitimate child'. The law on infanticide was moderated where a woman was shown to be 'suffering from the effects of her confinement'; the laws were strengthened concerning adoption and relations between men and under age girls; better pensions and children's allowances were agreed for widows; and provision was made for the registration and regulation of nurses, midwives and maternity homes. The age of marriage was raised to sixteen for both sexes. And in 1928, feminists rejoiced in the passage of the Equal Franchise Act.[79]

This mass of legislation, which owed much to careful feminist pressures in the two countries, reflected both equal rights and social feminist objectives. Nevertheless, the way forward remained strewn with perils, and American activists felt that they had to move especially cautiously because of conservative post-war attempts to associate them with support for communism and political subversion. While the 1920s saw the development of reactionary politics on both sides of the Atlantic, the British response to the worldwide spread of communism was less extreme than that of elite Americans unsettled by economic and ethnic tensions, and by their country's new prominence on the world stage. Although

British Conservatives did associate feminism with the left, and made much of a Bolshevik conspiracy allegedly being furthered in Britain by the first Labour government (1924), the Labour Party was, in fact, moderate. Furthermore the Conservatives, in power between 1924 and 1929, were determined to show themselves 'as fit as any Liberal or Labour Government to legislate on social problems'.[80] But in neither Britain nor America was it easy, after the late 1920s, to achieve the sort of changes that feminists wanted.

Under these circumstances, full co-operation between America's white and black women reformers would have been highly desirable. Their established tendency to operate separately aggravated the tendency of local administrators of welfare measures such as mothers' pensions and the Sheppard-Towner Act to discriminate against black women in need of assistance, because they disapproved of their mores or simply held them in contempt. In the case of mothers' pensions, it has been estimated that by 1931 'only 3 per cent of pensions recipients nationwide were black, with even lower proportions in the southern states'. Of course most reform measures, regardless of country, are undermined by conservative or inadequately funded implementation, and those that British and American women had a hand in procuring from the nineteenth century are no exception, albeit the 'cost of government as ladies want it' was held against them in both countries. But the full support of white women for their black sisters in the unpromising political climate of the 1920s would have been a fitting mark of the whites' true emancipation, and would have strengthened black women's position in the national reform networks which taxed their limited resources more than did local endeavours. Integrated efforts would also have been of practical advantage to feminist associations – black and white – whose influence was being challenged by changing intellectual and social fashions, as well as by professional and working-class women's organisations.[81]

As it was, when women did collaborate across the racial divide, in bodies like the Committee on Women's Work of the male dominated Commission on Inter-Racial Cooperation of the Methodist Episcopal Church South (CIC, 1920) and the YWCA, the results were disappointing. Black women could hardly enthuse over organisations which, though they expressed support for improving the child welfare facilities, living and working conditions, educational opportunities, media representation, court and political rights of African Americans, were suspicious of the black masses and lacked any clear idea of how to move forward once personal contacts had been made, information gathered and goals set. The conservatism of most of their prosperous white members meant that the bi-racial associations largely left the improvement of black community facilities to blacks. Such conservatives had no intention of challenging the racial system from which whites of both sexes benefited. Women of the two races perforce learned more about each other, but black and white were even segregated within the organisations' own ranks. Inter-racial co-operation did not, in other words, bless the more radical aspirations of black club women: rather they were forced to work for familiar objectives, appealing to a familiar maternalist ideology, and accommodating a familiar white determination to control the forces of social change.[82]

It is thus the more surprising that black and white women were able to come together between the wars to publicise and deplore the persistence of lynching, and to support sheriffs who stood out against the barbarity. Some female activists also helped to sustain a determined if ultimately fruitless lobbying campaign for a federal anti-lynching bill. Like the child labour amendment, the measure met with particularly strong opposition in the South, where lynching was most common and Progressive reform had flowered late.[83] Yet while traditional southern opposition to outside interference was once again in evidence, the intensified anti-lynching movement revealed some new emphases in race relations. In the first place, black women collectively became more assertive, forming a Committee of Anti-Lynching Crusaders in 1922, whose publicity drive 'influenced the passage of antilynching laws in thirteen states, including Alabama and Tennessee, by July 1925'.[84] Second, black women – who had reproached black men for their failings as reformers – now attacked privileged white women for their failings; and because of the growth in the size and confidence of the black middle class, they were able to do so as members of the same respectable stratum in society. 'When Southern white women get ready to stop lynching', declared the Crusaders, 'it will be stopped and not before.'[85] Third, while the earlier campaign of Ida B. Wells had undermined lynchers' claims to be chivalrously defending white women against menacing black men, and had exposed their self-indulgent cruelty and prejudice, opponents now pointed out more vigorously that women were among the victims of lynching, that their social reform ideals must be imposed 'on the larger society', and that the disreputable persons who took the law into their own hands were perpetuating 'the galling image of the benighted South'.[86]

This last line of attack may have shaken white women into setting up their own Association for the Prevention of Lynching (ASWPL) in 1930, but to many conservatives their action was merely an unacceptable response to ideas about white male characteristcs and power that men had defensively elaborated from the end of the nineteenth century in the face of unsettling religious trends, racial theories and feminist claims.[87] Links were sustained between the ASWPL and African American women, and the courage, commitment, organisational skills and modernising thrust of association members is not in question. But it is indicative of the conventional side of ASWPL's Texan leader, the suffragist and feminist campaigner Jessie Daniel Ames, and her middle-class co-workers, that they saw separatism as the only sure way of avoiding racial conflict with African American women and drawing support from the country's established reform groups.

The ASWPL did win the support of these groups, with the national and regional federations of Jewish women in particular demonstrating the reform instincts that characterised their internationalism between the wars. By the early 1940s, Philip Dray points out, 'more than a hundred national women's groups had endorsed the ASWPL's mission'.[88] White activists could not, however, suppress black criticism of the separatist policy. Since the generally conservative National Council of Women had in 1922 endorsed black women's efforts against lynching, who can say that a racially integrated approach to the practice would not have secured even greater backing for change?[89] Unfortunately, relying as it did on church-based female institutions, the ASWPL was not a sufficiently feminist association to put female solidarity before 'women's traditional religious and domestic concerns'; and it was not sufficiently free of race prejudice to force a change in the commonplace and unhelpful opinions about black women which even many southern liberals entertained.[90] The reluctance of prominent social feminists of both races to relinquish their hard won positions of intellectual leadership in their own communities for less secure roles in the inter-racial groups was another reason why substantial ideological development regarding race was not provoked by the white women's campaign against lynching.[91]

Two other problems which adversely affected black and white women reformers after the First World War were the tension between egalitarian and social feminists (also discussed in chapters 4 and 6); and the cultural challenge to feminist maternalism. On both sides of the Atlantic, as we have seen, women appealed to politicians most successfully when they stressed their special qualities and their roles as wives and mothers. In Britain, social feminism was strengthened after the war by women activists who pressed for measures like family allowances, birth control and protective legislation in the belief that these were issues that addressed 'the potentialities of their own natures' and 'the circumstances of their own lives'. Looking at their problems 'through men's eyes and discussing them in men's phraseology' was dismissed by activists like Eleanor Rathbone as a 'me too' form of feminism which did not meet the needs of the majority of women.

The objections of egalitarian feminists to such arguments reflected both their sense that the approach they offered was far more wide ranging than jibes about man-apeing conceded, and that the social feminists were pushing women back towards the separate sphere to which they had been confined in the nineteenth century. In the opinion of the egalitarian Lady Rhondda, feminism was 'a kind of groping forward to find the new equal world and to try to discover how we can make its laws work. We don't quite see how yet, even the foremost of us – and the ordinary woman has scarcely begun to think' about its challenges. Extraordinary women like her fellow egalitarian Vera Brittain, who had thought about them, believed that the feminist aim could be 'summed up in one sentence addressed to mankind: "Recognise our full humanity, and we will trouble you no more".' But Brittain acknowledged the opposition that existed to feminism as she understood it, and the dispute about its true meaning was conducted in the feminist press, between and within feminist organisations, as well as provoking the creation of the Open Door Council (1927) to oppose protective legislation that affected working-class women.[92]

Still more spirited was the comparable debate in the United States, where social feminism was more elaborately mobilised among black and white women, and so had more to defend; where the feminists of the NWP were more disinclined to moderation than any of the British egalitarian groups; and where, from 1923, the NWP's proposed Equal Rights Amendment gave the quarrel an enduring focus that was lacking in Britain.[93]

A debate about the meaning of egalitarianism and the intellectual basis of feminism was both predictable and necessary in a new era. It was conducted with most urgency among British and American activists after the First World War, and again in Britain after the granting of full female suffrage in 1928; but it rumbled on throughout the decade, matching the ongoing speculation among politicians, popular writers and intellectuals about how post-suffrage women would behave. And in Britain, certainly, its polarising impact should not be exaggerated (see above, p. 54). That said, the altercations between the two countries' egalitarian and social feminists did take time that might have been spent on trying to heal old rifts and bring young recruits into the women's movement (albeit this support was sought in the 1920s during the renewed British suffrage campaign).[94]

It is hard to be confident that an infusion of young blood would have improved feminism's image with the public since, as Law maintains, the pejorative term 'flapper' was widely used in the British press to describe young women, 'who were characterized as feckless and immoral'.[95] A similarly exaggerated representation of flappers was to be found among American commentators.[96] Such an infusion might, however, have broken down the ungenerous aversion of some young women to what the aspiring American writer Lillian Hellman termed the 'stale stuff' of feminism. Members of her generation, she declared, were 'too young to be grateful' for how much they owed to feminists who had fought 'the battle of something-or-other in the war for equality'.[97] These self-consciously modern American women of the 1920s have been brilliantly placed in context by Ann Douglas, in her study of post-war New York. According to Douglas, such women 'were at least as eager as their male peers to seize the liberties of adventurous autonomy, creative and rigorous self-expression, and full exposure to ethnic and racial diversity, . . . liberties against which the Victorian matriarch had, as her descendants saw it, ruthlessly campaigned'.[98] A comparable desire to break with the past found expression in Britain; as one young woman put it, 'we have torn down the musty hangings which the Victorians erected. We talk of everything, we consider everything . . . We are determined to let in the air – to ventilate every corner of our mansion.'[99]

The revolt against maternalism was, in fact, less complete and less beneficial to women than its proponents hoped it would be. The 1920s saw no repudiation of women's primary homemaking role, even if marriage was to be companionate, and working outside the home and sexual activity before marriage were more acceptable than they had been in the pre-war era. Greater social freedom to pursue personal satisfaction did not exempt women from their key roles as consumers, responsive to post-war advertising pressures to invest in the new mass production goods on which much of the decade's economic prosperity depended. Despite the claims made in the 1920s about the mental and sexual equality of men and women, activists were unable to win tolerance for lesbian relationships, for economic equality between the sexes or for substantial female influence in politics. And notwithstanding the publicity given to flappers, post-war culture in the United States and Britain was influenced by memories of men's wartime exploits and orientated towards a frank embrace of urban pleasures usually associated with men.[100]

In this context, black women leaders faced an especially difficult challenge. What became known as the 'Negro Renaissance' in Harlem may have increased white awareness and appreciation of black culture, and created liberating opportunities for black intellectuals and artists, but the majority of its patrons were white men. While black women were a memorable presence on stage and as blues singers, the main creators of the renaissance were black men who enjoyed the company of other men.[101] Its influence was nevertheless felt by the numerous post-war black migrants to the cities. Hence, White has established, the black activists who still took pride in social feminism's emphasis on sexual control and the uplifting power of organised motherhood found themselves ideologically undermined by this brand of modernism. And they were not granted a compensatory voice and role in civil rights organisations such as UNIA, the National Urban League and the NAACP, which, though they were prepared to admit, protect and glorify black women, were not prepared to see them as equal co-workers.[102]

Yet if internationalism, party politics and reform in the 1920s had been unable effectively to bring black and white women together, or to involve more than a fraction of either group, the Great Depression of the 1930s created new reform opportunities for social feminists in which African American women shared. Such was the enormity of the national economic crisis and the pragmatism of the Roosevelt administration that relief was targeted at all the major interest groups in American society. Women were among the plethora of experts who were welcomed in Washington to advise on the New Deal's burgeoning programmes for recovery and reform, and they made their mark particularly on the Social Security Act of 1935, the Fair Labor Standards Act of 1938, and the efforts to find work for the unemployed. Moreover, both the demands of black activists and the value of the northern black vote (expanded by increased migration from the South) were considered seriously by the Democratic Party, as it sought to strengthen its base of support in the face of Republican opposition.

Even the South somewhat relaxed its traditional hostility to federal intervention in its affairs, and by the end of the 1930s white liberals were once again confronting the enormities of its racial system: this time through the Southern Conference for Human Welfare (SCHW, 1938). But while the inter-racial SCHW recruited female members, and though prominent women such as Louise Charlton, Mollie Dowd, Mary McLeod Bethune, Lucy Randolph Mason and Virginia Durr played a vital part in its proceedings, the conference's growing attack on racial discrimination and segregation meant that race concerns took precedence over gender issues, as was so often the case in organisations where the two were ostensibly united. Given the criticism levied against the SCHW by moderates and conservatives, because of its liberalism on race, any other course would probably have been ill judged; as it was, its commitment to educational improvements, registering voters and abolishing the poll tax could be seen as helpful to all African Americans.[103]

Black women advanced their concerns more directly by reorganising themselves nationally and by working through an exceptional campaigner whose political skills equalled those of the Democratic Party's white female fixers, Sue Shelton White and Molly Dewson. That campaigner was Mary McLeod Bethune, who, like White and Dewson, came to politics via female reformism and networks. In founding the National Council of Negro Women (NCNW) in 1935, Bethune drew on her long experience as an educator and club woman in the South; but her acquaintance with poverty, her dark colour, her visionary confidence in the purchasing power of African Americans, her awareness of their needs as workers, and her own potency as an orator enabled her to reach out to the black masses in a manner reminiscent of Marcus Garvey. Unlike Garvey, however, she held and exploited a position in government (head of the Division of Negro Affairs in the National Youth Administration) that gave her access to the President and his wife Eleanor, as well as to members of Roosevelt's black cabinet, over which she presided and for whom she spoke with motherly determination. Connected as she was, other politicians responded to her and she was able to raise racial questions at highly publicised conferences and through persuasive personal lobbying.[104]

Mrs Bethune's race did, of course, generally exclude her from the tightknit group of white feminists whose influence was enhanced by the New Deal. But not all white women turned away. Hence the sheltered southerner, Virginia Durr, who during the 1930s was a volunteer in the Women's Division of the Democratic National Committee and a tireless worker against the poll tax, testified to Bethune's 'commanding presence' and was grateful that she 'took a great deal of trouble with me . . . she really did. She tried hard to teach me the facts of life' at a time when 'there was no talk even about the black vote. That wasn't even discussed. It was a matter of trying to get white women represented.' More importantly, Mrs Bethune developed a close rapport with Mrs Roosevelt, another white feminist who outgrew her privileged background. Both women enjoyed politics and recognised that it required compromises scorned by ideologues. Both were social feminists who saw the need to get on with men, stressed the importance of racial and economic justice, and did not push the president to move on matters like anti-lynching legislation, where he believed action was politically impossible. Both women were blessed with boundless energy and a care for people throughout the nation, and both placed their concerns in an international context.[105] They thus communicated better from the outset than did Mrs Roosevelt and another important black contact: the young feminist and civil rights campaigner, Pauli Murray, who conceded that the First Lady initially served as the lightning rod for her anger with the racial status quo.

But if Murray chafed at the caution on race showed by Mrs Roosevelt, who in turn felt that Murray pushed too hard, they eventually established a friendship of 'respect and affection' that lasted for twenty-two years. As Murray recalled, they found 'common ground in our status as women and it was in this area that we were able to transcend our political differences on racial strategies'. It was none the less profoundly important to Murray that Eleanor Roosevelt shared her deep interest in the civil and women's rights movements, and could see that it was the same prejudice which prevented 'both Negroes and women from realizing their capabilities'. And while Roosevelt was careful not to overplay her hand and alienate the power brokers she needed, Murray commented admiringly on the older woman's belief that it was 'Better to light one candle than to curse the darkness'.[106]

Such friendships showed black women leaders reaffirming the interest in national politics that the disappointments of the 1920s had undermined. Whereas the NACW president and anti-lynching stalwart, Mary Talbert, had been forced to appeal to white women 'for moral and financial support',[107] Bethune was helped by the greater assertiveness of African American men in the black cabinet, the NAACP, the National Urban League and the Negro Industrial League, and by her own confidence in what the federal government could deliver.[108] She and the NCNW were emboldened by the state of African American protest and the state of the economy to seek an increase in 'black female employment and economic opportunity', which aim included full black participation 'in all New Deal welfare and jobs programs', and the appointment of black professionals to the national, state and local agencies which administered these programmes.[109]

Although Bethune stressed the importance of black women helping themselves and avoiding reliance on bodies like the white dominated National Council of Women, when the need arose she was willing to work with white organisations – among them the LWV and the National Consumers' League.[110] But Bethune and the NCNW were disadvantaged within the black community by their reliance on the sororities, church and professional bodies, since this reliance laid them open to the charge of pandering to the light skinned elites.[111] Members of the NCNW were often at odds with NCAW activists, who questioned the need for the new council and the focus it adopted,[112] just as white egalitarian feminists denounced social feminists such as Mrs Roosevelt.[113] And despite her contacts, her organisational base, her high profile and the president's willingness to see more women in government office, Bethune was unable to secure a large increase in black female appointments.[114] Moreover, if black women activists, like their male equivalents, now relied less on community campaigning and more on pressure group methods and patronage jobs from the Democrats, black men still had the advantage of more elective offices upon which to build a base in that party.[115] There was little comfort to be drawn from the fact that white American and British women likewise found winning political office more difficult after 1931 than in the 1920s,[116] once feminist causes came to seem less important to many people than national economic crises and international threats, particularly from organised fascism. Feminists did see the danger of fascism and condemned its reactionary features.[117] However, as we shall see (below, chapter 7), refuting its tenets was a divisive distraction from their main objectives.

Conclusions

During the interwar years and regardless of race, American and British feminists faced a number of common difficulties in internationalism, politics and reform. These included reassessing their ideology; getting out the women's vote; reviewing their relations with the political parties; sustaining and adding to their organisations; procuring new legislation; and making an impact on the theory and practice of international relations. But the sense of solidarity produced by such shared challenges was undermined by the Americans' preoccupation with their domestic race problems and the British concern with race in the imperial context.

Women of colour, like their white counterparts in both countries, found that they could make headway in terms of influence and legislation by embracing social feminist goals. But on the whole they were obliged to operate separately from white women. They did reap some benefits from this separation, namely continuing community power, leadership opportunities, a degree of freedom to adopt their own ideological emphases, and the facilitating of contacts with activist men of their race. Furthermore, closer relations with white feminists would not have averted many of the difficulties associated with poverty, minority status, recent enfranchisement, and women's enduring reservations about political partisanship. But racial solidarity might have helped them to move the anti-lynching campaign further along, to increase their profile nationally, and to enhance the legislative gains they were able to obtain. There were novel opportunities for women of colour in internationalism, and their presence at its meetings gave them contacts and encouragement, besides improving the sensitivities and enlarging the agenda of the once overwhelmingly white movement. Yet their small numbers and elite status limited their impact, whether they acted through well established bodies like WILPF and the Alliance, or in newer organisations like the ICWDR and the BCL.

Between the wars, women of colour could not have mobilised themselves to much better effect, given that no American government was committed to desegregation, no British government was willing to hasten the end of empire, and white race liberals on both sides of the Atlantic remained few in number, relatively powerless, and wedded to giving race priority over gender. Before substantive benefits could be received by most women of colour, they would also need to share more fully in the economic and educational advantages of modern, urban society; and national power brokers would need to question the moral justification and economic necessity for racial discrimination.[118]

6 Feminism and class during the interwar years

By the outbreak of the First World War, the governments of Britain and the United States had for over two decades been alarmed by the growing chasm separating corporate capital and labour, and by the emergence of an assertive trade union and socialist/labour movement which sought political as well as economic clout. In both countries, liberal reformers and concerned politicians had supported the passage of welfare legislation and the extension of the suffrage in order to mitigate workers' unrest. Where such methods failed, state coercion had been applied, with the years before 1914 witnessing peculiarly bitter clashes between the opposing groups.

Feminists were adversely affected by these developments, since through publicly ignoring the existence of complicated class differences among women they had initially been able to present their cause as more coherent, wide-ranging and humane than it actually was. Out of the public gaze, however, middle-class women had eventually moderated their censorious condescension towards working women, and had helped them to benefit from improved local amenities and state services: the 'brutal "humbling of inferiors" . . . [was no longer] thought necessary to the maintenance of social order'.[1] For their part, working women had increased their contacts with elite women and learned how to profit from them. But by the 1930s, despite a serious attempt by activists of all political persuasions to work together in a Popular Front to combat fascism and help its victims, it became fully apparent that women could not normally co-operate across class lines.[2] It also became clear that the conspicuous separation of working-class and middle-class feminists that marked this period brought only the same mixture of advantages and disadvantages that had been inherent in women's pre-1914 cross-class endeavours. Why, how, and with what consequences this separation occurred, and why it was more pronounced in Britain than in the United States, the present chapter will seek to establish. It will begin with an assessment of women's thinking about class in the two countries. It will then offer an account of leftwing feminine involvement in internationalism, with special reference to labour organisation and protective legislation. And it will conclude with a review of class politics, focusing first on birth control, and then on work and social welfare issues.

Attitudes to class

Although by popular convention American society is as classless as Britain is class-ridden, the concept of class has always been complicated and controversial on both sides of the Atlantic. Accordingly David Cannadine's recent study of class in Britain shows it to be of enduring interest and presents a threefold model of class as a seamless web of hierarchical relations; as a tripartite division of society into 'upper, middle and lower collective groups'; and as an adversarial division in society between 'us' and 'them'. None the less, he also sees among modern scholars a tendency to 'stress the relatively high degree of consensus which seems to have prevailed in Britain', making it hard for them to privilege class identity or analysis in their interpretations.[3]

Class thinking and practice are similarly complex in the United States.[4] Its government and citizens have certainly avoided the overt acknowledgement of class, because of their commitment to a founding ideology which elevates individual rights while abhorring strong government and class legislation. But during the twentieth century, the nation's immense middle class has come to determine social mores in a way that may be resented or despised by those below or above it. Moreover, the very fluidity of their civilisation – based on the growth of the land base, economy, political democracy, personal freedom and equality of opportunity – can make Americans particularly anxious for enduring individual and group marks of respect. And as Neville Kirk has argued, the alleged exceptionalism of the United States with regard to class has been exaggerated, since by the First World War, notwithstanding its ethnic and racial diversity and large agricultural sector, the American labour force had become more homogeneous and self-aware. As a result, in 'industrial struggles, . . . [in] the formation and growth . . . of a socialist rather than a labour party, and in the . . . spectacular successes of syndicalist organising drives', American workers might actually be regarded as 'more militant, indeed more class conscious, than their British cousins'.[5] All societies in fact produce class divisions and class thinking, whether or not these phenomena are frankly acknowledged or discussed in the Marxian terms of opposing economic interests. Historians simply disagree about their nature, impact, and development over time.

As far as interwar feminists are concerned, class was openly important in Britain, with labour unrest culminating in the General Strike of 1926, and with the coming to office of the Labour Party in 1924 and 1929–31. Despite the unifying power of its mass culture and egalitarian ideology, class was also more than usually salient in the United States, as the *laissez-faire*, pro-business federal governments of the 1920s gave way in the 1930s to reformism with what Richard Hofstadter has called a 'social-democratic tinge', reflecting the 'demands of a large and powerful labor movement . . . [and] the interests of the unemployed'.[6] And both countries – though to different degrees – felt the unsettling impact of a fragile international economy, the establishment of Soviet communism and the rise of fascism. Under these testing new circumstances, feminists had to take account of class without giving it more importance than the complex condition of women, and without conceding the long familiar leftwing allegation that feminism was a deluded and narrowly focused bourgeois sideshow which unhelpfully distracted women from the class struggle.

In the United States, the accusation of narrowness was sometimes met directly by middle-class campaigners. Thus the socialist feminist Florence Luscomb firmly dismissed the allegation as false, pointing to the efforts women had made to give feminism an 'all-inclusive character'. Such efforts were necessary, she thought, because the capitalist system discriminated against any group that was weak.[7] Often, however, bourgeois American feminists chose not to highlight either their personal views on class or their own class membership. In the recollection of the veteran campaigner Mary Dewson, influential women were not 'communicative about their inner life and personal thoughts, nor did they pry into yours'; yet they were 'kind, thoughtful, considerate, upright and energetic'.[8] Female reformers, confident that they could if necessary transcend class, tended to discuss it obliquely and partially in terms of the poverty of labour women; the alien quality of immigrant culture; or the resentful outlook of those not organised for self-help – as when the settlement house and health care leader, Lillian Wald, warned audiences that 'what is called "class feeling" has been intensified' by oppressive industrial conditions.[9] And who can wonder at reformer circumspection, since openly to believe in the class system or class consciousness was to risk seeming un-American even in good times, let alone during a period when conservatives rallied feverishly to defend 'the family and the state against feminism and socialism'.[10]

None the less, the American social feminists of the interwar years were, like all reformers, sustained by a sense of belonging to a class apart, whose well educated members wrote to each other, worked, travelled and even lived together;[11] and in this supportive order of the saved, middle-class women might find unselfish personal fulfilment and escape from the constraints of the world into which they were born. In that world, after all, women traditionally had been cast as second class citizens, lumped 'without exception with children, idiots, and criminals', or 'no class at all after we were married'.[12] For much of the time, women activists could take for granted their ability and need to serve, and their support for 'the modern emphasis upon social well-being as contrasted with individual prosperity'.[13] And if they no longer blamed the poor for poverty, they had not lost earlier activists' sense of *noblesse oblige* towards 'the most helpless group of the great industrial army of America'.[14] Working women, declared the national WTUL stalwart Mary Dreier needed to be 'helped over the hurdle of masculine power'; and prosperous but democratic individuals like her colleague Mary Winslow, who made the ascent possible, deserved high praise.[15] It was not an option to ignore working women; for besides being genuinely interested in 'the least privileged', feminists believed that 'Women workers, unorganized, are unwittingly one of the most serious dangers to the standards of industry the world over'.[16] All would be assisted, they claimed, if the disadvantaged were assisted.

American social feminists therefore encouraged labour women to seek advancement through unions, and were willing to co-operate with male unionists in advocating legislation to protect women in the workplace. In other words, whereas many members of the middle class feared labour activists as socialists, white bourgeois feminists made an effort to do business with them, finding their relationship easier than that which had developed with African Americans, because the fluid characteristic of class was more negotiable in the United States than the ascribed characteristic of race. Hence white women reformers achieved some collaboration with working-class women in urban clubs and settlement houses, in the national WTUL, and in the New Deal female network analysed by Susan Ware (albeit the WTUL was careful not to embroil itself in purely theoretical debates about the link between feminism and class, and only three of the twenty-eight women in Ware's sample were from working-class backgrounds).[17]

For their part, American labour women usually articulated their awareness of the class/sex connection by indicting those middle-class feminists who made a name or living from their expertise about the poor, and whom unionist Rose Schneiderman disparagingly christened 'the Mink brigade'.[18] Members of the NWP were a special source of annoyance because they opposed industrial legislation for women and were 'not members of the working class'; rather, they were women 'whose economic interest . . . runs counter to the intent of this legislation, and who derive their support from persons and groups whose own financial interest is admittedly in opposition to any regard for the welfare of the workers of the country'.[19]

According to social feminists and labour women, the typical equal rights critic of protective laws was 'an individualist, asserting the laissez-faire philosophy and her own political liberty without realizing the hardships it imposes upon women in modern industry'. They, however, were convinced that for millions of vulnerable women, 'group conditions must be treated by group action, and the labor woman therefore has a collective ideal, with a program which may sometimes restrict individual liberty'.[20] Even a successful working-class reformer like Mary Anderson, of the US Department of Labor's Women's Bureau, attached great importance to the security which she associated with belonging to a labour organisation; 'through the trade union movement', she maintained, 'we working women could get better conditions and security of mind'.[21] In addition to feeling affronted by affluent women's business backing and limited practical 'knowledge of social conditions',[22] working-class women were likely to envy and resent their education, leisure, enjoyment of autonomy, social pull, claims to reform leadership and pursuit of professional status.[23]

In Britain, where unemployment, trade union membership, economic cleavages and class consciousness remained higher, feminists were forced candidly to reassess the problematical relationship between class and feminist objectives. But candour simply revealed, without reconciling, a range of opposing views. For some middle-class campaigners, among them the independent MP Eleanor Rathbone, it was not a matter for embarrassment that feminism, like 'every other political and social movement', had 'depended and must necessarily depend, largely on women who have some money and leisure to spend on something besides the struggle for existence'.[24] The feminist internationalist Margery

Corbett Ashby agreed and reflected that elite women, often endorsed by their governments, also came to head the women's movements in Asian and African countries, where it was thought necessary to show that there were leading women in positions of authority.[25]

Middle-class activism included women who thought that the British had been 'harmlessly class conscious'[26] in the early part of the twentieth century, and those who believed that they rose above conventional categorisations – as witness suffragette Grace Roe's assertion that there was 'no such thing as class with me'.[27] It included feminists like the writer Vera Brittain, who reflected the commonplace prejudices of the privileged, and those like Winifred Holtby and Lady Rhondda, who largely avoided them. Rhondda's feminist journal *Time & Tide* expressed impatience with rigid class barriers, declaring that it 'is as ridiculous as it is impossible to segregate women into classes and to tell one class that it has no right to take any interest in the doings or the restrictions placed on another class'.[28] And in personal terms one can see why such a course seemed foolish, since reforming women, irrespective of class, commonly displayed the same mixture of drive, discipline, self-control and unflagging faith in social evolution.

Yet middle-class British and American feminists, though loyal to their class, were also determined to assert their individuality,[29] a course that they might regard as too ambitious and risky for poorer women. Hence, since the nineteenth century, some bourgeois British campaigners had taken the line that vulnerable labour women should try to better themselves collectively, primarily through joining the separate economic organisations of the working class.[30] By 1920, unlike the Americans, they were willing to see the end of Britain's cross-class WTUL. The male hierarchy of the British Labour Party naturally agreed that working-class men and women should stick together; and after the First World War, by tying women's rights more firmly to the class struggle, they successfully increased the support of working women for party politics at the expense of non-partisan feminism. As a result, complained Mrs Corbett Ashby, people were made class-conscious in a 'very stupid way'.[31]

Insofar as bourgeois British feminists gave a feminine dimension to class, it was by reaffirming the link between their class and service to women and children. Updating nineteenth-century ideas and practice, they highlighted women's needs in both the home and the paid workplace, and envisaged greater state as well as reformer intervention in women's lives to bring about social reconstruction. Their focus, which was shared by American social feminists, meant that they were gradualists rather than revolutionaries: vehemently hostile to the prospect of a class war, just as they invariably denied any intention of provoking a sex war and remained opposed to shooting wars anywhere in the world. Both the British Labour Party and the ILP, despite their differences, were condemned by many feminists and non-feminists alike for allegedly advocating 'force and violence' to achieve the overthrow of capitalism. The newly formed (1920) Communist parties of the United States and Britain, and even the weakened and non-revolutionary American Socialist Party, were likewise censured on these grounds.[32]

The key contribution of increasingly politicised British working-class women to the interwar debate about class was to strengthen and clarify the commitment of their class to social justice, particularly through striving 'for better conditions for women and children'. In the words of one contemporary, working women 'belong to the class that, consciously or unconsciously, stands for the reconstruction of society'.[33] Anxious for practical gains, Labour Party women – like middle-class feminists – frequently shunned the strident language of class warfare; and, as the veteran working-class activist Hannah Mitchell pointed out, not having had to 'fight so hard for self expression' as the older generation of women, the young had 'escaped the hardening process that we went through'.[34] None the less, Labour Party feminists did offer a concerted body of ideas about women's subordination,[35] and some did deploy a fearless class rhetoric, among them the union organiser and Labour MP Ellen Wilkinson. Willing to criticise her party on the one hand, and 'you middle-class people' on the other, she never lost either her interest in the masses or her dismay that 'the orthodox teaching for women' involved submission and ignored 'them as human beings'.[36] The socialist feminists of the ILP – 'always in the van of socialist thought' – were still more outspoken, more committed to equality between the sexes, less bound by Labour Party discipline and from 1932 disaffiliated from it in their search for an 'equitable distribution of the world's wealth'.[37]

British socialist and labour women were, in addition, drawn into the conflict over protective industrial legislation that had divided American middle-class feminists, and alienated American elite women from their working-class sisters. And while there was a familiar note of resentment directed by labour women against prosperous women who had the temerity to interfere in a question beyond their firsthand experience,[38] it was given a much sharper class and party twist in Britain. This was particularly unfortunate, since, as Pat Thane has shown, the British women's labour associations 'cut across classes' and 'were conscious and proud of their mix'.[39] They were, however, equally aware of the need for working-class solidarity if the Labour Party's newfound political power was to be made permanent.

In neither country were women, as ideologues, able to devise a feminised version of classic Marxism that recognised women's unique difficulties and needs but offered no threat to this desired solidarity. Although female artists and writers were active in the elaborate culture of the left, women were unwelcome in political leadership positions. The majority were therefore obliged to take whatever political roles they could in the socialist/labour movement, and these roles were – as was the case with other social movements – largely subordinate and practical. By the late nineteenth century, a number of peripatetic female agitators had emerged who did offer inspiration to those contemplating or engaged in organised protest. They also highlighted female grievances in articles written for movement journals, and they benefited from the exchange of ideas at movement workshops and summer schools. But by the 1930s such stump speakers were starting to seem old-fashioned, while devising substantial essays or books took time and money that most women activists lacked; besides which the role of lecturer, organiser or ideologue was often lonely and invariably embattled.[40]

As Hannah Mitchell recalled, 'When I first began to speak, and kept to general Socialist propaganda, I was often told flatteringly that I had a male mind, but when I began to concentrate on sex equality, my male friends began to look askance, and avoid my company. I was often asked to change my subject when I proposed to speak on feminist topics; this I always firmly refused to do.'[41] Mitchell's experience was similar to that of the American communist Mary Inman whose book *In Woman's Defense* (1940) analysed the continuing oppression of women through separate socialisation, unequal marriages, and the low value placed by society on female work in the home. While gender issues continued to be debated in the communist press after 1940, the focus of Inman's study proved unacceptable 'to the CP's top leadership', as indeed did any arguments questioning the solidarity of working-class men and women, or the wisdom of seeing the trade unions as the main vehicle for producing revolutionary action.[42] In fact women radicals were and remained divided, just like their male comrades: notably over the merits of evolutionary and revolutionary socialism; over the relative importance of economic and party activities; and over the consequences of the Russian Revolution.[43]

Amid such faction fights, it is not surprising that there were few campaigners with the intellectual confidence of British socialist women Hannah Mitchell, Ellen Wilkinson, Stella Browne, Selina Cooper and Margaret McCarthy, and their American counterparts Charlotte Perkins Gilman, Emma Goldman, Crystal Eastman, May Woods Simon, Lena Morrow Lewis and 'Mother' Mary Harris Jones. Those who did emerge could find themselves unhelpfully isolated both from the leaders of mainstream feminism and from prominent male radicals.[44] The best way of avoiding isolation – other than through marriage to a fellow radical – was by accepting the primacy of economic issues, by stressing socialism's commitment to 'the collective ownership of the means of wealth', and by educating 'the worker to a sense of the wrongs he has had to suffer, and does suffer'.[45] Accordingly, American and British labour women who sought to give meaning to socialism's theoretical endorsement of equality between the sexes tended to avoid blunt criticism of the major themes or founding exponents of socialist dogma – something which was extremely unwelcome even when it came from male intellectuals.[46]

The position of left-wing female radicals was especially difficult in the United States, because of the historical American association of socialism's great names (Marx, Engels, Bebel, Lenin and Stalin) with distant cultures, and their support with unassimilated immigrants. Yet the size of the United States, the welcome given by isolated communities to travelling speakers, and the regional strength of radical movements (in the Mid-West and Far West), gave distinctive opportunities to American women socialists. British radical women were, for their part, adversely affected by their country's preference for the practical over the philosophical, which meant that the middle-class British intellectuals who supported Marxism did not challenge its established theory. Instead, they operated on Keir Hardie's rule that 'Socialism is more of an affair of the heart than of the intellect'.[47]

Avoiding these various quagmires, feminine activists within the diverse classes of Britain and the United States encouraged and appealed to women's sense of community. But though female community builders, in return, contributed to the growth of working-class consciousness in the face of hostility from the 'preying' classes', difficult conditions for unions on each side of the Atlantic continued to inhibit the development of a fully fledged socialist feminism and to foster a potentially restrictive view of women's distinctiveness.[48] The truth, as the intrepid unionist 'Mother' Jones admitted in 1930, was that neither working men nor women had learned effectively to use the power they possessed.[49] Even when union strength increased in the two countries during the ensuing Depression, as did the influence of the Left in the American labour movement,[50] women could not force a fresh look at the socialist argument that they were an integral part of the 'social problem', which would only be solved by socialist-induced economic change. What is more, the crisis of capitalism and the rise of the Popular Front led to a temporary downplaying of theory and a focus upon practical action which, it was hoped, would recruit more support for the labour movement in all its manifestations.[51]

American and British women were, then, divided among and between themselves by interwar debates on class, to which they contributed. Female activists lacked the numbers and power to change accepted political thinking about class, and considerable advantages followed, as always, from faithfulness to the party line. Only male and female fascists in Britain claimed that their ultra-patriotism transcended class divisions: a claim undermined, as Julie Gottlieb has shown, by the clear domination of the British Union of Fascists by middle- and upper-class elements.[52] While all women activists accepted the importance of gender, middle-class feminists often sought to minimise the importance of class, whereas their working-class counterparts emphasised it. Americans also remained convinced that Britain was a class ridden country, and that they enjoyed better relations with labour women. None the less, in both the United States and Britain, working-class campaigners felt they could still reach out to each other in internationalism. And it is to their international activities that we now turn.

Labour women, socialism and internationalism

The international ramifications of trade unionism, socialism and feminism were seriously disrupted by the First World War, but after 1918 all three firmly set about renewing their international organisations and refashioning their international objectives. In chapter 4 we have seen that the issue of protective industrial legislation complicated the overseas efforts of middle-class feminists, and that – without checking the expansion of such efforts – the different foreign policy objectives of Britain and the United States put a strain upon the relations of activists previously held together by the suffrage campaign. Were labour/socialist women any more fortunate in their endeavours? The answer must be a firm no, since they too quickly encountered a daunting blend of environmental, ideological and organisational problems.

At first, however, the prospect of replacing wartime paper contacts with personal communications and serious agendas was an exciting one. The Paris Peace Conference at the end of the First World War established an International Labour Organisation (ILO) as part of the machinery of the League of Nations, and at the conference women lobbyists made their views known about both the ILO and the League. Representatives of the American and British WTULs also played a vital role in ensuring that an international Congress of Working Women (ICWW) met in Washington, DC, in 1919, to coincide with the first conference of the ILO. Although it was committed to social justice and the 'principle that men and women should receive equal remuneration for work of equal value', the ILO further pledged itself to the 'protection of children, young persons and women'. This had been a concern of international bodies since the 1890s; but it was one which was guaranteed eventually to produce friction between the ILO and internationally mobilised egalitarian feminists.[53] A second potential irritant was the ILO's vague assurances about how women would be deployed in its operation. Other problems were also apparent from the outset. Juggling, as it did, the broad interests of its constituent government, union and employer representatives, the ILO was unlikely to be able to give women the attention and power that female activists desired. Furthermore, besides lobbying the ILO, ICWW women might additionally be involved in the affairs of the International Federation of Trade Unions (IFTU, 1901, Amsterdam). In other words, like bourgeois feminists, they were obliged to weigh the sometimes conflicting claims of gender, class and country.

Nevertheless, like their bourgeois sisters, the women caught up in labour internationalism generally knew each other well and had long been concerned with the issues they debated – notably 'women's employment, especially in relation to childbirth, night work, and jobs involving dangerous substances . . . ; child labor; the eight-hour day; and the problems of unemployment'.[54] They might differ on these questions, influenced by the conditions and practices in their respective nations; but, like the bourgeois feminists, they found that international meetings facilitated the exchange of information, the setting of priorities and the promotion of female solidarity. Confident and interested enough to want to make the ICWW a permanent organisation, promoters of the congress secured it a base first in Washington and then in London, fashioned for it a constitution and secretariat, and renamed it the International Federation of Working Women (IFWW, 1921). Its 1921 conference vigorously debated familiar topics, checked on the progress of resolutions agreed two years earlier, and considered such broader developments as the Russian Revolution and pressures for disarmament.[55] A respectable and predictable future among labour organisations seemed assured.

However, while IFWW's American supporters sidestepped one possible area of friction by declining to provide open-ended funding for the new body after its launch – IWSA's experience having shown that American wealth could promote resentment abroad rather than internationalism – they were for years unable to engage fully with the ILO because the United States was not a member. A similar challenge to the Americans was posed by IFTU, which the United States had not rejoined when it was revived after the First World War, largely because Samuel Gompers of the American Federation of Labor (AFL) objected 'to IFTU policies on dues, decision making, and socialism'. Leaders of the American WTUL had their own doubts about the genuineness of IFTU's concern for women's issues; but, embarrassingly, European labour women made clear their support for IFTU, 'the recognized nongovernmental trade union organization working with the ILO'. Accustomed to acting within an extraordinarily elaborate and successful social feminist network, prominent American WTUL women – epitomised by the affluent reformer Margaret Dreier Robins – were convinced that the IFWW should be an independent and feminist association. Once raised, its status could be neither ignored nor compromised, since many European women – including the British Labour Party politician Marion Phillips – believed that through transforming the IFWW into a female auxiliary of IFTU, 'we may get a wider and more powerful movement of women than we can under our own scheme[,] without losing any of the essentials'.[56]

Between 1923 and 1925, the absorption of the IFWW by IFTU was achieved at the prompting of the former and despite the broad opposition of the American WTUL. In 1924, the American women formally withdrew from the IFWW and ended their links with IFTU. Although the WTUL's official reason for opposing the merger was an unwillingness to be part of an organisation to which the AFL did not belong, a state of affairs that would have denied it voting rights in IFTU, Jacoby has argued persuasively that the real objection of the American activists was to being brought under the direction of labour men. The distinctive problems of working women, maintained the American WTUL's executive board, 'need to be emphasized by women in women's own way'; it was therefore unfortunate that European labour movements 'emphasize class-consciousness and deprecate a woman movement within their class'. As Jacoby concludes, we cannot know whether an independent IFWW would have improved the lot of British and American women workers.[57] We do know that the initial American WTUL support for such a body would have been hard to sustain.

During the 1920s, the WTUL struggled to retain its own membership and influence because of the reactionary attacks made in the United States on left-wing and feminist groups. It also suffered because these were generally poor years for American labour and socialism, in which divisions among the working class flourished. And it was hampered by the domination of the AFL by 'conservative and narrowly exclusive white male views[,] . . . clearly manifested in the failure to recruit large numbers of black workers and women'.[58] Although Robins and the WTUL's executive board opposed the IFWW merger with IFTU, her successor favoured it.[59] The dissenting feminists, even if they had carried the day with their veto, might have found American as well as European union women hard to keep on an independent feminist course.

The British, too, ran into difficulties with the IFWW, proposing unsuccessfully that, in addition to trade union women, federation membership should include working-class women who were not part of the paid workforce. Labour women in Britain had found such collaboration possible through their Standing

Joint Committee of Industrial Women's Organizations, which welcomed associations like the Women's Cooperative Guild (described by its General Secretary as 'a sort of trade union for married women').[60] Despite considerable American support for the British proposal, it fell before Canadian and European fears that a mixed membership would divisively politicise their efforts.[61]

Yet the United States and Britain seldom made common cause over IFTU, and we should not be surprised. After all, British labour women, drawing confidence from a stronger national labour movement, were willing to wind up their WTUL and independent political leagues to help integrate British labour endeavours after the First World War. It was predictable that they would be equally willing to accept integration within IFTU, which had been making sympathetic gestures towards the IFWW since 1921. From 1925 onwards, however, though IFTU honoured its promise to form an International Women's Committee and support conferences on the problems of women workers, these seem to have been underfunded debating opportunities which failed to influence the parent body. As was the case in the international associations of bourgeois women, national loyalties drove the women who were involved.[62] But British labour activists – among them the energetic unionist and MP Margaret Bondfield – could at least take comfort from their prominent role in international labour conferences.[63]

The ILO was in a stronger position than IFTU, being, from its foundation, linked to the League of Nations. But though it consequently became a natural target for women lobbyists from many organisations, they found it no easier to deal with than IFTU. Male directed, the ILO welcomed women's participation in its affairs but seemed content with the low attendance of women at its conferences and their small numbers on its staff and standing committees. If in 1928 its director acknowledged that the women's movement was 'one of the great forces working for justice', and was making 'steady progress', he also observed that it 'sometimes seemed disjointed or incoherent'.[64] Disjointed it certainly was.

Thus on the one hand, egalitarian feminists criticised the priority the ILO gave in its early years to international protective legislation regarding, for example, hazardous and night work for women. Given female employment difficulties after the First World War, during the Depression, and with the rise of anti-feminist fascist regimes, they warned against the passage of measures that, 'in spite of any temporary advantage, *may* develop into a very real tyranny and result in the segregation of women workers and the imposition of fresh handicaps on their capacity as wage-earners'.[65] On the other hand, many British and American social feminists – whether bourgeois or working class – praised the ILO as 'a symbol of welfare politics', and feared that contributing to the weakening of ILO protective labour conventions might undermine protective legislation at home and destroy their credibility abroad. Accordingly, as we have seen (above, chapter 4), they resisted the international agitation mounted by the NWP, IWSA, ODI, ERI and other egalitarian women's groups between the wars for an Equal Rights Treaty and Equal Nationality Treaty.[66]

Buffeted by irreconcilable forces, the ILO moved on women's issues with great caution: an understandable reaction in a newly formed body ultimately dependent for its effectiveness on the goodwill of the national governments it represented. Specifically, it conceded that women's maternal responsibilities were perennially at odds with their roles in the paid workforce: a problem that had so far defied solution. Without going out of business, the ILO could hardly abandon its basic protectionist stance; and protectionists within the organisation were in fact strengthened once the United States joined it in 1934, with strong backing from two leading American social feminists – Mary Anderson of the Women's Bureau and the Secretary of Labor, Frances Perkins. Thereafter, United States support was forthcoming for ILO conventions, which it had previously ignored. In 1937, the ILO did appear to hold out hope to those pressing for change by calling on all governments to reassess women's status 'with respect to their political rights and opportunities, economic conditions, and protection from economic exploitation'. But while the approach of the Second World War saw the ILO debate about women's rights broadened, it was in no way transformed.[67]

Other prominent international organisations, notably the Communist International (Comintern), the Labour and Socialist International (LSI), the International Co-operative Women's Guild (ICWG) and the League of Nations, afforded activist women a similar mixture of hope and disappointment.

Established in 1919 and surviving until 1943, Comintern was initiated by Moscow to counteract the influence of reformist socialists, to promote world revolution and to secure support from foreign workers.[68] Clara Zetkin might have assured Emma Goldman in 1921 that she was 'working to rally the support of the women of every country for the world revolution',[69] but Comintern was an overwhelmingly male body, as authoritarian in structure as it was exclusive in its membership. Its habit of 'substituting Soviet experience for critical inquiry'[70] was generally unfortunate and particularly unappealing to Americans. And its historian, Kermit McKenzie, has noted that 'Relatively little information can be found in Comintern materials about such matters as the family, education, religion, or culture in the broad sense'. Power politics and economics reigned supreme, although the Programme of 1928 did 'give the barest outlines of the policies and reforms that the Communists expected to pursue' in other fields. Aiming at equality between the sexes, partly through an educational drive that would eradicate the 'ideology and traditions of "female bondage"', Comintern was opposed to the creation of separate, national feminist organisations to act on its programme. Yet it failed to show how changes in the traditional family and the extension of state care for children could be achieved outside the exemplary Soviet Union.[71] Ellen DuBois has rightly concluded that 'in the whole history of the Left, the Third International stands out for its failure to generate a corollary feminist movement'.[72]

The existence of the LSI between 1923 and 1940 did not bring about a much better deal for women, since its affairs were dominated by the conflict between communism and social democracy: by its divisive and futile efforts to achieve 'the restoration of workers' unity'.[73] The International's concern to defend peace, democracy and workers' social benefits did, however, make it of interest to social feminists.[74] British labour and socialist women were for once keen for separate female mobilisation in response to an international initiative, and by 1925 they had agreed with European colleagues to constitute an International Advisory Committee of Women to meet annually, at least, and to advise the LSI 'about the aims and methods of Socialist women in various countries'. It was, in addition, committed to holding an international conference to coincide with meetings of the LSI. This it did in 1928 and 1931, with the British delegation including Marion Phillips and her fellow Labour Party politician, Susan Lawrence. The focus of the conferences was on the needs of mothers and children, and on 'women in the economic system'. After 1931, however, activity by the Advisory Committee declined as European economic and political conditions deteriorated.[75]

The experiences of women in relation to socialist internationalism in some ways resembled those of persons of colour. The Comintern was staunchly committed to overthrowing imperialism and supported 'the freedom movements of the colonial peoples'.[76] Just as it denounced sexual discrimination, it 'condemned any kind of discrimination against nationality, nation, or race'.[77] But action proved difficult, while consistency proved impossible. Comintern expected workers seeking freedom to accept Communism as the only way forward,[78] and it was largely driven by unpredictable world events and pressing Soviet needs.[79] Its attacks on British imperialism served mainly to strengthen the determination of the British authorities to defend the empire.[80] And its eventual move from supporting Pan Africanism to focusing on educational work with black labour groups divided and destabilised black activism, and resulted in the dismissal of Garveyism – the only mass movement among black Americans before the Second World War – as 'petty-bourgeois radicalism'. Altogether, socialist internationalism offered something to black activists looking for intellectual stimulation, personal contacts, lobbying opportunities, and additional means of rousing domestic opinion. It was more concerned with race than it was with gender; but in each case it offered no substitute for domestic action and sometimes gave a steer in unhelpful directions.[81]

The International Co-operative Women's Guild ran into similar difficulties. It was founded in 1921 by the Women's Co-operative Guild which, since 1883, had been bringing English women together not 'to rail against existing evils' but 'to remedy them wherever possible by applying to them the power of a well-directed Co-operation'. The Co-operative movement from which it sprang had, from the 1840s, contested 'the ways in which private retailing exploited working people', and, as Black observes, necessarily required the participation of women consumers and household managers.[82] However, the guild developed both a social feminist focus and a remarkably wide-ranging programme which included campaigns to secure equality between the sexes in the co-operative movement; to shun goods made by non-union labour; to support female unionisation; to encourage women to seek local political office and the national suffrage; and to investigate and seek action on public health laws, divorce reform and maternity allowances. As independent and successful activists who were appalled by the economic upheavals and human ravages of the First World War, it was understandable that WCG women came to see themselves as capable of contributing both to 'our national progress' and, in the world at large, to 'a new social civilization' built on peace, disarmament and international economic co-operation. As the WCG's first General Secretary, Margaret Llewelyn Davies, enthused: 'We can see before us an economic League of Peoples . . . which, operating naturally, is a far surer guarantee for Peace than a legally-devised association of Governments, and is the only social framework for an enduring League of Nations'.[83]

Yet though ICWG women believed that 'true friendship' and 'a real understanding' with other countries would secure their ends, achieving this solidarity was a different matter entirely. The conferences of the ICWG – like those of middle-class female internationalists – were enjoyable occasions for networking and talking. Participants (from 27 countries in 1931) learned about each other's approaches to shared problems and discussed a wide range of matters interesting to women: among them their situation in and outside the home; low prices; pure food; and the need for disarmament. Guild activists also kept in touch by correspondence. And thanks in good part to the efforts of Davies, in their early years they had a coherent internationalist ideology and strategy to keep them going. Women, they argued, were bound and entitled to repudiate war, since it was a killer of their children and a relic of the past, like slavery. It followed that they should, in the first instance, seek to drive militarism out of the educational system. They were enjoined to try to eradicate 'the spirit which breeds hate and war'; and they were also to show 'unflinching hostility to all policies, economic or militarist, which may provoke war' and prevent economic co-operation. In putting their views before politicians at home and the League of Nations abroad, they were mindful of the warning: 'woe betide them and the world if foreign politics are left in the hands of Governments'. And as individuals, they were exhorted to pledge that 'under no circumstances whatever' would they 'take part in, or help towards, the propagation of war'.

The ICWG did not help itself, however, by declining – as did the women's section of IFTU – a place on the Joint Standing Committee of the Women's International Organisations (1925), whose purpose was to get women appointed to the League of Nations. The ICWG position is understandable; membership of the Joint Standing Committee would have taken it into very middle-class company. Furthermore, it might have jeopardised the independence of guild women, who were convinced that 'it was not till an organisation of their own came into existence that women's power in Co-operation became an effective force', and that such autonomy was needed 'so long as there is class and sex inequality'. On the other hand, since the ICWG *did* join the League of Nations Peace and Disarmament Committee, a consistent involvement in the interwar superinternational coalitions of women would probably have been worth the risk, strengthening groupings that badly needed support and challenging the willingness of bourgeois British internationalists to leave their working-class sisters alone in their own 'very strong international cooperative movement', on the grounds that this separatism was something that had just happened, and was not willed.[84]

Nor did it prove possible to strike a close relationship with the United States, even though the ICWG rejoiced in 1920 'to hear of the splendid enthusiasm for Co-operation' that was arising there.[85] Advertisers in both countries flatteringly courted women as consumers, particularly in their capacity as housewives and in the desperate conditions of the 1930s. But neither country developed what June Hannam and Karen Hunt have termed a feminine 'politics of consumption', designed to challenge the centrality of the politics of production.

In Britain, co-operative guild women's consumer activities came over time largely to reaffirm women's domestic image rather than 'to problematiz[e] women's oppression within the home'. And when consumer matters moved to the fore during the First World War, concerned women's groups were unable to establish a 'gendered understanding' of them or to sustain their increased importance. In America, wartime and post-war efforts by labour women to organise around such consumer issues as the cost of living did not manage seriously to alter the main priorities of the labour movement. Middle-class female consumerism had greater vitality. As Rhodri Jeffreys-Jones has pointed out, it was a loosely linked fourfold movement which variously directed American women to 'boycott goods and services supplied by businesses that exploited women and children'; to keep their spending high to 'redeem U.S. economic fortunes'; to 'protect consumers from the unscrupulous production of dangerous items'; and to press for the reduction of tariff levels to restrain prices and help America's trading partners.[86] Yet, while concerned with the unstable international economy and the priorities of United States foreign policy, it lacked an international organisation through which to express its complex consumerist goals. Female associations straightforwardly concerned with peace often did better and seemed more relevant in the 1920s than long-established bodies like the American consumer leagues, which struggled to retain their supporters as women looked outwards and some, at least, became 'weary of being treated as social problems'.[87]

When countries turned to autarkic policies in the face of post-war financial and trading difficulties, the ICWG's admirable economic objectives seemed as unrealistic as did American women's consumerist campaign for tariff reductions during the 1920s.[88] The guild believed in promoting trade with Russia – an objective that was hardly helped along by the WCG's hostility towards communists within and outside its ranks. Its aim of 'forwarding international co-operative trade', so that commerce became 'a bond of friendship instead of a cause of jealous rivalry', led naturally to advocacy of international machinery to govern trade and banking. But it took the acrimonious collapse of the interwar debts and reparations system, a depression of frightening dimensions and duration, and another world war before international economic co-operation could be realised. The ICWG favoured strengthening international conventions seeking minimum labour standards;[89] hence it added to the difficulties of egalitarian feminism by opposing the Equal Rights Treaty, on the grounds that 'a hard and fast rule as to complete equality can be specially dangerous to protective legislation affecting women as mothers . . . where there is no equality of function, legal equality cannot exist'.[90]

There were other problems. Germany remained outside the ICWG, and continental European women remained aware of how they differed from the British, acknowledging that much that was done in Europe by political organisations was done by economic organisations in Britain.[91] Moreover, the guild's stand on peace failed to promote unity among British women. While initially it served as an effective recruiting tool, and by 1939 the WCG had eighty-seven thousand members,[92] Gillian Scott has established that the uncompromising backing for pacifism of the guild leadership eventually became a source of internal disagreement and external friction. Some guild members endorsed collective security and found that the menace of fascism forced them to distinguish between just and unjust wars. Pacifism brought their organisation into conflict with the Labour and Progressive parties, which officially supported collective security, and it increasingly marginalised guild women in the late 1930s debates over foreign policy and possible female war work.[93] While they argued that 'Co-operators are and must be revolutionary', it was also stressed that they should be constructive radicals. Pacifism could make them look like negative extremists, as members of peace associations were often alleged to be. In the words of an exasperated guild woman: 'one's arguments and points of view often receive more consideration and carry more conviction when one is unattached and not regarded as a "crank"'.[94] When Davies warned in 1927 of the danger the WCG ran of 'getting into grooves',[95] she was more than usually prescient. Every enduring reform campaign faces this danger, and for guild women rigidity was particularly evident in their handling of the peace question.[96]

Equally disappointing was the failure of the League of Nations to develop into the kind of democratic organisation that the ICWG idealistically envisaged. Like the ILO, the League had to galvanise its agenda and machinery, and to learn where it could act without trampling on the sensitivities of the member nations it hoped to influence. Despite much lobbying, women remained a token presence within the League throughout the interwar years, just as they did in the ILO. And as with the ILO, they had to learn the rules of foreign politics as played by men: to discover what was acceptable in 'the club', to prove their political ability, and to work alongside diplomats who – recollected the internationalist Helena Swanwick – were limited by their 'backward-looking minds, their fears, their suspicions, [and] their little plots'.[97] Although, as Miller has shown, the League listened to and consulted the women's voluntary associations – for example through the Liaison Committee of Women's International Organisations (1931) – it expected them to work for its broad objectives, looking most kindly on social feminists, and upholding the ILO line on protective legislation. It was not a negligible achievement that, by 1937, both the League and the ILO had been persuaded of the need for an ambitious worldwide study of the status of women, a review which finally led to the establishment in 1946 of the United Nations Status of Women Commission.[98] The pressure exerted internationally by labour women contributed to this positive outcome, and their activism forced middle-class feminists to take their views more seriously.

Thus IWSA, while valuing its independence, urged its auxiliaries to contact working women's organisations 'so that there may be a freer interchange of views on industrial and economic questions', and to convince them that the work of the Alliance was 'really in their interests'.[99] It was, after all, concerned about the economic situation of all women, and acknowledged that 'No question is of greater importance than economic status. Inferior economic status, the persistent idea that women workers are on a different footing from men workers, more than any other single factor prevents the full and equal participation of women in the whole life of . . . [their countries], trammels them in private life and cramps their influence in international relations and in the cause of peace.'[100] If IWSA's Committee on Like Conditions of Work for Men and Women initially failed to reconcile proponents and opponents of protective laws for women, it facilitated international debate on the issue and by the late 1930s most Alliance auxiliaries had come round to a compromise position which advocated 'identity of legislation for women and men', combined with 'the protection of maternity through insurance'.[101]

Among other, largely middle-class, organisations active in internationalism, the American LWV similarly acknowledged the importance of working women's opinions on industrial legislation. Such legislation, it declared, 'must be drawn not on the basis of hypothesis nor of successful solution in other countries but on the basis of fact in the particular country concerned with reference to the needs and wishes of the working women of that country'.[102] In class-conscious Britain, the outward looking Six Point Group was still more exercised to show that equality was 'no class matter'; pointing out that British women 'who believe in the principle and practice of equality, believe also in the protection of the worker'.[103] And the Open Door International, which upheld the right of both sexes to paid work, urged that the regulation and conditions of employment should be made dependent 'on the nature and not on the sex of the worker',[104] and campaigned for a charter of economic rights for women,[105] was similarly at pains to show its concern for women of all classes.

Like the internationally active working women's organisations, the ODI was alarmed that 'Attacks on the economic status of women have come from many quarters in many countries'.[106] But achieving an effective cross-class response to an agreed dilemma remained impossible. Despite the revival of labour and socialist internationalism between the wars, the bulk of female international lobbying still fell upon 'leisure class women, . . . not the professional or industrial women',[107] and the assumption of elite women that they should lead remained divisive. There were additional difficulties. Given the varied pressures upon them, even the British and American women who played a key role in internationalism found it difficult to stay as closely in touch as was desirable.[108] Nor did the NWP's uncompromising stance on protective legislation endear it to British and American working women, notwithstanding the party's proud claim that it was 'leading women to stand together'.[109] In reality, rather than 'raising the position of women' so that they could 'control life as much as men control life',[110] the NWP stimulated a fresh debate about equality which could not be settled in the international arena any more than it could be resolved at the national level. And at that level, American and British activists' shared interest in birth control, work and welfare could not bring them closer together in the face of very different political and economic circumstances.

Testing issues

Birth control

Birth control is an important indicator of the state of British and American feminism between the wars because, though it aroused widespread publicity and open support for the first time in the history of the two countries, women activists proved unable fully to determine the course of its provision or to realise its radical potential. This was an area where feminists in the United States and Britain had always had much in common. But even here, their practical co-operation was made extremely difficult by national differences relating to obscenity laws, race, class and religion, as well as by personal tensions between the two leading women of the national campaigns.[111]

Take the common ground first. For much of the nineteenth and early twentieth centuries, only a handful of American and British political radicals, social theorists and feminists advocated women's right to limit their fertility for personal and social reasons. Opposing them were doctors who thought that contraception was risky and selfish, unpleasantly associated with abortion, and a matter properly managed by men of science. Religious leaders also condemned it as flouting the divine purpose of matrimony; and they were especially vocal in the United States – a less secularised society than Britain and one with a more powerful Catholic church. In addition, defenders of the patriarchal family, already dismayed by successful feminist campaigns to reform the marriage laws, feared that birth control would further undermine male authority over women.

Feminists on both sides of the Atlantic were themselves divided about birth control, with most distinguishing between natural methods (abstinence, the use of coitus interruptus and the 'safe period'), and artificial checks upon reproduction (sheaths, sponges, douches and diaphragms). Sharing non-feminist convictions that artificial restraints were repulsive, might promote illicit sex, and were liable to encourage further demands on women already obliged to yield sexual rights to their husbands, feminists generally extolled voluntary motherhood achieved by natural means. If all children were wanted children, they argued, women would be able to preserve their health, do right by their offspring and generally assist their families.

However, in Britain and the United States alike by the last quarter of the nineteenth century, the birth control debate was facilitated as well as complicated by a number of significant social developments. The declining birth rate among the late marrying upper and middle classes, and the high incidence of abortion (especially among the urban poor and despite the tightening up of anti-abortion laws), indicated an interest in sexuality and family limitation which writers, publishers and manufacturers of contraceptives were happy to promote. But for governments and supporters of eugenics – that is, of selective breeding to produce fine children – birth control was not a straightforward question. Its most demonstrable effect, after all, seemed to be enabling the 'fit' to reduce their fertility while the 'unfit' continued to reproduce unabated. For feminist birth controllers, embracing eugenicism likewise presented complications. As McCann has pointed out, although they benefited from its 'scientific authority[,] . . . expertise . . . in population studies . . . [and] sexually neutral language', they also became associated with elitism at best and racism at worst.[112] This happened because increasingly the poor were equated with the 'unfit', as were members of non-white racial groups whose members were said to be inferior on hereditarian grounds. It followed that, to improve the white race, such 'inferiors' should be discouraged or prevented from breeding, if necessary by sterilisation. Under these circumstances, poor women and women of colour often regarded birth control advocacy with suspicion as well as gratitude.[113]

The social purity movement created another paradoxical situation for American and British feminist birth controllers. It is true that they profited from the movement's insistence that sex was not simply a private matter, and from its concern for the vulnerable, the combating of sexually transmitted diseases, sexual self-control by men, enlightened child rearing, and law reform. Nevertheless, social purists were often hostile towards women's power to regulate reproduction, and their backing for censorship and legal intervention to control individuals and activities they judged to be irredeemably corrupt had a restrictive effect on the circulation of contraception information.[114]

After the First World War, birth controllers in the two countries continued to face a similar mixture of opportunities and disadvantages. Thus on the one hand, the war had stimulated greater sexual licence, and more relaxed sexual relations between men and women persisted during the post-war period. Working-class women's interest in family limitation, expressed in pre-war letters to the WCG, was also sustained after 1918. On the other hand, many middle-aged and middle-class social feminists still hesitated to speak about sex in public, and proved loath to abandon the self-denying maternalist philosophy which had served them so well as reformers. Working-class male leaders were similarly reticent, despite the pressure upon them from rank-and-file labour women.[115] Nor had medical and religious opposition to contraception been vanquished.

And so birth controllers seeking to persuade doubters once more alternated between radical and conservative arguments. Accordingly, they set women's right to limit their fertility and enjoy their sexuality as men did theirs against the benefit to society from a decline in maternal mortality and a drop in the number of unwanted children. Gains would, it was stressed, be particularly marked among needy but previously uninvolved members of the working class: among 'the mothers of the child laborers and . . . the wives of the wage slaves'.[116] The focus on married women meant that heterosexuality was assumed, and that the sexual needs of single women were ignored.[117]

This balanced approach was employed by the two individuals – the nurse Margaret Sanger in America and the scientist Marie Stopes in Britain – who became the best known publicists of the cause during the 1920s and 1930s.[118] Both women emphasised the insights that followed from the female advocacy of birth control: its earlier proponents had frequently been male radicals. Both women put their careers first and had no intention of living 'a quiet, mediocre married life'.[119] Both women recognised that information about contraception had to be scientific not sensational, and arrived at 'in the sunlight of frank and open discussion'.[120] They saw, too, that reform must be institutionalised to be secure. In the case of birth control, this meant clinics – private and public – that at last fitted women with a reliable contraceptive for which they were responsible. To make the clinics respectable, Sanger and Stopes agreed that they should be staffed by doctors and nurses, and should gather data about their clients, thereby improving the service offered and assisting the public debate on population planning.[121]

Both women were impressed by the 'distinguished minds' and academic approach of eugenicists, and believed that they could draw strength from them without prejudicing the individual rights of the vast majority of poor women whom they sought to help.[122] Both saw themselves as feminists and hoped for the endorsement of feminist organisations.[123] Both were very willing, in the early stages of the birth control struggle, to exchange information and engage in friendly competition for the leadership of a movement they were determined to make international in scope.[124] Both, in fact, found their initial pre-eminence undermined by the growing number of middle-class health and social work professionals that the birth control clinics required.[125]

Furthermore, their personal comradeship was not to last. Since Sanger and Stopes were hostile to competing birth control providers in their respective countries, it is scarcely surprising that they managed to quarrel with each other.[126] Partly the rift came from personal resentments;[127] but, more seriously, the tensions between Stopes and Sanger reflected their divergent backgrounds. Thus Sanger's nursing experience of the sufferings of the poor, her connections with pre-war American labour, and her links with British radical eugenicists and members of Britain's Malthusian League (which since 1877 had emphasised the economic need for birth control), all gave her greater warmth towards the working class than the academic and more privileged Stopes possessed.[128]

National differences are also crucial in explaining the history of birth control, and are acknowledged by Stopes and Sanger. Pointing out that Britain had prepared the ground for the modern birth control movement 'through years of ploughing by . . . scholars and thinkers', Sanger added that workers in the field had been helped after the First World War by British tolerance, 'moral courage' and candour. She was less generous about the feminist and socialist contemporaries she lobbied in the United States, reproaching them for subordinating birth control to their other interests. Overall, Sanger concluded, the situation for birth controllers was better in Britain than in the United States.[129]

For her part, Stopes was willing to concede that the law allowed British campaigners a freedom of manoeuvre that was unknown across the Atlantic. Birth controllers in both countries had long fallen foul of obscenity legislation, with Americans following the English common-law tradition and influenced by 'Lord Campbell's law of 1857, the successful effort in England to strengthen laws against obscenity'. Moreover, Stopes lost when she sued for libel after her work was attacked as a 'monstrous', immoral and harmful 'experiment on the poor'.[130] But as the social purity movement declined in Britain between the two world wars, there was, Frank Mort has shown, a retreat from 'the criminalising approach to sexual regulation'.[131]

In America, by contrast, Sanger bemoaned 'the eternal barrier of our laws'; and through the National Committee on Federal Legislation for Birth Control (1928) she felt obliged to protest against a situation in which the efforts of the birth control clinics were hindered by conflicting federal and state laws on the subject, and by federal 'prohibition on the importation and interstate transport of contraceptive information and devices'.[132] Although federal laws were less rigorously enforced than they had been, it was 'only in the United States [that] it was illegal to circulate information about birth control'.[133] In conservative states like Massachusetts, where the Catholic presence was strong, birth controllers such as Lucile Lord-Heinstein continued to risk arrest, 'unpleasant publicity' and harassment by 'the mediaeval police' during the 1930s.[134]

Being a martyr 'for an important cause' was something that might appeal to a white middle-class woman, secure in her personal and social circumstances,[135] but the Sangerists' enthusiasm for militant direct action alienated moderates of both sexes, just as suffrage militancy had done.[136] It had no British parallel and there are two reasons for this, besides the more favourable legal situation. In the first place, radical tactics were not needed in Britain because moderate feminist groups (with a few exceptions) campaigned for birth control during the 1920s in a way that their counterparts declined to do in the United States.[137] Having a period of pre-war radical birth control activism to live down, an era of post-war conservatism to endure, and other maternalist measures to pursue, American feminists accepted the exclusion of a birth control provision from the 1921–9 Sheppard-Towner Act, which was designed to improve educational programmes concerned with the welfare of mothers and children. For the same reasons, they failed to press for the inclusion of birth control advice in New Deal public relief and maternal programmes, where they remained a limited and discretionary service; state and city programmes were comparably meagre.[138] A second explanation for the absence of militant birth control tactics in Britain after the First World War was that the cause made a modest degree of progress there. For just when American socialism was in decline, British labour women's associations supportive of birth control – including the Women's Co-operative Guild and the Workers' Birth Control Group – saw their lobbying of local authority clinics rewarded. Accordingly, in 1930 the second Labour government permitted such clinics 'to give birth control advice, in restricted circumstances'.[139]

Of all the various national differences, those to do with class and race were the most significant. In Britain, class was vital in determining the fate of birth control. Despite the attempt by Stopes to distance herself from the Malthusians and to stress the scientific perspective on birth control, she did not manage to avoid its class implications.[140] Sanger was right in declaring that 'the trend of the movement in England was economic'.[141] When the Labour Party conference in 1925 declined to make support for birth control official, it argued that it was not a party matter but one on which people should be 'free to hold and promote their individual convictions'.[142] The party also wished to reassure opponents within its ranks;[143] and, as a result, it found itself in agreement with middle-class feminists who similarly presented contraception as 'an issue of personal liberty affecting all members of their sex'.[144] In fact, the ability to practise effective birth control was overwhelmingly shaped by class. Middle-class feminists who took up the advocacy of birth control in the 1920s, and abortion reform in the 1930s, did so because they were aware of working-class suffering and vulnerability. Labour women pressed for contraceptive instruction as a class measure. The poor were the chief beneficiaries of the new clinics and of the only government legislation on the subject. As Gittens has established, working-class women responded to improved prospects of limiting their fertility according to their own family circumstances and changing patterns of labour market participation. And the prosperous classes continued to be able to make their own advantageous birth control arrangements, as they had since the nineteenth century.[145] Eugenical arguments in Britain, though powerful in a period when race consciousness and imperial pride remained strong, complicated but could not conceal class calculations.

In the United States, race did come to loom larger than class in the birth control campaign, albeit the two always reinforced each other. Eugenicism's ostensibly scientific take on birth control was highly appealing to American conservatives who saw the 'new' immigrants arriving in America from the 1890s as inferior to the old stock in terms of race and religion. They were also fearful of a black population which, contrary to racist predictions in the nineteenth century, had not died out following the abolition of slavery. As many African Americans moved from the South to the North during and after the First World War, joining the immigrants already crowded into American cities, tensions exploded into race riots and race thinking received a new fillip. Birth control had relevance in this context because it simultaneously appealed to racists interested in limiting the fertility of non-whites and ethnic groups, and to black leaders who saw a way of assisting black mothers and black families. However, in establishing a clinic in Harlem 'for the special use of the colored people', Sanger was capitulating to just the kind of entrenched prejudice that had driven her to take up birth control.[146]

McCann has argued persuasively that Sanger herself was a liberal, not a bigot, on matters to do with race; she saw separate provision for African Americans as being necessary to ensure that they were not excluded from birth control, and she recognised that black suspicion of white motives and direction might be a problem. Unfortunately, in identifying poor black women as being in special need of help, Sanger shared the patronising attitudes towards the poor of many middle-class black and white social feminists. And as McCann also points out, Sanger and her fellow birth controllers failed to relate the contraceptive concerns of women of colour to the full range of sexual and racial factors that shaped their lives. That said, the difficulties facing the reformers should not be underestimated.[147]

Even in the 1930s, when the enormity of the Depression fostered the resurgence of environmentalist explanations of misfortune, and racial grievances were taken seriously by the American Left, black women received a disappointing degree of birth control assistance. As Robert Shaffer has shown, while the Communist Party for a time worked closely with reformers, trade unions and councils of the unemployed to distribute birth control information, the party turned away from this issue once it became embarrassingly at odds with the Soviet Union's moves to expand its own population.[148] The Democratic Party followed a similarly calculating line. Though pledged to consider the welfare needs of mothers, New Dealers were ambivalent about promoting birth control while it remained offensive to their Catholic supporters in the North and complicated by race in the South, where some states saw it as a means of tackling the high black birth rate. Black and white women activists were neither numerous nor motivated enough to challenge racial discrimination in birth control wherever it occurred: and it occurred nationally.[149]

The birth control movement, like suffragism in the early twentieth century, was an international movement whose time had come. But like suffragism, it deployed some arguments that now repel; and, like suffragism, its tactics can be faulted. The best outcome as regards state intervention was achieved in Britain, where female pressures procured action in 1930 from a Labour government. However, not all local authorities used their power under the 1930 legislation to give contraceptive advice in public health facilities.[150] And on both sides of the Atlantic, the private clinics operated by labour and middle-class women reached too few women to offset disappointments at the government level.

Could the British and American birth controllers have done better, in view of the enduring notoriety attached to their cause and the enduring fear of politicians that improved contraceptive knowledge would be dysgenic in effect? The answer is no. A single-issue campaign of the sort activists mounted, using a broad range of arguments and seeking a wide array of allies, succeeded organisationally in a way in which specialist feminist associations devoted to birth control could not have done in the hostile social climate of the 1920s and 1930s. But for poor women and women of colour, the campaign became one more sign of the caution and divisions that prevailed among their sex.

Work and welfare

If the time for internationalism and birth control had come in the post-war women's movements, the time for economic equality between men and women emphatically had not. A 1936 survey of 'the pace of transformation' for women since the war concluded that it was 'slowest of all in regard to financial standing'. From the beginning of first wave feminism, men had resisted changes that threatened male economic supremacy. Hence while female employment outside the home was gradually accepted, it was accepted on men's terms. In other words, the sexual division of labour already established in the family economy was extended under capitalism. Priority was therefore given to a 'family wage' paid to men, while women were largely segregated in poorly paid jobs, accorded low priority by labour unions, and expected to retire either on marriage or with the advent of children. If female workers were eventually thought to deserve protection as wives and mothers, Kessler-Harris has shown that it was men who were accorded individual economic rights which were extended over time.[151] Nevertheless, in the United States and Britain alike, there were many women who objected to inadequate pay and barriers to their employment; who were concerned about their union standing and working conditions in industry; and who welcomed payments from the state that recognised the importance of their domestic roles. And the question that now concerns us is, how did they best secure action on these matters? Was it through the union movement, the political parties of the Left, or the feminist organisations? Events were to prove that it was through the feminist groups, which alone put women's interests first; but they, of necessity, had to seek links with the other two.

In both the United States and Britain, female workforce experiences were conditioned by age and skill, by region and industry, by race and ethnicity, and by the overall state of the economy, employer attitudes and government policies. The 1920s also saw unionists on the defensive in the two countries, while the situation improved for them in the 1930s. None the less, American and British working-class women were affected by entrenched differences as well as shared difficulties. Thus, for example, racial factors were more significant in the United States than in Britain, where the black population was small but diverse and the labour issues that erupted focused on the unfair treatment of seamen in the port cities.[152] American labour activists were less enthusiastic than their British counterparts about links with international labour efforts; and nor did they display the British reluctance to work through independent female associations. Instead they believed, as the legislative secretary of the American WTUL put it, that 'the organized working women of the United States have always had most cordial relations with the nation-wide woman movement'.[153] Furthermore, if British women acknowledged in the 1920s that 'America is the paradise of the employed woman',[154] Americans reflected enviously on the fact that British unions 'didn't have to fight and suffer the way we had to against big business here'.[155]

Big business was indeed in the saddle in America during the 1920s. Women were driven out of male jobs that they had held during the First World War, and workers' collective bargaining rights were not secure. As the decade wore on, the fact that no public, political or court support could be mustered for the liberal interpretation or extension of labour welfare legislation frequently had a 'paralysing' effect on reform efforts. While some women found employment in white-collar occupations, light industry, domestic service and agriculture, many more struggled to make a living and were hit by the decline of union militancy and membership.[156] The union organising side of the WTUL's operation suffered in this climate and support for the League dwindled, despite its promotion of the social feminist agenda and its endorsement of working-class leaders, training of labour activists, and maintenance of links with the generally unsympathetic southern states and the generally hostile AFL. The YWCA and women's clubs, which encouraged the investigation and protesting of exploitative industrial conditions at the state level, found cross-class endeavours similarly hard going. And although unionists of both sexes, activists from the Women's Bureau and women reformers joined together to oppose the ERA, their combined efforts could not silence NWP claims that legislative protection meant the economic subordination of women based on their special characteristics.[157]

American female unionists faced an exceptionally challenging combination of problems after the First World War, and simply lacked the numerical, organisational and ideological strength to combat them. Theoretically advocating 'equal rights for equal ability in politics and industry', in practice women organisers were expected to put the union line first, despite not being accepted fully by union men, who yielded as little as possible to female concerns and questioned the strength of female loyalty. Critical of the individualism of bourgeois women reformers in other associations, female unionists had less time for involvement in diverse causes than the privileged members of those associations. They felt obliged to seek the opinions and approval of male breadwinners, while activism for married women tended to come late, since they were 'much more home-centred' than their middle-class sisters and so had 'a deeper sense of guilt' about leaving their families. Recruitment might be hindered because some women – office workers, for instance – did not believe that unionisation was relevant for them.[158] And race was an even more troubling issue than class – indeed, in the South, it was 'the most visible social category that divided women from one another and determined the men with whom they could form acceptable relationships'.[159]

Intrepid female organisers might have capitalised upon the novelty value of their gender in the southern states, alleging that they were able 'to do more and exist in a community longer than a man'. However, it was unhelpful that, in unionism, they represented a movement that had devised a class indictment but only skeletal gender and racial analyses of their oppression. Although more women (including married women) entered the paid labour force after the First World War, workplace solidarity could scarcely develop in communities where the two races were segregated at home and at work, and where even whites who accepted black unionists as dues payers found black activism unpalatable. Furthermore, worries about employer intimidation were not easily overcome in a region where company towns were common and capitalists were unusually anti-union. Conditions in the South were not uniform, and it witnessed growing interwar campaigning by women tobacco, textile, agricultural and railway workers, and consequent improvements in female pay and conditions. But white fear of competition kept black women 'completely excluded from operative positions in the textile mills and restricted to seasonal handwork in tobacco factories' until the 1960s. Ninety per cent of African American women were concentrated in poorly organised farm and domestic occupations as late as 1930.

Black and white women were a force in the industrial unions of the 1930s. Yet if the focus of these new unions was more helpful than that of the craft orientated AFL, their style was dauntingly masculine and the 'warfare between [the] A.F. of L. and [the] C.I.O.' was alarming. American women generally may have sustained their employment level better than men for much of the Depression, but scholars have shown that this phenomenon followed from their concentration in occupations that were not as badly affected as those employing men. It certainly did not come from exceptional union action on behalf of women, and only served to reinforce traditional notions about the distinctiveness of women's and men's work. And though the New Deal produced a political realignment of interest groups, economic solidarity between minority group women was unattainable owing to their different settlement patterns and cultural traditions, and the strength of assimilationist pressures. Mexican American women in the west, for instance, were tied into family labour contracts which had no parallel among African Americans.[160]

At the end of the First World War, women in Britain, as in the United States, were obliged to give up their lucrative war work. But the expansion of new industries and white collar jobs that had helped American female workers was slower in Britain, and unions regarded the poorly paid young women who took such jobs as unpromising prospects for organisation. They also resisted the recruitment and employment of married women sooner than American unionists, and Pedersen has demonstrated that a divided Trade Union Congress eventually joined the opposition to making monetary payments (family allowances) to working-class mothers for their children, fearing that they might lead employers to cut wages and generally 'undermine the principles and power of trade unions'. Female union membership dropped by 38.5 per cent between 1920 and 1923; a setback after a period of unusual expansion, but not one with which male unionists could be expected to have much sympathy, given the decline of 34.1 per cent in male union members during the same years. British women unionists seem to have faced the sort of male and employer hostility that their American equivalents encountered without receiving any help from bodies like the WTUL, the YWCA and the women's industrial clubs they promoted. Furthermore, the National Federation of Women Workers, which had an established record as a strike organiser and campaigner for female interests, lost its independence and its impact in 1921 by merging into the National Union of General Workers.

British women did participate in union protests against employer cost-cutting measures and unequal employment benefits, notably in the textile sector, at the time of the General Strike, and through the National Unemployed Workers Movement (NUWM). In the 1930s, as they had done before and during the First World War, they also took part in rent strikes, with Jewish women playing a crucial part in community mobilisation. And British unions as a whole were, as Kirk observes, 'more deeply and broadly based and generally more resilient' than their American counterparts. Yet female unionists gained little from these actions and advantages, and tended to remain relatively isolated and patronised within the larger labour movement. Thus, for example, while they were included in the Standing Joint Committee of Industrial Women's Organizations, which helped to strengthen the protection of women under the Labour Party's proposed factory act of 1924, unionists were not to the fore in the British debate about protective legislation any more than they were in the American. British female labour leaders, and British and American middle-class feminists all felt entitled to speak on behalf of women unionists.[161]

American and British women did little better economically when they turned to the parties of the Left, which were – theoretically at least – pledged to sexual equality. During the 1920s, the Communist parties of the United States and Britain failed to address women's interests specifically, although their 'work among industrial workers, the unemployed, and blacks' was sometimes incidentally helpful. But from 1935, with the launching of the Popular Front, party workers on each side of the Atlantic formed women's groups and collaborated with unions, non-Communist socialists, liberals and women's associations. In Britain, Communists gave some backing to the NUWM, and in America from late 1936 they helped to promote a Women's Charter whose demands aimed both at full female equality and at protective legislation involving 'maternity insurance, minimum wages, and maximum hours'. Membership of the party increased, and in both countries Communist support was given to striking women workers; to the establishment of female committees and auxiliaries; to direct action by women against such oppressive Depression conditions as unemployment and high prices; and to measures designed to improve maternal and child welfare. These efforts lasted until the coming of the Second World War.[162]

Communism's assistance to women should not, however, be overrated. The period of coalition building was short and old suspicions of Communists among conservatives and non-Communist leftwingers were not easily overcome. The Women's Charter proved disappointing; failing to attract substantial cross-class support from women, its demands on government were too great for the times. Communist Party grassroots assistance drew gratitude from recipients, but could not transform traditional ways of thinking and doing among male unionists and employers. Female participants in the NUWM courageously argued 'for equal employment benefit, a national minimum [wage] for all and the right to work', but the rise in unemployment raised opposition to women's labour market involvement among the dominating male labour leaders; predictably, the 'women marched separately from the men'. Most importantly, the switch of tactics by Communists during the Popular Front era was driven by a particular set of circumstances, not an intellectual conversion to the merits of feminism. Old attitudes survived in the party, just as they did outside it – as witness the sweeping dismissal of the NWP as 'a narrow, anti-labor sect', and of the New Deal as just a 'prop for a dying system', by the prominent American Communist, Ella Bloor. Only in the Soviet Union, she asserted, could 'women enjoy to the full their right to motherhood, as well as pursuing whatever career they choose'.[163] But if the Communist Popular Front had its limitations, so too did the work and welfare programmes of the American Democrats and the British Labour Party.

In the United States during the 1930s, we have noted that the severity of the Depression drove liberalism to the left, and that women helped to shape New Deal reforms and benefited from them. The Democratic Party did more than the British governments of the decade. Unemployed female workers found training and work through the relief agencies, which also employed women administrators. Employed women as well as men were helped by the maximum hour and minimum wage standards in codes applied to a range of industries by the National Recovery Administration (NRA) between 1933 and 1935. The Fair Labor Standards Act (FLSA, 1938) made permanent for both sexes the hours and wages regulation started by the NRA. Under the Social Security Act (SSA) of 1935, federal-state support for the unemployed and federal provision for the aged was established, together with programmes and grants for mothers with dependent children. And the 1935 National Labor Relations Act outlawed various unfair employer practices, and set up a board to oversee and ensure employees' right to collective bargaining. The board's positive attitude to labour encouraged unions to increase their recruiting of women.

All these measures were welcome and all were flawed from women's point of view. In practice, as Mettler demonstrates, the New Deal's supposed universalism was undermined for women in various ways, not least those posed by a federal political system. Hence relief operations provided them with 'women's work'; produced fewer opportunities than were found for men; and encouraged the view that recipients should be household heads, who were presumed to be men. Domestic servants and agricultural workers, many of them women, were excluded from the benefits of the SSA, and the NRA and FLSA likewise covered only a fraction of the female workforce.[164] The New Deal was designed to get men back to work and to restore their pride. Hastily devised and committed to free market capitalism, it aimed to aid recovery in the key sectors of the economy as swiftly as possible. These were dominated by men. Although the NRA and the FLSA did extend the kind of workplace protection to men and women which the NWP had long advocated, such measures were not a tribute to feminist clout, but rather an unsatisfactory compromise between economic interests and regions.[165]

The Labour Party in Britain similarly gave priority to male interests without totally ignoring those of women. While the party was willing to stress its commitment to sexual equality during the 1920s, Graves has shown that by the 1930s, having secured the support of labour women, 'the subject of gender disappeared' from its public discourse. Yet if the Depression strengthened class awareness, the interwar years as a whole showed the pre-eminence of class, masculine concerns and electoral considerations for Labour leaders who were only briefly – and then precariously – in power. Thus in 1919, Labour supported legislation which forced women out of wartime jobs. It came into office in 1924, having promised to move on the widows' pensions for which labour women and men alike had campaigned. But the Chancellor of the Exchequer did not include them in his first budget and the government fell before they could be achieved. The party resisted the efforts of labour women on behalf of family allowances. And in 1931 it got behind the party's minister of labour, Margaret Bondfield, in her promotion of an act officially designed to cut down on false claims for unemployment relief, even though it became apparent that the legislation would be used to deprive married women of unemployment benefit.

Labour women protested, pressing for equal employment benefits for married women. But mostly they kept party considerations carefully in mind. Hence – as Pat Thane and Pamela Graves have established – though they worked vigorously on community issues and local government issues of benefit to women, they also collaborated with labour men nationally, notably in opposing the means test 'introduced in August 1931 to cut the cost of supporting the long-term unemployed'.

The ILP is commonly seen as more determined than the Labour Party in its promotion of women's issues, and it was committed to the involvement of both sexes at its meetings. However, as an elite group within the socialist movement, it did not operate under the same constraints as Labour. Nor did the ILP attract large numbers of working-class women. It was, in fact, unable to offer a viable alternative to the Labour Party.[166]

The record of the American and British feminist groups on economic matters was, like that of the unions and leftwing parties, stronger on advocacy than delivery. We have seen (in chapter 5) that after achieving an impressive post-war range of legislation in both countries, feminists found it more difficult to secure action on behalf of women. Opposition to change was especially strong in the male dominated economic sphere. In harsh economic times and with the resurgence of conservative views about women's place, there was predictable hostility towards activists' concern with women's right to work; equal pay for equal work; an end to discrimination against married working women; financial aid to mothers; and protective industrial legislation. Egalitarian and social feminists, labour women and women further to the right all supported this balanced agenda, designed to rescue women from involuntary economic subordination to men and to confirm the importance of motherhood. Only protective legislation provoked enduring disagreements. And while female tactics – meetings, speeches, fact-finding investigations, publications and lobbying – were not new, they were practiced and professional. They did not, like suffrage militancy, divert attention from ends to means; and as Eleanor Rathbone declared, they were well suited to contemporary complexities and the need to move feminism away from what some women perceived as a narrow egalitarianism. But they were not enough.

The right to work was a bold claim when feminists first advanced it in the mid-nineteenth century, and it remained so in the twentieth. Activists themselves could not provide women with jobs; and the unionists, employers and politicians who could, saw female employment difficulties as a second order issue at a time of high male joblessness. Equal pay for equal work was regarded as an even greater potential threat to male earnings, but given the widespread segregation of the sexes in industry, its main practical relevance in the short term appeared to be to middle-class professional women such as civil servants and teachers. Yet on each side of the Atlantic, inadequate and unequal pay 'plagued female workers in every job category'. This was not just an issue of interest to bourgeois feminists, though since middle-class women were not making great strides in 'male' professions – and, indeed, had only been admitted to some since 1919 in Britain – it made sense to challenge pay deficiencies in fields where women had numerical strength and might welcome external support.

Discrimination against married women similarly concerned a wide range of female activists, despite the fact that married women constituted only a small (if rising) percentage of the paid workforce, and that their employment was controversial among women as well as men. During the 1930s in Britain, more than a quarter of a million married women had their claims for unemployment benefit disallowed and the 'marriage bar' was enforced by local authorities, just as it was by companies, state legislatures and the federal government in America. There, women's groups contributed to the repeal of the National Economy Act (1932–7), which had operated against married women in government jobs, but hostile state actions continued, with President Roosevelt declining to be drawn into the controversy.

Social feminists having mobilised in both countries before the First World War to help shape the early welfare state, it was predictable that they would push their case for maternalist legislation between the wars, and that non-feminist women's groups would support them. They met with disappointments in Britain and the United States alike, notwithstanding the dramatic extension of welfare provision under the New Deal. Thus while the SSA established a federal programme of direct aid for American mothers and children, it endorsed the conventional sexual division of labour and the family wage, prohibited maternal employment, and confined itself to the poor. All these drawbacks reflected the general exclusion of women reformers from the economic policy making departments of the New Deal, and especially the powerlessness here of black activists who – Linda Gordon has established – were orientated towards 'universal programs' and 'mothers' employment'. In Britain, stresses Pat Thane, labour women activists worked to see the 1918 Maternity and Child Welfare Act put into practice, while the Labour government in 1929 expanded the provision of pensions for widows and orphans, and in the 1930s sustained a commitment to improved urban healthcare, 'slum clearance, and municipal services in general'. But the campaign for family allowances failed. It did so because of union opposition; because of politicians' backing for the existing system of assistance for mothers in kind rather than cash; and because of the conflicting and often controversial arguments put forward by the advocates of change. In particular, on this as on many other questions, the different ideological emphases of British feminists and labour women undermined their formal agreement over ends and limited co-operation between them by the 1930s.

Proposals for protective legislation also produced controversy among women activists in the two countries, separating British feminists from labour women and different clusters of American feminists from each other. The sustained intensity of the NWP in defending the ERA is perhaps the most remarkable aspect of the quarrel, and reflects more than either the commanding personalities of its leaders, important as they were, or the party's realisation that it needed great persistence by the 1930s, when 'the Federal administration, with all its power', was 'behind the legislation'. Experience in suffragism had shown the NWP that a state by state approach to tackling an established evil could delay victory indefinitely, while the emphasis on 'a permanent female helplessness unrelated to specific economic circumstances' that was required for the constitutional justification of protective legislation was clearly a most unattractive position to be locked into. British participants in the dispute could afford to be more flexible, since no ERA was in contention. Nevertheless, they could not escape some acrimony when debating the tension between protection as the defence and protection as the restriction of women: the tension between women acting as self-interested individuals and women under 'domestic tutelage' in a family unit that preserved male supremacy, social stability and the future of 'the race'.[167]

Conclusions

Class was important for all groups of feminists in the United States and Britain between the wars. Even in America, where it was customarily overshadowed by gender and race considerations, the 1920s attacks on women as political radicals 'organized for social and industrial betterment',[168] the calamitous Depression, and the revival of the Left all made class an unavoidable concern. If British and American working women highlighted class in a way in which bourgeois women did not, both contributed to the feminisation of class thinking by stressing women's distinctive needs at home and in the paid workforce; and by playing up the importance of social reconstruction and playing down the primacy of class warfare. But in neither country did activists manage to challenge the basic Marxist view of feminism as a bourgeois distraction from the class struggle, or to alter the fact that their acceptance in leftwing parties and trade unions depended upon their support for male leaders and priorities. Nor did feminists and working women on each side of the Atlantic manage to avoid a well publicised debate over the value of protective industrial legislation. And labour internationalism – despite its idealism and useful impact on bourgeois campaigners – could not break free from the class attitudes prevailing at the national level.

There were, none the less, differences between American and British activists that would influence the course of their movements in years to come. In the United States, no formal split occurred between working women and feminists, and the cross-class WTUL was sustained alongside the nationally mobilised network of social feminist groups. Internationally, American WTUL campaigners attempted to take an independent female line through the International Federation of Working Women, whereas their British counterparts elected to work through the international labour organisations that involved men. The Americans were unsuccessful here: the women's federation was absorbed by the male dominated International Federation of Trade Unions, and failure confirmed the contrast between American and European activists that was rooted in their different political and economic circumstances, different levels of affluence, and different degrees of involvement with the League of Nations and the International Labour Office. In Britain, the post-1918 split between middle-class feminist groups and women in the Labour Party increased during the 1930s. While the divide did not put an end to female activism during the Depression,[169] it did leave 'labour women convinced that feminists were hostile to the workers' movement and feminists scornful of the patriarchal Labour Party'. It also obliged them to campaign separately 'for the same welfare programmes'.[170] The scope for co-operation between British and American activists was, in these circumstances, predictably limited.

Despite their differences, however, British and American activists alike found few economic gains between the wars. Those they did make were achieved by an emphasis on female distinctiveness that was fraught with dangers. Women's shared interest as consumers, for instance, could easily be used to reinforce their traditional rather than their public roles. Similarly, birth control could be advanced with reference to maternal and social benefits, but at the expense of individual female emancipation. Unions, leftwing parties and feminists all understandably achieved more for women in terms of welfare than in terms of jobs or equal pay, though they agitated for both. And the circumstances of the Depression were peculiarly daunting on both sides of the Atlantic. Altogether, one must agree with the exclamation of one British commentator, that 'a woman honestly struggling to work on the same basis as a man, can have a very cruel time of it'.[171]

7 The Second World War

A turning point for women?

When the Second World War erupted in 1939, the women of Britain and the United States faced problems which the 1914–18 war had made familiar: ideological and practical challenges to internationalism and pacifism; the assumption that war required male dominance and the subordination or abandonment of female concerns; and strains on the Anglo-American relationship. Women none the less responded to the war as an opportunity as well as a tragedy and constraint; and this chapter will examine how they did so, and how far their responses were shaped by considerations of class, race, gender and nation. Overall, it will seek to show whether, in hostilities more far reaching than those of 1914–18, the forces of continuity still remained more powerful for women than the forces of change.

The coming of war: anti-fascism disrupts the women's peace movement

In 1939, American and British feminists were better prepared and better organised to meet the challenges of war than feminists had been in 1914. While they had lost the mass support that they had achieved in the last stage of the suffragist campaign, suffragism no longer embarrassed their responses to war (see chapter 3). Moreover, the major women's organisations were better informed about world affairs, having taken up the cause of peace and internationalism with enthusiasm during the interwar years. The 1930s, especially, had shown how vulnerable women were in the face of global economic upheavals and expansive nationalism. International campaigners for female civil and economic rights had been driven by the knowledge that 'things are very bad for the women everywhere'. Being 'more than ever exposed to persecution, expulsion and deportation on political, racial and social grounds', women were felt to need the help of other women, and to be duty bound to try to counterbalance 'a world point of view' that was 'so extremely national'.[1]

With the establishment of dictatorships in Italy, Germany and Spain, fascism constituted a challenge to democracy which feminists could not ignore. The dominant fascist organisation in Britain, the British Union of Fascists (BUF, 1932), appalled them by its exaggerated patriotism, militarism, masculinism and hero worship. Equally appalling was the fact that women were actually attracted to the movement by these features, as well as by BUF emphasis on women's importance as mothers who sustained the race and nation. The union's flattering depiction of domesticity and claim that women, though complementary to men, were also their equals, appeared well judged at a time when feminists themselves were highlighting the importance of women's maternal roles. Belonging to an energetic rightwing organisation that demanded a high level of commitment seems to have compensated female BUF members for the fact that the aims and direction of British fascism were determined by men, and for the divisions which existed within its ranks. However, the BUF criticisms of feminism as misguided, decadent and ineffectual forced feminists to defend themselves yet again. In the process, they were able to expose fascism's distinctive form of oppressive patriarchy and intolerance of Jewish, Communist and other minorities.[2] But as Bruley and Joannou have pointed out, British feminists found no single, unifying mode of opposing fascism. Hence if some focused on practical help to its victims, making fact-finding visits to Germany and lobbying politicians on their return, others offered a literary rather than a political resistance.[3]

Although the far right organisations which flourished in the United States between the wars included such fascist, anti-semitic groups as the Silver Shirts, Black Legion and the German-American Bund, they were never as significant for women or for the country as a whole as the BUF. Roosevelt's widespread popularity allowed him to ride out attacks on Jewish influences within the New Deal, but he privately regarded Nazis and other fascists as 'gangsters who ultimately would have to be restrained'. Meanwhile Eleanor Roosevelt was also convinced, by 1939, that the fascist menace would force America to fight.[4] The noisy activities of the German-American Bund were an embarrassment to the German authorities, and Italian and German Americans largely resisted the fascist propaganda directed at them.[5] Female voluntary associations offered a home for women of every persuasion, thereby reducing the attraction of the fascist splinter groups, as did the position of the American wife, which was deemed to be that of 'pampered goddess' as opposed to the central European 'household drudge'.[6] Moreover, the open anti-semitism that existed among British female fascists was discouraged in the United States by the stronger mobilisation of Jewish American women and the deeper national sympathy for the Jewish cause at home and abroad. In this situation, there was a danger that Americans would not take fascism sufficiently seriously, while female internationalists who did, found it as difficult as their British counterparts to decide on the best way of combating anti-semitism and all the awful implications of fascism. Like them, they frequently turned to helping persecuted individuals as a practical way out of the dilemma.[7]

For British and American feminists who were convinced – in Winifred Holtby's words – that 'the pendulum is swinging backwards, not only against feminism, but against democracy, liberty and reason, against international co-operation and political tolerance',[8] perhaps the best opportunity to oppose fascism came with the Spanish Civil War: a conflict which – from 1936 to 1939, and because of its overthrow of a legitimate democratic government – proved as emotive for white liberals and radicals as the fate of Ethiopia had been for black activists.

Americans were mobilised through their League Against War and Fascism (ALAWF, 1933), a spin-off from a world committee formed the year before to oppose these two evils. A large American delegation headed by the Communist leader, Ella Bloor, had also attended the 1934 anti-fascist women's conference in Paris, which led to the formation of the Women's World Committee Against War and Fascism, one of whose sections rallied British women. Although according to Bloor, only the Communist Party 'saw that fascism had to be fought on both a national and world scale', actually all manner of progressive individuals and groups were engaged in the fight – including, with some misgivings, a number of African Americans. But American Communists did help women to become involved on action committees which might otherwise have remained male dominated, and worked with them to publicise the threat of fascism, to defend its victims and to raise money for the Spanish Republicans. In Britain's branch of the Women's World Committee, Communists were similarly energetic partners with the feminist, religious, labour and party political women who worked tirelessly to assist refugees (including children), to raise money, food and clothing, and to keep debate about the Spanish conflict alive. Additionally, as in all wars, women volunteered to help the injured, their efforts being managed by an International Medical Service.[9]

World opinion was deeply engaged in the outcome of Spain's Civil War, and for that, feminist activists can take some credit. In Britain and America, the working together of female Communists and non-Communists was an uncommon achievement, as was the close collaboration of feminist, labour and conservative women, and of labour women and men on a mainstream issue.[10] A second world conference of women against fascism was held in 1938, and the Women's World Committee was relaunched as the Women's Committee for Peace and Democracy, both developments indicating that female peace campaigners had not lost hope, despite the fears entertained by 1938 of 'a waning of that international spirit which alone can make a peaceful world practicable'.[11] But that waning signified the difficulties for women inherent in 1930s anti-fascism.

Collaboration between feminists and diverse political elements over specific foreign policy issues did not convert the latter to feminism, whose broader goals were subordinated in the process, just as they had been when diverse peace proponents attempted to come together during the First World War (see chapter 3). Having been denounced as 'red' for much of the 1920s, American and British women reformers – whether in the WCG, WILPF, ALAWF or the Women's World Committee – worried about aligning themselves with Communists during the 1930s, and pacifists were well aware that their new comrades opposed 'only those wars waged by capitalist countries and those dictatorships termed "fascist"'. The 1939 Nazi–Soviet Pact simultaneously justified their anxieties and made a nonsense of such popular front coalitions against fascism. Relief activities may have given those who undertook them a welcome sense of being useful and were acceptable as an extension of women's caring role; they did not, however, change the foreign policies of Britain and the United States. The Spanish Civil War, Ceadel reminds us, also dramatically hardened the division which existed among peace supporters between, on the one hand, pacifists who opposed any involvement in war; and, on the other, pacificists (usually internationalists) who wanted action to distinguish between aggression and its victims, between democracy and fascism. Furthermore, the wisdom of peace groups' support for disarmament – and, in America, for neutrality legislation – was called into question once fascist regimes had armed themselves and weaker nations were left in need of military and economic help. In Britain, as we have already seen (in chapter 6), the Women's Co-operative Guild was particularly badly hit by this debate about the meaning and proper course of pacifism; but it affected activists everywhere. And, finally, Anglo-American relations became increasingly strained in the second half of the 1930s.[12]

If concerned citizens in both countries deplored the First World War and fervently wished to avoid another such catastrophe, the involvement of Britain and the United States in that war had been very different and distinctly alienating. As a result, John Moser and others have shown, they disagreed not only about the future of the British Empire, the deployment of American economic might, and their contrasting diplomatic styles, but also over Britain's role in drawing the United States into the First World War; over British war debt repayments to the United States; naval construction; American neutrality legislation; Japanese expansion in Asia; and British appeasement of Germany and Italy. British statesman Austen Chamberlain's exclamation about Americans – 'What a difficult people they are to live with!' – might have been the verdict on Britons of any of his American counterparts. For much of the decade, British politicians actually found it hard to persuade either Roosevelt or the American population that appeasement was not merely designed to disguise Britons' lack of will to fight against the fascist evils they ostensibly deplored.[13] In Margaret Bondfield's indignant observation, 'whether Britain likes it or not she is not taken at her own valuation in the USA. "Britain is played out" is a phrase which makes me hot when I hear it'.[14] Women like Bondfield, the Duchess of Atholl, Lady Astor, Mrs Corbett Ashby and the feminist pacifist Dr Maude Royden, did their best when in the United States to explain Britain to America and to promote 'Anglo-American accord'. But Royden's experiences as a popular lecturer in the United States were disappointingly typical. Thus despite attracting good audiences and disarming them with criticism of Britain's post-war politicians, her appeals to American women to act on their pacific feelings and her flattering hopes that Americans generally would 'provide leadership for real world peace' failed to galvanise the mass of people whom she hoped were opposed to war.[15]

Under these trying circumstances, what were peace-minded British and American women activists to do during the final slide to global war? On the positive side, within their different groupings they publicly emphasised the positions they could agree upon, as WILPF's Emily Balch had always urged them to do.[16] This meant, for example, supporters of the American section of WILPF – which represented 'every creed, degree of education, level of economic life and racial inheritance possible in this country' – continuing to back the organisation's 'philosophy as the common denominator'. It meant WILPF members and other internationalists continuing to denounce appeasement, to press for the strengthening of the League of Nations, and to reaffirm their faith in a new international order which rejected the inevitability of war. It meant pacificists and pacifists continuing to assure doubters that peace thinking did not deal in abstractions but offered a 'courageous initiative for a constructive policy of just peace'.[17] In Britain, where the need to get these pro-peace points across was most urgent, they were hammered home by women of diverse outlooks, with Virginia Woolf, Vera Brittain and Helena Swanwick proving eloquent in defence of pacifism and isolationism, while the internationalist Eleanor Rathbone appealed to head and heart in her 1938 tract, *War Can Be Averted*. Candidly admitting the weaknesses of the League of Nations, of the Left and of the peace movement, she maintained that it was possible to pursue the 'collective defence of peace' more 'persistently and realistically' than hitherto, not least by building up within the League a group of nations which were willing to take action; by targeting rank-and-file Labour Party supporters still opposed to collective security; and by forcing pacifists to recognise that their stance might be the less than entirely heroic 'means of combining fidelity to conscience, moral adventure and relative physical security'.[18]

By the late 1930s, however, the factors working against internationalism and pacificism were infinitely stronger than those working in their favour. The League of Nations remained underpowered and unrepresentative. Ineffective in the Manchurian, Ethiopian and Spanish crises, it alienated by its deficiencies many of the British activists whose best hopes it had once carried; and it did so, ironically, just when many American campaigners were looking forward to their country's eventual involvement in such a supranational body, the voluntary pacts against war that they had once favoured having proved fruitless. The purposes of the Second World War seemed clearer and nobler than those of the First World War, giving oxygen to 'the popular argument (advanced during every period) that war as a whole is wrong, but *this* war is the outstanding exception'.[19] The American and British peace societies, which had once drawn strength from their varied and overlapping memberships, were, with the onset of hostilities, undermined by their divisions and loss of supporters. And all these societies were obliged to weigh the merits of principled futility (as embraced by the WCG) against those of uncomfortable patriotism (as adopted by the CCCW and WILPF).[20]

Moreover, as Chatfield has demonstrated, the peace movement had not moved far enough from its liberal origins to fashion a new ideology for a new era: to transform its concern about the individual and the concentration of economic power into a new programme for largescale, non-violent direct action designed to produce social change and to benefit the underprivileged – a programme of the kind threatened by the civil rights movement in the 1940s and delivered in the 1950s.[21] Admittedly, 'consumer co-operation as it developed in England, provided a genuinely international as well as feminist rationale for women's peace action', but the pacifism of the WCG was not shared by the larger co-operative movement.[22]

The important contribution women commentators made in this daunting situation was to point out that modern wars had destroyed the old, stark division of interest between men and women. With such conflicts deploying unprecedented propaganda methods and technological power, and affecting the civilian population to an unprecedented extent, it was argued that war had ceased to be 'a masculine occupation' and that its costs clamoured for more serious examination than they had traditionally been afforded. Unfortunately, as Vera Brittain admitted, British peace advocates wrongly assumed that the keen enthusiasm of an energetic minority signified a desire for peace on the part of the whole nation. A similar assumption was made among their more elaborately organised counterparts in America, where pacifism was strengthened by isolationism to a degree that was impossible in imperial Britain. But the impressive female lobbying, demonstrations and educational activities produced by that enthusiasm for peace did not compensate for women's inability to act effectively on their ideas about the nature of modern warfare and the need for economic change. In the short term, their emphasis on its all-embracing impact merely served to undermine women's traditional claim to have a distinctive perspective on war. In the short term, they were simply under increased pressure to become 'peacetime pacifists' and to throw in their lot with men. And in the short term, from the pacifist viewpoint, there were too many women like Nancy Astor, who described herself as 'interventionist . . . but . . . also . . . realist', and too few like the steadfast Montana proponent of peace and neutrality, Jeannette Rankin, who, like Astor, was the first woman to be elected to her national legislature.[23]

Activists did manage to persuade their contemporaries that peace was an issue of special interest to women, despite the strength of male pacifism, women's changing views on the impact of war, and divergent female opinions on the precise link between feminism and pacifism. With the coming of the war, British and American politicians were accordingly wary of the distinguished peace women who had emerged to pressure them. Advocates as formidable as Eleanor Roosevelt, Caroline O'Day and Dorothy Detzer in the United States, and Margery Corbett Ashby, Ellen Wilkinson and Helena Swanwick in Britain were acknowledged by masculine legislators, and American women's groups united in the Committee on Women in World Affairs (1942) pushed 'for female appointees to international organisations and conferences'. Yet women still lacked the clout that they needed inside their countries' foreign policy establishments.[24]

Ever sensitive to the power of public opinion, President Roosevelt may have been at pains to head off women's protests 'against actions that are too military' and 'against giving too much help to the allies'. He did so by making a 'token [female] appointment to his war advisory commission'. The President was, however, only willing to contemplate sending women diplomats to countries 'not likely to be drawn into a European conflict': in which spirit, dispatching

Ruth Owen to Denmark in 1933 as the first US female overseas minister had seemed safe enough.[25] In Britain, women were even more distanced from the heart of foreign policy making. When, in 1943, parliament debated the continuing exclusion of women from the diplomatic and consular services, it was suggested that 'intuition and sympathy were the two main feminine virtues, and each of these was of little value in diplomacy'.[26] Whereas helping interwar refugees was generally thought to be an appropriate outlet for female virtues, controversy attended fearless women who, though not apolitical, put conscience before party. There were no better examples of this unsettling type than the ascetic Jeannette Rankin; the intrepidly independent Eleanor Rathbone; and the fastidious Duchess of Atholl – who, when a campaign required it, was willing to work with feminists and non-feminists, political insiders and outsiders alike.[27]

Women's activism and women's work in wartime

Once their two countries had been drawn into war, female pacifists and internationalists on both sides of the Atlantic faced a new period of heart searching. As they did so, those who opposed armed conflict at least avoided being lumped together as the dupes of the dangerous Left – their common fate during the First World War. This was because they were now to be found on the left and right of British and American politics, with the former represented in both countries by WILPF, and the latter by the BUF and the Peace Pledge Union (PPU, 1936) in Britain and by the America First Movement (AFM, 1939) and the America First Committee (AFC, 1940) in the United States. However, rightwing peace endeavours presented their own problems, since by opposing war and accepting support from extreme conservatives, the PPU, AFM and AFC laid themselves open to the charge of endorsing fascism. Furthermore, only the small numbers of unambiguously pacifist women on the left and right alike allowed them to escape the sort of state regulation that was meted out to BUF women between 1940 and 1945.[28]

The first duty of female activists was to give each other the strength to face their diverse circumstances. Some campaigners had hoped until 1941 that the neutral nations could help the allies without themselves becoming embroiled, and could start by initiating a conference 'to offer terms of mediation to the countries now at war looking towards a negotiated peace'.[29] Rather more women had just felt overwhelmed by events. After all, enlightened public opinion had not decided the course of events,[30] and the 'noble aims of humanity' extolled by the Women's World Congress for Peace and Liberty (1939) [31] had been flouted on every side. The head of the Peace and Disarmament Committee of Women's International Organisations frankly admitted that her group was reduced to impotence and that the problems ahead were 'too big and complicated for me'.[32] The Women's Peace Union ceased to function. But internationalists were, of necessity, committed to staying in touch with people and problems beyond national boundaries. Pacifists were accustomed to failure. And feminists were inured to periods of modest progress made tolerable by the warmth of fellowship

– by the consciousness of having enlisted in a long struggle. Organisational roadblocks and personal attacks were felt to produce 'strong independent characters',[33] who would not be silenced.

In this spirit, the Committee on the Cause and Cure of War, despite being faced with diminishing funds, drew up an elaborate list of 'Issues Requiring Earnest Study and Immediate Action' which pledged members to work for civil liberties at home, to alleviate the suffering of victims of persecution, war and forced migrations, and to participate in efforts for a fair and permanent peace. Mrs Catt, the perennial politician, suggested that if the CCCW decided to disband 'it would be well to draw up a statement as to what they have accomplished regarding the causes of war and concerning the possible cures of war. This would give the Committee some excuse at least to say it had finished its duty and could be disbanded with honor.'[34] The suggestion was unnecessary. By 1943 the CCCW had transformed itself into the Women's Action Committee for Victory and Lasting Peace, and was trying 'to reach women of every group in every community' so as to rally them behind 'the basic principle of America's full participation in [a] world organization to secure a just and lasting peace'.[35] Notwithstanding the hostility towards their politics, radicals like Florence Luscomb kept going in the cause of peace and freedom;[36] the LWV committed itself to studying war needs at the state and national levels and supporting the proposed United Nations;[37] and the World Woman's Party (WWP, 1938, incorporating the Equal Rights International from 1941), undertook to press Congress to accept the ERA and gave its support to the launching of a new union of nations.[38] The WCG did not let internal divisions over pacifism prevent it from undertaking all war work;[39] the British and American sections of WILPF pledged their backing for a combination of national and international activities; and the Liaison Committee of International Women's Organisations shook off the impact of wartime disruption to 'press the case for the equal status of women and their share in post-war reconstruction'.[40]

Realisation of these ambitious aims was another matter. Although the governments of Britain and the United States needed female support in all kinds of ways, social programmes were immediately subordinated to military needs. Nor could the strained Anglo-American relationship be made trouble-free at any level for the duration of the war. There were some positive aspects to trans-Atlantic reformer relations. American financial generosity was, as always, to the fore – paying for WILPF's Gertrud Baer to move to the United States so that she could more effectively keep in contact with the League of Nations and ILO operations.[41] Mrs Catt also stayed in touch with Mrs Corbett Ashby throughout the conflict, to show solidarity with European feminists and to help fund future initiatives to benefit the world's women.[42] And American admiration was expressed for British women who did 'magnificent work' under 'impossible circumstances', suffering to an extent that 'will give us who are Americans an inferiority complex'.[43] Less likely to please Britons was the patronising tone of the executive committee of the CCCW, which believed that other countries had now turned to the United States for leadership, and that it might be necessary for Americans 'to save the more democratic nations [that is, the British Empire and France] in order to insure our own freedom'.[44] And while the British and US sections of WILPF made sincere attempts to find common ground, American activists felt they got on better with their government than did the British with theirs;[45] shared its anti-imperialism;[46] and complained about the British restrictions on visitors to the United States – a development which made Americans believe that Britain was censoring what they were allowed to hear.[47]

Rising above these irritants, a small minority of women on each side of the Atlantic held steadfastly to their pacifist convictions, some as registered conscientious objectors.[48] Many more women internationalists chose to follow the example of women legislators in the United States and Britain, and to support their democratically elected governments without abandoning their own principles.[49] Practically this involved them in efforts to alleviate suffering, defend individual rights and promote a debate about peace terms. General intellectual inquiry was encouraged by extensive correspondence and by the study groups of WILPF, which also sent out questionnaires to its national sections with the aim of tapping and focusing opinion.[50]

Conscious that their country could have acted in 'a less cold-hearted and self-regarding' fashion towards persecuted Jews,[51] American activists assisted Jewish and other refugees and helped to secure the setting up of a War Refugees Board. Peace minded women were acutely aware of whites' need 'to educate themselves out of the superiority complex which is a Nazi–Fascist idea',[52] and one that could be used to buttress racial discrimination in the United States. Accordingly, WILPF members attempted to recruit and integrate more women of colour within the league,[53] and protested at 'the great wrong' done after 1942 by the relocation and internment of 112,000 Japanese Americans. Co-operating with the Japanese community, WILPF, along with bodies like the YWCA, sought to combat adverse propaganda, to defend the internees' civil rights, to foster their participation in the war effort, and to improve their living and working conditions.[54] The league also extended aid to conscientious objectors. And it backed the committee that – helped by public indignation – successfully agitated against the introduction of female conscription. Given America's historic aversion to standing armies and the draft, this successful opposition – which had no British equivalent – was to be expected. It was likewise predictable, as Alonso has pointed out, that the National Committee to Oppose the Conscription of Women (1942) used distinctly traditional arguments about women's proper family and social roles.[55]

In Britain, women were similarly concerned to aid conscientious objectors and refugees. Eleanor Rathbone appropriately became the Honorary Secretary of the Parliamentary Committee on Refugees and worked with various voluntary refugee associations, trying to humanise the internment bureaucracy and to make sure that it distinguished between the innocent and the dangerous. In addition, Rathbone set up the National Committee for Rescue from Nazi Terror, acting as its deputy director, strengthening her links with British Jewry, and taking a special interest in the fate of Polish Jews and deportees. The British section of WILPF successfully lobbied the Ministry of Labour to give women conscientious objectors the same rights as men.[56]

Yet there were disappointments for American and British activists in both the domestic and international arenas. The drive which WILPF joined to secure the liberalisation of America's immigration laws was only partially successful; and its plea for an end to the discriminatory use of the poll tax failed.[57] So did women's attempts to force a clarification of war aims that would commit the allies to avoiding 'vindictiveness and recrimination', and to recognising racial equality, individual 'rights and liberties', and 'the integrity of small as well as great nations'. The Anglo-American declaration at the Casablanca Conference (1943) that total surrender would be demanded from all enemies did not bode well for the future, and offset the idealistic but vague statement of principles known as the Atlantic Charter (1941), made by the United States and Britain before the Americans formally entered the war.[58]

On the other hand, immigration policy reform was overdue, furthered during the Second World War (with the 1943 repeal of the Chinese Exclusion Act), and would subsequently accelerate as racial thinking changed. Agitation against the poll tax, though not effective until the passage of the Twenty-Fourth Amendment to the Constitution in 1964, was an admirable part of WILPF's stand against racism and one which had found growing support among American reforming politicians and civil rights campaigners since 1920. And that hopes for a largely defensive war and a different kind of peace were sustained by internationalists, despite their hard experiences of international politics between the wars, is at the very least a tribute to their resilience and sense of historical responsibility. They had not forgotten the commitments made at the Hague Congress of 1915, and if they had a better sense of their immensity, they were also convinced that the consequent 'widespread determination to put an end to war . . . [was] a new thing in history'.[59]

This determination existed on both sides of the Atlantic, and even the habitually pragmatic President Roosevelt formally conceded that he could not ignore the body of idealistic opinion which had grown up in favour of a new international organisation to ensure peace. He accepted, in the words of his Secretary of State Cordell Hull, that 'we in this country have moved from a deep-seated tendency toward separate action to the knowledge and conviction that only through unity of action can there be achieved in this world the results which are essential for the continuance of free peoples'.[60] And most particularly, Roosevelt could not ignore the voice given to idealistic opinion by his social feminist wife, who was determined to act on her conviction that 'We had to win the war, but we will have to work to keep the peace. The alternative is too appalling to even contemplate.'[61]

When the United Nations was launched in San Francisco in June 1945, it therefore already carried a heavy freight of hopes and was burdened with several contentious features. Although the conference that gave it life was attended by fifty nations, proceedings were dominated by American–Russian disagreements. And while member states of varying degrees of influence were to be represented in the General Assembly, substantive decisions in the Security Council – which was primarily responsible for 'the maintenance of international peace and security' – were to require the assent of its five powerful permanent members, among them the United States and Russia. On the other hand, like British and American peace women, the United States government was very conscious of the legacy of the First World War, and so in 1943 had secured congressional support for America to 'take the lead in establishing the United Nations Organisation'. As a result, the UN did not get entangled in the peacemaking process, as the League of Nations had done. Roosevelt also took care to see that the American delegation was a bipartisan affair. The reward for these prudent initiatives was the acceptance of the UN by the American Senate and by the US public, large sections of which had opposed internationalism as late as 1941.[62] A leading member of the British WILPF was soon able to report that 'America is far more "United Nations" minded than we are. Natural, of course, because its headquarters are there': a nice reversal of the interwar situation.[63] Yet while WILPF's hope that those headquarters would not be located within the borders of any major power had been disappointed,[64] women's international organisations did manage to promote female concerns at the San Francisco meeting.

Their main achievement was to get the principle of equality between men and women included in the charter of the United Nations, and in so doing to demonstrate the continuing importance to women's causes of independent female pressure groups. The main dispiriting feature of the gathering was the continuing evidence of rivalry and ill feeling among women's associations. Thus, for example, the WWP's claim to have been 'instrumental' in the victory was disputed by the International Alliance of Women, whose Brazilian delegate, Bertha Lutz, reported that 'The women's movement is at a very low ebb in the USA and international complications arise from the feud between the Woman's Party and the rest'.[65] Furthermore, Lutz had hoped for Anglo-American leadership of the movement once peace was restored.[66] It was therefore both a disappointment and a challenge to her to think that at San Francisco British and American delegates were more cautious than, say, the Latin American or Australian women.[67] Certainly Virginia Gildersleeve representing the United States and Ellen Wilkinson representing Britain showed how easily the formal inclusion of a handful of women in any UN endeavour could lead to their support for the official line – Wilkinson even allegedly saying that her position proved 'that women had arrived' and that 'nothing further was needed'.[68]

The WWP, at least, was under no such illusion, pressing for the creation of a Commission on the Status of Women under the auspices of the UN's Social and Economic Council: a sub-commission was initially obtained. But as Leila Rupp has shown, the old division again emerged between activists who opposed and activists who favoured special bodies run by women to protect women's interests. Opponents of female separatism advocated the consideration of those interests by the UN Commission on Human Rights, and it was this body that accepted the 1946 programme of the women's sub-commission (made a full commission in June 1946): namely to raise 'the status of women to equality with men in all fields of human enterprise'.[69]

After 1946, Lutz grumbled that 'we have not had much help from the more conservative North American groups, including Mrs Roosevelt when she was a member of the United Nations' (1945–52).[70] Lutz's suspicion of these social feminists and their First Lady ally is understandable. During the 1930s, they managed to ease the egalitarian Doris Stevens out of her headship of the Inter-American Commission of Women and to replace her with one of their own – the WTUL's Mary Winslow – who was happy to see the commission reduced in power and devoting itself to promoting hemispheric goodwill and democracy rather than equal rights. If Stevens's personal flamboyance made her vulnerable, she had appreciated the domestic and international concerns of Latin American activists and her removal was resented as a political and social feminist manoeuvre.[71] It certainly was; yet Eleanor Roosevelt cannot easily be pigeonholed. By the late 1940s, she was enjoying her independence and high profile, which she cultivated through extensive travel, in the press and on the radio. Her work for peace and a better world stemmed from her convictions as a liberal reformer as well as a Democrat. The sheer scale of Mrs Roosevelt's ambition and activities, her awareness of America's new world role, and her horrified resolution in the wake of the Holocaust to promote human rights, meant that she could not concentrate on Latin America or the demands of any particular feminist undertaking. As a lobbyist and diplomat, she was undeterred by defeat. As a pragmatist, she saw the need for concessions to opponents. Bertha Lutz notwithstanding, she was no longer the conservative that her upbringing had first made her.[72]

Fashioning her UN social, humanitarian and cultural committee into a power base rather than the harmless 'female' backwater it was intended to be, and also working effectively as chair of the Human Rights Commission on Refugees, Eleanor Roosevelt played a vital part in devising and guiding through the UN Assembly the 1948 Universal Declaration of Human Rights. In Blanche Weisen Cook's skilful and long needed analysis of Mrs Roosevelt's foreign policy role, it is noted that the inclusion of economic and social as well as civil and political rights in the declaration was a concession to the Soviet Union; but it was, in addition, a reflection of her social feminism and the impassioned determination to tackle social injustice in the United States that she had developed during the 1930s. Its thirty articles were designed as a standard for 'all peoples and all nations', and remain 'the most far-reaching of all UN declarations on behalf of fundamental freedoms and economic and social rights'.[73]

Taken together, the effort of Mrs Roosevelt and the female international groups (which sensibly applied for consultative status) guaranteed that the overwhelmingly male composition of the United Nations in its formative years was balanced by the frequently different politics of women.[74] As far as the rest of the peace settlement was concerned, female voices were less audible than they had been during the First World War. This state of affairs owed something to the small number of female activists and their well known quarrels; however, it owed far more to the way in which the allies had agreed not only to short-term plans but also to major post-war arrangements at a series of conferences from 1941. Despite the strains on the Grand Alliance, the Allies worked together more closely than their counterparts in the 1914–18 conflict, and from 1945 their efforts were supplemented by meetings of a Council of Foreign Ministers. Hence, for example, it was possible to produce draft treaties for Germany's satellite countries in 1946 which 'were ratified without substantial change' by the Paris peace conference.[75]

Gallantly, WILPF sent resolutions to the conference appealing for the co-operative and peaceful management of atomic energy; for peace treaties 'based on human rights'; for frontiers drawn with 'regard to economic and social consequences'; and for the avoidance of punitive treatment of Germany.[76] While the actual peace – little resembling either the Atlantic Charter or WILPF's ideals – drove the league's Mildred Olmsted to denounce its 'incredibly horrible and stupid terms',[77] the earnest WILPF search went on for issues over which the American and British sections could collaborate, with anti-imperialism seen as a likely (if controversial) unifier and the Anglo-American Committee of Inquiry on Palestine as an immediate test.[78] But the sudden post-war collapse of British power and the equally swift development of the Cold War presented peace advocates everywhere with massive challenges to which they needed to find measured new responses. Even as American power in the world reached its zenith, the dominance of female internationalism by English speakers and, most importantly, by American money and organisational capacity, was ending. It had been symbolised at its height by the award of the Nobel Peace Prize to Jane Addams (1921); it was symbolised as it drew to a close by the award of the prize to Emily Balch (1946).[79]

Infinitely less problematical on each side of the Atlantic was the female activism that found expression in voluntary war work. Whereas women's internationalism and pacifism largely continued to be seen by politicians and civil servants as inappropriate and unhelpful, female war work was eventually regarded as suitable and necessary. In Britain and America alike, voluntary war service also appealed to women's sense of civic duty, and allowed pacifists and opponents of conscription to show solidarity with combatants without surrendering their convictions.

Co-operating with government authorities, British women served enthusiastically in such specially created organisations as the Women's Voluntary Service for Civil Defence (WVS, 1938), which had a membership of over a million by 1942. They laboured, too, through existing groups like the Townswomen's Guilds and Women's Institutes: bodies long experienced in improving 'the material circumstances of women's lives' locally, and glad now to turn to the country as a whole. Women exempt from compulsory war service because of age or family obligations received training in everything from first aid to fire fighting, and assisted refugees and evacuees; prepared meals and ran rest centres; provided every kind of help during air raids; collected needed items and money; distributed information about diet and fuel; made and mended blankets, clothes and knitted goods; and produced drivers and vehicles for a multitude of tasks. In short, where a need was perceived, female voluntarism tried to meet it. In the process, its practitioners shook off old associations with charity and middle-class condescension, and drew in women from all classes. Lady Reading, the formidable leader of the WVS, is a good case in point; for though she was a titled and politically well connected figure, it has been shown that Reading shunned elitism and was described as 'a feminist, of course', though 'in the old-fashioned sense'.[80]

In the United States, where wartime conditions were easier than in Britain and there was no female conscription to make women regard the alternative of voluntary work with unusual favour, it was none the less expected and undertaken. And as in Britain, what is striking is the range of the jobs that were tackled and the provision of on-the-job training which helped some women to expand their horizons. Thanks to the volunteers, civil defence activities were assisted; war bonds sold; hospitals, Red Cross efforts and child care centres supported; salvage collection was undertaken; and advice and help given over housing and rationing problems, food production and conservation, appliance maintenance and first aid. Furthermore, women were employed without pay by the expanded government agencies, among them the Office of Price Administration.[81] In America as in Britain, such war work attracted attention and gratitude without challenging conventional views about gender.

What had greater impact on entrenched opinion concerning women was the level of their commitment to paid work during the war, and their determination to continue with it once peace was restored. Naturally, female responses to the new opportunities thrown up by the war varied according to their circumstances and temperament, and these opportunities related to the erratic economic shift towards a female orientated consumer economy which had been underway well before the conflict. Yet if most feminist historians would agree that neither of the world wars dramatically altered the overall position of women, there is general acceptance of William Chafe's contention that, with regard to paid work, change after 1945 was permanent and profound.[82] On both sides of the Atlantic, the Second World War resulted in increased female involvement in the paid labour force, with the participation of married women no longer encountering the hostility it had provoked in Depression conditions and women undertaking a wider range of jobs than they had in the First World War. In the United States, between 1940 and 1944 there was a 47 per cent increase in female employment, and the participation rate of married women rose from 15.2 to 23.0 per cent.[83] By the end of the 1940s, the gains for women – and particularly for older women – had been sustained, despite post-war readjustments.[84] In Britain, one and a half million more women worked in essential industries in 1943 than had done so in 1939; the demand for women's labour was maintained after 1945, and the opposition to married women working abated, for example in nursing, teaching and clerical work. Nor was demobilisation 'as abrupt for most [British] women' at the end of the Second World War as it had been in 1918.[85]

There were other similarities between the two countries with regard to female employment. Women workers were actively sought by government, notwithstanding the countervailing desire to strengthen the family and women's crucial role in it during a time of national crisis. For the women who responded willingly, or were coerced into the paid labour force in Britain after 1941, there were several advantages. Some managed to escape from poorly remunerated women's jobs – notably in domestic and personal service – into more lucrative government, industrial and white collar work. And for some, there were also better child care facilities, provided by employers, the government and local authorities in Britain, and (less extensively) by the federal government in the United States under the terms of the Lanham Act of 1943. Moreover, unions which had once ignored or slighted women were obliged to recognise them as a group worth recruiting – and even promoting. During the Second World War in the United States, the number of women enrolled in unions rose from 800,000 to three million, and in Britain female membership of unions went from a little under half a million to one and one-third million. Women moved into unions' organisational hierarchies, took part in strikes for better conditions, and benefited from the TUC in Britain and the willingness of CIO unions in America to deal with specifically female concerns.[86]

For African American women, as Giddings has recorded, the Second World War entailed the familiar struggle 'against discrimination, the relegation to the worst jobs in industrial plants, and unfair wages'. But between 1940 and 1944 – assisted by Roosevelt's Fair Employment Practices Commission (FEPC, 1941) banning discrimination in employment by companies carrying out defence contracts – black women tripled their involvement in the industrial sector, 'while during the same four years the percentage of domestics dropped from over 60 percent to 45 percent'.[87] The number of black women employed in badly paid farm jobs declined from 20 per cent to 7 per cent during the conflict, which has been described as 'in some ways a second emancipation'.[88] Serving in the armed forces of the United States and Britain was a further opportunity, grasped by about 200,000 American and about half a million British women.[89] It has been estimated that 3,961 enlisted African American women were serving in the Women's Army Corps (WAC) by the summer of 1945, together with 120 black officers.[90]

Women during the war: the case for continuity

For all the activism of the small band of female pacifists and internationalists, and for all the benefits that their countries derived from female voluntary and paid work, women's advances between 1939 and 1945 were limited by class and race factors, as well as by the domestic weakness of organised feminism in Britain and the United States.

Class

The union gains made by various groups of British and American labour women during the Second World War 'provided both the inspiration and the resources for mobilization in the post-war era'. But the growth of wartime class solidarity between women and men was hindered by the separation of the sexes in the workforce and the survival of old anxieties among labour leaders. These flourished even though the numbers of men kept in strategic occupations were substantial; even though the jobs that women did were frequently deemed subordinate to those done by men and graded accordingly; even though equal pay for equal work was accepted in principle but often denied in practice; even though the number of women in union leadership positions remained small; and even though it was understood that women doing men's jobs would be removed at the end of hostilities (an undertaking reinforced in Britain in 1942 by the Restoration of Pre-War Practices Act). As they had in the First World War, male unionists found it unsettling that women could do work for which they were supposed to be innately unfitted. It was likewise tiresome to have to respond to women's desire for part-time work, and to devise regulations to cover female employees which would at one and the same time help the newcomers, reassure male workers, and take account of the interests of servicemen who expected to return to their jobs at the war's end.[91]

Nor did the Second World War encourage the growth of cross-class solidarity among British and American women, although in the United States the class gulf commonly appeared as a race divide. Middle-class and working-class women remained apart in the paid workforce,[92] and middle-class women accustomed to servants fretted about the threat to domestic service posed by more lucrative war jobs.[93] If working-class women were used to making their own child care arrangements, the inadequate state facilities provided in wartime did little to transform their lives, while the combined pressures of paid and home work weighed more heavily on them than on their middle-class sisters, who were not totally bereft of their customary 'help'.[94] And in voluntary work and the women's branches of the armed forces, the class system replicated itself.

Thus if Lady Reading was never isolated by class snobbery, throughout 'the 1940s, 30–40 per cent of the regional administrators [of the WVS] were titled ladies'. The leaders of American voluntary organisations were likewise privileged individuals, who could afford to work without pay and were accustomed to wielding influence in their localities.[95] The better off in Britain gravitated to the Women's Royal Auxiliary Air Force, Women's Royal Naval Service and Women's Land Army in preference to the Auxiliary Territorial Services (ATS).[96] Linked class and race prejudices similarly affected black British women. It was not until 1943 that the British War Office reluctantly agreed to admit black West Indian women to the ATS: some 600 were accepted.[97] In the United States, class and race also determined the armed forces experiences of African American women, who were steered into the WAC, segregated and frequently confined to menial assignments. It was not until 1945 that President Roosevelt yielded to domestic black pressures and sent a unit of 850 African American WACs to Britain.[98] Most of these young women seem to have been well received – after all, they were intent upon helping the British war effort. However, Bousquet and Douglas have pointed out that black service women in Britain, regardless of their qualifications, encountered the expectation that they would do 'all the dirty work' and would be willing to clean the officers' houses.[99]

As had been the case before the Second World War, there was only a limited amount that the International Labour Organisation could do to help hard pressed and still disunited working women. Relocated in Canada for most of the conflict, and endorsing the Atlantic Charter and the allied cause, the organisation did try to continue doing business as usual. It mounted conferences and meetings, and produced reports, in 1941 adopting a social mandate which reaffirmed its commitment to 'such items of concern to women as the elimination of unemployment, [and the] improvement and extension of social insurance to all classes of workers'. The mandate stressed, especially, the need for 'greater equality of economic opportunity', and for 'a minimum living wage for those too weak to secure it for themselves'. By the time of its 1944 conference, note Lubin and Winslow, ILO recommendations foreshadowed what would be a growing emphasis on principles of equality – an important shift away from its pre-war preference for social feminism. None the less, the ILO remained male dominated, and feminist groups showed little interest in 'the role of women on the staff of international organizations'. Furthermore, much of the organisation's time was perforce taken up with sorting out its role as just one among many inter-governmental bodies in the post-war world. Individual women did keep in touch with each other by means of the ILO conferences, and at the end of the war an Anglo-American exchange of labour leaders included Maida Springer Kemp, 'the first American Negro woman to represent American labor abroad'. Information was exchanged about war production questions, and the hope was to 'cement relations between working women of America and England'.[100] Despite such links, the struggle to retain the economic advantages obtained by workers during the war had to be conducted in the context of national conditions and labour relations.

The Second World War was indeed 'a people's war' in a way in which the First World War was not. There was a greater community of interest among the British and Americans alike, because of the nature of the Nazi regime and because civilian suffering was more widespread. Since there were fewer conscientious objectors than there had been in the First World War, fears about internal divisions were eased somewhat, and the objectors were treated more humanely. The United States was more completely engaged and for longer, and supported a propaganda emphasis on what united its population. And in Britain – which had experienced no New Deal in the 1930s – there was a clear expectation of social reform at the end of hostilities. But long established social patterns were not to be uprooted in six years, however traumatic those years might have been.[101]

Race

It was in the area of race that old images and behaviour were hardest to shake. This was, however, also the area which, in terms of organised protest, offered most to African American women. Unlike white feminists, black activists were openly aware of the need both to prove their loyalty and to obtain a *quid pro quo* for full participation in the war, so as not to repeat the bitter experiences of the First World War.[102] According to a 1942 conference of black leaders: 'We believe the Negro today is not unreservedly, whole-heartedly, all-out in support of this war'. Their aim was the double 'V' of victory abroad and victory over racism at home.[103] Their strong card was the ability to embarrass the government at a time when Nazism had raised awareness of the appalling consequences of discrimination, and American foreign policy – for example in the Atlantic Charter – was committed to defending rights and freedoms in the world at large that it did not uphold for its own black citizens. The threat of a mass march on Washington by A. Philip Randolph, head of the Brotherhood of Sleeping Car Porters, led to the creation of the FEPC. Once African American leaders had fought 'for the right to fight', their pressures brought improved terms for black involvement in the armed forces. The NAACP – helped by a wartime leap in membership from 50,000 to 450,000 – kept up the attack on segregation and discriminatory practices, playing a key part in the outlawing of exclusively white primary elections in 1944. In 1943, the Congress of Racial Equality was formed, anxious to increase the pace of change and pledged to non-violent direct action. And as they had done before the war, the NCNW and the black sororities campaigned vigorously for racial justice, recognising that the chief female beneficiaries from expanded economic opportunities were white, but co-operating with white women when they could. Although the FEPC remained weak, and the armed services remained segregated until 1954, the prospects for black organisations were evidently beginning to improve, whereas WILPF and the mainstream feminist groups were overstretched and limited in impact[104] (see below, next section).

What is more, given their developing internationalism (see above, chapter 5), African American women had much to gain during the 1940s from association with anti-colonial black 'political leaders, intellectuals, journalists, and activists who articulated the bonds between black Americans, Africans, and all oppressed peoples'. As Penny Von Eschen has shown, they 'saw race at the heart of the processes shaping the modern world'. They wanted to articulate 'a democratic and internationalist politics' which attempted to influence 'the relationship of the United States to emerging Asian and African nations'; and they sought to debate how 'political, economic, and civil rights were to be defined and who in America and across the globe was to have access to those rights'. Mrs Bethune was therefore wise to throw the support of her NCNW behind the male led NAACP, as did the California journalist and civil rights campaigner Charlotta Bass, and organisations ranging from the Delta Sigma Theta Sorority to the National Association of Ministers Wives.[105] But there were serious limitations to the race solidarity policy, and these quickly manifested themselves.

If Pan Africanism had drawn in women from the 1920s, it was frequently because of its ideology rather than the advanced behaviour of its male leadership, and this remained true in the 1940s. Hence when Walter White, DuBois and Bethune went as consultants to the founding conference of the United Nations, the two men resented Bethune's involvement, cast doubts on her ability, and went their own way in San Francisco.[106] Black activists may have been as eager to influence that conference as feminists, and may have succeeded in securing a commitment to racial equality in the UN Charter and the Declaration of Human

Rights. However, the official delegations to San Francisco were short on non-whites, unionists and women alike;[107] and African American men were no more ensconsed in influential State Department posts than white or black women.[108] While the Charter and Declaration were major achievements, and the definition of rights would be invaluable to future UN lobbyists, they would prove difficult to enforce and national self-interest still loomed larger in the world than internationalism, whatever its source.[109] Furthermore, in the wartime context there was an inhibiting suspicion among American policy makers that highlighting the rights of one disaffected group could lead to the claims of others being raised, and that the whole process might be embarrassing at home and abroad.[110] Black connections with the political Left and criticisms of the American and British records on race and colonialism created an awareness that black activism was, at the very least, potentially subversive, and this awareness was to intensify with the Cold War. In addition, while the emphasis upon labour activities in 1940s Pan Africanism was understandable, as it recognised the need to move away from its former elitism, the link had disadvantages once post-war conservative fears mounted about the activities of leftwing unions.[111]

There is no issue that better reveals the reluctance of American and British authorities to change on matters to do with race than their treatment of the black armed services personnel in Britain. In the opinion of General Eisenhower, Britain was 'devoid of race consciousness'.[112] Yet in the opinion of the NAACP and the American black press, race prejudice flourished on each side of the Atlantic, a view shared by such black British commentators as Una Marson and the League of Coloured Peoples (see above, chapter 5), as well as by WILPF, which wanted the 'abolition of all forms of the colour bar'. These differing judgements reflect, of course, their very different sources; but they also indicate the sensitive situation that faced policy makers, who were unhelpfully divided in Britain.

As Reynolds has argued, the majority of Britons were unacquainted with the black population concentrated in the port cities and numbering about 8,000 in 1939. An informal colour bar did exist in urban areas, offensive racial stereotypes did circulate, and social contacts between the races were expected to be distant. Crucially, however, there was no widespread system of legalised, public racial segregation of the kind that characterised the American South and which many white American soldiers from the southern states who were stationed in Britain would have liked to see operating in their host country. While there is considerable evidence that the black American troops were for the most part cordially treated, British respect for their civil rights did not prevent inter-racial awkwardness and violence increasing in a period when the number of non-whites doing service and civilian jobs in Britain was doubling, the number of non-white women remained small, and many British men were away from home. In this situation, political and military officials in the United States and Britain alike wanted to manage the troops in a way which would suggest enlightenment and changing times without moving changes along or publicising their private prejudices. They wished to respect each other's customary arrangements and domestic interests regarding race without running into trouble with the cosmopolitan network of black activists and white liberals who hoped that the war was being fought to recognise human rights, and to defend them through a new international order.[113] There was nothing to suggest that the greater British informality and tolerance on matters to do with race would survive the influx of large numbers of Commonwealth citizens after the war.

Feminism

In both countries, women legislators tended to co-operate 'across partisan lines for the advancement of their sex'.[114] In both countries, such co-operative efforts met with limited success, but the situation for American feminists was particularly disappointing. Some disappointment was to be expected: women activists had enjoyed considerable gains during the New Deal, and it was desirable that black rights at home and abroad should be given increasing prominence. Eleanor Roosevelt's ideological shift of focus from gender and peace concerns to race and civil rights epitomises the trend.[115] What was also predictable but not desirable was the way in which American women were largely excluded from policy making roles in the war agencies and relegated to advisory roles, while protests by women leaders were ignored.[116] The research expertise and data of the Women's Bureau could have been extensively tapped in the drive to achieve 'the most efficient utilization of women workers in war industries'.[117] Even without encouragement, the bureau did press effectively for better factory facilities for women.[118] But its head, Mary Anderson, complained about the lack of consultation over women's employment matters.[119] When a Women's Advisory Committee was eventually created by the War Manpower Commission, it lacked research staff and its advice, too, went unsolicited.

Although American women's organisations set up a new committee to promote female appointees at all levels of government, progress was slow and the New Deal feminist network, analysed by Ware, was no longer a force by the 1940s, because of retirements, deaths and an undue reliance on exceptional individuals.[120] But it was still possible for an able woman to make an impact on behalf of her sex, provided she had a secure political base from which to work. Two good examples are the nationally known Democrat, Mary Bethune, and the Republican legislator from Maine, Margaret Chase Smith. Due to her exertions through the National Youth Administration, Bethune secured a commitment from defence firms to hire black women – and some did so.[121] As a member of the powerful House Committee for Naval Affairs, Mrs Smith was in a position to protect female war workers from alarmist complaints about their absenteeism and immorality, and to influence the provision of practical assistance for such workers. In her vindication of working women's morals, she resembled the British feminist MP, Dr Edith Summerskill.[122]

Yet Mrs Smith was not readily accepted as a member of the Naval Affairs Committee: when she asked to join, the response had been – what would a woman do with it? Her tactful reply was that she would work for her state, for budget management, and for the welfare of husbands and brothers in the service.

Once appointed, she was able to take up the 'pathetic' situation of navy nurses, and to counter the resistance to treating them well that was based on 'the general feeling . . . that women were there more for looks and companionship than for duty'.[123] It seemed that in the United States – and the same is true of Britain – women had to begin all over again to prove themselves in wartime. Notwithstanding their contributions during the First World War and their arguments about the all-inclusive features of modern war, the hostilities were seen as an overwhelmingly masculine business.

Mobilised through the NCNW, the national WTUL, the NWP, and the National Federation of Business and Professional Women's Clubs (BPW), the American Association of University Women (AAUW) and many other bodies, American feminists took advantage of public awareness of women's importance to the war effort to push for state improvements in the legal status of women 'as citizens, married women, and workers'. While they enjoyed considerable success, egalitarian campaigns fared poorly at the federal level. Equal pay proposals provoked employer hostility and political caution, and the ERA provoked disagreements among feminists themselves. As Rupp and Taylor have noted, support for the amendment grew during the Second World War. The ERA was included in the Republican Party's platform for the first time in 1940, and in the Democratic platform for 1944. It was voted on in the Senate in 1946, after being introduced annually in Congress since 1923. State groups favouring the ERA began to appear from 1943, and the NWP set up three new organisations in 1943–4 to demonstrate and extend support for the amendment, especially among working-class and Catholic Americans. In the unusual wartime conditions, the ERA campaign was taken sufficiently seriously to prompt the formation of a National Committee to Defeat the Un-Equal Rights Amendment, and the promotion of an (ultimately unsuccessful) alternative bill designed to 'end discrimination on the basis of sex except where reasonably justified by differences in physical structure or biological or social function'.[124] The chief dangers facing the NWP were in fact all too familiar: that is to say, the ERA was still seen as threatening needed labour laws; and, in addition, its programme seemed too narrow, its leaders too privileged, its concern for international affairs a distraction, and its focus on the national scene neglectful of the community activism which was women's greatest political strength. 'The state branches', observe Rupp and Taylor, 'served the organization primarily as names on letterheads to use in lobbying senators and representatives'.[125]

In Britain, female activists were able to show modest gains both on equal rights and on women's welfare issues, without having to grapple with the disarray of a once powerful peace movement, a still contentious ERA campaign, and a newly energised drive for black civil rights. Feminists in parliament took up the interests of working women more vigorously than in the 1930s, and were helped – as in the First World War – by male unionists' concern that women who substituted directly for men in the wartime economy should receive the man's rate. As Summerfield reminds us, they 'made three major parliamentary attempts to secure equal remuneration for women'. But their effort to secure equal pay for certain groups of conscripted women was rejected. They did manage to obtain equal compensation for female war injuries, with sympathetic unionists suggesting that an injured woman deserved help because of her reduced chances of marriage or remarriage. However, when their efforts resulted in the insertion of a clause proposing equal pay for teachers in the 1944 Education Act, and provoked a broader debate on the principle of equality, the matter was referred to a royal commission which did not report until 1946, when the wartime case for improved treatment of women no longer applied. Its finding that equal pay for work of commensurate worth was applicable only to the junior levels of the civil service, local government and teaching was buttressed by traditional arguments about women's home and family responsibilities, and anxiety about the economic implications of even limited change persuaded the new Labour government to reject its findings. The women members of the commission proved powerless.[126]

Wartime conditions encouraged non-parliamentary female activists to meet and air their grievances. New organisations sprang up – notably the Women's Group on Public Welfare (1939), which raised the welfare needs of women and children; the Women Power Committee (1940), to advise the government on women's employment; the Equal Pay Committee (1943); and the Women for Westminster committee, to promote female candidates for parliament. And existing bodies remained active – among them the British Federation of Business and Professional Women (BFBPW) and the Six Point Group (SPG). But feminists generally found it hard to produce a forward-looking agenda of the kind they had supported during the interwar years (see chapter 6), [127] even if they hoped that women's wartime labours would be rewarded when peace came.

As one would expect from the widespread belief in women's distinct destiny, there was most political enthusiasm for the pro-family legislation long urged by social feminists. Servicemen's wives were financially supported, as they had been during the First World War, and family allowances were finally introduced in 1945, beginning with the second child in a family and paid to the mother – not the father, as was originally intended by the government. This shift of focus came after the impassioned intervention of Eleanor Rathbone and representation from social feminist groups. As with the equal rights gains, there was no general political conversion here to feminism of any description. Susan Pedersen's definitive study has established that action on welfare provision was, during the Second World War and the interwar years alike, taken by those who believed in the family wage, limited state interference in the wage system, and 'compensating men *and their families* for loss of wages'. New wartime legislation came amid worries about the inadequacy of the family wage, and about the need for full employment to allow men to meet their responsibilities. Such thinking and such anxieties survived the hostilities. Thus, even though Sir William Beveridge's Report on Social Insurance and Allied Services (1942) had benignly acknowledged the social importance of housewives, and had supported the family allowances and national health service from which they would soon benefit, the 1946 National Insurance Act discriminated against those housewives, who received on marriage – and with it dependency – reduced pensions, sickness and unemployment benefits.[128]

It is hard to see that the connection between American and British feminists would have been much closer, or the performance of feminists in the two countries much more effective, if activists had been differently organised and more united. They would still have felt the constraining influence of different wartime, international, class and race conditions. It is in this light that we must view the better child care facilities secured for British women, rather than in the light of the (admittedly damaging) conflicts about their provision among American feminists. Some feminist coalitions were attempted on each side of the Atlantic; but reformer coalitions are notoriously hard to sustain, and British labour women were usually opposed to them. The efforts made by bodies of privileged women like the AAUW, BPW and BFBPW to further their members' professional advancement can be condemned as narrow and selfish.[129] However, in an era when specialist women's associations were strong and wide-ranging feminist associations were not, such efforts were more likely to succeed than 'blanket' equal rights measures and universalist claims.

Conclusions

The First and Second World Wars have both been presented as great modern wars, whose modernising influence was felt by women as well as men.[130] However, it now seems clear that fitting wartime women into a single conceptual framework is unwise, whether the stress is upon their emancipation or their subordination. As Brabon and Summerfield point out, the two world wars were very different in terms of civilian involvement, military technology, the nature of the American role, global reach, and public attitudes to the conflict.[131] And with respect to the Second World War, Summerfield's wide researches have demonstrated that the responses of women to the hostilities were as varied and complex as the pressures placed upon them.[132]

This chapter has tried to show that though there was no overall transformation of women's position in the United States and Britain, and though government, union and class attitudes proved hard to alter, the Second World War was nevertheless profoundly significant for the American and British women's movements in four main ways. In the first place, it ushered in a new era of less Eurocentric and more loosely organised female internationalism. Second, the war years strengthened the link between African American women and the civil rights movement: a link which had been slowly developing since the early twentieth century, and which benefited both. Third, while the labour movements of the two countries were able to offer women wartime gains, and female activists fought, and would continue to fight, against sexual discrimination in the workplace, organised labour failed to establish its appeal to more than a minority of working women. Finally, the war confirmed United States ascendancy within the Anglo-American connection – a long maturing power shift which permanently affected relations between British and American reformers.

Throughout the years leading to war in 1939, women pacifists and internationalists displayed in vigorous anti-fascist activities the organisational strength that they had built up since the First World War. Moreover, in the cause of antifascism they showed that willingness to co-operate with other like-minded bodies and individuals that can sometimes be crucial to the success of pressure groups and social movements, and which had not normally been their hallmark between the wars. Unfortunately, the Spanish Civil War aggravated the division between pacificist and pacifist women, leaving pacifists to make a weakened stand against militarism at the onset of the Second World War. The mass of women may have opposed pacifism in the 1914–18 war, as Richard Evans maintains;[133] but the association of suffragism, socialism and pacifism during that conflict did give peace activists the power to alarm politicians. With more public support existing for the Second World War, and fewer conscientious objectors to focus dissent, women campaigners in the 1940s enjoyed no such power and had to make the best of a low profile, undertaking carefully chosen war work, and lobbying for a just peace and a new international organisation to make sure that it endured. In addition, they drew on their interwar experiences in internationalism to press successfully for a commitment to sexual equality in the UN Charter, for a UN Commission on the Status of Women and for a UN Universal Declaration of Human Rights.

The last of these three achievements also owed much to agitation by African Americans and representatives of the developing nations, and there was a risk from the outset that international work for human rights – like women's interwar campaigns for citizenship rights – might ignore women's special concerns. National self-interest was not vanquished but rather given a new forum by the creation of the United Nations, and the task of translating fine words into meaningful action remained. Nor had the machinery of the new internationalism or the conduct of foreign policy among the world's nations been feminised by the end of the war. However, American and British internationalists looked forward to tackling the huge challenges that lay ahead, and at least in 1946 Britain belatedly agreed to admit women to the Foreign Office on a permanent basis. The war had helped to bring about a reappraisal of female abilities, albeit opponents of the move still argued that women 'were less objective than men, less capable of keeping secrets, less good at teamwork, more liable to allow authority to go to their heads and more prone to let enthusiasm run away with them'.[134]

In the area of work – voluntary and paid – the British and American governments saw the need to mobilise women and to deal with their societies. Yet they were committed at the same time to upholding traditional female roles and had no wish to involve women as equal partners in the war planning agencies. In both Britain and the United States, female legislators co-operated across party lines in their desire to help women. But their efforts often had only a wartime relevance, and the women's movements no longer commanded enough support to pose a threat to male power brokers. Race questions were more worrying to politicians, with the British government exercised about the impact of increasing numbers of persons of colour in Britain, and the United States government anxious about the power of African Americans to expose the gulf between America's international ideals and domestic racial practice. The fact that black American organisations were gaining strength and that their leaders were prepared to demand a reward for their loyalty made it sensible for black women activists to support them. From this point onwards, there was no prospect of them transferring their allegiance to the white dominated women's groups, except on an occasional basis for a specific campaign.

Women did follow their own wishes and needs by claiming a larger share in the paid workforce than they had enjoyed between the wars, with more older and married women employed – a development of enormous significance. So, too, was the separation of women activists by class. Established by the early twentieth century, though denied in the United States, it was strengthened during the interwar years and continued through the 1940s in both countries, notwithstanding the survival until 1950 of the American WTUL. Although the Second World War was represented as 'a people's war', workplace and social contacts between the classes were not transformed on either side of the Atlantic, and only in Britain was reform anticipated with the coming of peace.

While American and British women alike were affected by the wartime elevation of all things masculine, by the changing fortunes of internationalism, by improved opportunities in the paid labour force and union movement, and by the greater salience of race, the impact of the Second World War on the Anglo-American connection meant that in the long as well as the short term, women activists in the two countries were destined to go their own ways. Between 1939 and 1945, their different priorities can be seen in the focus of American feminists on equal pay and the ERA, and of their British counterparts on a combination of equal rights and welfare legislation. Furthermore, the British were aware of American power, and for all their sympathy with British suffering, the Americans were aware of it too. This superior power can be seen in the eventual post-war resurgence of feminism.

8 The post-war women's movements

Old themes and new emphases

For those who lived through them, the women's movements that had emerged by the 1970s seemed very different from their pre-Second World War predecessors in terms of style and objectives. Stressing the importance of their women's liberation shock troops, they signalled at the outset that familiar efforts for women's rights were to be buttressed by something more assertive and less respectable. Often ignorant of the actual range, achievements and survival of first phase feminism, uninhibited campaigners set out to remedy its perceived omissions, and they were buoyed up by a sense that social circumstances were encouraging, and hence that feminism was once again practical politics. It will be the purpose of this chapter to show, however, that old problems endured throughout the exciting years of resurgence, among them divisions caused by race, class and internationalism. And most attention will be given to race, since this was the most disruptive of the three issues.

Feminism's context and main features

Social circumstances by the 1970s were indeed hopeful. Even in the 1950s, female activism had not disappeared in either Britain or the United States. Despite the constraints imposed by post-war political conservatism, and the pressing need for young recruits, more leverage in party politics, and greater co-operation among surviving women's groups and legislators, feminists still worked for peace and internationalism, equal pay, more women in positions of influence – and, in America, for the ERA and civil rights. The decade was, in fact, a caretaker period for feminism, not a blank. That period ended and new hopes were kindled during the 1960s. In both countries the kind of liberal to left politics then flourished that has generally been necessary for feminist advances. The widespread use of the contraceptive pill; more tolerant attitudes towards unconventional sexual preferences and sex outside marriage; greater indulgence of the young; the high level of female employment; some equal pay gains; and women's awareness of their power as consumers: all these were factors suggesting that further change might be achieved, once new feminist leaders and organisations had emerged. In the United States, encouragment could be derived from the returning interest in feminist concerns of such established women's bodies as the women's clubs and the League of Women Voters, and from the growing number of educated women who were concerned with both public issues and private advancement. Moreover, the achievements of the American civil rights movement stimulated reformers of all kinds, and British women were likewise affected by the other social movements of their time.[1]

The gains of the new feminists were swift and varied. Discovering that what they had to say was deemed interesting and newsworthy, they spread their message through leaflets, books, journals, consciousness-raising groups, and existing and new women's organisations. The range of viable women's associations meant that they could focus on the national as well as the local scene, on specific issues as well as goals that united a cross-section of women.[2] The vast ethnic, racial, geographical, and political diversity of the United States had always guaranteed that it would sustain a legion of pressure groups, and the elaborate organisation of the American feminist movement by the end of the nineteenth century was a special source of strength, even if the separation of women by race was an enduring reproach to white women. Second wave feminism dramatically boosted this separatist trend among white and African American women alike. Notwithstanding the growing numbers of newcomers it received in the course of the nineteenth century from Ireland and continental Europe, and via the settlements of black political radicals and seamen, Britain had remained a far less cosmopolitan country than the United States, responding warily to colour questions during the Second World War (see chapter 7) and to Commonwealth immigration from the 1950s to the 1960s. It traditionally afforded black women fewer female organisational outlets, obliging them to join male dominated black British societies (see chapter 5). With the resurgence of feminism, however, black activists in Britain were able to turn to female community groups which raised interest and funds for local projects. They involved themselves in the National Organization of Women of Asian and African Descent (1978–82). And they raised their voices – frequently angry – in black feminist tracts.[3]

Besides creating a new literature and new organisations, women set about refashioning feminist ideology. For many years, discussions had focused on the allegedly bourgeois nature of white feminism, the definition of feminist aims and the reconciliation of women's demands for public rights with their acceptance of a special role relating to motherhood and the care of the private home. Campaigners in the later twentieth century, faced with criticisms about the offensiveness and inaccuracy of early feminism's universalist claims, but determined to strengthen their sense of sisterhood, supported a range of ideological emphases which acknowledged and capitalised upon feminist diversity. These included radical feminism, which aimed to substitute a female culture for the patriarchy which dominated all aspects of society; socialist feminism, which stressed the patriarchal nature of capitalism, exposed the elaborate exploitation of women in their productive capacity, and urged their need to work with other oppressed elements in society; black feminism, which recognised that race, class and gender considerations interlocked to subordinate black women; liberal feminism, which largely accepted the status quo but updated and enlarged the women's rights agenda; and an analysis of the role of language in constructing and sustaining the patriarchy. To critical commentators, the main danger here was that feminism, like the first New Left in Britain (1956–62), appeared to display 'an excessive intellectual pluralism' that was no more helpful to it than the simpler equality versus difference debate had once been.[4]

Sexual issues had not been neglected by first wave feminists; rather this group became bolder, with the passage of time, about what they were willing to raise and work for. Second wave feminists were none the less more radical in this area, playing down the importance of biological differences between the sexes, abandoning the old feminist glorification of motherhood, debating instead the implications of women's domestic labour, and highlighting the concept of sexual liberation. If women's concern for control over their own bodies had emerged in the nineteenth century, the late twentieth century gave an unprecedented boost to efforts to achieve abortion reform; to get rape and sexual harassment to be taken seriously; to generate a frank debate about lesbian aims and ideas; and to discredit women's disparaging treatment as sexual objects.[5]

Familiar women's rights objectives were taken up in a new way and with a new determination. Thus, for example, in the United States President Kennedy created a National Commission on the Status of Women (NCSW) in 1961, with Eleanor Roosevelt as its powerful chair and the head of the Women's Bureau, Esther Peterson, as its driving force. Notwithstanding its carefully balanced, mixed sex composition, the commission proved willing to produce an agenda to improve women's circumstances, to reach out to women's associations, and to see the formation of similar commissions at the state level. The NCSW also gave rise to the National Organisation of Women (NOW, 1966), which – headed by the best selling feminist author, Betty Friedan – became the effective mouthpiece for American liberal feminism. Its efforts were helped by the Equal Employment Opportunity Commission (EEOC). Set up by the 1964 Civil Rights Act, it got off to a slow start but was given power to go to the courts on its own account in 1972, by which time it sympathised with NOW's campaign to eradicate national discriminatory employment practices. Although abortion reform efforts had seemed to make similarly slow progress, in *Roe* v *Wade* (1973), 'the first abortion case to reach the Supreme Court', a sympathetic but subsequently controversial decision ruled that abortion 'was a fundamental right, guaranteed by the right to privacy and the clause of the Fourteenth Amendment' (1868).[6]

British progress was less dependent on court and executive action and more on the exertions of a few dedicated legislators (to be found in America, too), and the work of women's groups such as the Fawcett Society. There was no equivalent of NOW in Britain, whose unitary political system and powerful establishment fostered lobbying by small cadres dedicated to specific reforms. None the less, between 1967 and 1969 feminists in Britain contributed to the legalisation of abortion, the removal of the barrier to the provision of birth control help on the National Health Service, and divorce law reform; and a British women's liberation movement had emerged by the late 1960s. It has been persuasively assessed by Eve Setch, who, though stressing that it displayed complex and sometimes bitter ideological divisions from the outset, sees these as educative, directly linked to feminist practice, and not a barrier to co-operation between the different elements of the movement. In 1970, some six hundred British women assembled for an influential conference on women's liberation at Ruskin College, Oxford, and adopted as their goals equal pay; equal education and opportunity; twenty-four hour nurseries; free contraception; and abortion on demand. The Labour Party's women MPs proved willing to act on part of this programme at least, and for a while they and women in the larger labour movement were able to work together. The Conservative Party, anxious to increase its share of the female vote, was also interested in furthering women's interests.

In consequence, women gained from the Equal Pay Act of 1970, which conceded equal pay for the same or similar work; the Sex Discrimination Act (SDA) of 1975, which 'made it illegal for a woman to be treated less favourably than a man, because she was a woman, in the areas of housing, employment, education and training and the provision of goods and services'; and the Equal Opportunities Commission, established by the SDA and designed to oversee the Equal Pay Act and SDA by 'promoting equal opportunities and fighting cases of discrimination'. Legislation improving women workers' maternity leave and pension rights, giving women equal guardianship of their children, acknowledging their 'non-financial contribution to a marriage', improving the enforcement of 'court-ordered maintenance payments against husbands', and allocating child benefit as a universal cash payment made straight to mothers, were additional British achievements of the 1970s.[7] In both countries, campaigns to elect more women legislators were undertaken. And in both countries, renewed national political endeavours were supplemented by women co-operating with local authorities, and with state and local governments, on projects which could make an impact in the short term: for example, programmes to tackle poverty, to curb violence against women, to offer job training and to provide child care.[8]

In the encouraging conditions of the 1960s and 1970s, the ERA at last seemed like a serious political proposition. Taken up by the NCSW and NOW, it apparently aroused less opposition within labour circles and the American women's movement than it had ever done before. The National Council of Jewish Women, for example, had once condemned it, but had shifted its position by 1970, working at the state and federal level for a measure it had come to see as 'a human rights issue which will be to the benefit of every citizen'. But the amendment, though it had been approved by Congress by 1972, could not muster the same degree of support in the states, where it lost momentum and hence allowed opponents to mobilise. Especially was this the case in the South, which still feared the ERA as an assault on its sexually and racially segregated society: the proponents of the amendment, after all, claimed that it would benefit black women because of their unequal circumstances and that it would help in the fight against 'other oppressions'.[9] The feminist focus on the ERA was understandable: if secured, the amendment would have had both a 'tremendous symbolic value' and a major impact upon judicial decisions and state laws. On the other hand, the fallout that would follow from going down to defeat with the

ERA – as eventually happened in 1982 – was bound to be great, and some activists were beginning to pin their hopes for challenging, modifying or striking down discriminatory laws on the 1964 Civil Rights Act, the EEOC, and the equal protection clause of the Fourteenth Amendment.[10]

Throughout all their organising and campaigning, feminists on each side of the Atlantic were, for the first time, generally free of embarrassment about being feminist – free of that self-deprecation which has not afflicted, say, socialists or pacifists, and which has allowed women's critics to deride their lack of conviction as reformers. Indeed, as Janet Radcliffe Richards has pointed out, some new wave feminists even used to claim – often with the confidence of youth – that feminism was the primary struggle among struggles, and male supremacy the oldest and worst form of discrimination. They thereby alienated those who were ready to accept feminism if it were more reasonably presented as a reaction against a type of '*systematic social injustice*' directed against women '*because of their sex*'.[11] Yet reason had been the hallmark of early women's rights campaigns, producing at best a stalled revolution. The second wave black feminist lawyer and lecturer Florynce Kennedy turned away from liberal conciliation, declaring that the 'last thing an oppressed person can afford is to be reasonable . . . the minute you get a bit out of hand, they've got to start listening to you because you've gotten in the way of the smooth functioning of the system'. Kennedy was not alone. Many feminists of the 1960s and 1970s were angry, and this certainly gained attention but also proved as unacceptable to society at large as black militancy. The last angry feminists had been the British suffragettes, who, though attracting worldwide attention, always endured more censure than praise. Even the fairly modest level of direct action and street theatre sustained by women's liberation and radical peace women produced hostility as well as publicity. Women's liberation was associated with 'things like bra burning and marching', just as the suffragettes were invariably remembered as being chained to railings. None of these protests involved more than a minority of militants, but since to critics they seemed to be quintessentially unfeminine, they quickly assumed iconic status.[12]

Race

If the civil rights movement was one of the forces that helped to ignite 1960s feminism, was it strong enough finally to reconcile the two great forces of gender and race, as far as American women were concerned? Were minority groups, under the impact of the civil rights struggle, able to come together and surmount old prejudices? The answer must be no. The career of the distinguished black American writer, educator, lawyer and activist Pauli Murray (see also chapter 5) is an excellent illustration of what was involved in seeking such a reconciliation. Murray devoted much of her life to striving for an 'adequate consideration of the inter-structuring of racism, sexism and economic exploitation'.[13] She recognised, however, the enormity of the task she had set herself in a world where most people did 'not want to carry the burden of justifying their existence'.[14] As part of the generation that had lived through the Depression, the Second World War and 1960s militancy, Murray always took the wider view, but she was aware that she had to co-operate with upcoming activists who were 'so lacking in historical perspective that they seemed destined to repeat all the errors of other movements which have become the God that failed'.[15]

Murray relied on spreading her ideas through NOW and on the lecture circuit, trying to convince her audiences that revolutionary movements 'feed one another', and that it was vital that they did, since the powerful had a 'habit of playing one group of the disadvantaged against another'.[16] Arguing that women were frequently overlooked by elites which monitored matters of concern to them, Murray was clear that self-absorption was not the answer, either for them or for minorities. She declared that the way forward for groups like the Japanese Americans was to move beyond their desire for civil rights and to 'take an active interest in other minority problems'. And despite the fact that when white women proclaimed themselves to be their non-white women's 'sisters in the struggle for women's equality', they 'were too often strangers across a cultural chasm', Murray was emphatic that they should 'communicate and cooperate . . . wherever possible'. Their common problems and interests as women, she believed, provided 'a bridge to span initial self-consciousness' – and the 'cultural chasm'.[17]

Murray was also able to devise policies in line with her desire to unite embattled elements in society. As a member of the NCSW, encouraged to reconcile women's conflicting attitudes towards the ERA, she highlighted the possibility of uniting women *and* advancing their struggle for constitutional equality by mobilising them behind the equal protection clause of the Fourteenth Amendment.[18] Another novel suggestion was that minority activists should seek emancipation through focusing on their broad human rights. These had been defined by the United Nations in 1948, and Murray recommended that everyone read the UN Declaration in their homes and make 'themselves as familiar with it as we are with our own Constitution'. A human rights amendment could then be substituted for the ERA and would, Murray contended, 'reduce tensions between the Civil Rights (black, Hispanic, Oriental, etc.) movements and the Women's Movement'. Such a shift of focus would require a different way of thinking: 'Whites must become a little Blacker and Blacks a little whiter . . . Women must become a little more Male and Men must become a little more Female'; in short, 'all of us must become a little more human'.

Determined to do as well as to think, Murray worked for her new order through the American Civil Liberties Union. And she was quite right to stress the adaptable nature of the American Constitution: politicians had long perceived it to be a vehicle for growth in the nation and the progress of the civil rights movement provided proof of this on a grand scale. Yet most women were probably unaware of the ERA until the ratification campaign, and were even less likely to have been familiar with the equal protection clause of the Fourteenth Amendment and the UN's Universal Declaration of Human Rights.[19] Moreover, Murray's ambitious aims were threatened by her courageous criticisms of other activists. She declared, for instance, that the revered Dr Martin Luther King was limited by his 'historical patriarchal conditioning'. As a result of that conditioning, he 'was never quite able to integrate the women of his movement into positions of leadership, thereby robbing his collective effort of half its strength and wisdom'. She censured other black male leaders for monopolising the gains derived from civil rights activism, and for their increasingly authoritarian temper. And she faulted them for their preoccupation with 'collective advancement' and the 'maximisation of group power' – a tendency that risked obliterating the 'respect for human personality which we have so long demanded from others'.[20]

Notwithstanding Murray's youthful radicalism, her subsequent desire for inclusion in the social mainstream limited the 'inter-structuring' role that she could play among minorities. In fairness, however, no person or group could have persuaded the African, Native, Mexican, Chinese and Japanese Americans substantially to alter their relations with each other, even if they all took whatever benefits they could from the civil rights upheavals of the 1960s and 1970s. They were separated by settlement patterns, language, history and economic competition, and were loyal to their own representative organisations. Their efforts for self-improvement were for a long time expected to be conducted in the context of achieving assimilation into the larger American society, an objective which primarily benefited the state but which afforded those leaders who publicly supported it respectability and a legitimate claim to be mediating between two worlds. Increasingly in the twentieth century, however, acculturation became the goal of racial minorities. Whichever process they embraced, minority groups were not encouraged to make common cause.[21]

Of course all minorities had an interest in increasing their involvement in politics. Yet for the most part their activists were too few and their loyalty to the Democratic Party too unwavering to buy them much return. Hence difficulties generally faced those feminists of colour who did advocate political 'coalition building with individuals engaged in similar social justice projects', just as they had faced the coalitions of white feminist and labour organisations which pushed for agreed legislative goals during the interwar years. Probably the best way of achieving a new level of woman-friendly political exchange between American minorities would have been through informal networks committed to a few clear aims and locally relevant projects, but they would obviously have taken time to build up, and would have distracted the minority women who were forming their own feminist operations (such as Asian Women United and Asian Sisters in Action).[22]

Members of minority groups have naturally disliked being lumped together, even when greater collaboration might have brought some advantage: Native Americans, for instance, did not see Red Power as a spinoff from Black Power, but as a product of their own warrior traditions. A link with the African American community did, however, offer real benefits to any disadvantaged group, and whatever others might say, black leaders were clear that 'most of these people pattern their resistance after blacks'.[23] Murray herself, though wanting a voice for all minority women, was keen to speak for the African American women who (in

1970) constituted 93 per cent of all nonwhite American women. And, as an African American, she was also proud to declare that 'It is our destiny as the largest and most controversial minority in the United States to be the barometer of the state of democracy in our own country'.[24] The black minority was special because of its experience of slavery, the southern caste system and urban unrest: all of concern to opinion outside America. It was special in the degree of guilt it aroused among white liberals, whose support was crucial to the passage of civil rights legislation.[25] And it was special because black disenchantment with the leadership of the Democratic Party had led to a high rate of black defection from the party by the middle of the 1950s. In other words, African Americans constituted a minority large and confident enough to question (albeit briefly) its customary political allegiance.[26] Could black women capitalise upon these advantages?

Alas, a number of entangled race, class and gender factors conspired to make this impossible. Black women had an established role in the civil rights movement, which grew with the movement and which they had long linked to their concerns as women. But the involvement of often privileged young white women in the civil rights campaign via the Student Nonviolent Co-ordinating Committee (1960), and their strong objections to being subordinated by black male leaders, produced unhelpful tensions between white women and black men as well as between white and black women. The latter did not see this as a key issue and objected to white women reproving black men. Some alienated white women moved away to pursue feminist goals in groups of their own devising. And African American women were in due course themselves embarrassed as well as energised by the emergence of the authoritarian Black Power movement, with its emphasis on violence, confrontation and masculinity. Black women, by contrast, continued to excel as initiators and sustainers of local projects, including the organisation of voter registration drives and boycotts, logistics management and the mounting of freedom schools. Such activities were, by the 1960s, recognised to be vital to racial and gender advancement; but it was not conceded by men that women's sustaining of communities and men's public representation of the cause were equally important. African American women who could no longer tolerate such a state of affairs looked for opportunities in separate associations, notably the National Black Feminist Organisation (1973), the National Alliance of Black Feminists (1976), and the National Association of Black Professional Women (1977).

Black and white feminists failed to come together at this critical juncture. But the gulf between them did not simply follow from civil rights experiences; it was also the consequence of habitual mutual mistrust and, increasingly, of non-negotiable differences over feminist ideology and political priorities. Under the circumstances, most black women were wise to retain their civil rights connection and – as black professor Dr Julianne Malveaux put it – to 'develop [their] . . . consciousness without viewing black men as the enemy'; after all, nurturing them was a task made much easier by the fact that they 'are not the economic oppressor (though their attitudes may be oppressive, which is another story)'.[27]

Black and white female American activists were not alone in finding it difficult to strike a satisfactory balance between race and gender interests. In a recent study, Elizabeth Anne Castle has examined the role of women campaigners and the tensions between men and women in the American Indian Movement. As far as AIM women are concerned, Castle has clearly established their important responsibilities as activists, in addition to discussing the difficulties involved in trying to tackle the issue of gender inequality within Indian activism at large. Castle further shows that the organisational separation of the sexes afforded Native American women a way of strengthening their position in their various communities.[28] The same could be said of Asian and Chicana feminists, emerging by the 1970s. As analysed by Alma Garcia, Chicana feminists were obliged to place their discourse in the larger Chicano movement; to clarify their position on sexism in that community; to gain acceptance for the centrality of racial oppression in explaining women's oppression; to rebut the familiar charges that feminism was anti-men and subversive of cultural nationalism; and to work out their relationship with white middle-class feminists. While in theory they favoured linking with the white movement, all these troublesome issues meant that in practice Chicana feminists prudently 'stressed the importance of developing autonomous feminist organisations that would address the struggles of Chicanas as members of an ethnic minority and as women'.[29]

In Britain and America, women of colour had aims and burdens in common. Most attractive was their attempt to fight sexism within the context of a larger battle against race and class exploitation, at home and abroad. Less attractively, the gender prejudices of many British men of colour matched those of the Americans; and white British feminists, like their American counterparts, were inclined to give undue priority to their own objectives. Thus in the eyes of women of colour they paid too much attention to such issues as abortion and legal rights, and gave insufficient time to low wages, working conditions, domestic violence, inadequate educational facilities, and police and racial harassment. And even those who avoided these prejudices were aware that the variety among American and British activists, and their regrouping in the face of changing circumstances, posed formidable problems for would-be organisers.

Conversely, there were Anglo-American differences that made a difference. In the first place, black British feminists owed a greater debt to the writings of black American radicals and the practice of Black Power than did their American sisters. The imports did not lose their drawbacks with travel, and a home-grown radicalism might have been more helpful to activist women of colour, not least by proving less short-lived. Second, whereas British women of colour frequently hesitated to call themselves feminists, because the term was not associated 'with any serious politics' and was even used 'in a derogatory way, as a term of abuse', poll evidence showed their African American sisters to be strongly in favour of feminism. Their longer experience of what it involved allowed them to rise above contemporary quarrels in a way that black British newcomers could not quickly do. Third, the Commonwealth immigrants had to grapple with problems that southern blacks migrating to the northern United States had faced decades previously, including getting on terms with established non-whites. Women of colour throughout Britain were drawn into new protest groups from the 1960s.[30] But their efforts evolved behind those of white feminists, without the ideological and personal links that whites – and African American activists – had been building since the nineteenth century.

Internationalism

If race remained a divisive force among both British and American feminists, internationalism had become an even more contentious area than it had been between the two world wars. While the domination of its activities by white westerners was clearly over, it was not immediately apparent how women of colour and non-western women would exert their influence and what the role of the United Nations would be. Although the old hostility to women taking any interest in foreign affairs had gone, it remained to be seen whether they would develop a distinctive approach to the external world. Women had once again to determine their best way of organising for peace, with American activists facing two special and consuming challenges in anti-Communism and the Vietnam War. And after 1945, American and British feminists had to see whether their relationship in reform would dwindle further as the United States strengthened its superpower status and took up new causes.

The pre-war internationalists had supported regular conferences, for the personal and information exchanges they made possible and the publicity they attracted. But with huge numbers of official representatives and non-governmental organisations to accommodate, the conferences through which the UN highlighted women's concerns were less sedate and manageable affairs. Indeed, in 1975 and 1980, bitter resentments surfaced between women of colour and white women over western women's assumption that they could define feminism, treating as universal that which was culture bound and locally generated. Similarly controversial was the widespread tendency to sidestep lesbians' existence and concerns. By the time of the 1985 UN Conference, women activists had come to terms with each other; but the public reaction was mixed and critics were not won over by signs of greater harmony among the feminists. The explanation for this wariness among conservatives seems to have been that the conference movement – buttressed by the UN's Decade for Women (1975–85) – both reflected and encouraged the growth of feminism and pacifism. It forced feminists to review their programmes and tactics at the national level, where new contacts were made between women and new groups formed. And it obliged national governments to give women's activism more attention than normal by encouraging them 'to change discriminatory policies and promote gender equality'.[31]

WILPF's preparation for the International Women's Year that opened the UN Decade for Women showed that even an association that was small and slow to change could catch some fire from a fresh approach. Its proposals for 1975 covered peace; education; national self-determination and development; the

United Nations; and equality 'in society, in legislation, and in reality', not one of which 'just falls into women's laps'. According to WILPF, women were not overwhelmed by familiar enemies but commanded possibilities for action in 'women's and youth organisations, in trades unions, in parliamentary bodies and local government, in religious, social and cultural institutions, in factories and offices, in villages and towns, in national and world-wide organisations'.[32] Unfortunately, progress on identified international problems eventually depended not only on sympathetic internationalist politicians but also on favourable economic conditions and effective follow-up action in the countries concerned: a combination of factors which was immensely hard to secure.

In neither Britain nor the United States did women develop a collective foreign policy orientation that moved much beyond the early emphasis of activists on the need for international institutions, arbitration, peace and disarmament, and action on issues of particular interest to women such as the reform of married women's nationality rights (a campaign which achieved success in 1957 when the UN endorsed independent nationality rights for women as an international standard). Women's agenda of domestic spending priorities that would be facilitated by a reformed foreign policy was only just emerging. Yet in both countries there was a discernible tendency for women to be more hostile to militarism than men;[33] and this 'gender gap' helped to keep the post-war women's peace movement going, despite its frequent lapses into obscurity. Peace organisations supported each other as their fortunes fluctuated, highlighting the enormity of the nuclear arms race, mounting days of protest, staging marches and demonstrations, producing petitions, distributing literature, and lobbying established and prospective politicians. While some peace groups concentrated their focus, others, like WILPF, remained convinced that security from war required not only disarmament but also 'economic progress and social justice, respect for human rights and basic freedoms, genuine interaction among peoples, and tolerance'. Radical activists emerged on each side of the Atlantic and, influenced by a profound concern for the impact of militarism on the environment, they showed a particular flair for theatrical protests. Their best known creations were the peace encampments situated near depositories for the Cruise and Pershing II nuclear missiles; and they included the American Seneca army depot and the British Greenham Common airbase. The world of the suffragettes was conjured up by camp women's imaginative propaganda and willingness to endure fierce clashes with authority. Peace encampments appropriately began in Britain (in 1981), and in their course they changed the widespread image that existed of peace women as ineffectual and vaguely comical.

The radicalisation of female peace activism did, however, carry some obvious risks, as Liddington has shown. Its growing association with feminism alarmed those who thought the connection to be distracting without being likely to bring in many supporters. Other critics wanted to shift pacificism's focus away from male violence directed by the state in wartime and towards the domestic and sexual aspects of male violence against women. Although earlier peace women had debated the connection between men's public and private power and violence, they had more often been concerned to pursue the link between maternalism and peace. And this approach alienated younger activists who were hostile towards universalist claims, opposed to setting women apart and treating them as victims, and anxious to inject a new degree of militance into peace advocates' non-violence.[34] Additional problems had a more familiar ring: among them the need to recruit more young women and more women of colour; the need to show that their small numbers did not necessarily consign peace supporters to impotence; the need to operate as insiders as well as outsiders; the need to raise more money for movement operations; the need to work harmoniously with men and non-feminists; and the need to strike a balance between retaining left-wing support and not being dismissed as disloyal extremists.[35]

Under these trying circumstances, it would have been unreasonable to expect overall Anglo-American reformer relations to have blossomed. On the peace front, the Americans continued to be stronger, and news of American events and debates reached Britain quickly and sometimes helped British debates along. But in the debates generated from the 1970s, American arguments 'did not always translate smoothly to Britain'.[36] Intellectual exchanges between British and American women in the feminist movement as a whole were similarly significant but problematical. In particular, the determination of many British activists to locate feminism within a European socialist tradition distanced them from American feminists who from the 1960s were influenced by their country's New Left, with its indifference to political dogma and argument that the personal was political. There were also Anglo-American differences over radical feminism, for British feminists found it hard to accept the rejection or drastic reformulation of Marxist ideas in the interest of redefining the primary nature of women's oppression. And the quarrels that had swiftly developed in American feminism over sexual issues (especially lesbianism and rape) offered the British a warning about the danger of being over dependent, intellectually, on the dynamic American movement.[37] This was not always easy to heed, given the larger number of United States feminists whose work was known beyond their own boundaries – beginning in 1963 with Betty Friedan's *The Feminine Mystique*, an analysis of the grievances of middle-class women which produced a huge trans-Atlantic impact. The earlier start of second wave feminism in America was part of the explanation. So, too, was the vast size of the country, its powerful publishing industry, and its support for women's studies as an academic discipline. However, long after second wave feminism had peaked, American celebrity feminists found a good reception for their ideas on the lucrative lecture circuit.[38] And notwithstanding American media dominance, in both countries the legitimacy and popularity of studying women had been accepted, with publishers responding eagerly to the work they produced.

Despite the growth of feminist communication via the United Nations and other new organisations, there was still room for trans-Atlantic goodwill exchanges by individual internationalists like the American peace advocate Mary Dingham and the British journalist Monica Whately; for scholarships and educational visits to enlarge the outlook of the young; and for lecture tours sponsored by such bodies as the Carrie Chapman Catt Memorial Fund and the British–American Associates.[39] After all, thanks to the media, some British women apparently thought that their American counterparts led 'lives of indolence, ease and glamour and that our children run the streets', while others still made false assumptions about the closeness of the United States and Britain because of their shared language.[40]

None the less, the foreign policies of America and Britain were further apart than they had been during the already strained interwar years, and this shaped what individuals thought and did in the two countries. While the loss of the empire and status rankled bitterly with Britain, the United States assumed the costs of power, dispensing aid with care, co-operating with Britain in some parts of the world when it suited but usually seeking to pursue its own economic advantage in the post-imperial era. As the American labour internationalist Maida Springer Kemp saw matters, it was vital that the United States took every opportunity of involvement with the 'underdeveloped' world, since America's 'own hugely productive system depends, in part, upon the rise of productivity and living standards' of overseas workers. It was also deemed necessary, during the Cold War, when the Communist opponents of the United States were said to be 'making a drive for the support of women, particularly in the East and Arab nations', to bring to the world 'a knowledge of the leadership that America has always given to the movement for the liberation of women' and to link female activism abroad more closely with the process of Americanisation.[41] Nationalism might always be an intrinsic part of internationalism, but to Britons living in austerity and increasingly dominated by American popular culture, American assertiveness appeared in a less than amiable light. This was not the time to hope for closer Anglo-American links on public questions of common concern, such as race. Accordingly, as the American civil rights revolution gathered force, the Americans needed no spur from the British; and as Commonwealth immigration to Britain increased, British conservatives chose to focus negatively on the urban dimension of America's 'race problem', associating it with over-crowding, violence and the enlargement of the working class, and deploring the prospect of such problems occurring in Britain.[42]

Class

If race and international issues were incapable of uniting women, it would have been remarkable if economic questions had been capable of doing so. In both Britain and America, progress was made, but in neither country could activists greatly intensify the advantages to be derived from unionism or socialist feminism. This was partly the result of environmental factors. In the United States, union gains made during the 1930s came under attack during the Cold War, while working women were said to face 'bitter discrimination'. And on both sides of the Atlantic, although the female paid workforce continued to grow from the 1970s, and women generally were able to gain entry to a wider range of occupations, most of the new jobs were 'low-paid, unskilled, part-time and temporary', disadvantaging the older women and women of colour who tended not to be offered training for advancement.[43]

There was another – and familiar – obstacle in the way of change. Women in the unions recognised the importance of solidarity with male allies, especially where they belonged to vulnerable groups like the Chicanas and Mexicanas.[44] But bourgeois feminists allegedly remained wedded to the pursuit of individual self-interest. In the judgement of American activist Mary Callahan, of the International Union of Electrical Workers, feminists and unionists 'don't see eye to eye on a lot of the ways to reach a goal. I think those women can't understand that a contract is a benefit to a woman as well as to a man. They are of the opinion that you go in and you pick out certain things that are just for us and you set up a dual line, you know, just for women and the men are something else. Union women don't see it that way. They see it that a union is a union, that's what it is, unity of the sexes, of the races, what have you.' Other activists were of like mind, suggesting that women still did not understand the value of a union as well as men, or appreciate the difference between membership of voluntary organisations and of unions which, representing a certain job, demanded strict adherence from their workers, who were not 'necessarily cause-minded . . . or wanting to change anything'. Despite their interest in equal pay, it was said still to be tempting for women to keep silent in unions where they did not have the weight of numbers and were not accustomed to sharing power with men. By contrast, a successful female organiser had to make herself heard; as one American unionist reflected, 'I am the Protest Queen'.[45]

Encouragingly, there was some evidence that younger women 'have more initiative; . . . They are more optimistic about their own future'. Such women were at least aware of the positive gains to be had from resurgent feminism, though they were 'probably five or six years behind the rest of the Women's Movement'.[46] The result was a cautious degree of backing for NOW; female unionist action through Title VII of the 1964 Civil Rights Act, which forbade sex discrimination in employment; and the creation of new, independent, women's labour groups in the United States – a welcome but not a startling development, given that the WTUL had survived there until 1950. Efforts to help British women workers nationally were channelled through the TUC, reflecting the continuing hostility to an independent feminism that prevailed in Britain's labour circles.

In 1974, America's Coalition of Labour Union Women (CLUW) brought together from fifty-eight unions some 3,000 women who were pledged to working within the established labour movement to improve their circumstances both as workers and as unionists. Specifically, this meant organising unorganised women into unions; working with unions in support of affirmative action; involving more union women in political campaigns to improve the conditions of women workers (including the campaign for ERA ratification); and encouraging participation of women within their unions.[47] In the next ten years, CLUW attracted 15,000 members, set up sixty local chapters, secured a place for its president on the AFL–CIO executive council, and proved itself sympathetic to feminism. Yet as Milkman has established, the organisation primarily attracted women union leaders rather than rank-and-file unionists. Given old labour's denunciation of feminists for helping individual women rather than the group, this outcome was ironical.[48] Feminists were also involved in the creation of independent working women's organisations among office workers, the most prominent of which was 9 to 5 (1973). The creation of public awareness of office workers' concerns was 9 to 5's initial aim, but after two years it was granted a charter from the powerful Service Employees' Industrial Union (SEIU), which took as its goal the national unionisation of clerical workers.[49] Did this mean 9 to 5's absorption in the main trade union movement? Milkman thinks not, since 9 to 5 retained some autonomy within SEIU, adopted a democratic organisation and sought to recruit rank-and-file members rather than female leaders.[50]

With the emergence of bodies like CLUW and 9 to 5, many lingering prejudices about feminists among American labour women were finally dispelled. There was nothing comparable to these organisations in Britain, although the American idea of affirmative action did spread across the Atlantic. Recognising the complexity of the factors that might inhibit working women's progress, positive action programmes were set for specific firms which devised hiring and training schedules, and laid down goals and timetables. Close monitoring of the programmes was vital and there were not enough of them to make a substantial impact; but they were a valuable new initiative in a movement that tended to work in terms of the protection of established benefits and differentials.[51]

In Britain, the American positive action initiative found its way into the SDA and was eventually promoted by the TUC, its Women's Advisory Committee and its Women's Conference.[52] Anxious to control the pressures for change sparked off by feminism, the TUC in 1975 updated its charter, Aims for Women at Work. From the mid-1970s, it supported the feminist defence of abortion rights. In 1978, it produced a charter which called for flexible hours for working parents, and for a 'comprehensive and universal service' of care and education for children from birth to five years. In 1981, the TUC Women's Conference highlighted the problems caused for women by the unequal division of work in the home, and the TUC recognised that the family wage was an outmoded concept which was contributing to female unemployment. However, while officially in favour of 'an end to all pay discrimination against women workers', the TUC did nothing to produce the 'intensive industrial campaigns' it knew were necessary to transform aims into reality.[53]

Individual unions often held out more hope for women. After all, in the United States and Britain alike, but especially in Britain, female membership of unions had increased. It was also likely to become more significant as manufacturing declined, while women's jobs and occupational concentration increased. A typical response from a sympathetic union was that of Britain's local government union, NALGO, which adopted guidelines for the achievement of sexual equality, workplace nurseries and rights for working parents.[54] Working women in Britain and the United States – with women of colour fully involved – also proved their willingness to take collective action, and they did so regardless of the renewed resistance to unionisation encountered in the southern United States during the 1950s and 1960s.[55] But however important women activists were on the picket lines, as fund raisers and organisers, they were no more able than the authors of new union guidelines to transform the basically conservative nature of the union movement.

In two other areas – labour internationalism and the unions' relationship with the political left – we find a comparable pattern of modest gains and stubborn obstacles. The International Labour Organisation, back in Geneva by the end of the 1940s, was transformed by the demands of the Latin American countries and the rise of independent countries in Africa, Asia and the Middle East. Technical assistance became more important than ever, and in due course most of the ILO's members came from developing areas. This did not mean that women's interests, which had been gaining ground in the organisation, were now slighted. The ILO supported initiatives on women, and in 1985 at its own conference and the women's international conference in Nairobi it endorsed 'equal opportunities and equal treatment for men and women in employment', and warned that the 'neglect or exclusion of women in decision-making processes could seriously jeopardize economic and social progress'. It was most important that the composition and preoccupations of all kinds of internationalism should be liberalised, but the domestic impact of ILO reforms on American and British workers was probably small.[56]

Could the political left do any better for women? On both sides of the Atlantic, the growth of socialist feminist debate in the early years of second wave feminism was helpful in enlarging contemporary understanding of women's oppression. In particular, it pointed out the crudeness of old socialism's assumption that the inclusion of women in the paid workforce would lead directly to their liberation, indicted its inadequate treatment of sex, and censured its enduring association of women with the private sphere. Second wave feminism also searched for a fresh way of defining women as a group, accepting that they could neither be ignored within the concept of class nor simply lumped together as a class. Gayle Rubin's term sex/gender system acknowledged the importance of gender as 'a significant category of social analysis', interacting in a complicated fashion with class and race.

The intensity of socialist feminist debate in books and journals was extremely heartening, given the long association of women with action rather than ideology. Yet a familiar problem quickly emerged. The new socialist activists, whose chief impact was predictably in Britain, were aware that working women and women of colour frequently needed immediate, material help – over, say, medical matters and welfare benefits. But providing it might become all consuming. The best that could be done in Britain was the extension of a limited amount of direct help – for example in the early 1970s strikes among low-paid women – and the offering of a radical perspective to those pressing for economic legislation.[57]

Conclusions

By the end of the 1970s, it was apparent that second wave feminism still provoked public interest on both sides of the Atlantic. But interest did not usually involve warmth, perhaps because the feminists had pitched their claims too high, failed to contain their most controversial elements, or been unable to show the wisdom of the diversity for which they had fought. All protest movements must be prepared for any charges of disunity that can plausibly be brought against them. But fearless second wave feminism was singularly rich in quarrels and schisms, which in due course encouraged anti-feminism in the two countries. In Britain, where anti-feminism was entrenched but often low profile, its proponents became organised and vocal on the issue of abortion, agitating against the grain of public opinion for limits to the 1967 act. In the United States, where conservatism was often crusading, where campaigners could generally find support in the South, and where the ERA had been sent for ratification in 1972, anti-feminism had a more vigorous existence. And ironically, Phyllis Schlafly, the best known and highly successful opponent of the ERA, would have made a wonderful feminist campaigner: confident, forthright, intelligent and well informed (with a rare interest in and expertise on foreign affairs).[58] Moreover, though her universalist maternalism could seem old-fashioned, Schlafly had an advantage not enjoyed by second wave feminists, namely security in an uncontested women's culture.

These and other difficulties warned that the 1980s would be bracing times for British and American feminists, even without the political lurch to the right in their two countries. But the race, internationalist and labour activists we have looked at here had at least held their own, just as they would in the decades to come.

Race remained a divisive force among British and American feminists. The opportunity of a coming together of all women of colour and ethnic background was not lost since it was never real. Established black activists were willing to do business with white women, even while challenging their pronouncements on race in the past and in the present. White women responded by upholding segregation, dealing with token African Americans, and generally begrudging them any gains that might be forthcoming from the civil rights movement.[59] On the whole, therefore, black feminists were obliged to pursue their varied objectives through a range of organisations: civil rights (generally with men, where they were crucially important but inadequately acknowledged); long established black women's groups (like the NCNW and the sororities); new black women-only associations (such as the National Black Feminist Organisation); and white dominated groups (when a shared concern made this worthwhile). Although black women found sexism quite unacceptable, many were prepared to handle it, when it occurred, without making it a public issue and humiliating their men, whom they had always absolved from being their oppressors. In this spirit, the complaints by white female civil rights activists about the discriminatory behaviour of their black male counterparts were treated as a second order issue.

No racial coalitions of the sort proposed by Pauli Murray and some women's minority groups proved possible. African American men opposed them as unnecessary, given the size of the black community and the achievements of its civil rights campaigners. Old established minority group organisations, which had struggled to establish their identity and ability as power brokers, had little obviously to gain from coalition politics. And young minority group feminists, who could see the value of co-operating with other groups interested in similar reform projects, found that differences with their proposed allies were alienating. Such feminists had the further burden of having to rebut accusations that their efforts were anti-men and unhelpful to the larger freedom movements sustained by their communities.

Activist women of colour in Britain had much in common with their non-white American sisters. Willing to work with their own men, they were none the less sometimes discomfited by the sexism they encountered. They shared with American activists a desire to place their struggle in the largest possible context, and an admiration for the beliefs and tactics of Black Power. They, too, operated within a racially diverse society whose cultural differences could not easily be set aside for the purpose of political campaigning. But they did not enjoy the advantage of large numbers and the support of a long established feminist network. They therefore could not make the overall impact on their country's feminist movement that African American women activists could on theirs.

Post-war internationalism mirrored the diversity and volatility of the post-war world. Women's international efforts were galvanised by the UN's promotion of interest in women's conferences, and by the involvement in these gatherings of women from all parts of the world. The early conferences were marred by well publicised quarrels over sexual issues and the assumption of white feminists that they could still tell the story of feminism and set its agenda. However the system settled down, and the activists of global feminism settled down to tackle the problem of persuading their national governments to act on the international agreements they endorsed.

The notion that women had no part to play in foreign policy had been swept away by the Second World War but women had yet to determine if they had any distinctive foreign policy voice. In both countries, there is evidence that women were more hostile to militarism than men, and certainly there were women in the American and British peace movements who provided proof of this. Attempting to update female pacifist ideology, some women also emphasised that male power not only damaged them as mothers who lost children to war, but also hurt them when it found connected expression in men's domestic and sexual violence. On both sides of the Atlantic, in reaffirming the link between feminism and peace campaigns, activists produced tactics that were reminiscent of the suffragettes and were capable of firing the public imagination. The American peace movement remained the stronger of the two, despite the fluctuating fortunes of both and the assertiveness of British women in the Campaign against Nuclear Disarmament. If American ideas moved swiftly across the Atlantic, they did not always suit the British scene.

Anglo-American reformer relations reflected the growth of American power that Britons had feared for so long. American feminist ideologues were more numerous and influential than those of Britain. And while relations between the two women's movements remained cordial, with individual internationalists, scholarships and cultural exchanges working to keep them so, American internationalism was increasingly concerned, not with Britain, but with extending technical assistance to the developing countries.

In view of the enduring difficulty involved in meeting feminists' economic demands, greater union activism on the part of women was unexpected and welcome. In Britain and the United States alike, the activism was encouraged by the resurgence of socialist feminism (especially in Britain), and by the unions' realisation that the growth of 'women's jobs' behoved them to reassess a traditionally neglected constituency. American women created new, independent union organisations to exploit the situation; and if they chiefly benefited the female union elite, they were another tribute to the vitality of American separatist feminism. In Britain, the TUC became more active on behalf of women, while on each side of the Atlantic individual unions and groups of women strikers played an important part in change. And feminists such as Sheila Rowbotham, Juliet Mitchell and Shulamith Firestone introduced a debate about women and class which was long overdue in both countries.

Although women of every kind produced every kind of innovation in the early phase of second wave feminism, the position of women of colour, internationalists and labour women as separate elements within the women's movement did not basically alter. Their utility as such had been established beyond changing by the Second World War, and unfortunately they did not manage to find a new security in politics or to forge new, independent and powerful cross-race and cross-class coalitions.

9 Conclusion
Sisterhood questioned?

> I rather dislike united fronts, not because I dislike unity but because forming such a front always means such a terrible amount of machinery and organisation; but again I know that this is often worthwhile.
>
> Kathleen Courtney, 1931[1]

Kathleen Courtney's heartfelt comment would have found wide support among the American and British feminists studied here. Although such fronts were created from time to time,[2] particularly in the United States, the machinery involved was indeed hard to sustain. Differences developed because they were too big, ambitious and diverse, with member organisations feeling the loss of independence and co-operation thus being too cautious to be effective. But even groups unencumbered by such commitments found it taxing to maintain their internal unity and achieve their overall aims when environmental factors proved unhelpful, opponents proved formidable, interim successes proved few, members proved elusive, and charismatic leaders proved scarce. All of which would suggest that a united feminist movement, however desirable, was impractical. In summarising activists' difficulties and achievements in my conclusion, the shaping context of the Anglo-American relationship has been borne in mind, and the contribution of women activists to ideological debate has been highlighted.

A special relationship?

The Anglo-American relationship which framed the efforts of British and American feminists did not exert an oppressive influence upon them. As they had done since the nineteenth century, activists from the two countries amicably exchanged ideas, information and visitors, besides working together in feminist internationalism. But as early as the First World War, when Britain was forced to seek substantial financial help from the United States, there was British unease about the threat posed by American economic power and hostility towards the British Empire. During the 1920s and 1930s, differences became more pronounced over a host of foreign policy issues, as well as over American aloofness from the League of Nations. Despite the closeness of the United States and

Britain for most of the Second World War, the shift of power in the special relationship by 1945 was irreversible, and as satisfactory to Americans as it was galling to Britain.

Reformers on both sides of the Atlantic were conscious of these developments, with British activists acknowledging American generosity but envying American wealth, feeling that they wanted too much influence for their money and finding their geographical and political distance from the League a considerable hindrance to women's lobbying activities in Geneva between the wars. For their part, American feminists recognised British jealousy of their power. It was therefore eminently sensible that a good deal of the feminist internationalism of Britain and the United States focused on their national priorities, and that, when they ventured abroad, activists went to countries closely connected to their own: that is, to Latin America and the British Empire. Once America passed from being an outsider in the affairs of the League to becoming the major player in the United Nations and the new order it ushered in, British campaigners readily accepted that American women would have to lead in the post-war world. They continued to promote goodwill contacts and were intensely interested in the manifestations of second wave feminism in the United States. However, they were also well aware of the dangers inherent in borrowing too much from their powerful neighbour, whose potent popular culture already dominated much of the globe. It was a nice irony that feminist militancy, associated with Britain in the later stages of suffragism, had crossed the Atlantic and become the hallmark of American feminism by the 1970s.

Ideology

The inability of feminists to produce an ideology to which all women could subscribe, and which reconciled their often conflicting views about the distinctiveness and similarity of women and men, may well have inhibited the development of a united movement. But such an ideology is always likely to remain elusive, since ideas about women are fashioned when required and added to over time, durability and utility being better tests of value than consistency.[3]

The women studied in *Sisterhood Questioned?* have certainly produced ideas about the groups they supported, and have influenced feminist writing over the last twenty years. In the area of internationalism, activists asked themselves how the respective claims of nationalism and internationalism could be balanced, recognising the destructive force of nationalism yet aware that women in some parts of the world were the beneficiaries – at least to a certain extent – of male dominated national liberation movements. Activists also replied to the vehement attacks on feminism by fascism, opposing its militarism, exaggerated patriotism, intolerance of minorities and subordination of women. In addition, they began the process of re-examining the purpose of female internationalism: a process which scholars have recently taken further.

In explaining why women should seek a common interest greater than their separate national interests, feminists stressed that they brought a fresh perspective to internationalism and an awareness that wars increasingly involved the population at large and could no longer be left for male militarists alone to manage. They did continue to stress women's responsibilities as homemakers, mothers and protectors of the vulnerable, when asserting their interest in the peace movement; but they indicted men for their domestic violence as well as for their international war making. For their part, modern authorities like Tickner, Keohane, Grant, Newland and Peterson have welcomed the prospect of feminist theory pushing international relations away from its traditional focus on men's special qualities and duties and towards an appraisal of the impact of international factors on women, and an assessment of the inadequacy of subsequent state policies affecting them.[4] Feminists in our period, however, engineered no such beneficial shift but did provoke male efforts to reassert masculine values and equate them with civilisation. In the process, women's arguments for an international role might be dismissed as at worst advocating a dangerous pacifism and at best sinking into an unsophisticated sentimentality that proved their unfitness for the world's work.[5]

Making a contribution to debates about class was more difficult for women. With the rise of Marxian socialism, they confronted a founding doctrine whose male propagators dismissed feminism as a bourgeois sideshow and did not welcome ideological challenges, even from men. Class thinking by women was none the less a feature of both countries. American feminists were willing to do business with labour leaders and groups and to create their own organisations for the purpose, the relatively fluid characteristics of class being more negotiable than the ascribed characteristics of race. A more candid acknowledgement of the importance of class by British feminists did not enable them to stay on close terms with labour women, whatever organisational means they tried; courtship by a Labour Party officially pledged to women's equality proved impossible to resist. The role of the union movement in advancing needed change was not clarified in the United States or Britain, whereas feminists did manage to make clear their abhorrence of class warfare, their commitment to social justice, and their support for the development of working women's sense of community. Class rhetoric was consequently somewhat softened in both countries, with middle-class women predictably playing down class and working women playing it up if advantage beckoned. When second wave feminists looked again at the possibility of promoting a viable socialist feminism, British activists were to the fore. But feminists on each side of the Atlantic were anxious to escape from the notion of women as being a class apart, and determined to recognise gender as a vital social variable which interacted in a complicated fashion with class and race, and which required a reappraisal of women's lives and a rewriting of their histories.

Race is the area, especially in the United States, where feminists' ideas have been most contentious, since their social advantages have made any displays of prejudice, and any rejection of overtures by women of colour, seem intolerably selfish and damaging to those affected and to feminism as a whole. While they were not the architects of nineteenth-century racial thinking, white activists adapted it to the requirements of gender, with British women doing so most commonly in the connection of imperialism and Americans in the context of slavery and its aftermath. Race arguments were accordingly used to justify women's missionary outreach to less fortunate females at home and abroad, and to entitle white feminists to a voice in contemporary debates about matters ranging from the meaning of civilisation to the essence of nationalism, thereby strengthening their claims to full and equal citizenship. It was convenient to whites, however, to collapse black women's interests under the umbrella of race and to urge them to work through their race organisations; and it was helpful that black men took the same view.

Such pressures notwithstanding, for African American women race and gender problems were seldom separable. Hence they urged the need for co-operation with white feminism even while developing their own brand, which stressed female strength rather than weakness and took distinctive positions on 'the' family, reproduction rights and paid work. Sharing white feminists' maternalist ideology and social feminist goals, and sometimes even their elitism, middle-class black activists used arguments about their morality, intelligence and reform credentials to gain the attention of white women and black leaders alike. In the bi-racial anti-lynching campaign of the interwar years, black women moved from the political margins to take the lead, reproaching white women for their timidity on the question and southerners for supporting a practice which victimised women as well as men, and stamped the South as benighted. Although new arguments in the drive against lynching did not convert powerful opponents at the state and federal levels, a vigorous bi-racialism did prove possible in the decades after the Second World War, as political, economic and international circumstances changed. However, American women of colour remained at odds with white feminists over the need to connect gender, class and race, and black feminists in Britain eventually expressed similar concerns, besides owing a considerable debt to American black nationalism. In both countries, protest by activists encouraged a debate among scholars about race and feminism,[6] just as it had done about feminism and internationalism.

Practical matters

At the practical level, women in my three groupings were similarly divided and enjoyed similarly mixed success. Taking internationalism first, and beginning with the positive, activists achieved organisation and publicity, exploiting women's role as mothers and consumers. Winning acceptance for the association of women with the cause of peace, they helped to promote the 'gender gap' that was appearing between men and women over this and related issues. Efficient female public servants and lobbyists made it impossible to maintain beyond the 1940s the case against women being unsuited to employment in the foreign service. American women, bolstered by their numerous separate associations, were particularly prominent, with Jewish activists finding the cause highly congenial. Feminists attempted to broaden the base of their organisations to include more women of colour and working-class women, and they took advantage of UN support for women's interests and human rights after the Second World War. British and American activists gave some support to indigenous women's movements and they received some thanks for this. International meetings provided activists with useful information, a standard of comparison, a wider range of friendships, and confirmation of their belief that sisterhood, like female oppression, was universal. In an era regularly torn by international conflicts, women who had worked together regularly in good times rallied efficiently to help the victims of these conflicts.

On the other hand, internationalism also produced a number of tensions. The radicals of America's NWP took abroad their opposition to protective industrial laws, reanimating the debate over protection among British feminists and further distancing them from pro-protection British labour women. Differences over the NWP drive for 'blanket' equal rights treaties weakened internationalism and put a strain on Anglo-American feminist relations. Feminists found it difficult to co-operate in a popular front with other anti-fascists, and keeping the various components of the peace movement in harmony proved hard. The main organisations of female internationalism remained dominated by white women until the Second World War, and overseas activists were increasingly touchy about the interference of such women in their affairs. And neither in the United States nor in Britain did women of colour manage to sustain satisfactory alternative associations: the International Council of Women of the Darker Races had limited means and a short life, and was obliged to concentrate on educating its constituency, always a slow job; while the British Commonwealth League involved too many white, pro-empire women to offer a comfortable base for a black feminist such as the poet, playwright and lecturer, Una Marson.

After the disruption of the First World War, unionists and socialists set about reviving their international objectives and associations, but they could no more break free from attitudes prevailing at home than could their middle-class counterparts. American and British working women, having opposite opinions about organising separately from labour men, predictably differed about the need for an International Federation of Working Women. The Federation was speedily absorbed by the International Federation of Trade Unions (IFTU), against the wishes of the American WTUL; thereafter, IFTU sidelined women's interests and the WTUL struggled to retain its members and influence. Unity between American and British activists might not have prevented this unsatisfactory state of affairs, but their differences certainly contributed to it. Other international associations also proved disappointing. The International Labour Organisation, though usefully linked to the UN, was a cautious body, slow to advance female demands until after the Second World War, and unable to avoid the row over protective legislation. The UN itself, if it recognised the activism of labour women and inclined to their social feminist goals, did not give women more than a token presence and expected their backing for its broad objectives. The Communist International and the Labour and Socialist International opposed 'female bondage' but concentrated on power politics and economics. And the International Women's Co-operative Guild, despite its attractive ideology, found that its proposals were ahead of their time in the autarkic interwar years.

However, internationalism was a minority pursuit for women of all backgrounds. The domestic manifestations of class had a greater impact on working women. Different levels of class consciousness prevailed in Britain and the United States, and American unionism was affected by southern conservatism, federal legislation and extreme anti-Communism, whereas in Britain the close links between organised labour and the Labour Party were significant. None the less, female unionists in the two countries encountered similar problems, one of which was being regarded as a problem. Among embattled male leaders, the frequently offered answer to working women's vulnerable position in the labour market was a 'family wage', paid to male breadwinners and sufficient for the support of a family. This was difficult for men to achieve and for women to challenge, given their minority status within the union movement and their suspicion of possible feminist allies. Hence commitment to the family wage was not seriously threatened until the rise of second wave feminism. Female union membership and activism increased during the Second World War, but by then it was plain that the basic conservatism of the unions would prevent them from becoming a major vehicle for the advancement of women. The subsequent expansion of the female workforce, and the increase in 'women's jobs' in a changing economy, did create a more favourable environment for female unionism, and one that feminists were able to exploit. Independent women's labour groups were formed in America in the 1970s, and efforts to help British women were channelled through the TUC, reflecting the continuing labour hostility to separatist feminism that prevailed in Britain. Individual unions likewise attempted to promote women's interests. But to change their position fundamentally, women unionists needed allies beyond the labour/socialist movement, and that movement's ingrained suspicion of feminists made this impossible on both sides of the Atlantic.

The Labour Party in Britain, the Democrats in America, and socialist groups in both countries were also problematical as far as women were concerned. Thus, for example, during the First World War, all reformers could endorse programmes for improved welfare provision for women. But the short involvement of the United States in the war led to the neglect there of female welfare; while in Britain, despite the passage of the important Maternity and Child Welfare Act of 1918, the conservatism of male labour leaders and their support by labour women contributed to the provision of two key pieces of welfare legislation that acknowledged the absence of British men rather than the vital female service of motherhood. During the interwar years, the Communist Party in the United States and Britain assisted striking women workers, supported measures to improve maternal and child welfare, and backed direct action by women against unemployment and high prices; but the party's demands on government were too great for the times; its reputation for radicalism limited its recruitment of women; and its rhetoric was more impressive than its achievements. A variety of measures from the radicalised Democratic Party in America gave women assistance during the Depression; all were welcome but all were flawed from the feminist point of view. And in Britain, though glad to enlist women, the political leftwing could not do much for them between the wars and into the 1940s. Preoccupied with class, masculine and electoral considerations, the Labour Party proved unable to act before 1929 on the women's pensions it officially favoured; resisted women's campaign for family allowances; condoned the denial of unemployment benefit to married women; and opposed action on equal pay. The Independent Labour Party, notwithstanding its promotion of women's issues and the female participation in its meetings, remained too small and male dominated to make a practical difference for most women. Not until the 1960s and 1970s did the Democrats and the Labour Party manifest a truly helpful interest in pro-women measures.

From the First World War, middle-class feminists – sometimes alongside labour women – regularly attempted to achieve both egalitarian and welfare measures for women. During the war, they helped women at work and those who had been displaced from their jobs. After 1918, they pushed for an array of legislative measures to help women and children, with remarkable success until politicians learned not to fear feminism's numerous but frequently non-partisan petitioners. They then pressed for action on a balanced programme which included birth control, work and welfare issues. In these challenging areas, they often proved better at advocacy than at delivery, being unable to make progress on equal pay and dividing on protective laws for women. But in the United States they helped to ease restrictions on married women working and to shape parts of the New Deal. And in Britain and America alike, they contributed to progress over birth control, despite its daunting class ramifications in the former and race complexities in the latter. By the Second World War, although British and American feminists were similarly determined to take advantage of the public's awareness of women's importance to the war effort to push for improvements in their position, the two women's movements were growing apart under the stress of the conflict and the influence of differing social conditions. Their contrasting emphases can be seen when Americans resumed their long campaign over the ERA and British feminists in parliament again sought a mixed range of legislation; their need to convert just one legislature was a feature of British life that American activists did envy.

Race remains: an area of great moral reproach to white feminists but organisationally one of achievement as well as division. African American women had an elaborate network of associations throughout our period, operating first at the local level and then, from the 1890s, at the national. Such clubs, sororities, church and professional bodies afforded their members company, help, stimulation and a sense of community, and their leaders had the opportunity to develop their own agenda, free from intervention by white women who thought they knew best. African American women involved themselves in politics during the 1920s, despite the opposition to their voting, and responded when Mary McLeod Bethune – black activist and New Dealer – created the National Council of Negro Women in 1935 as a personal platform and one from which she could reach out to the black masses. The earlier snubs of black organisation women by their white counterparts were ignored by black female leaders when it would advance their cause; but even if white female New Dealers had responded by facilitating closer collaboration across the racial divide, it is unlikely that women would have been able to secure a more central role in an administration that was so sensitive to the opinions of the South and so concerned with economic imperatives. As it was, black women's political weakness allowed local administrators to discriminate against them in the distribution of relief, work and welfare.

Belonging to civil rights rather than women's organisations was not the easy answer to black women's difficulties, since though they found a welcome there, it was accompanied by political subordination and indifference to their proud maternalist ideology. None the less, by the 1950s African American women had clearly established their importance within the civil rights movement, particularly as sustainers of communities: managers of local projects, organisers of boycotts and voter registration drives, and the mainstay of freedom schools. The underestimation of their roles, as well as sexism on the part of male civil rights activists, drove some black women to withdraw and form their own organisations in the 1970s. But many retained their civil rights connection and were probably wise to do so, since allies were either not forthcoming or unlikely to be an asset. Native American, Asian and Hispanic minorities had only begun to take an interest in mainstream politics during the interwar years, and were initially too separated by their distinctive settlement patterns, history and culture to ally with others in protesting poverty and discrimination. When in the 1960s, women in such minorities became increasingly interested in joining forces with white feminists to advance shared objectives, they found that these dividing factors still existed and that, moreover, their interest put them at odds with the established, male dominated ethnic pressure groups. Women of colour in Britain, vigorously organising by the 1970s, shared with their American sisters the disadvantages attached to minority status, and they too gave high priority to mobilising at the community level.

Destructive differences?

In 1928, a British woman journalist visiting the United States complained that 'women are so rarely loyal to one another'.[7] She offered no evidence for this statement and I would dispute it. Having found themselves categorised and socialised by race, class and gender, women were impressively loyal to the organisations that sustained these divisions, producing leaders who were reluctant to retire and perhaps thereby impeding the regular recruitment of the young. When in the 1940s Doris Stevens was advised by her old comrade, Lucy Burns, to 'Put the trunk in the cellar' and settle for tranquillity, Burns recognised that Stevens was too 'restless and dynamic and . . . socially minded' to relish, as she did, 'peace, poverty, and the private life'. Stevens was not alone in wanting friends to press her into service.[8]

There are several factors more important than disloyalty in explaining why sisterhood was hard to achieve. In the first place, activists separated by race, class and gender did not usually work together and saw little of each other socially, so that a desire to collaborate did not arise naturally out of firsthand knowledge and personal sympathy. And second, in almost all areas where women activists encountered major difficulties, it was because of unhelpful social circumstances, depleted resources, and a temporary decline of interest in feminism rather than female quarrels. Anglo-American differences are also primarily to be explained in terms of context, not cantankerousness. The notorious dispute over protective industrial legislation between Britons and Americans, feminists and labour women, and different groups of feminists is the exception that proves the rule.

Of course single issue and professional women's associations could be selfishly limited in their approach; social and egalitarian feminists differed; class and race organisations denounced the attitudes and efforts of middle-class feminists; British and American activists frequently chided each other; and the range and vigour of feminist disputes increased impressively from the 1960s. But individual women reached out to each other regardless of their primary groupings. Separate associations effectively nurtured those who might have achieved nothing in uncongenial mixed company. And feminist goals influenced women in race, class and welfare bodies that were often loath to call themselves feminist. By the Second World War, indeed, race and class associations were too long and too securely established seriously to contemplate new alliances with 'outsider' women. None the less, always quarrelsome American and British feminism has survived; and the last words should be left to a 1933 letter writer to the editor of the *New York Times*: 'while appreciating your point that it would be much better for all women to agree, wouldn't it be much better if all men could agree? Yet no one expects them to, or condemns them because they don't, as it is clearly recognized that progress will always result in controversy, until an ideal state is reached.'[9]

Notes

1 Introduction

1 F. Kennedy, *San Francisco Examiner*, 17 September 1985, Folder 1, Florynce Kennedy Papers, The Arthur and Elizabeth Schlesinger Library on the History of Women in America (in future SL), Radcliffe College, Cambridge, MA; interview with Catherine Conroy by Elizabeth Balanoff, Institute of Labor and Industrial Relations, The University of Michigan, Wayne State University, Oral History Project, *The Twentieth Century Trade Union Woman: Vehicle for Social Change*, 1978, p. 56, SL.

2 First wave feminism is a term of convenience applied to women's activism from approximately the 1840s to 1920. Second wave feminism is shorthand for the women's movements which developed from the 1960s, and the phrase implies that feminism was moribund in the period between the two waves. Throughout this book, however, the continuity of feminist activism is underlined, and the significance of the interwar years of the twentieth century is stressed. Although the emphases within feminism changed over time, while the term was not widely used until the early 1900s, I have taken it generally to mean the advocacy of women's self-definition, personal autonomy and collective consciousness; promotion of respect for women's distinctive qualities and needs; and a search for equality with men regarding opportunities, rights and esteem. I have included in the women's movements *both* individual feminists and their associations, *and* women reformers – usually called social or welfare feminists by historians – who pursued women's interests in separate all-female groups or alongside men.

3 V. L. Ruiz and E. C. DuBois (eds), *Unequal Sisters: A Multi-Cultural Reader in U.S. Women's History*, New York, Routledge, 1994, second edition, p. xii; A. Basu (ed.), *The Challenge of Local Feminisms: Women's Movements in Global Perspective*, Boulder, CO, San Francisco and Oxford, Westview Press, 1995.

4 Christine Bolt, *The Women's Movement in the United States and Britain from the 1790s to the 1920s*, London and Amherst, Wheatsheaf and the University of Massachusetts Press, 1993, pp. 87–95; Christine Bolt, *Feminist Ferment: 'The Woman Question' in the USA and England, 1870–1940*, London, UCL Press, 1985, chapter 1; and see also O. Banks, *Faces of Feminism: A Study of Feminism as a Social Movement*, Oxford, Basil Blackwell, 1986, Part II. The vote was a broadly unifying issue despite the well publicised differences between its advocates.

5 Interview with Mrs Hazel Hunkins-Hallinan, in *Tapes of Interviews on British Women's History in the 20th Century*, recorded by Brian Harrison (Corpus Christi College, Oxford), from 1974 onwards, and financed by the Social Science Research Council, Tape 10, 8 February 1975, The Women's Library, London (in future WL).

6 'Doris Stevens to Betty Gram Swing', 8 January 1946, Doris Stevens Unprocessed Papers, Box 12, Folder 164, Doris Stevens Papers, SL.
7 Interview with Mary Callahan in Oral History Project, *The Twentieth Century Trade Union Woman*, *op. cit.*, p. 45, SL.
8 The term labour women is used throughout, for convenience, to encompass women in the labour movement, including trade unionists and supporters of the political Left.
9 Article by Kennedy, 1983, p. 353, Folder 1, Florynce Kennedy Papers, SL.
10 Article on Luscomb of 24 February 1976, Box 9, Folder 215, Florence Hope Luscomb Papers, SL. And see S. H. Strom, *Political Woman: Florence Luscomb and the Legacy of Political Reform*, Philadelphia, Temple University Press, 2001.
11 Hazel Hunkins-Hallinan, Tape 10, in *Tapes of Interviews on British Women's History*, *op. cit.*, WL; and tribute to Monica Whately in Six Point Group Papers, WL.
12 Given my focus, I have not highlighted geographical differences among feminists; nor have I written a detailed history of feminist and labour women's campaigns; much new work is being done in both areas.

2 The setting, 1880s–1914

1 M. M. Randall, *Improper Bostonian: Emily Greene Balch*, New York, Twayne, 1964, p. 308; Hazel Hunkins-Hallinan to Dr D. T. Hoffman, 20 April 1971, Box 548, M.19, Six Point Group Papers, WL.
2 L. Colley, *Britons: Forging the Nation, 1707–1837*, London, Pimlico, 1994, originally published 1992, pp. 132–45; F. Thistlethwaite, *America and the Atlantic Community: Anglo-American Aspects, 1790–1850*, New York, Harper and Row, 1963, originally published 1959, chapter 1.
3 Thistlethwaite, *America and the Atlantic Community*, chapters 2–5; D. Turley, *The Culture of English Antislavery, 1780–1860*, London and New York, Routledge, 1991, p. 123.
4 M. Bradbury, *Dangerous Pilgrimages: Trans-Atlantic Mythologies and the Novel*, London, Secker and Warburg, 1995.
5 A. Mann, 'British social thought and American reformers of the Progressive era', *Mississippi Valley Historical Review*, 1955–6, vol. 42, pp. 672–92; S. Anderson, *Race and Rapprochement: Anglo-Saxonism and Anglo-American Relations, 1895–1904*, Rutherford, Madison and Teaneck and London and Toronto, Fairleigh Dickinson University Press and Associated University Presses, 1981.
6 Useful introductions are A. P. Dobson, *Anglo-American Relations in the Twentieth Century*, London and New York, Routledge, 1995; and R. Renwick, *Fighting With Allies: America and Britain in Peace and War*, London Macmillan, 1995.
7 A. T. Vaughan, *Roots of American Racism: Essays on the Colonial Experience*, New York and Oxford, Oxford University Press, 1995, particularly chapter 1; Christine Bolt, *Victorian Attitudes to Race*, London and New York and Toronto, Routledge and Kegan Paul and Toronto University Press, 1971; W. Jordon, *White Over Black: American Attitudes toward the Negro, 1550–1812*, Chapel Hill, University of North Carolina Press, 1968; D. MacLeod, *Slavery, Race and the American Revolution*, Cambridge, Cambridge University Press, 1974; L. Tise, *Proslavery: A History of the Defense of Slavery in America, 1701–1840*, Athens, University of Georgia Press, 1988; L. Friedman, *The White Savage: Racial Fantasies in the Postbellum South*, Englewood Cliffs, NJ, Prentice Hall, 1970.

8 Bolt, *Victorian Attitudes to Race*.

9 C. Bolt, 'Race and the Victorians', in C. C. Eldridge (ed.), *British Imperialism in the Nineteenth Century*, London, Macmillan, 1984, pp. 127–30; Bolt, *Victorian Attitudes to Race*, chapter 1; D. A. Lorimer, 'Race, science and culture: historical continuities and discontinuities, 1815–1914', in S. West (ed.), *The Victorians and Race*, Aldershot, Scolar Press, 1996, p. 32; G. M. Frederickson, *The Black Image in the White Mind: The Debate on Afro-American Character and Destiny, 1817–1914*, New York, Harper and Row, 1971; Anderson, *Race and Rapprochement*, pp. 11–12; E. W. Said, *Orientalism*, New York, Pantheon Books, 1987; Rosenberg, *Beyond Separate Spheres*, p. 40; C. Bloom 'The politics of immigration, 1881–1905', *Transactions of the Jewish Historical Society of England*, 1992–4, vol. xxxiii, pp. 187–214.

10 E. Fox-Genovese, *Within the Plantation Household: Black and White Women of the Old South*, Chapel Hill, University of North Carolina Press, 1988; S. Lebsock, *The Free Women of Petersburg: Status and Culture in a Southern Town, 1784–1860*, New York and London, W. W. Norton, 1984, p. 241, and pp. 224f. on the uneasy relationship of white men and women in charitable work; D. G. White, *Ar'n't I a Woman? Female Slaves in the Plantation South*, New York and London, Norton, 1984, stresses the independence of black women. The degree to which women accepted planter paternalism is in fact disputed by scholars: see, for instance, J. W. Harris (ed.), *Society and Culture in the Slave South*, London and New York, Routledge, 1993, originally published 1992, p. 8 and *passim;* A. F. Scott, 'Women's perspective on the patriarchy in the 1850s', in C. Clinton (ed.), *Half Sisters of History: Southern Women and the American Past*, Durham, NC, and London, Duke University Press, 1994, pp. 77–92.

11 M. Ferguson, *Subject to Others: British Women Writers and Colonial Slavery, 1690–1834*, New York and London, Routledge, 1992, p. 4 and *passim*; C. Midgley, *Women Against Slavery: The British Campaigns, 1780–1870*, London and New York, Routledge, 1992, pp. 196–7.

12 Midgley, *Women Against Slavery*, pp. 87–9, 39–40, 142–5; Bolt, *The Women's Movements*, pp. 67–8; b. hooks, *Ain't I a Woman? Black Women and Feminism*, London and Winchester, South End Press and Pluto Press, 1992, originally published 1982, pp. 125, 128; J. F. Yellin and J. C. Van Horne (eds), *The Abolitionist Sisterhood: Women's Political Culture in Antebellum America*, Ithaca and London, Cornell University Press in co-operation with the Library Company of Philadelphia, 1994, Part Two especially.

13 Ferguson, *Subject to Others*, conclusion; Midgley, *Women Against Slavery*, pp. 196–7; D. G. Faust, *Mothers of Invention: Women of the Slaveholding South in the American Civil War*, Chapel Hill and London, University of North Carolina Press, 1996, pp. 253–4.

14 E. C. DuBois, *Feminism and Suffrage: The Emergence of an Independent Women's Movement in America, 1848–1869*, Ithaca and London, Cornell University Press, 1978, particularly pp. 178–9; E. Griffith, *In Her Own Right: The Life of Elizabeth Cady Stanton*, New York and Oxford, Oxford University Press, 1984, p. 124; and see L. M. Newman, *White Women's Rights: The Racial Origins of Feminism in the United States*, New York, Oxford University Press, 1999.

15 hooks, *Ain't I a Woman*, chapters 4 and 5; P. Giddings, *When and Where I Enter: The Impact of Black Women on Race and Sex in America*, New York, William Morrow, 1984; R. Terborg-Penn, 'Discrimination against Afro-American women in the women's movement, 1830–1920', in S. Harley and R. Terborg-Penn (eds), *The Afro-American Woman*, Port Washington, Kennikat Press, 1978, pp. 17–27;

B. H. Andolsen, *Daughters of Jefferson, Daughters of Bootblacks: Racism and American Feminism*, Macon, Mercer University Press, 1986; D. and C. J. Schneider, *American Women in the Progressive Era, 1900–1920*, New York, Facts on File, 1993, chapter 5; B. Guy-Sheftall, *Daughters of Sorrow: Attitudes Toward Black Women, 1880–1920*, New York, Carlson, 1990, chapters 2 and 4; A. Douglas, *Terrible Honesty: Mongrel Manhattan in the 1920s*, London, Picador, Macmillan Books, 1995, chapter 7; C. Neverdon-Morton, *Afro-American Women of the South and the Advancement of the Race, 1895–1925*, Knoxville, University of Tennessee Press, 1989; E. Brooks-Higginbotham, *Righteous Discontent: The Women's Movement in the Black Baptist Church, 1880–1920*, Cambridge, MA, Harvard University Press, 1993; J. A. Rouse, *Lugenia Burns Hope: Southern Reformer*, Athens, Georgia University Press, 1989; D. G. White, *Too Heavy a Load: Black Women in Defense of Themselves, 1894–1994*, New York, W. W. Norton, 1999; S. J. Shaw, *What a Woman Ought to Be and to Do: Black Professional Women Workers during the Jim Crow Era*, Chicago, University of Chicago Press, 1996; D. Salem, *To Better Our World: Black Women in Organised Reform, 1890–1920*, Brooklyn, NY, Charlson Publishing, 1990, chapters 2–6; N. Caraway, *Segregated Sisterhood: Racism and the Politics of American Feminism*, Knoxville, University of Tennessee Press, 1991, chapter 5.

16 Bolt, *The Women's Movements*, pp. 196–8; M. S. Wheeler, *New Women of the New South: The Leaders of the Woman Suffrage Movement in the Southern States*, New York, Oxford University Press, 1993, especially pp. 20f. and chapter 4; Guy-Sheftall, *Daughters of Sorrow*, pp. 99f.; L. G. Kusmack, *Woman's Cause: The Jewish Women's Movement in England and the United States, 1881–1933*, Columbus, Ohio University Press, 1990, pp. 38–40.

17 P. H. Collins, *Black Feminist Thought: Knowledge, Consciousness, and the Politics of Empowerment*, New York and London, Routledge, 1991, originally published 1990; Lebsock, *The Free Women of Petersburg*, pp. 111, 225; V. Amos and P. Parmar, 'Challenging imperial feminism', *Feminist Review*, 1984, vol. 17, pp. 3–19; D. G. White, 'The cost of club work: the price of black feminism', in N. A. Hewitt and S. Lebsock (eds), *Visible Women: New Essays on American Activism*, Urbana and Chicago, University of Illinois Press, 1993, pp. 252–7; G. R. Puryear, 'The black woman: liberated or oppressed?', in B. Lindsay (ed.), *Comparative Perspectives of Third World Women: The Impact of Race, Sex, and Class*, New York, Praeger, 1980, pp. 251f., observes that black women's acceptance of the need to work outside the home does not necessarily involve a 'radical sex ideology', and that their reputation for strength could result in their unhelpful portrayal as the 'antithesis of the ultrafeminine woman in society'; Giddings, *When and Where I Enter*, pp. 98–102, 113–17, quotation from p. 113, notes the tensions between black women and men when black women tried to assert race leadership; hooks, *Ain't I a woman?*; Salem, *To Better Our World*, especially chapters 3, 5 and 6; Caraway, *Segregated Sisterhood*, chapters 2 and 3.

18 D. C. Hine, 'Reflections on race and gender systems', in P. A. Cimbala and R. F. Himmelberg (eds), *Historians and Race: Autobiography and the Writing of History*, Bloomington and Indianapolis, Indiana University Press, 1996, p. 61, stresses that black women's mission was informed by their distinctive 'consciousness of the complex and interconnected nature of the struggle against racial, sexual, and class systems of dominion'; E. Boris, 'The power of motherhood: black and white activist women redefine the "political"', *Yale Journal of Law and Feminism*, 1989, vol. 2, pp. 25–49; Giddings *When and Where I Enter*, pp. 97–8; Salem, *To Better Our World*, chapters 1 and 2; White, 'The cost of club work', *op. cit.*, pp. 258–64;

N. I. Painter, 'Difference, slavery and memory: Sojourner Truth in feminist abolitionism', in Yellin and Van Horne (eds), *The Abolitionist Sisterhood*, pp. 140–58, especially, pp. 156–7 on Truth's distance from the style of her ladylike black sisters; the Mary Church Terrell Papers, Manuscript Division, Library of Congress (in future LC), Washington, DC, read on microfilm at the Lamont Library, Harvard University, give a good indication of the concern of a highly educated, middle-class black activist with personal achievement and racial uplift, with the emphasis on 'the purification of the home': see in her correspondence for 1901–3 a clipping from the *New York Age*, 4 January 1900; quotation from Article II of the Program and Constitution of the NACW for 1897, in folder on the National Association of Colored Women. See also B. W. Jones, *Quest for Equality: The Life and Writings of Mary Eliza Church Terrell, 1863–1954*, Brooklyn, NY, Carlson, 1990; and E. L. Davis, *Lifting as They Climb*, Introduction by Siegelinde Lemke, New York, G. K. Hall and London, Prentice-Hall International, 1996, quotations from pp. xvii, xix, 383.

19 L. Bland, *Banishing the Beast: English Feminism and Sexual Morality, 1855–1914*, London, Penguin Books, 1955, pp. 229–35, 296; M Valverde, 'The concept of "race" in first-wave feminist, sexual and reproductive politics', in F. Icovetta and M. Valverde (eds), *Expanding Boundaries: New Essays in Women's History*, Toronto, University of Toronto Press, 1992; A. Davin, 'Imperialism and motherhood', *History Workshop Journal*, 1978, vol. 5, pp. 9–65; A. Burton, *Burdens of History: British Feminists, Indian Women and Imperial Culture, 1865–1915*, Chapel Hill, University of North Carolina Press, 1994; Kusmack, *Woman's Cause*, chapters 2–4; G. Bederman, *Manliness and Civilization: A Cultural History of Gender and Race in the United States, 1880–1917*, Chicago, IL, Chicago University Press, 1995; C. F. Kessler, *Charlotte Perkins Gilman: Her Progress Toward Utopia With Selected Writings*, Syracuse, Syracuse University Press, 1995; V. Ware, *Beyond the Pale: White Women, Racism and History*, London, Verso, 1992; K. Dodd, 'Cultural politics and women's historical writing: the case of Ray Strachey's *The Cause*', *Women's Studies International Forum*, 1990, vol. 33, nos 1–2, pp. 127–37, for an example by a feminist of this placing technique; L. A. E. Nym Mayall, P. Levine and E. C. Fletcher (eds), *Women's Suffrage in the British Empire: Citizenship, Nation and Race*, 'Introduction' and chapter 7 by Christine D. Myers, London, Routledge, 2000; S. Ledger and S. McCracken (eds), *Cultural Politics at the Fin-de-Siècle*, Cambridge, Cambridge University Press, 1995; R. Lister, *Citizenship: Feminist Perspectives*, New York, New York University Press, 1997; Newman, *White Women's Rights.*

20 C. Midgley, 'Ethnicity, "race" and empire', in J. Purvis (ed.), *Women's History: Britain, 1850–1945*, London, UCL Press, 1995, pp. 247–76; Ware, *Beyond the Pale*, pp. 197–221.

21 Bolt, *Feminist Ferment*, p. 42; I. B. Wells, *Crusade for Justice: The Autobiography of Ida B. Wells*, Chicago, IL, University of Chicago Press, 1970, (ed.) A. M. Duster, p. 140; see also P. A. Schechter, *Ida B. Wells-Barnett and American Reform, 1880–1930*, Chapel Hill, University of North Carolina Press, 2001.

22 J. Hunter, *The Gospel of Gentility: American Women Missionaries in Turn-of-the-Century China*, New Haven, CT, Yale University Press, 1984; P. R. Hill, *The World Their Household: The American Woman's Foreign Mission Movement and Culture Transformation, 1870–1920*, Ann Arbor, University of Michigan Press, 1985; A. F. Scott, *The Southern Lady: from Pedestal to Politics, 1830–1930*, Chicago, IL, University of Chicago Press, 1970, pp. 136f.; A. F. Scott, *Natural Allies: Women's Associations in American History*, Urbana, University of Illinois Press, 1991, pp. 86f.

23 Greenville Methodist Episcopal Church, Women's Auxiliary, Corresponding Secretary's Notebook, 9 January 1885; report of September 1889 meeting; report of October 1895 meeting, vol. 22, Somerville Howorth Papers, SL.

24 Hill, *The World Their Household*, pp. 8, 195–6.

25 *Ibid.*, chapters 4 and 5; Hunter, *The Gospel of Gentility*, pp. 230, 232, 255; R. P. Beaver, *American Protestant Women in World Mission: A History of the First Feminist Movement in North America*, Grand Rapids, William B. Eerdmans, 1980; J. J. Brumberg, 'Zenanas and girlless villages: the ethnology of American evangelical women, 1810–1910', *Journal of American History*, 1982, vol. 69, pp. 347–71.

26 Hill, *The World Their Household*, pp. 34–6, 50, 52–4, 137; the suffragist internationalist, Carrie Chapman Catt, apparently met only one feminist missionary during her world tour of 1911–12: see M. G. Peck, *Carrie Chapman Catt: A. Biography*, New York, Octagon Books, 1975, originally published 1944, p. 201.

27 See Hunter, *The Gospel of Gentility*, on missionary women's embrace of self-denial not self-advocacy, pp. 87–9, 148, 162–4, 167–76, 204, 228; B. J. Loewenberg and R. Bogin (eds), *Black Women in Nineteenth-Century American Life*, University Park, PA, and London, Pennsylvania State University Press, 1976, pp. 166, 171; E. B. Tompkins, *Anti-Imperialism in the United States: The Great Debate, 1890–1920*, Philadelphia, University of Pennsylvania Press, 1970, pp. 11–12, notes that the acknowledged advocates of imperialism among American missionaries appear to have been male. For other women connected with African American missionary work, see for instance Davis, *Lifting as They Climb*, pp. 175, 203, 221–2.

28 L. E. Burgess, 'The Lake Mohonk Conferences on the Indian, 1883–1916', PhD dissertation, Claremont Graduate School, 1972, pp. 58–9; F. E. Partington, *The Story of Mohonk*, Mohonk Salesrooms, 1911, p. 29.

29 B. L. Epstein, *The Politics of Domesticity: Women, Evangelism, and Temperance in Nineteeth-Century America*, Middletown, Wesleyan University Press, 1981, p. 124; N. Boyd, *Emissaries: The Overseas Work of the American YWCA, 1895–1970*, New York, Women's Press 1991, pp. 3, 5, 246f.; F. Willard, *Glimpses of Fifty Years: The Autobiography of an American Woman*, Chicago, WCTU publications, H. J. Smith, 1889, chapter 6; A. A. Gordon, *The Beautiful Life of Frances E. Willard*, London, Sampson Low, Marston, 1898, chapter 9; M. Earhart, *Frances Willard: From Prayers to Politics*, Chicago, University of Chicago Press, 1994, pp. 272, 340; I. Tyrell, *Woman's World, Woman's Empire: The Woman's Christian Temperance Union in International Perspective, 1880–1930*, Chapel Hill, University of North Carolina Press, 1991, pp. 29, 63, 81–113, 131–2, 143, 169, 253.

30 *English Woman's Review*, October 1872, no. xl, p. 268.

31 Quoted in F. Bowie, D. Kirkwood and S. Ardener (eds), *Women and Missions: Past and Present Anthropological and Historical Perceptions*, Oxford, Berg, 1993, p. 8.

32 *Ibid.*, Introduction and chapters 5, 6, 10 and 11 especially.

33 See, for instance, Judith Tucker, *Gender and Islamic History*, Washington, DC, American Historical Association, 1993, p. 25.

34 Burton, *Burdens of History*, p. 2, and Burton, 'British Feminists and the Indian Woman, 1865–1915', *Women's Studies International Forum*, 1990, vol. 13, pp. 295–308.

35 A. E. Wright, *The Unexpurgated Case Against Woman Suffrage*, London, Constable, 1913, p. 33; M. Pugh, *Votes for Women in Britain, 1867–1928*, London, The Historical Association, 1994, p. 14.

36 Burton, *Burdens of History*, p. 210.

37 P. Tuson (ed.), *The Queen's Daughters: An Anthology of Victorian Feminist Writing on India, 1857–1900*, Reading, Ithaca Press, 1995; K. Ballhatchet, *Race, Sex and Class Under the Raj: Imperial Attitudes and Policies and Their Critics, 1793–1905*, London, Weidenfeld and Nicolson, 1980; E. W. Andrew and K. C. Bushnell, *The Queen's Daughters in India*, London, Morgan and Scott, 1898; Burton, *Burdens of History*, chapter 5.

38 See, for instance, Bowie, Kirkwood and Ardener (eds), *Women and Missions*, chapter 10; M. A. Lind, *The Compassionate Memsahibs: Welfare Activities of British Women in India, 1900–1947*, Westport, Greenwood Press, 1988; L. Flammang (ed.), *Women's Work for Woman: Missionaries and Social Change in Asia*, San Francisco, Westview Press, 1989; P. Barr, *The Memsahibs: The Women of Victorian India*, London, Secker and Warburg, 1976; M. Strobel, *European Women and the Second British Empire*, Bloomington, Indiana University Press, 1991.

39 M. G. Fawcett and E. M. Turner, *Josephine Butler: Her Work and Principles: and Their Meaning for the Twentieth Century*, London, The Association for Moral and Social Hygiene, 1927, pp. 112–13; and E. M. Bell, *Josephine Butler: Flame of Fire*, London, Constable, 1962, and J. Jordan, *Josephine Butler*, London, John Murray, 2001, chapter 9, for further discussion of Butler's European work.

40 Bolt, *The Women's Movements*, pp. 153, 195–6; L. J. Rupp, 'Constructing internationalism: the case of transnational women's organizations, 1888–1945', *American Historical Review*, 1994, vol. 99, pp. 1574–5; Rupp's article (pp. 1571–1600) is an invaluable introduction to this subject; M. Bosch and A. Kloosterman (eds), *Politics and Friendship: Letters from the International Woman Suffrage Alliance, 1902–42*, Columbus, Ohio State University, 1990, chapter 1, quotation from p. 9; R. Evans, *The Feminists*, London, Croom Helm, 1984, originally published 1977, Appendix.

41 Carrie Chapman Catt to Belle Sherwin, 30 October 1925, Box 51, series II, League of Women Voters Papers, LC; Peck, *Carrie Chapman Catt*, pp. 181–211.

42 C. Phelps, *The Anglo-American Peace Movement in the Mid-Nineteenth Century*, New York, Columbia University Press, 1930, p. 188.

43 On America, see 'Women in foreign affairs', 1976 clipping from the Department of State *Newsletter*, Folder 2258, Pauli Murray Papers, SL; H. Calkin, *Women in American Foreign Affairs*, Washington, Department of State, 1977; and on Britain, 'Women in diplomacy: the FCO, 1782–1994', *History Notes*, Historical Branch, LRD, no. 6, May 1994, pp. 1–11.

44 Kuzmack, *Woman's Cause*, pp. 29f., 45, 48, 51, 65, 74–6, 82, 163, 180–1. See folder on The International Council of Jewish Women in Box 26, Group II, Records of the National Council of Jewish Women, LC; and booklet on the International Council in the folder on that subject, Hannah G. Solomon Papers, Box 3, LC.

45 Giddings, *When and Where I Enter*, p. 214; M. C. Terrell, *A Colored Woman in a White World*, Washington, DC, Ransdell Inc., 1940, reprint by Arno Press, New York, 1980, chapters 21, 33, 37; Loewenberg and Bogin (eds), *Black Women*, pp. 277–8, 318, 330–1; G. Bederman, 'Civilization, the decline of middle-class manliness, and Ida B. Wells's anti-lynching campaign, 1892–94', in B. Melosh (ed.), *Gender and American History Since 1890*, London, Routledge, 1993, pp. 213–17; E. Barley Brown, 'Womanist consciousness: Maggie Lena Walker and the Independent Order of Saint Luke', in Ruiz and DuBois (eds), *Unequal Sisters*, p. 270.

46 Bosch and Kloosterman (eds), *Politics and Friendship*, chapter 2, quotations from pp. 37 and 40; Tyrell, *Woman's World, Woman's Empire*, pp. 12–13, 182; Hunter, *The Gospel of Gentility*, pp. 152–3, 156; M. Banta, *Imaging American Women: Idea

and Ideas in Cultural History, New York, Columbia University Press, 1987, pp. 549, 553f.

47 Bederman, *Manliness and Civilization*, p. 157; E. Showalter, *Sexual Anarchy: Gender and Culture at the Fin de Siècle*, London, Virago, 1992, originally published 1990, chapter 1; J. A. Mangan and J. Walvin, *Manliness and Morality: Middle-Class Masculinity in Britain and America, 1800–1940*, Manchester, Manchester University Press, 1987; M. Roper and J. Tosh (eds), *Manful Assertions: Masculinities in Britain Since 1800*, London, Routledge, 1991; G. L. Mosse, *The Image of Man: The Creation of Modern Masculinity*, Oxford, Oxford University Press, 1996.

48 S. Cooper, 'The work of women in nineteenth century continental European peace movement', *Peace and Change*, 1984, vol. 9, pp. 11–28, quotation from p. 11; Phelps, *The Anglo-American Peace Movement*; J. Liddington, *The Long Road to Greenham: Feminism and Anti-Militarism in Britain Since 1820*, London, Virago, 1989, chapters 1 and 2; L. Rupp, *Worlds of Women, The Making of an International Women's Movement*, Princeton, NJ, Princeton University Press, 1997, p. 19; Bolt, *The Women's Movements*, pp. 70–1, 254.

49 *Woman's Journal*, 16 April 1898.

50 Peck, *Carrie Chapman Catt*, p. 97.

51 For important pioneering studies of women and foreign policy, see E. P. Crapol, *Women and American Foreign Policy: Lobbyists, Critics and Insiders*, Westport, CT, Greenwood Press, 1987, p. 1; J. Papachristou, 'American women and foreign policy, 1898–1905: exploring gender in diplomatic history', *Diplomatic History*, 1990, vol. 14, pp. 493–509, especially p. 495; R. Jeffreys-Jones, *Changing Differences: Women and the Shaping of American Foreign Policy*, New Brunswick, NJ, Rutgers University Press, 1995, p. 2; Rupp, *Worlds of Women*; C. Miller, 'Lobbying the League: women's international organisations and the League of Nations', D. Phil. thesis, University of Oxford, 1992. For the introduction of women in imperial history in the context of sexual attitudes and behaviour in the colonies, see, for instance, R. Hyam, *Empire and Sexuality: The British Experience*, Manchester, Manchester University Press, 1991, originally published 1990; R. Hyam, *Britain's Imperial Century, 1815–1914: A Study of Empire and Expansion*, London, Macmillan, 1993, originally published 1976, pp. 291–4, quotation from p. 292; L. James, *The Rise and Fall of the British Empire*, Boston, Little, Brown, 1994, pp. 222, 435–6; D. Judd, *Empire: The British Experience, from 1765 to the Present*, London, HarperCollins, 1996, pp. 171–86. For recent writing re-evaluating women, see Burton, *Burdens of History;* Lind, *The Compassionate Memsahibs;* H. Callaway, *Gender, Culture and Empire: European Women in Colonial Nigeria*, Urbana, University of Illinois Press, 1987; N. Chaudhuri and M. Strobel (eds), *Western Women and Imperialism: Complicity and Resistance*, Bloomington, Indiana University Press, 1992, Introduction and *passim*; C. Knapman, *White Women in Fiji, 1835–1930: The Ruin of Empire?*, Sydney, Allen and Unwin, 1986; K. Sangari and S. Vaid (eds), *Recasting Women: Essays in Colonial History*, New Delhi, Kali for Women, 1989; N. Chaudhuri and M. Strobel, 'Western women and imperialism: introduction', in *Women's Studies International Forum*, 1990, vol. 13, no. 4, pp. 289–93; and in *ibid.* 1990, vol. 13, nos. 1–2, pp. 105–15; J. Haggis, 'Gendering colonialism or colonising gender? Recent women's studies approaches to white woman and the history of British colonialism'; also in *ibid.*, B. N. Ramusack, 'Cultural missionaries, maternal imperialists, feminist allies: British women activists in India, 1865–1945', pp. 309–21.

52 A. Gorren, *Anglo-Saxons and Others*, London, David Nutt, 1900, pp. 3, 6–9, 37.

53 Anderson, *Race and Rapprochement.*

54 Tompkins, *Anti-Imperialism in the United States*, p. 255; R. E. Welch, Jr., *Response to Imperialism: The United States and the Philippine–American War, 1899–1902*, Chapel Hill, University of North Carolina Press, 1979. Women did not gain a foothold on the executive board of the Anti-Imperialist League until 1904.

55 *Woman's Journal*, 30 April 1898.

56 *Ibid.*, 14 May 1898.

57 Quoted in Griffith, *In Her Own Right*, p. 259.

58 *Woman's Journal*, 30 April 1898.

59 Papachristou, 'American women and foreign policy'; C. R. Marchand, *The American Peace Movement and Social Reform, 1898–1918*, Princeton, Princeton University Press, 1972, pp. 11–13; J. M. Craig, 'Lucia True Ames Mead: American publicist for peace and internationalism', in Crapol (ed.), *Women and American Foreign Policy*, pp. 72–3, 79–80; quotation from an article on 'Justice to the Negro', by the feminist Caroline Maria Severance, Box 14, Severance Papers, Huntington Library, San Marino, California; and Susan B. Anthony to Elizabeth Cady Stanton, 2 December 1898, Anthony Family Collection, Huntington Library.

60 *Woman's Journal*, 30 April 1898.

61 I. H. Harper, *The Life and Work of Susan B. Anthony*, Salem, MA, N. H. Myer, 1983, originally published 1898, vol. 3, p. 1,199.

62 *Woman's Journal*, 14 May 1898; Susan Anthony to Clara Colby, 20 April 1898, Colby Collection, Huntington Library.

63 Harper, *The Life and Work of Susan B. Anthony*, vol. 3, pp. 1,129–30, 1,376; *Jus Suffragii*, 15 September 1907; women were enfranchised in Hawaii in 1920, in Puerto Rico in 1937, and in the Philippines in 1946.

64 Even in 1898, notwithstanding its general welcome to speakers on race and foreign affairs, the prestigious New England Women's Club concentrated on lectures with a domestic flavour: see Secretary's Annual Report, 1898, pp. 3–4, Box 8, New England Women's Club Papers, SL.

65 *Woman's Journal*, 16 April 1898.

66 See letter of 15 July 1898 from the corresponding Secretary in General Correspondence, Box 3, Hannah G. Solomon Papers, LC; Records of the National Council of Jewish Women, LC; and in *ibid.*, National Council of Jewish Women-American, Folder 9, Sadie, 1894–1910, flier addressed to 'Dear sisters', n.d.

67 Papachristou, 'American Women and foreign policy', p. 505; Marchand, *The American Peace Movement*, chapter 6; Craig, 'Lucia True Ames Mead', p. 80.

68 B. Porter, *Critics of Empire: British Radical Attitudes to Colonialism in Africa, 1895–1914*, London and New York, Macmillan and St. Martin's Press, 1968, pp. 240f.; D. Birkett, *Mary Kingsley, Imperial Adventuress*, London, Macmillan, 1992; A. Blunt, *Gender and Imperialism: Mary Kingsley in West Africa*, New York, The Guilford Press, 1994; H. Callaway and D. O. Helly, 'Crusader for Empire: Flora Shaw/Lady Lugard', in Chaudhuri and Strobel (eds), *Western Women and Imperialism*, pp. 79–97, quotation from p. 81; S. Foster's *American Women Travellers to Europe in the Nineteenth and Early Twentieth Centuries*, Keele, Keele University Press for the BAAS, 1994, is an excellent introduction to its subject, and see also her *Across New Worlds*, Hemel Hempstead, Harvester Wheatsheaf, 1990; S. Mills, *Discourses of Difference: An Analysis of Women's Travel Writing and Colonialism*, London, Routledge, 1991; D. Middleton, *Victorian Lady Travellers*, London, Routledge and

Kegan Paul, 1965; J. Wallach, *The Extraordinary Life of Gertrude Bell: Adventurer, Adviser to Kings, Ally of Lawrence of Arabia*, London, Phoenix, 1997; I. Grewal, *Home and Harem: Nation, Empire and the Cultures of Travel*, Leicester, Leicester University Press, 1996; M. L. Pratt, *Imperial Eyes: Travel Writing and Transculturation*, London, Routledge, 1992.

69 P. Grimshaw, *Women's Suffrage in New Zealand*, Auckland, Auckland University Press, 1972; R. E. Paulson, *Women's Suffrage and Prohibition: A Comparative Study of Equality and Social Control*, Glenview, Scott, Foresman, 1973, chapter 6; Mayall, Levine and Fletcher (eds), *Women's Suffrage in the British Empire*; A. Oldfield, *Woman Suffrage in Australia: A Gift or a Struggle?*, Cambridge, Cambridge University Press, 1992.

70 P. Jalland, *Women, Marriage and Politics, 1860–1914*, Oxford, Clarendon Press, 1986, p. 227.

71 Quoted in Anderson, *Race and Rapprochement*, pp. 140, 208.

72 R. G. Martin, *Lady Randolph Churchill: A Biography*, London, Cassell, 1972, originally published 1971, vol. 2, pp. 61–2.

73 *Ibid.*, p. 131.

74 *Ibid.*, pp. 159f.

75 Porter, *Critics of Empire*, pp. 112f.; S. Howe, *Anticolonialism in British Politics: The Left and the End of Empire, 1918–1964*, Oxford, Clarendon Press, 1993, pp. 35–7.

76 J. Trollope, *Britannia's Daughters: Women of the British Empire*, London Pimlico, 1994, originally published 1983, pp. 64–5, 109–10; A. J. Hammerton, *Emigrant Gentlewomen: Genteel Poverty and Female Emigration, 1830–1914*, London, Croom Helm, 1979.

77 *Imperial Colonist*, 1902, 1, no. 1, p. 6, WL.

78 Reports of the South African Colonisation Society for 1906 and 1913–14, WL; J. Goodman, '"Their market value must be greater for the experience they had gained": secondary school headmistresses and empire, 1897–1917', on teachers who went overseas: in J. Goodman and J. Martin (eds), *Gender, Colonialism and Education: The Politics of Experience*, London, Woburn Press, 2002, chapter 8.

79 R. West, *1900*, London, Weidenfeld and Nicolson, 1996, originally published in 1982, p. 56; J. Bush, *Edwardian Ladies and Imperial Power*, Leicester, Leicester University Press, 2000.

80 Anderson, *Race and Rapprochement*, pp. 130–2; Balfour to Mrs Fawcett, 14 March 1900, Autograph Letter Collection, WL.

81 R. First and A. Scott, *Olive Schreiner*, London, Andre Deutsch, 1980, pp. 97, 197, 219f.

82 B. Roberts, *Those Bloody Women: Three Heroines of the Boer War*, London, John Murray, 1991; P. M. Krebs, '"The last of the gentlemen's wars": women in the Boer War concentration camp controversy', *History Workshop Journal*, 1992, vol. 33, pp. 38–56; S. B. Spies, 'Women and the war', in P. Warwick (ed.), *The South African War: The Anglo-Boer War, 1899–1902*, London, Longman, 1980, pp. 161–85; Boer War letters, vol. 7, Leonard and Kate Courtney Collection, Archives Division, British Library of Political and Economic Science, London School of Economics (in future LSE); Liddington, *The Road to Greenham*, chapter 3, looks at the Boer War.

83 Martin, *Lady Randolph Churchill*, pp. 156, 219.

84 D. Rubinstein, *A Different World for Women: The Life of Millicent Garrett Fawcett*, Columbus, Ohio University Press, 1991, p. 120.

85 B. Caine, *Victorian Feminists*, Oxford, Oxford University Press, 1992, pp. 174–5,

213–14; M. G. Fawcett, *Women's Suffrage: A Short History of a Great Movement*, London, n.d., pp. 59–60.

86 J. Butler, *The Native Races and the War*, London, Gay and Bird, 1900; Jordan, *Josephine Butler*, p. 283.

87 Rubinstein, *A Different World for Women*, pp. 121–30; Roberts, *Those Bloody Women*, p. 274, source of quotation; Krebs, ' The last of the gentlemen's wars'; R. Van Reenen (ed.), *Emily Hobhouse's Boer War Letters*, Cape Town, Human and Rousseau, 1984.

88 See, for instance, W. O'Neill, *Everyone Was Brave: A History of Feminism in America*, New York, Quadrangle, 1969; R. Muncy, *Creating a Female Dominion in American Reform, 1890–1935*, New York, Oxford University Press, 1991; Scott, *Natural Allies;* L. Gordon, 'Black and white visions of welfare: women's welfare activism, 1890–1945', *Journal of American History*, 1991, vol. 78, pp. 559–90; S. Koven and S. Michel (eds), *Mothers of a New World: Maternalist Politics and the Origins of Welfare States*, London, Routledge, 1993; K. K. Sklar, *Florence Kelley and the Nation's Work: The Rise of Women's Political Culture, 1830–1900*, New Haven, Yale University Press, 1995; N. Frankel and N. S. Dye (eds), *Gender, Class, Race and Reform in the Progressive Era*, Lexington, University Press of Kentucky, 1991; T. Skocpol, *Protecting Soldiers and Mothers: The Politics of Social Provision in the United States, 1870s–1920s*, Cambridge, MA, Belknap Press, 1992; Schneider and Schneider, *American Women in the Progressive Era*; S. Pedersen, *Family, Dependence, and the Origins of the Welfare State*, Cambridge, Cambridge University Press, 1993; A. Gutman (ed.), *Democracy and the Welfare State*, Princeton, Princeton University Press, 1988; J. Lewis, *Women and Social Action in Victorian and Edwardian England*, Aldershot, Edward Elgar, 1991; G. Bock and P. Thane (eds), *Maternity and Gender Politics: Women and the Rise Of European Welfare States, 1880s–1950s*, London, Routledge, 1991; E. J. Clapp, *Mothers of All Children: Women Reformers and the Rise of Juvenile Courts in Progressive America*, University Park, PA, Pennsylvania State University Press, 1998; Bolt, *The Women's Movements* and '*Feminist Ferment*'; E. J. Yeo (ed.), *Radical Femininity: Women's Self-Representation in the Public Sphere*, Manchester, Manchester University Press, 1998; E. Jordan, *The Women's Movement and Women's Employment in Nineteenth-century Britain*, London, Routledge, 1999.

89 E. C. DuBois, 'Working women, class relations, and suffrage militance: Harriot Stanton Blatch and the New York woman suffrage movement, 1894–1909', *Journal of American History*, 1987, vol. 74, pp. 34–58; E. C. DuBois, *Harriot Stanton Blatch and the Winning of Woman Suffrage*, New Haven, Yale University Press, 1997; R. M. Jacoby, 'Feminism and class consciousness in the British and American Trade Union Leagues, 1890–1925', in B. A. Carroll (ed.), *Liberating Women's History: Theoretical and Critical Essays*, Urbana, University of Illinois Press, 1976, pp. 137–60; N. S. Dye, *As Equals and Sisters: Feminism, the Labor Movement and the Women's Trade Union League of New York*, Columbia, University of Missouri Press, 1980; J. Gaffin and D. Thoms, *Caring and Sharing: The Centenary History of the Co-operative Women's Guild*, Manchester, Co-operative Union, 1983; J. Liddington and J. Norris, *One Hand Tied Behind Us: The Rise of the Women's Suffrage Movement*, London, Virago, 1978; R. S. Neale (ed.), *Class and Ideology in the Nineteenth Century*, London, Routledge and Kegan Paul, 1972, pp. 143–68; Bolt, *The Women's Movements*; S. Alexander (ed.), *Women's Fabian Tracts*, London, Routledge, 1988, especially Tract no. 175; Kuzmack, *Women's Cause*, chapters 4–5.

90 On the importance of women to industrialisation, and of industrialisation to the fashioning of gender, see K. Honeyman, *Women, Gender and Industrialisation in England, 1700–1870*, Basingstoke, Macmillan, 2000, pp. 146–7 and *passim*; first quotation from 'Why wage-earning women should vote' by Maud Younger in Elizabeth B. Harbert Collection, Huntington Library; see also A. Kessler-Harris, *Out to Work: A History of Wage-Earning Women in the United States*, New York, Oxford University Press, 1982; and A. Kessler-Harris, *In Pursuit of Equity: Women, Men, and the Quest for Economic Citizenship in 20th-century America*, New York, Oxford University Press, 2001; B. M. Wertheimer, *We Were There*, New York, Pantheon, 1977; M. Tax, *The Rising of Women: Feminist Solidarity and Class Conflict, 1880–1917*, New York, Monthly Review Press, 1979; N. C. Soldon, *Women in British Trade Unions, 1874–1976*, Dublin, Gill and Macmillan, 1978; E. Roberts, *A Woman's Place: An Oral History of Working-Class Women, 1890–1940*, Oxford, Basil Blackwell, 1984; H. Benenson, 'The "family wage" and working women's consciousness in Britain, 1880–1914', *Politics and Society*, 1991, vol. 19, no. 1, pp. 71–108; B. Drake, *Women in Trade Unions*, London, Virago, 1984, originally published 1920; E. Jordan, *The Women's Movement and Employment in Nineteenth Century Britain*, London, Routledge, 1999; S. Pennington and B. Westover, *A Hidden Workforce: Women Homeworkers in Britain, 1850–1985*, London, Macmillan, 1983; A. V. John (ed.), *Unequal Opportunities: Women's Employment in England, 1800–1918*, Oxford, Basil Blackwell, 1986; S. O. Rose, *Limited Livelihoods: Gender and Class in Nineteenth Century England*, London, Routledge, 1992; A. Clark, *The Struggle for the Breeches: Gender and the Making of the British Working Class*, Berkeley, University of California Press, 1995; H. Bradley, *Men's Work, Women's Work: A Sociological History of the Sexual Division of Labour in Employment*, Cambridge, Polity Press, 1989; D. Valenze, *The First Industrial Woman*, Oxford, Oxford University Press, 1995; P. Sharpe (ed.), *Women's Work: The English Experience, 1650–1914*, London, Arnold, 1998; E. Gordon, *Women and the Labour Market in Scotland, 1850–1914*, Oxford, Clarendon Press, 1991; S. Lewenhak, *Women and Trade Unions*, London, Ernest Benn, 1977; L. Holcombe, *Victorian Ladies at Work: Middle Class Working Women in England and Wales, 1850–1914*, Newton Abbot, David and Charles, 1973; K. Gleadle, *British Women in the Nineteenth Century*, Basingstoke, Palgrave, 2001, p. 36 (source of second quotation), chapters 1–2, 7–8; C. Collette, *For Labour and for Women: The Women's Labour League, 1906–1918*, Manchester, Manchester University Press, 1989.

91 J. Hannam and K. Hunt, 'Gendering the stories of socialism: an essay in historical criticism', in M. Walsh (ed.), *Working Out Gender: Perspectives from Labour History*, Aldershot, Ashgate, 2000; L. Sargent (ed.), *Women and Revolution: The Unhappy Marriage of Marxism and Feminism, A Debate on Class and Patriarchy*, London, Pluto, 1981; S. Rowbotham, L. Segal and H. Wainwright, *Beyond the Fragments: Feminism and the Making of Socialism*, London, Merlin, 1979; J. Hannam and K. Hunt, *Socialist Women: Britain, 1880s to 1920s*, London and New York, Routledge, 2002, 'Introduction', chapter 1 and *passim*; M. J. Buhle, *Women and American Socialism, 1870–1920*, Urbana, University of Illinois Press, 1981; Banks, *Faces of Feminism*, chapter 4; H. Scott, *Does Socialism Liberate Women? Experiences From Eastern Europe*, Boston, Beacon Press, 1975, originally published 1974, chapters 2, 3 and 10; M. J. Boxer and J. H. Quataert, *Socialist Women: European Socialist Feminism in the Nineteenth and Early Twentieth Centuries*, New York, Elsevier, 1978; Z. Eisenstein (ed.), *Capitalist Patriarchy and the Case for Socialist Feminism*, New York, Monthly Review Press, 1979; C. A. Mackinnon, 'Feminism, Marxism, method

and the state: an agenda for theory', in N. G. Keohane, M. Z. Rosaldo and B. Gelpi (eds), *Feminist Theory: A Critique of Ideology*, Brighton, Harvester, 1982, pp. 1–30; A. Phillips, *Divided Loyalties: Dilemmas of Sex and Class*, London, Virago, 1987.

92 Quoted in Scott, *Does Socialism Liberate Women?*, p. 59.

93 See 'Why you should be a socialist' by Theresa Malkiel in Alice Park Collection, Huntington Library; Hannam and Hunt, *Socialist Women*, chapter 7, is the best introduction to their internationalism, and stresses that 'the potential points of fracture' for that internationalism 'were suffrage politics and party loyalty'. The First International was known to contemporaries as the International Workingman's Association.

94 On the complexities of class in Britain, see D. Cannadine, *Class in Britain*, New Haven and London, Yale University Press, 1998.

95 Quoted in L. Garner, *Stepping Stones to Women's Liberty: Feminist Ideas in the Women's Suffrage Movement, 1990–1918*, London, Heinemann Educational Books, 1984, p. 4 – quotation from Lily Gair Wilkinson's c. 1910 book, *Revolutionary Socialism and the Women's Movement;* E. C. DuBois, 'Woman suffrage and the Left: an internationalist socialist-feminist perspective', *New Left Review*, 1991, vol. 186, pp. 20–45, especially p. 33.

96 S. Bernstein, *The First International in America*, New York, Augustus M. Kelley, 1962, p. 286; Buhle, *Women and American Socialism*, p. xiv.

97 Jacoby, 'Feminism and class consciousness'; J. A. Baer, *The Chains of Protection: The Judicial Response to Women's Labor Legislation*, Westport, CT, Greenwood Press, 1978, p. 5 and *passim*; S. Lehrer, *Origins of Protective Legislation for Women, 1905–1925*, Albany, State University of New York Press, 1987; Scott, *Does Socialism Liberate Women?*, p. 60; P. M. Graves, *Labour Women: Women in British Working-Class Politics, 1918–1939*, Cambridge, Cambridge University Press, 1994, pp. 142f.; DuBois, 'Woman suffrage and the Left' p. 32; R. Feurer, 'The meaning of "sisterhood": the British women's movement and protective labour legislation, 1870–1900', *Victorian Studies*, vol. 31, winter, 1988, pp. 233–60.

98 B. Taylor, *Eve and the New Jerusalem: Socialism and Feminism in the Nineteenth Century*, London, Virago, 1983; G. Malmgreen, *Neither Bread Nor Roses: Utopian Feminism and the English Working Class, 1800–1850*, Brighton, Harvester, 1978; S. Te Selle (ed.), *The Family, Communes and Utopian Societies*, New York, Harper and Row, 1971; A. E. Bestor, *Backwoods Utopias: The Sectarian and Owenite Phases of Communitarian Socialism in America, 1663–1829*, Philadelphia, University of Pennsylvania Press, 1980; J. F. C. Harrison, *Robert Owen and the Owenites in Britain and America: The Quest for the New Moral World*, London, Routledge and Kegan Paul, 1969.

99 See, for instance, P. Levine, *Victorian Feminism, 1850–1900*, London, Hutchinson Education, 1987, pp. 16–17; Buhle, *Women and American Socialism*, chapters 3 and 4; D. Powell, 'The New Liberalism and the rise of labour', *Historical Journal*, 1981, vol. 29, no. 3, pp. 392–3.

100 R. Strachey, *The Cause: A Short History of the Women's Movement in Great Britain*, London, Virago, 1989, originally published by Virago in 1978, p. 245.

3 The impact of the First World War

1 P. Summerfield, 'Women and war in the twentieth century', in J. Purvis (ed.), *Women's History: Britain, 1850–1945, An Introduction*, London, UCL Press, 1995, p. 307.

2 For a sample of the huge literature, see A. Marwick, *The Deluge: British Society and the First World War*, Harmondsworth, Penguin, 1967, first published 1965, p. 9; A. Marwick, *War and Social Change in the Twentieth Century*, London, Macmillan, 1974; S. Constantine, M. W. Kirby and M. B. Rose (eds), *The First World War in British History*, London, Edward Arnold, 1995; D. Mitchell, *Women on the Warpath: The Story of the Women of the First World War*, London, Jonathan Cape, 1966; G. Brabon and P. Summerfield, *Out of the Cage: Women's Experiences in Two World Wars*, London, Pandora, 1987; M. Eksteins, *Rites of Spring: The Great War and the Birth of the Modern* Age, London, Black Swan, 1990; M. Higonnet *et al.*, *Behind the Lines: Gender and the Two World Wars*, New Haven, Yale University Press, 1987; J. M. Winter, *Socialism and the Challenge of War: Ideas and Politics in Britain, 1912–18*, London, Routledge and Kegan Paul, 1974; J. M. Winter, The *Great War and the British People*, Cambridge, Harvard University Press, 1986; D. M. Kennedy, *Over Here: The First World War and American Society*, New York, Oxford University Press, 1980; N. A. Wynn, *From Progressivism to Prosperity: American Society and the First World War*, New York, Holmes and Meier, 1986; M. Greenwald, *Women, War and Work: The Impact of World War One on Women Workers in the United States*, Westport, CT, Greenwood Press, 1982; N. Fligstein, *Going North: Migration of Blacks and Whites from the South, 1900–1950*, New York, Academic Press, 1982; B. Steinson, *American Women's Activism in World War One*, New York, Garland, 1982.

3 M. Ceadel, *Pacifism in Britain, 1914–1945: The Defining of a Faith*, Oxford, Clarendon Press, 1980, p. 60; C. Chatfield, *For Peace and Justice: Pacifism in America, 1914–1941*, Knoxville, University of Tennessee Press, 1971, p. 9.

4 S. Pankhurst, *The Home Front: A Mirror to Life in England During the World War*, London, Hutchinson, 1932, pp. 31, 39, 66–7.

5 *Ibid.*, p. 169.

6 Buhle, *Women and American Socialism*, p. 222.

7 *Ibid.*, pp. 222–41, and chapters 5, 7 and 8; Scott, *Does Socialism Liberate Women?* p. 61; DuBois, 'Woman suffrage and the Left', p. 31.

8 Scott, *Does Socialism Liberate Women?* pp. 61–2; Pankhurst, *The Home Front*, p. 31; J. Braunthal, *History of the International, 1914–1943*, London, Nelson, 1967, translated J. Clark, originally published 1963, vol. 2, pp. ix, 1, 34–5: the four parties were the British ILP, the two Russian parties, and the Serbian Social Democrats; Ceadel, *Pacifism in Britain*, p. 5.

9 Pankhurst, *The Home Front*, p. 148.

10 Buhle, *Women and American Socialism*, pp. 318–23, quotation from p. 322; DuBois, 'Woman suffrage and the Left', pp. 42–3; Braunthal, *History of the International*, p. x; D. G. Daniels, *Always a Sister: The Feminism of Lillian D. Wald, A Biography*, New York, The Feminist Press, 1995, originally published 1989, chapter 9, on superpatriots' activities; Hannam and Hunt, *Socialist Women*, pp. 177–80; B. Winslow, 'Sylvia Pankhurst and the Great War', in I. Bullock and R. P. Pankhurst (eds), *Sylvia Pankhurst: From Artist to Anti-Fascist*, London, Macmillan, 1992, pp. 115–16. In March 1916, the ELFS was renamed the Workers' Suffrage Federation. Christabel Pankhurst, by contrast, dismissed 'the struggle for freedom in Russia' as 'a man's movement': see E. S. Pankhurst, *The Suffragette Movement*, London, Virago, 1997, originally published 1931, p. 337.

11 Pedersen, *Family, Dependence and the Origins of the Welfare State*, p. 46; Mrs. Fawcett in *Jus Suffragii*, 15 November 1907.

12 M. Walker, 'Labour women and internationalism', in Middleton (ed.), *Women in the*

Labour Movement, pp. 84–5; Hannam and Hunt, *Socialist Women*, p. 177; K. Hunt, 'The immense meaning of it all', pp. 32f., 36, 38 (source of quotation), 39.

13 Graves, *Labour Women*, p. 14; Pankhurst, *The Home Front*, p. 33; Marwick, *The Deluge*, p. 166.

14 A. Wiltsher, *Most Dangerous Women: The Feminist Peace Campaigners of the Great War*, London, Pandora, 1985, p. 60.

15 *Ibid.*, pp. 129, 137 and *passim.*

16 G. Bussey and M. Tims, *Pioneers for Peace: Women's International League for Peace and Freedom, 1915–1965*, London, WILPF, 1980, p. 23.

17 S. Oldfield, *Spinsters of This Parish: The Life and Times of F. M. Mayor and Mary Sheepshanks*, London, Virago, 1984, p. 178.

18 Wiltsher, *Most Dangerous Women*, p. 23.

19 *Ibid.*, chapters 1–3 and pp. 58–9; Mary Sheepshanks to Alice Park, 10 May 1915, Autograph Letter Collection, WL; Oldfield, *Spinsters of This Parish*, p. 185.

20 Oldfield, *Spinsters of This Parish*, p. 177; Wiltsher, *Most Dangerous Women*, chapter 4; J. Vellacott Newberry, 'Anti-war suffragists', *History*, 1977, vol. 62, pp. 417–18; J. Vellacott, 'Feminist consciousness and the First World War', *History Workshop Journal*, 1987, vol. 23, pp. 88–90 (source of first quotation), 92–3; Mrs Fawcett to Carrie Chapman Catt, 15 December 1914 and 21 July 1915, Autograph Letter Collection, WL, and Mrs Fawcett to Secretaries of Federations and Societies (of the NUWSS), 23 April 1915, in Women's International League for Peace and Freedom Papers, 4/1, LSE; Rubinstein, *A Different World for Women*, pp. 216–17.

21 See resignation letters of members of the NUWSS executive in Women's International League for Peace and Freedom Papers, 4/1, LSE.

22 Wiltsher, *Most Dangerous Women*, pp. 78–81; Rubinstein, *A Different World for Women*; J. Alberti, *Beyond Suffrage: Feminists in War and Peace, 1914–28*, London, Macmillan, 1989, chapter 3.

23 Ceadel, *Pacifism in Britain*, pp. 3, 5; Wiltsher, *Most Dangerous Women*, pp. 75, 80; S. Holton, *Suffrage Days: Stories From the Women's Suffrage Movement*, London and New York, Routledge, 1996, pp. 215–16, identifies three positions among NUWSS members: pacifism; advocacy of 'an educational campaign on the causes and prevention of war in general'; and patriotism leading to support of the war effort. The first two positions were held by the internationalists.

24 S. Oldfield, *Women Against the Iron Fist: Alternatives to Militarism, 1900–1989*, Oxford, Blackwell, 1989, pp. 29, 45, 58–9.

25 Oldfield, *Spinsters of This Parish*, p. 189; Alberti, *Beyond Suffrage*, pp. 40–1, 69.

26 Wiltsher, *Most Dangerous Women*, pp. 82–3; Oldfield, *Spinsters of This Parish*, p. 307; Vellacott, 'Feminist consciousness and the First World War', p. 93; H. Swanwick, *I Have Been Young*, London, Gollancz, 1935; Wiltsher, *Most Dangerous Women*, Introduction; Vellacott Newberry, 'Anti-war suffragists'; Alberti, *Beyond Suffrage*, chapter 2; Oldfield, *Women Against the Iron Fist*, chapters 2 and 3; S. Fletcher, *Maude Royden*, Oxford, Blackwell, 1989.

27 Wiltsher, *Most Dangerous Women*, chapters 5 and 6; Bussey and Tims, *Pioneers for Peace*, chapter 1; J. Addams, E. G. Balch and A. Hamilton, *Women at the Hague: The International Congress of Women and Its Results*, New York, Garland, 1972, originally published 1915.

28 Bussey and Tims, *Pioneers for Peace*, pp. 21–2.

29 Wiltsher, *Most Dangerous Women*, pp. 126, 210.

30 Ceadel, *Pacifism in Britain*, p. 61.

31 Wiltsher, *Most Dangerous Women*, pp. 127, 191.
32 *Ibid.*, chapter 7 and p. 193.
33 *Ibid.*, p. 131; but (see p. 242) the individual membership of the Union of Democratic Control, to which all British peace groups were affiliated, was only 6,000 in 1915: the UDC then had 300,000 associated members.
34 Pankhurst, *The Home Front*, p. 153.
35 Oldfield, *Spinsters of This Parish*, pp. 181–5.
36 Wiltsher, *Most Dangerous Women*, p. 193; Holton, *Suffrage Days*, p. 221; Hannam and Hunt, *Socialist Women*, p. 183f.; Winslow, 'Sylvia Pankhurst and the Great War', pp. 88f.
37 At the practical level, conscientious objectors were particularly helped by the women (and men) of the No Conscription Fellowship (1915). This paragraph has drawn on Wiltsher, *Most Dangerous Women*, chapters 7 and 9; Liddington, *The Long Road to Greenham*, pp. 109–19; J. J. Smyth, 'Rents, peace, votes: working-class women and political activity in the First World War', in E. Breitenbach and E. Gordon (eds), *Out of Bounds: Women in Scottish Society, 1800–1945*, Edinburgh, Edinburgh University Press, 1982, pp. 174f.; Mitchell, *Women on the Warpath*, pp. 332–44; M. L. Davies, (ed.), *Life As We Have Known It, By Co-operative Working Women*, London, Virago Press, 1977, originally published 1931, p. 65.
38 J. Vellacott, *Bertrand Russell and the Pacifists in the First World War*, Brighton, Harvester Press, 1980, p. 23; C. Law, *Suffrage and Power: The Women's Movement, 1918–1928*, London, I. B. Tauris, 1997, pp. 16–21, 30–6; Winslow, 'Sylvia Pankhurst and the Great War', pp. 112–13.
39 Wiltsher, *Most Dangerous Women*, p. 180; Holton, *Suffrage Days*, p. 209.
40 Marchand, *The American Peace Movement*, chapters 1 and 5.
41 *Ibid.*, pp. 144–5 and chapter 5 generally.
42 Daniels, *Always a Sister*, pp. 125–8; Marchand, *The American Peace Movement*, pp. 182–5.
43 Garlin, 'We women of the United States', p. 2, in Anna Garlin Spencer Papers, Swarthmore College Peace Collection (in future SPC), Swarthmore, Pennsylvania.
44 Steinson, *American Women's Activism in World War One*, pp. 16–23, 28 (source of quotation); E. Pethick-Lawrence, *My Part in a Changing World*, London, Victor Gollancz, 1938, pp. 308–10.
45 L. B. Costin, 'Feminism, pacifism, internationalism and the 1915 International Congress of Women', *Women's Studies International Forum*, 1982, vol. 5, p. 308; B. J. Steinson, '"The mother half of humanity": American women in the peace and preparedness movements in World War I', in D. R. Berkin and C. M. Lovett (eds), *Women, War and Revolution*, New York, Holmes and Meier, 1980, p. 261.
46 Marchand, *The American Peace Movement*, chapter 6; Mitchell, *Women on the Warpath*, p. 316; M. L. Degen, *The History of the Women's Peace Pact*, Baltimore, Johns Hopkins University Press, 1939; Daniels, *Always a Sister*, pp. 128–31; Schneider and Schneider, *American Women in the Progressive Era*, chapter 8; S. R. Herman, *Eleven Against War: Studies in American Internationalist Thought, 1898–1921*, Stanford, Stanford University Press, 1969; J. Addams, *Peace and Bread in Time of War*, New York, Macmillan, 1922; H. H. Alonso, *Peace as a Women's Issue: A History of the U.S. Movement for World Peace and Women's Rights*, Syracuse, Syracuse University Press, 1983; B. S. Kraft, *The Peace Ship: Henry Ford's Pacifist Adventure in the First World War*, New York, Macmillan, 1978; Foster, *Women for All Seasons*, p. 18 (source of quotation).

47 Marchand, *The American Peace Movement*, chapter 7.
48 Daniels, *Always a Sister*, p. 131.
49 *Ibid.*
50 *Ibid.*, pp. 207–8.
51 Rubinstein, *A Different World for Women*, pp. 230–2; Bosche and Kloosterman (eds), *Politics and Friendship*, p. 141.
52 Wiltsher, *Most Dangerous Women*, p. 82; Marchand, *The American Peace Movement*, p. 213.
53 Marchand, *The American Peace Movement*, p. 218; Bolt, *The Women's Movements*, pp. 183–204, 237–49 on suffragism in the two countries.
54 *Ibid.*, p. 217; R. B. Fowler, *Carrie Catt: Feminist Politician*, Boston, Northwestern University Press, 1986; Steinson, *American Women's Activism*, pp. 111–12.
55 Jeffreys-Jones, *Changing Differences*, chapter 2.
56 Marchand, *The American Peace Movement*, p. 219.
57 B. Wiesen Cook (ed.), *Crystal Eastman on Women and Revolution*, New York, Oxford University Press, 1978, p. 14.
58 Marchand, *The American Peace Movement*, chapter 7.
59 *Ibid.*, pp. 294–322; H. H. Alonso, 'Gender and peace politics in the First World War United States: the People's Council of America', *International History Review*, 1997, vol. xix, pp. 83–102; DuBois, 'Woman suffrage and the Left', p. 43; N. Cott, 'Feminist politics in the 1920s: the National Woman's Party', *Journal of American History*, 1984, vol. 71, pp. 43–68; see also K. Kennedy, *Disloyal Mothers and Scurrilous Citizens: Women and Subversion During World War I*, Bloomington, Indiana University Press, 1999.
60 Marchand, *The American Peace Movement*, p. 263.
61 Craig, 'Lucia True Ames Mead', p. 81.
62 *Ibid.*, p. 83.
63 Bolt, *The Women's Movements*, p. 254.
64 Daniels, *Always a Sister*, p. 132; Marchand, *The American Peace Movement*, p. 259.
65 Wiltsher, *Most Dangerous Women*, p. 201, and Bussey and Tims, *Pioneers for Peace*, p. 29, for slightly different figures about attendance and national sections.
66 373 Congress members voted for war; in the Senate the vote was 82 to 6 in favour of war.
67 Bussey and Tims, *Pioneers for Peace*, pp. 31–2; 'Women's International League for Peace and Freedom, 1915–1938: the War Years, 1915–1918', in Mary Nuttall WILPF files, Add. 1, p. 9, LSE.
68 Alberti, *After Suffrage*, p. 87.
69 Craig, 'Lucia True Ames Mead', p. 84.
70 Bussey and Tims, *Pioneers for Peace*, p. 32.
71 Wiltsher, *Most Dangerous Women*, p. 210.
72 Bussey and Tims, *Pioneers for Peace*, p. 33.
73 Alberti, *After Suffrage*, pp. 88–9, source of second quotation; Bosche and Kloosterman (eds), *Politics and Friendship*, p. 142; 'The sixth quinquennial of the International Council of Women held in Washington, May 4–14, 1925', pp. 1–2, by Fannie Fern Andrews, in Folder 275, Box 21, Fannie Fern Andrews Papers, SL. See also C. J. Snider, 'Peace and politics: Fannie Fern Andrews, professional politics and the American peace movement, 1900–1941', *Mid-America*, vol. 79, no. 1, winter 1997, vol. 79, pp. 71–96, on Andrew's growing inability to balance her gender and political interests, and to launch an international education bureau.

74 Summerfield, 'Women and war', pp. 319–23; Greenwald, *Women, War and Work*, chapter 1; Giddings, *When and Where I Enter*, chapter VIII; C. Griffiths, *Women's Factory Work in World War I*, Stroud, Alan Sutton Publishing, 1991, see p. 13 for a different figure for women industrial workers in Britain to that quoted in Summerfield, p. 321; G. Brabon, *Women Workers in the First World War*, London, Routledge, 1989; Pedersen, *Family, Dependence and the Origins of the Welfare State*, chapter 2; B. Thwaites, *A Class Society at War: England, 1914–18*, Leamington Spa, Berg, 1987; M. F. McFeely, *Lady Inspectors: The Campaign for a Better Workforce, 1883–1921*, Oxford, Blackwell, 1988, chapters 15–16; Kessler-Harris, *Out to Work*, chapter 8; Strachey, *The Cause*, p. 340.

75 Quoted in Davies (ed.), *Life As We Have Known It*, p. 65.

76 Rubinstein, *A Different World for Women*, pp. 215, 233–4; Graves, *Labour Women*, pp. 5, 9 (source of quotation); Pankhurst, *The Home Front*; Mitchell, *Women on the Warpath*, sections on 'Women in Factories' and 'Our Sylvia'; Pedersen, *Family, Dependence and the Origins of the Welfare State*, chapter 2; Jacoby, *The British and American Women's Trade Union Leagues, 1890–1925*, Brooklyn, NY, Charlson Publishing, 1994, pp. 105–14; Winslow, 'Sylvia Pankhurst and the Great War', pp. 100f.

77 Peck, *Carrie Chapman Catt*, pp. 267–9, 271–2, 274–5; Schneider and Schneider, *American Women in the Progressive Era*, pp. 223–4.

78 See, in National Trade Union League of America Papers, SL, account of 1917 convention in Folder 3, Box 1; also account of the league training schools in Folders 4 and 5, Box 1; Dye, *As Equals and as Sisters*; R. M. Jacoby, 'The Women's Trade Union League and American feminism', *Feminist Studies*, 1975, vol. 3, pp. 126–40; and Jacoby, *The British and American Women's Trade Union Leagues*, pp. 131, 133; the Women's Bureau survived: see K. A. Loughlin, *Women's Work and Public Policy: A History of the Women's Bureau, U.S. Department of Labor, 1945–70*, Boston, MA, Northeastern University Press, 2000, on its history, work and links.

79 Schneider and Schneider, *American Women in the Progressive Era*, pp. 215, 228; Steinson, *American Women's Activism in World War One*; Greenwald, *Women, War and Work*, pp. 39–44, 234–6, 240–1.

80 For a stimulating introduction to women's role, see Skocpol, *Protecting Soldiers and Mothers*, Part III; L. Gordon, *Heroes of Their Own Lives: The Politics and History of Family Violence, Boston 1880–1960*, London, Virago, 1989, first published 1988, p. 137.

81 See K. K. Sklar, 'The historical foundations of women's power in the creation of the American welfare state, 1830–1930', in Koven and Michel (eds), *Mothers of a New World*, pp. 43–93; S. Koven and S. Michel, 'Womanly duties: maternalist politics and the origins of welfare states in France, Germany, Great Britain, and the United States, 1880–1920', *American Historical Review*, 1990, vol. 95, pp. 1076–1108; T. Skocpol, *Social Policy in the United States*, Princeton, Princeton University Press, 1995, Introduction, chapters 1 and 3, and *passim*.

82 A. Douglas, *Terrible Honesty: Mongrel Manhattan in the 1920s*, London, Picador, 1996, originally published 1995, chapter 6 and *passim*; R. Rosenberg, *Beyond Separate Spheres: Intellectual Roots of Modern Feminism*, New Haven and London, Yale University Press, 1982.

83 See the following essays in Koven and Michel (eds), *Mothers of a New World*: A. Klaus, 'Depopulation and race suicide: maternalism and pronatalist ideologies in France and the United States', pp. 188–212; S. Michel, 'The limits of maternalism: policies toward American wage-earning mothers during the Progressive era', pp. 277–320, especially

pp. 279 and 300–3; E. Boris, 'The power of motherhood: black and white activist women redefine the "political"', pp. 213–45, especially p. 232; see also L. Gordon, 'Black and white visions of welfare: women's welfare activism, 1890–1945', *Journal of American History*, 1991, vol. 78, p. 560; J. L. Goodwin, 'An American experiment in paid motherhood: the implementation of mothers' pensions in early twentieth century Chicago', *Gender and History*, 1992, vol. 4, pp. 323–42; M. Ladd-Taylor, *Mother – Work: Women, Child Welfare, and the State, 1890–1930*, Urbana and Chicago, University of Illinois Press, 1994, especially pp. 55–63, 159–60 and Conclusion; L. Gordon (ed.), *Women, the State, and Welfare*, Madison, University of Wisconsin Press, 1990: especially L. Gordon, 'The new feminist scholarship on the welfare state', pp. 9–35; V. Sapiro, 'The gender basis of American social policy', p. 36f; G. Mink, 'The lady and the tramp: gender, race, and the origins of the American welfare state', pp. 92–122; B. Nelson, 'The origins of the two channel welfare state: workmen's compensation and mother's aid', pp. 123–45; R. Feldstein, *Motherhood in Black and White: Race and Sex in American Liberalism*, Ithaca, NY, Cornell University Press, 2000.

84 See Pedersen, *Family, Dependence and the Origins of the Welfare State*, chapter 2; S. Pedersen, 'Gender, welfare, and citizenship in Britain during the Great War', *American Historical Review*, 1990, vol. 95, pp. 983–1005; S. Pedersen, 'The failure of feminism in the making of the British welfare state, *Radical History Review*, 1989, vol. 43, pp. 86–110; S. K. Kent, 'The politics of sexual difference: World War I and the demise of British feminism', *Journal of British Studies*, 1988, vol. 27, pp. 232–53; D. Dwork, *War Is Good For Babies and Other Young Children: A History of the Infant and Child Welfare Movement in England, 1898–1918*, London, Tavistock, 1987; J. Lewis, 'Models of equality for women: the case of state support for children in twentieth-century Britain', in Bock and Thane (eds), *Maternity and Gender Policies*, pp. 73–92; and in *ibid.*, pp. 93–118, P. Thane, 'Visions of gender in the making of the British welfare state: the case of women in the British Labour Party and social policy, 1906–1945': quotation from p. 106; on the class and political complexities mentioned here, see, for instance, Hannam and Hunt, *Socialist Women*, *passim*; Scott, *Feminism and the Politics of Working Women*, chapter 6 and *passim*; J. Hannam, *Isabella Ford, 1855–1924*, Oxford, Basil Blackwell, 1989; J. Hannam, 'Women and politics', chapter 9 in J. Purvis (ed.), *Women's History: Britain, 1850–1945, An Introduction*, London, UCL Press, 1995, especially pp. 230–1, 238.

85 See, for instance, S. Holton, *Feminism and Democracy: Women's Suffrage and Reform Politics in Britain, 1900–1919*, Cambridge, Cambridge University Press, 1986; E. C. DuBois, 'Working women, class relations, and suffrage militance: Harriot Stanton Blatch and the New York women suffrage movement, 1804–1909', in Ruiz and DuBois (eds), *Unequal Sisters*, pp. 228–46.

86 See S. M. Buechler, *The Transformation of the Woman Suffrage Movement: The Case of Illinois, 1850–1920*, New Brunswick, NJ, Rutgers University Press, 1990, chapter 5; Cott, 'Feminist politics', especially, p. 55; Rupp, *Worlds of Women*, pp. 31, 35–6; Hannam and Hunt, *Socialist Women*, pp. 190–1, 195. Some socialist women had, of course, themselves been prepared to accept a limited suffrage for tactical reasons: see Hannam and Hunt, *Socialist Women*, chapter 5; Holton, *Feminism and Democracy*, chapter 7.

87 Tax, *The Rising of Women*, pp. 200–1.

88 'English women in the labor and co-operative movements: three speeches delivered before the seventh biennial convention of the National Women's Trade Union League, Philadelphia, June 2–7, 1919', pp. 5–13, in National Women's Trade Union

League Papers, Box. 6, SL; Jacoby, *The British and American Women's Trade Union Leagues*, pp. 149f.

89 Giddings, *When and Where I Enter*, chapters VII–X.

90 See Christine Bolt, 'Was there an Anglo-American feminist movement in the earlier twentieth century?', in F. M. Leventhal and R. Quinault (eds), *Anglo-American Attitudes: From Revolution to Partnership*, Aldershot, Ashgate, 2000, chapter 10; and see Lucy Burns's tribute to Christabel Pankhurst in a letter to Doris Stevens, Folder 79, 31 December 1958, Doris Stevens Unclassified Papers, Doris Stevens Papers, SL.

91 Quoted in Mitchell, *Women on the Warpath*, p. 323.

92 Quoted in *ibid*., p. 313; see also Holton, *Suffrage Days*, p. 218, for one woman's complaint about the sentimentality of the peace movement; N. Black, 'The mothers' international: the Women's Co-operative Guild and feminist pacifism', *Women's Studies International Forum*, 1984, vol. 7, p. 474.

93 See, for instance, Steinson, 'The mother half of humanity'; Kennedy, *Women on the Warpath*; Davis, *Lifting as They Climb*, pp. xxii, 60 (source of quotation), 62, 351, 393; Schneider and Schneider, *American Women in the Progressive Era*, pp. 213f.; Strachey, *The Cause*, pp. 237f.; K. Roberts, 'Gender, class, and patriotism: women's parliamentary units in First World War Britain', *The International History Review*, 1997, vol. XIX, p. 65.

94 See J. Sutherland, *Mrs Humphrey Ward: Eminent Victorian, Pre-eminent Edwardian*, Oxford, Clarendon Press, 1990, pp. 350–1, 354.

95 West, *1900*, p. 162.

96 On Addams's independence see, for instance, Wiltsher, *Most Dangerous Women*, p. 122; Garlin's independence has been noted earlier in this chapter; on the financial consequences of the war, and their impact on the Anglo-American relationship, see P. J. Cain and A. G. Hopkins, *British Imperialism: Crisis and Deconstruction, 1914–1990*, London and New York, Longman, 1993, pp. 58–63; D. C. Watt, *Succeeding John Bull: America in Britain's Place, 1900–1975*, Cambridge, Cambridge University Press, 1984.

4 Feminist internationalism and nationalism between the wars

1 Quotation from article, 'What will the world-wide suffrage congress do?', *The Woman Citizen*, 15 May 1920, p. 1277.

2 Doris Stevens, national vice-president of the Woman's Party, quoted in Cook (ed.), *Crystal Eastman on Women and Revolution*, p. 197.

3 L. J. Rupp, *Worlds of Women*, pp. 38–40, 108.

4 Ruth Vandeer Litt, New York, to Crystal Macmillan, London, 2 August 1935, Folder 1370, Alice Paul Papers, SL.

5 R. McKibbin, *The Ideologies of Class: Social Relations in Britain, 1880–1950*, Oxford, Clarendon Press, 1990, chapter 9 on the electoral success of the Conservatives between the wars; Cain and Hopkins, *British Imperialism*, especially p. 4 and chapter 5; Bagwell and Mingay, *Britain and America*, chapters 9 and 10.

6 Jeffreys-Jones, *Changing Differences*, pp. 35–6, 73, 98; M. Pugh, *Women and the Women's Movement in Britain, 1914–1959*, London, Macmillan, 1992, pp. 105–7; Alberti, *Beyond Suffrage*, chapter 8; Liddington, *The Long Road to Greenham*, pp. 132f.; Bussey and Tims, *Pioneers for Peace*, *passim* but especially p. 144; Randall, *Improper Bostonian*, p. 307 and chapters 13–15; the Kellogg-Briand Pact was compli-

cated for European women by the desire not to seem hostile to the rival Soviet peace initiative: see Oldfield, *Spinsters of This Parish*, pp. 250–1.

7 Even British suffragettes had been welcome in the United States: see Christine Bolt, 'America and the Pankhursts', chapter 9 in J. H. Baker (ed.), *Votes for Women: The Struggle for Suffrage Revisited*, New York and Oxford, Oxford University Press, 2002; B. Harrison, *Prudent Revolutionaries: Portraits of British Feminists Between the Wars*, Oxford, Clarendon Press, and New York, Oxford University Press, 1987, pp. 70, 75, 179; Cook (ed.), *Crystal Eastman on Women and Revolution*; A. John, *Elizabeth Robins: Staging a Life, 1862–1952*, London, Routledge, 1995; *Tapes of Interviews on British Women's History in the Twentieth Century*, interviews with Margery Corbett Ashby and Hazel Hunkins-Hallinan, WL; and, also in the WL, the Corbett Ashby Papers and the Six Point Group Papers (for Hunkins-Hallinan).

8 See Mrs Corbett Ashby's letters about her US Tour, 1925, in Margery Corbett Ashby Papers, WL.

9 Interview with Margery Corbett Ashby, 23 November 1976, in *Tapes of Interviews on British Women's History in the Twentieth Century*, WL.

10 Interview with Hazel Hunkins-Hallinan, 8 February 1975, in *Tapes of Interviews on British Women's History in the Twentieth Century*, WL; Hunkins-Hallinan to Dr D. T. Hoffman, 20 April 1971, Box 584, M19, Six Point Group Papers, WL; Hunkins-Hallinan to Wilma Scott Heide, 24 January 1973, in *ibid.*

11 Hunkins-Hallinan, 12 January 1948, in *ibid.*, N1; D. Spender, *There's Always Been a Women's Movement This Century*, London, Pandora Press, Routledge, 1983, p. 27.

12 Cook (ed.), *Crystal Eastman on Women and Revolution*, pp. 226–8; Graves, *Labour Women*, pp. 151–3.

13 Jacoby, *The British and American Women's Trade Union Leagues*, chapter 6.

14 See long letter of Carrie Catt to Belle Sherwin, 30 October 1925, in Box 51, Series II, League of Women Voters Records, LC; Emily Balch to Jane Addams, 5 July 1927 and 18 January 1928, Microfilm reel 19, Jane Addams Collection, University Microfilms International, SPC. There were, however, limits to American boldness, as witness the mixed reactions to British suffrage militancy.

15 Cook (ed.), *Crystal Eastman on Women and Revolution*, p. 165.

16 *Ibid.*, p. 170; S. D. Becker, *The Origins of the Equal Rights Amendment: American Feminism Between the Wars*, Westport, CT, Greenwood Press, 1981, p. 165. The Equal Rights Amendment proposed that 'Men and women shall have equal rights throughout the United States and every place subject to its jurisdiction'.

17 See 'Lady Rhondda', by D. M. Ford, *The Woman Citizen*, vol. 54, 1922–3, 9 September 1922, p. 13; Cook (ed.), *Crystal Eastman on Women and Revolution*, pp. 209–10.

18 Cook (ed.), *Crystal Eastman on Women and Revolution*, p. 199; Becker, *The Origins of the Equal Rights Amendment*, especially chapters 1 and 5; Rupp, *Worlds of Women*, pp. 139–46 and *passim*; Graves, *Labour Women*, pp. 139f.; Alberti, *Beyond Suffrage*, pp. 204–10; Miller, 'Lobbying the League', especially chapters 2 and 6, and pp. 284–5; C. Miller, '"Geneva – the key to equality": inter-war feminists and the League of Nations', *Women's History Review*, 1994, vol. 3, pp. 219–45, reference to p. 220; *Women's International League for Peace and Freedom, 1915–1938: A Venture in Internationalism*, Maison Internationale, Geneva, 1938, in Mary Nuttall WILPF Add.1, p. 19, LSE.

19 Note at Washington, 9 May 1925, US Tour 1925, Margery Corbett Ashby Papers; letters between Sherwin and Catt, Sherwin and Anna Wicksell, Paul and Corbett

Ashby, and Corbett Ashby and Catt, in Boxes 51 and 52, Series II, League of Women Voters Records.

20 Speech by Doris Stevens on 27 August 1931, tribute to Alice Paul as a doer, in Carton 12, folder 372, Speeches of Doris Stevens, Stevens Unprocessed Papers, Doris Stevens Papers, SL; Lady Margaret Rhondda to Helen Archdale, 4 June 1928; to Stevens, undated, on militancy; to Stevens, 11 June 1928; to Stevens, 28 May 1927; to Stevens, 9 July 1928, Folder 154, Lady Margaret Rhondda, 1927–50, in *ibid.*; Rhondda to Paul, 14 June 1926, folder 367 in *ibid.*

21 Alice Paul to Doris Stevens, Geneva, 9 October 1930, Carton 12, Folder 367, Stevens Unprocessed Papers, Doris Stevens Papers, SL; Helen A. Archdale, Geneva, to Mrs Hooker, editor, *Equal Rights*, 19 February 1934, Box 103, Folder 1362, in Alice Paul Papers, SL. Corbett Ashby was said to be 'terrified of . . . [Stevens] in the international field': see Rhondda to Stevens, 9 July 1928, cited in note 20 above. Also, on the tension between Archdale and Paul, see Archdale to Dorothy Evans, 26 July 1931, and to Flora Drummond, 20 June 1932, Box 331, Equal Rights International Papers, WL; Rupp, *Worlds of Women*, pp. 148–9, and Miller, 'Geneva – the key to equality', p. 226. Leaders like Paul were, of course, adored as well as admonished.

22 Alice Paul to Dorothy Evans, 2 April 1934, Box 103, File 1360, Alice Paul Papers, SL; Paul to Doris Stevens, 9 October 1930, Carton 12, Folder 367, Doris Stevens Papers, SL; letters of Corbett Ashby to her mother, 1, 9, 17 April, in US Tour 1925, Margery Corbett Ashby Papers, WL; Carrie Catt to Kathleen Courtney, 13 December 1932, in Carton 19, Committee on the Cause and Cure of War Papers, SL; Mrs O. H. P. Belmont to Alice Paul, 16 September 1929, Box 102, Folder 1335, Alice Paul Papers, SL; Chatfield, *For Peace and Justice*, p. 95; Rupp, 'Feminism, pacifism, internationalism', p. 1579.

23 Margaret Rhondda to Helen Archdale, 4 June 1928, Folder 154, Doris Stevens Papers.

24 Letter from 206 Church Street, Newton, Mass., to Stevens, n.d., Folder 168, Miscellaneous Correspondence, Doris Stevens Papers, SL.

25 See M. Levine, 'Anglo-Jewish foreign policy in crisis – Lucien Wolf, the Cojoint Committee and the war, 1914–18', *Jewish Historical Studies*, 1987–9, vol. xxx, pp. 185–94.

26 Margaret Rhondda to Stevens, 3 July 1928 and 8.3.31, Folder 154, Lady Margaret Rhondda, and Stevens to Jane Norman Smith, 2 August 1934, Folder 163, Doris Stevens Papers, SL.

27 Margaret Rhondda to Alice Paul, 14 June 1926, Folder 367, carton, 12, Stevens Unprocessed Papers, and Rhondda to Helen Archdale, 13 July 1928, Folder 154, Lady Margaret Rhondda, Doris Stevens Papers, SL.

28 Rupp, *Worlds of Women*, pp. 138–9; Becker, *The Origins of the Equal Rights Amendment*, pp. 173–4.

29 Becker, *The Origins of the Equal Rights Amendment*, pp. 23 and 186.

30 Margaret Rhondda to Stevens, 27 August 1928, in Folder 154, Lady Margaret Rhondda, Doris Stevens Papers, SL; Oldfield, *Spinsters of This Parish*, pp. 247–8, 261–3; Bussey and Tims, *Pioneers for Peace*, pp. 104, 127–8; Addams quoted in Chatfield, *For Peace and Justice*, p. 38; Ella Boynton to Jane Addams, 14 September 1927, on British–continental European differences, Microfilm Reel 19, Jane Addams Collection, University Microfilms International, SPC; see also Gustava Heymann to Addams, 4/11/1928, on such difficulties – Reel 19 in *ibid.*

31 B. Melman, *Women's Orients: English Women and the Middle-East, 1718–1918*, Ann Arbor, University of Michigan Press, 1992; J. Zonana, 'The sultan and the slave: feminist orientalism and the structure of *Jane Eyre*', *Signs*, 1993, vol. 18, pp. 592–617; R. Lewis, *Gendering Orientalism: Race, Femininity and Representation*, New York, Routledge, 1996; Tyrrell, *Women's World, Women's Empire*; Remusack, 'Cultural missionaries, maternal imperialists, feminist allies'; Burton, *Burdens of History*.

32 Quotation from Affidavit of National Chairman of International League for Peace and Freedom, by Hannah Clothier Hull, Microfilm Reel 55, Records of the Women's International League for Peace and Freedom, United States Section, 1919–59, SPC.

33 Said, *Orientalism*; K. Jayawardena, *The White Woman's Other Burden: Western Women and South Asia During British Rule*, New York, Routledge, 1995; A. Burton, 'Contesting the zenana: the mission to make "lady doctors for India", 1874–1885', *Journal of British Studies*, 1996, vol. 35, pp. 368–97; G. Forbes, 'Medical careers and health care for Indian women: patterns of control', *Women's History Review*, 1994, vol. 3, pp. 515–30; Burton, *Burdens of History*; Ramusack, 'Cultural missionaries, maternal imperialists, feminist allies'; Chaudhuri and Strobel (eds), *Western Women and Imperialism*, especially chapters by M. Sinha, A. M. Burton and N. L. Paxton.

34 Lady May Drummond-Hay to Doris Stevens, 23 July 1928, Folder 121, Unclassified Papers, Miscellaneous 'H' Correspondence, Doris Stevens Papers, SL; K. Mayo, *Mother India*, London, Cape, 1927; Rubinstein, *A Different World for Women*; E. F. Rathbone, *Child Marriage: The Indian Minotaur. An Object Lesson From the Past to the Future*, London, George Allen and Unwin, 1934, pp. 106f.; B. Harrison, 'Eleanor Rathbone', in *Prudent Revolutionaries*, pp. 99f; M. Stocks, *Eleanor Rathbone: A Biography*, London, Gollancz, 1950, first published 1949, pp. 125–6, 132–40, 148f., quotation from p. 173; 'Women suffrage and child marriage in India', manuscript (undated, probably 1930s) in Margery Corbett Ashby Papers, MICA/C4, WL; J. Liddle and R. Joshi, *Daughters of Independence: Gender, Caste and Class in India*, London, Zed Books and New Brunswick, NJ, Rutgers University Press, 1989, especially pp. 19–23, 26, 31.

35 R. K. Roy, 'Gandhi on women: their role in the world of politics', in A. Copley and G. Paxton (eds), *Gandhi and the Contemporary World: Essays to Mark the 125th Anniversary of the Birth*, Chennai, Indo-British Historical Society, 1997, p. 228; J. Jayawardena, *Feminism and Nationalism in the Third World*, London, Zed Books, 1989 edition, originally published 1986, chapter 6.

36 I. Harrison, *Agatha Harrison: An Impression By Her Sister*, London, Allen and Unwin, 1956, p. 52; *Englishwoman's Review*, no. VI, April 1871, pp. 86–90.

37 See, for instance, Emily Balch to Jane Addams, 5 July 1927, Microfilm Reel 19, Jane Addams Collection, University Microfilms International, SPC.

38 A. Basu and B. Ray, *Women's Struggle: A History of the All-India Women's Conference, 1927–1990*, New Delhi, Manohar, 1990, pp. 12, 54–8; Stocks, *Eleanor Rathbone*, pp. 167f.; M. Kaur, *Women in India's Freedom Struggle*, New Delhi, Sterling Publishers, 1992, especially chapters 3–10; Bussey and Tims, *Pioneers for Peace*, pp. 110–11; Harrison, *Agatha Harrison*, chapters 7–13, quotations from pp. 52, 80. And see, in WILPF papers, LSE: WILPF 4/2: Resolution passed by the Council of the WIL at its meeting on October 30th, 1919; Resolution passed by the Council of the Women's International League at its Meeting on October 30th, 1919; Resolution passed by the Women's International League at its Meeting on November 14th, 1919, at the Queen's Hall, London; Resolution passed by the Executive Committee at its Meeting on March 10th, 1931; Resolution passed at the meeting of the WI Executive

Committee on July 11 1933; Resolution passed at the Annual Council Meetings of the Women's International League on 8 February, 1935; Minutes of the Meeting of the India Sub-Committee held on Friday, October 31st, 1930; Minutes of the India Sub-Committee, Saturday, November 8th, 1930; Minutes of the India Sub-Committee held on April 27th, 1931; Minutes of the India Sub-Committee held on May 28, 1931; Minutes of the India Sub-Committee held on Thursday, June 18th, 1931; Minutes of Meeting of the India Sub-Committee held on Thursday July 30th, 1931; Minutes of Meeting of the India Sub-Committee held on October 8th, 1931; Minutes of the WIL Sub-Committee held on 22 November 1932; Minutes of the WIL India Committee held on 5 September 1933; Minutes of the WIL India Committee held on October 4th, 1934; Minutes of the WIL India Committee held on June 15th, 1936; Mary Nuttall WILPF files – WILPF Add. 1, Women's International League Monthly News Sheet, December 1939, 'India', by Agatha Harrison, p. 2, and Agatha Harrison to Edith Pye, 13 December 1930; WILPF Add. 2, Minutes of the WIL Committee held on 29 June 1932.

39 Letter to Emily Balch, and unfinished comments by Balch, Folder on India, 1930, The Papers of Emily Greene Balch, 1875–1961, SPC.

40 Harrison, *Prudent Revolutionaries*, p. 113; Moser, *Twisting the Lion's Tail*, p. 23.

41 *The Woman's Journal*, vol. 60, 1929, p. 40; and for the rejection of any presumption that British women could speak for Indian women, Rupp, *Worlds of Women*, p. 79.

42 'Nationality of married women', Box 103, File 1360, Alice Paul Papers, SL; and in *ibid.*, Box 103, File 1362, unsigned letter of 14 April 1934. to the Lord Chancellor; and 'Memorandum on the nationality of married women in the British Empire', January 1934. Issued by Chrystal Macmillan: File 1351 in *ibid.* Bussey and Tims, *Pioneers for Peace*, pp. 76–7, 108–9; Law, *Suffrage and Power*, p. 11. In WILPF Papers, LSE, the following – 4/2: Resolution Passed by the Council of the Women's International League at its Meeting on 30 October 1919; Resolution Passed at the Annual Council Meetings, March 1939; in WILPF 4/17: 'Africa in peace and freedom', Women's International League Conference, 20 November 1934, p. 2; letter to Dorothy Detzer, 17 November 1934, from the Hon. Sec. of the WIL Native Races Committee; Mary Sheepshanks to the Right Hon. Sir Philip Cunliffe-Lister, 20 April 1932; in WILPF 4/5: extracts from report by Mrs Marshall on the League of Nations, p. 3; in Mary Nuttall WILPF files – WILPF Add. 1: *Women's International League for Peace and Freedom, 1915–1938: A Venture in Internationalism*, p. 20; Delia Jarrett-Macauley, *The Life of Una Marson, 1905–65*, Manchester, Manchester University Press, 1998, pp. 74–9; letter of Helen Archdale to the Duchess of Atholl, 16 December 1929, and her reply, in File 1335, Alice Paul Papers, SL; A. S. Williams, *Ladies of Influence: Women of the Elite in Interwar Britain*, London, Allen Lane and Penguin Press, 2000, chapter 4.

43 Becker, *The Origins of the Equal Rights Amendment*, p. 163; 'A question of patriotism', on where women were voting in 1917, *The Woman Citizen*, vol. 49, 1917–18, 8 September 1917, p. 268; and, in *ibid.*, vol. 52, 1920–1, 12 June 1920, 'Mrs Catt to the women of Europe', pp. 44–5.

44 'Do women like politics? Ask Hawaii', *The Woman Citizen*, vol. 54, 1922–3, 15 July, 1922, pp. 11, 16.

45 Becker, *The Origins of the Equal Rights Amendment*, pp. 129, 164.

46 Carrie Catt to Maud (?), 31 January 1923, Box 52, Series II, League of Women Voters Records.

47 'Mrs Catt to the women of Europe', *The Woman Citizen*, vol. 52, 1920–1, p. 70.

48 Becker, *The Origins of the Equal Rights Amendment*, p. 172.
49 Address of Doris Stevens before the special plenary session of the 6th Pan American Conference, 7 February 1928, Havana, Cuba, reported in the *Congressional Record*, Seventy-Third Congress, Second Session, pp. 1–3, Folder 18, Box 2, Doris Stevens Papers, SL; resolution of Latin American women to Carrie Catt, 13 May 1935, Carton 50, League of Women Voters Records, LC.
50 Becker, *The Origins of the Equal Rights Amendment*, pp. 176f.; Rupp, *Worlds of Women*, pp. 139–50.
51 Speech to the Sixth International Conference of the Inter-American Commission of Women, University of Havana, 1930, p. 6, Folder 20, Box 2, Doris Stevens Papers, SL. See, on the work of the Commission, 'History of the Pan American conference of Women 1922–1926', Carton 50, League of Women Voters Records, LC.
52 'An apostle of action', an appreciation by Winifred Holtby, from *Time and Tide*, 26 October 1928, in Folder 29, Box 2, Doris Stevens Papers, SL.
53 Doris Stevens to Dan C. Casement, 19 February 1932, Miscellaneous 'C' Correspondence, Folder 92, Doris Stevens Papers, SL; Alice Paul to Mrs O. H. P. Belmont, 12 March 1930, Box 102, Folder 1337, Alice Paul Papers, SL.
54 Article on 'The Pan-American conference', *The Woman Citizen*, vol. 53, 1921–2, 6 May 1922.
55 Bussey and Tims, *Pioneers for Peace*, pp. 58–9.
56 Juanita Molina de Fromén of Nicaragua to Alice Paul, 21 March 1930, Box 102, Folder 1337, Alice Paul Papers, SL; L. M. Young, *In the Public Interest: The League of Women Voters, 1920–1970*, Westport, CT, Greenwood Press, 1989, p. 121.
57 Mildred Palmer to Alice Paul, quoting Bertha Lutz of Brazil, 14 June 1937, Box 104, Folder 1374, Alice Paul Papers, SL; press clipping from the *Times-Herald*, 21 February 1939, quoting Gabriela Mistral of Chile, Box 104, Folder 1378.
58 On the work of the Commission, see Box 104, Folder 1378, 'Inter American Commission of Women', in Alice Paul Papers, SL.
59 Article translated from *El País*, Havana, 28 February 1930, in Box 102, Folder 1337, Alice Paul Papers, SL.
60 Doris Stevens to Alice Paul, 15 April 1930, in Box 102, Folder 1341, Alice Paul Papers, SL.
61 See, in Alice Paul Papers, SL: letter of Muna Lee of Puerto Rico, 18 January 1934, Box 103, Folder 1351; Doris Stevens to Alice Paul, 2 March 1936, Box 104, Folder 1373; and in Doris Stevens Papers, SL: speech by Stevens at New York *Herald Tribune* conference on current problems, 1934, pp. 223–4, Folder 18, Box 2; Jon Mitchell to Talcott Parsons, 1 June 1959, Folder 110, Doris Stevens Unclassified Papers; Edith Houghton Hooker to Doris Stevens, 6 November 1937, Folder 122 in *ibid.*; Doris Stevens to John Milholland, 28 January 1933, Folder 136 in *ibid.*; see also Helen Hayes to Josephine Schain, 26 December 1938, from Buenos Aires, Committee on the Cause and Cure of War Papers, SL.
62 'A tree of good omen' by Carrie Chapman Catt, 27 June 1925, *The Woman Citizen*, vol. 57, 1925–6.
63 F. Miller, 'The international relations of women of the Americas, 1890–1928', *Americas*, October 1986, vol. 43, pp. 171–182.
64 Roy, 'Gandhi on women', pp. 228–33; Christine Bolt, 'Liberation movements', in the *Routledge Encyclopedia of Women: Global Women's Issues and Knowledge*, New York, Routledge, 2000, 4 vols., vol. 3, pp. 1230–4; P. Chatterjee, *The Nation and its Fragments: Colonial and Postcolonial Histories*, Princeton, NJ, Princeton University

Press, 1993; Jayawardena, *Feminism and Nationalism*, pp. 95–7; Report on the International Council of Jewish Women. Latin American Affiliates. Foreign Countries, General, 1966–81, p. 6, in Records of the National Council of Jewish Women, Group II, Box 22, LC, on its work in reaching out 'a helping hand to the great continent south of us' in the form of training in the United States for students and volunteer leaders.

65 Mary Beard, 'Women and the war habit', May 1930, *The Woman Citizen*, vol. 61, 1930.

66 Kathleen Norris, 'Worn out war talk', September 1930, in *ibid.*

67 See, in Committee on the Cause and Cure of War Papers, SL: 'Marathon round tables', 1934, subject: 'The evolving foreign policy of the United States', p. 2, National Conference Minutes, 1924–34; Marathon Study Kit, no. 3; 'Women's international boycott to prevent war'; Carrie Chapman Catt to M. Carey Thomas, 2 January 1925; Carrie Chapman Catt to Lillian D. Wald, 7 January 1925; letter to Hon. William H. Taft, 16 December 1924, in folder of Speakers' Addresses, 1925 etc.; Carrie Chapman Catt to Jeannette Rankin, 28 April 1932; The bodies involved in the CCCW up to 1940 were the American Association of University Women; the Council of Women for Home Missions; the Foreign Missions Conference of North America; the National Board of the YWCA; the General Federation of Business and Professional Women's Clubs; the National Council of Jewish Women; the League of Women Voters; the WCTU; the National Women's Conference of the Ethical American Union; and the National Women's Trade Union League. In 1940 the two mission societies were replaced by the National Committee of Church Women and the National Home Demonstration Council.

68 See, in Committee on the Cause and Cure of War Papers, SL: 'Women's international boycott to prevent war'; Marathon Study Kit, no. 3; Notes of July 12th meeting (1931), National Conference Minutes, 1924–34; Minutes of the Thirteenth Conference of the National Convention for the Cause and Cure of War, National Conference Minutes, 1935–40; and in *ibid.*, Minutes of the Second Conference of the Cause and Cure of War (1926); National Committee on the Cause and Cure of War, Program for 1939; Folder: Miss Kathleen Courtney, letter of 18 November 1939; Josephine Schain to Marie Ginsberg, n.d.; Frederick W. Peabody to Carrie Chapman Catt, 17 December 1926.

69 For quotation about membership figures, see Alonso, *Peace as a Women's Issue*, p. 108. And see, in Committee on the Cause and Cure of War Papers, SL: 'Report to the National Committee on the Cause and Cure of War on cooperation with the National Peace Conference', by Henrietta Roelofs, 23 May 1938; letter to Miss Roelofs from Kathleen D. Courtney, 13 February 1931; Josephine Schain to Eleanor F. Rathbone and Margery Corbett Ashby, 16 June 1936; Carrie Chapman Catt to Anna Steese Richardson, 11 August 1924.

70 See, in Committee on the Cause and Cure of War Papers, SL, Kathleen Courtney to Carrie Chapman Catt, 20 October 1931; Alonso, *Peace as a Woman's Issue*, pp. 142–3.

71 See, in Committee on the Cause and Cure of War Papers, 'History of the peace movement in the United States', radio talk, Letters to State Chairmen folder, 21 February 1936.

72 Jeffreys-Jones, *Changing Differences*, pp. 30–3; Young, *In the Public Interest*, chapter 12, on the efforts of the LWV.

73 Jeffreys-Jones, *Changing Differences*, p. 49.

74 *Ibid.*, p. 36.

75 *Ibid.*, chapter 5, figures from p. 67; D. Detzer, *Appointment on the Hill*, New York, Henry Holt, 1948, pp. 43–4, 107, 114f. and *passim.*

76 'Colored women and world peace', by Mary Church Terrell, in Committee on the Cause and Cure of War Papers, SL; flier from a Chicago newspaper, 25 January 1928, on the work of the National Council of Jewish Women, in Box 1, Hannah G. Solomon Papers, LC; and see, in Box 6, Folder 1, Programs and Activities, on 'Peace Education – Peace Action'.

77 Jeffreys-Jones, *Changing Differences*; Alonso, *Peace as a Woman's Issue*, especially p. 138; Bussey and Tims, *Pioneers for Peace*; J. M. Jensen, 'All pink sisters: the War Department and the feminist movement in the 1920s', in L. Scharf and J. M. Jensen (eds), *Decades of Discontent: The Women's Movement, 1920–1940*, Westport, CT, Greenwood Press, 1983, pp. 199–222, especially pp. 204–5; and Rupp, *Worlds of Women.*

78 Bussey and Tims, *Pioneers for Peace*, especially p. 120; *Women's International League for Peace and Freedom, 1915–1938*, WILPF Add. 1, Mary Nuttall WILPF files, LSE, especially p. 29; Miller, 'Lobbying the League', 'Extended Abstract', chapters 6–7, and pp. 279f.; see folder on Anglo-American Relations, 1928–9, in Box 31, Papers of Emily Greene Balch, SPC; 'As Lady Astor sees us', *The Woman Citizen*, 3 June 1922, vol. 54, 1922–3, p. 13; Swanwick, *I Have Been Young*, p. 321; Alberti, *Beyond Suffrage*, pp. 92–3; Liddington, *The Long Road to Greenham*, p. 132.

79 Carrie Chapman Catt, 10 December 1925, pp. 24–5, in National Conference Minutes, 1935–40, Committee on the Cause and Cure of War Papers, SL; and see R. Wieke's *Who We Are: A History of Popular Nationalism*, Princeton, NJ, Princeton University Press, 2001.

80 Liddington, *The Long Road to Greenham*, pp. 142–3.

81 See Anne O'Hare McCormick, 'The tariff – can we afford it?', in *The Woman Citizen*, October 1929, vol. 60, 1929, p. 35.

82 Letter of Mary Philbrook, Geneva, 5 May 1937, Box 104, Folder 1374, Alice Paul Papers, SL; and in *ibid.*, Box 104, Folder 1365, letter to Lola Maverick Lloyd, 4 May 1935; Mary Sheepshanks to Catherine Marshall, 21 May [1923?] WILPF Papers, British Section, WILPF 4/17, LSE.

83 Margaret Rhondda to Doris Stevens, 9 July 1928, in Folder 154, Stevens Unprocessed Papers, Personal Correspondence . . . Folders 123–68, Doris Stevens Papers, SL.

5 Feminism and race, 1920s–1930s

1 K. Hunt, *Equivocal Feminists: The Social Democratic Federation and the Woman Question, 1884–1911*, Cambridge, Cambridge University Press, 1996, is especially good on socialists' understanding of the woman question, but see also pp. 70–6 on their responses to race.

2 Davis, *Lifting As They Climb*, pp. 163–5; S. Harley, 'Mary Church Terrell: genteel militant', in L. Litwack and A. Meier (eds), *Black Leaders of the Nineteenth Century*, Urbana and Chicago, University of Illinois Press, 1988, pp. 307–21; Terrell, *A Colored Woman in a White World*, pp. 197–220; C. A. Foster, *The Women and the Warriors: The U.S. Section of the Women's International League for Peace and Freedom, 1915–1946*, Syracuse, Syracuse University Press, 1995, pp. 158–9; D. G. White, *Too Heavy a Load: Black Women in Defence of Themselves, 1894–1994*, New York and London, W. W. Norton, 1999, pp. 79, 93.

3 Terrell, *A Colored Woman in a White World*, especially pp. 330–6.

4 Davis, *Lifting As They Climb*, pp. 76, 173–83, 188–95, 205–6; R. Terborg-Penn, 'Discontented black feminists: prelude and postscript to the passage of the Nineteenth Amendment', in L. Scharf and J. M. Jensen (eds), *Decades of Discontent: The Women's Movement, 1920–1940*, Westport, CT and London, Greenwood Press, 1983, p. 270.

5 Davis, *Lifting As They Climb*, pp. 192–5.

6 Terrell, *A Colored Woman in a White World*, pp. 360–6; Rupp, *Worlds of Women*, pp. 73–4.

7 WILPF reports, Zurich 1919-Vienna, 1921, British Section, pp. 36–7, in WILPF 4/1, LSE; and in 4/5, Paper by E. G. B. (Emily Greene Balch) for report of the third WILPF conference, pp. 1–4.

8 Terrell, *A Colored Woman in a White World*, Preface by H. G. Wells, and Introduction; Foster, *The Women and the Warriors*, pp. 159–60, on Terrell's declining commitment after 1921.

9 Terborg-Penn, 'Discontented black feminists', p. 269; see also, for general background, J. Stein, *The World of Marcus Garvey: Race and Class in Modern Society*, Baton Rouge, LA and London, Louisiana State University Press, 1991: on Amy Jacques Garvey, see p. 151. Stein's otherwise excellent study says little about the role of women in UNIA, though see pp. 49, 63, 181–3, 202–3, 224, 227, 236, 242, 258. On Amy Ashwood Garvey, see Stein, pp. 32, 34, 36, 75, 150–1, 271; and see P. Fryer, *Staying Power: The History of Black People in Britain*, London, Pluto Press, 1989, first published 1984, p. 345; B. Bair, 'True women, real men: gender, ideology and social roles in the Garvey movement', in D. O. Helly and S. Reverby (eds), *Gendered Domains: Rethinking Public and Private in Women's History*, Ithaca, NY, Cornell University Press, 1992; White, *Too Heavy a Load*, pp. 138–40; interview with Frances Albrier by M. Chall, *Black Women Oral History Project: Interviews 1976–1981*, p. 256 on her activities as a Garveyite.

10 Alonso, *Peace as a Women's Issue*, pp. 100, 103–5, 148: quotations from pp. 104, 9; Hon. Sec. of WIL's Native Races Committee to Dorothy Detzer, 17 November 1934, WILPF records, 4/17, LSE.

11 Jarrett-Macauley, *The Life of Una Marson*, pp. 47, 50, 53, 72, 74–8, 95; B. Bush, *Imperialism, Race and Resistance: Africa and Britain, 1919–1945*, London and New York, Routledge, 1999, p. 220; A. M. Cromwell, *An African Victorian Feminist: The Life and Times of Adelaide Smith Casely Hayford, 1868–1960*, London, Frank Cass, 1986.

12 Jarrett-Macauley, *The Life of Una Marson*, p. 87.

13 *Ibid.*, p. 88.

14 *Ibid.*, pp. 89–90.

15 *Ibid.*, pp. 90–2; Marson's poem 'Nigger', quoted in *The Keys* (the official organ of the League of Coloured Peoples), vol. 1. no. 1, July 1933, pp. 8–9.

16 P. Clarke, *Hope and Glory: Britain, 1900–1990*, Harmondsworth, Penguin, 1997, p. 135; Jarrett-Macauley, *The Life of Una Marson*, chapter 10; Bush, *Imperialism*, pp. 256–8; B. G. Plummer, *Rising Wind: Black Americans and U.S. Foreign Affairs, 1935–1960*, Chapel Hill and London, University of North Carolina Press, 1996, pp. 6, 37f.

17 Jarrett-Macauley, *The Life of Una Marson*, chapter 19; interview with Virginia F. Durr, pp. 96–7, 99–102, Transcript of Oral History, 1974, Oral History Research Office, Columbia University, 1976, SL.

18 On DuBois's feminism, see D. L. Lewis, *W. E. B. DuBois: Biography of a Race*, New York, Henry Holt, 1993, pp. 381, 413, 418, 449–52: Lewis notes that DuBois was a 'theoretical feminist', whose feminism did not extend to his family life.

19 Jarrett-Macauley, *The Life of Una Marson*, pp. 50–1, 143 (source of quotation), and *passim*; Stein, *The World of Marcus Garvey*, pp. 268–9.

20 Fryer, *Staying Power*, pp. 326–34; and see *The Keys*, vol. 1, no. 1, July 1933, p. 2; no. 2, October 1933, p. 32; no. 3, January 1934, pp. 42, 61; no. 4, April–June, 1934, pp. 77–8 on African women; no. 5, 1934, pp. 1, 17 (on coloured nurses); next issue – no details, pp. 22, 32–3, 39; vol. 2, no. 3, January–March 1935, pp. 45–6, 51, 53, 64; vol. 3, no. 2, October–December 1935, p. 15; vol. 4, no. 2, October–December 1936, p. 15; no. 4, April–June 1937, pp. 48–50 (article by an Englishwoman on why she joined); vol. 5, no. 2, October–December 1937, pp. 31, 43–5 (on the position of women in the colonies); vol. 6, no. 1, July–September 1938, p. 9.

21 Terborg-Penn, 'Discontented black feminists', p. 268.

22 Rupp, *Worlds of Women*, pp. 74–5.

23 Terborg-Penn, 'Discontented black feminists', p. 269; E. B. Barnett, 'Nannie Burroughs and the education of black women', in S. Harley and R. Terborg-Penn (eds), *The Afro-American Woman: Struggles and Images*, Port Washington, NY, Kennikat Press, 1978, p. 103; C. Neverdon-Morton, *Afro-American Women of the South and the Advancement of the Race, 1895–1925*, Knoxville, University of Tennessee Press, 1989, pp. 200–1; White, *Too Heavy a Load*, p. 135; J. A. Rouse, *Lugenia Burns Hope: Black Southern Reformer*, Athens and London, University of Georgia Press, 1989, pp. 4, 131.

24 Barnett, 'Nannie Burroughs', p. 104; Stein, *The World of Marcus Garvey, passim*.

25 J. Jones, 'The political implications of black and white women's work in the South, 1890–1964', in L. A. Tilly and P. Gurin (eds), *Women, Politics and Change*, New York, Russell Sage Foundation, 1990, quotation from p. 126.

26 Rupp, *Worlds of Women*, p. 75.

27 See the following BCL publications, all in WL: 'BCL conference on the citizen rights of women within the British empire, 1925', pp. 22, 24, 35–6; 'Women and overseas settlement and some problems of government. Being a report of conference held . . . 1926', pp. 4–5, 6 8; 'Some problems of government in relation to women within the British empire. Being a report of conference held . . . 1928', p. 12; 'Women, power and policy, with special reference to the Imperial and Colonial Office conferences. Report of conference held . . . 1930', pp. 3, 9–10, 12.

28 'Women and overseas development', *op. cit.*, p. 11; 'Women, power and policy', *op. cit.*, pp. 15, 26; Mrs Fawcett in 'Foreword' to first BCL conference report, 1925, WL.

29 'Women and overseas settlement', *op. cit.*, pp. 4, 10–11, 15–17, 28–34, 61–6; 'Women, power and policy', *op. cit.*, pp. 7–8, 13–15, 42, 45–7; 'Some problems of government', *op. cit.*, pp. 67–8; '(a) The social and industrial condition of women of other than British race governed under the British flag; (b) Problems of government. Being a report of a conference held . . . 1927', pp. 41–2; 'Women and the future. (a) Women of the less forward races within the British Commonwealth. Their need and our responsibility. (b) The enfranchised woman and the future. Report of conference held . . . 1929', pp. 8, 16; '7th annual conference, 1931', pp. 5, 7; 'Report of ninth annual conference held . . . 1933. World unity and the British Commonwealth. The abolition of slavery celebrations centenary', pp. 30–1, 67; 'Marriage from the imperial standpoint. The civil rights of married women. Inter-racial unions. Report of conference held . . . 1932', p. 64; 'Report of tenth annual conference. Held . . . 1934', p. 82;

'Report of twelfth annual conference. Held . . . 1936', p. 38; 'Duties and rights of women under democracy. Contribution of democracy towards the peace of the world. Report of the thirteenth annual conference held . . . 1937', p. 8; 'BCL conference on the citizen rights of women', *op. cit.*, pp. 20–1; 'Report of fourteenth annual conference, 1938', pp. 5, 25, 71: all in WL.

30 'Women and the future', *op. cit.*, p. 8; 'Marriage from the imperial standpoint', *op. cit.*, pp. 52, 54, 74–5; 'Report of tenth annual conference. Held . . . 1934', p. 61; 'Report of fourteenth annual conference', op. cit., p. 71: all in WL; Jarrett-Macauley, *The Life of Una Marson*, p. 73; Bush, *Imperialism*, pp. 213–4.

31 Jarrett-Macauley, *The Life of Una Marson*, p. 76; Bush, *Imperialism*, pp. 183–4, 212, 215, 234–6.

32 Mary Sheepshanks to Right Hon. Sir Philip Cunliffe-Lister, 20 April 1932, WILPF records, 4/17, LSE.

33 'Africa in peace and freedom', Women's International League Conference, 20 November 1934, p. 4, WILPF records, 4/17, LSE; and in *ibid.*, Native Races Committee Annual Report for 1934.

34 Cain and Hopkins, *British Imperialism*, chapter 9: quotations from pp. 203 and 233; first quotation from Judd, *Empire*, p. 257; Bush, *Imperialism*, chapters 1–4, quotation from p. 71; and pp. 248, 252, 262–3.

35 Cain and Hopkins, *British Imperialism*, pp. 126–34; Judd, *Empire*, pp. 278, 291–3; Bush, *Imperialism*, chapters 5 and 10.

36 Mrs Corbett Ashby speaking on Tape 37, Side 2: *Tapes of Interviews on British Women's History in the Twentieth Century*, WL; Bush, *Imperialism*, pp. 64–5, 89–92, 103, 158.

37 See P. Fryer, *Staying Power*, pp. 321–46; Stein, *The World of Marcus Garvey*, pp. 266f.; S. Harley, 'Anna J. Cooper: a voice for black women', in Harley and Terborg-Penn (eds), *The Afro-American Woman*, p. 54; J. A. Langley, *Pan-Africanism in West Africa, 1900–1945*, Oxford, Clarendon Press, 1973, pp. 4, 27, 40, 49, 61, 66, 70, 73, 76–7, 326, 332, 340 and *passim*; Plummer, *Rising Wind*, p. 21; P. M. Von Eschen, *Race Against Empire: Black Americans and Anticolonialism, 1937–1957*, Ithaca and Cornell, Cornell University Press, 1997, pp. 45, 59; Jarrett-Macauley, *The Life of Una Marson*, pp. 54, 71; I. Geiss, *The Pan-African Movement in America, Europe and Africa*, New York, Africana, 1974; Bush, *Imperialism*, pp. 113–14, 120f., 159f., 219f., 239–40, 245 and chapter 9 generally.

38 Cain and Hopkins, *British Imperialism*, pp. 171–4; Judd, *Empire*, chapter 20.

39 Basu and Ray, *Women's Struggle*, p. 12 and chapters 2–4.

40 Cain and Hopkins, *British Imperialism*, p. 192, source of quotation; Clarke, *Hope and Glory*, pp. 183–4.

41 K. Jayawardena, *The White Woman's Other Burden: Western Women and South Asia During British Rule*, New York and London, Routledge, 1995, chapters 1–2, 5, 8, 10, 13, 14; Kaur, *Women in India's Freedom Struggle*, pp. 76–7, 94f., 113–38, 149, 187–9, 216–7; Chaudhuri and Strobel (eds), *Western Women and Imperialism*, chapter by N. L. Paxton.

42 Liddle and Joshi, *Daughters of Independence*, pp. 31–2, and Jayawardena, *The White Woman's Other Burden*, pp. 94–100, 237, on the angry reaction to Katherine Mayo's critique of certain Indian customs.

43 Jayawardena, *The White Woman's Other Burden*, pp. 154, 203.

44 Liddle and Joshi, *Daughters of Independence*, pp. 7, 19, 22, 49, 56; Basu and Ray, *Women's Struggle*, p. 11.

45 Liddle and Joshi, *Daughters of Independence*, pp. 33, 37–8.

46 Kaur, *Women in India's Freedom Struggle*, pp. 168, 199; Plummer, *Rising Wind*, pp. 72f.; Von Eschen, *Race Against Empire*, pp. 28–31; Basu and Ray, *Women's Struggle*, p. 57; Cain and Hopkins, *British Imperialism*, p. 184.

47 F. Miller, 'Latin American feminism and the transnational arena', in Bergmann *et al.*, *Women, Culture and Politics*, p. 21.

48 Kaur, *Women in India's Freedom Struggle*, p. 105.

49 See, for instance, Law, *Suffrage and Power*, pp. 42f. on Britain; and on the United States, Daniels, *Always a Sister*, pp. 142f.; Cott, *The Grounding of Modern Feminism*, chapter 8 and *passim*; Salem, *To Better Our World*, chapter 7.

50 Giddings, *When and Where I Enter*, pp. 129–30; A. Grimes, *The Puritan Ethic and Woman Suffrage*, New York, Oxford University Press, 1972, p. 65; Neverdon-Morton, *Afro-American Women of the South*, p. 204; Terborg-Penn, 'Discontented black feminists', pp. 261–2.

51 Mrs Terrell at the Fifteenth Biennial Session of the National Association of Colored Women, Oakland, California, August 1–5, 1926, p. 78; Guy-Sheftall, *Daughters of Sorrow*, pp. 108–14, 116–30; chapter 3 in Harley and Terborg-Penn (eds), *The Afro-American Woman*; Terborg-Penn, 'discontented black feminists', pp. 263–4.

52 M. S. Wheeler, *New Women of the New South: The Leaders of the Woman Suffrage Movement in the Southern States*, New York, Oxford University Press, 1993, *passim*; see also Caraway, *Segregated Sisterhood*, pp. 148f.; M. M. Thomas, *The New Woman in Alabama: Social Reforms and Suffrage, 1890–1920*, Tuscaloosa, University of Alabama Press, 1992; V. G. Lerda, '"We were no class at all": Southern women as social reformers', in M. Stokes and R. Halpern (eds), *Race and Class in the American South Since 1890*, Oxford, Berg, 1994, pp. 128f.; G. E. Gilmore, *Gender and Jim Crow: Women and the Politics of White Supremacy in North Carolina, 1896–1920*, Chapel Hill, University of North Carolina Press, 1996, pp. 204, 213.

53 Giddings, *When and Where I Enter*, pp. 123–9, 159–64, 166–70; Terborg-Penn, 'Discontented black feminists', p. 267; Cott, *The Grounding of Modern Feminism*, pp. 68–72; Gilmore, *Gender and Jim Crow*, pp. 210, 220, 223; Lewis, *W. E. B. DuBois*, pp. 418–19.

54 *The Woman Citizen*, 26 October 1918, p. 429.

55 White, *Too Heavy a Load*, pp. 36, 55–6, 66–7; Giddings, *When and Where I Enter*, pp. 122–3, 165; Gilmore, *Gender and Jim Crow*, pp. 211, 217–8, 221–3; Neverdon-Morton, *Afro-American Women of the South*, p. 204; P. Tyler, *Silk Stockings and Ballot Boxes: Women and Politics in New Orleans, 1920–1963*, Athens, University of Georgia Press, 1996, p. 25; White, *Too Heavy a Load*, p. 140.

56 I. H. Harper (ed.), *History of Woman Suffrage*, New York, Little and Ives for NAWSA, 1922; reprint for Source Book Press, New York 1970; vol. VI, 1900–1920, p. 606.

57 See, for instance, Dorothy Brown to Benjamin Carter, 29 March 192?, in Box 8 of Dorothy Kirchwey Brown Papers, SL; M. Dolan and C. Daley (eds), *Suffrage and Beyond: International Perspectives*, New York, New York University Press, 1994, p. 9; J. J. Camhi, *Women Against Women: American Anti-Suffragism, 1880–1920*, New York, Carlson, 1994, pp. 231–2; T. J. Jablonsky, *The Home, Heaven, and Mother Party: Female Anti-Suffragists in the United States, 1868–1920*, New York, Carlson, 1994, pp. 114–17; M. Pugh, *Women and the Women's Movement in Britain, 1914–1999*, Basingstoke and London, Macmillan, second edition, 2000, chapter 4 and pp. 141f.; Law, *Suffrage and* Power, pp. 120–3; P. Thane, 'What difference did the vote make?' in A. Vickery (ed.), *Women, Privilege, and Power: British Politics,*

1750 to the Present, Stanford, Stanford University Press, 2001, pp. 259–62; *The Woman Citizen*, 17 December 1919, p. 560.

58 K. Andersen, 'Women and citizenship in the 1920s', in Tilly and Gurin (eds), *Women, Politics and Change*, pp. 190–1; S. Baxter and M. Lansing, *Women and Politics: The Invisible Majority*, Ann Arbor, University of Michigan Press, 1980, p. 21.

59 J. Jones, 'The political implications of black and white women's work in the South, 1890–1965', in Tilly and Gurin (eds), *Women, Politics and Change*, p. 109.

60 Tyler, *Silk Stockings and Ballot Boxes*, p. 28.

61 Jones, 'The political implications', p. 117; Terborg-Penn, 'Discontented black feminists', p. 275.

62 *History of Woman Suffrage*, vol. VI, p. 606.

63 Cott, *The Grounding of Modern Feminism*, pp. 102, 104; Baxter and Lansing, *Women and Politics*, pp. 76–9, on the differences between black male and female voting; Plummer, *Rising Wind*, pp. 67–9; A. Barbrook and Christine Bolt, *Power and Protest in American Life*, Oxford, Martin Robertson, 1980, pp. 121f.; Christine Bolt, *American Indian Policy and American Reform: Case Studies of the Campaign to Assimilate the American Indians*, London, Allen and Unwin, 1987, chapter 6, and pp. 292f. on Native American reluctance to be lumped together with African Americans and treated accordingly; A. Bernstein, 'A mixed record: the political enfranchisement of American Indian women during the New Deal', *Journal of the West*, vol. 23, July 1984, pp. 13–20, quotation from p. 20; Alice Paul to Jessie Lee Muir of the Chinese Voters League of Fresno, Ca., 14 April 1934, Folder 1362, Alice Paul Papers, SL; correspondence about Native American affairs in Box 49, League of Women Voters Records, LC; Anna Garlin Spencer, 'What women can do for the city', 6 March 1921, pp. 11–12, in Anna Garlin Spencer Papers, on microfilm, SPC.

64 E. C. DuBois, *Harriot Stanton Blatch*, pp. 140–1; Baxter and Lansing, *Women and Politics*, pp. 53–4, 186.

65 D. McKay, *American Politics and Society*, fourth edition, Oxford, Blackwell, 1997, pp. 87–9, 99–100.

66 Becker, *The Origins of the Equal Rights Amendment*, chapter 1 and pp. 81f.; Cott, *The Grounding of Modern Feminism*, pp. 72–81; Camhi, *Women Against Women*, p. 11; letter of Marion L. Kenney, officer of the NWP, to Arthur A. Gaines, 9 January 1933, in Box 102, Folder 1344, Alice Paul Papers, SL; and in *ibid.*, Box 103, Folder 1357, Mildred V. Palmar to Alice Paul, 24 March 1934; M. F. Katzenstein and C. M. Mueller (eds), *The Women's Movements of the United States and Western Europe: Consciousness, Political Opportunity, and Public Policy*, Philadelphia, Temple Press, 1987, 'Introduction', p. 13. Note that in none of the countries studied had a women's movement produced its own political party.

67 Chafe, *The American Woman*, pp. 34–6 and *passim*; Cott, *The Grounding of Modern Feminism*, p. 112; E. B. Higginson, 'In politics to stay: Black women leaders and party politics in the 1920s', in Tilly and Gurin (eds), *Women, Politics and Change*, pp. 212–15; Baxter and Lansing, *Women and Politics*, p. 54, source of quotation. See also testimony of Ruth Dadourian in 'The Long March of the Suffragists', project no. 5147/2985, p. 6, SL, recorded in 1978 by Steven Peet for the British Broadcasting Corporation for the series 'Yesterday's Witness in America'; for a similar argument regarding the suffrage movement, see Mrs Hunkins-Hallinan, in the same project, p. 108; see also Rebecca Reyher's admission in her interview, p. 82, that the need to include black and working-class women in the feminist movement was seen belatedly.

68 *The Woman Citizen*, 10 July 1920; 20 November 1920, p. 687; 3 June 1922, p. 13;

9 September 1922, p. 23; 4 November 1922, p. 14; 15 December 1923, p. 14; April 1926, p. 42; April 1929, p. 18; January 1931, p. 45; March 1931, p. 29; K. Andersen, 'Women and citizenship in the 1920s', in Tilly and Gurin (eds), *Women, Politics and Change*, pp. 185–8; Law, *Suffrage and Power*, pp. 122, 150.

69 Pugh, *Women and the Women's Movement*, pp. 66–71; Law, *Suffrage and Power*, pp. 113–14, 131, 191, 209, 226; Harrison, *Prudent Revolutionaries*, p. 309; Atholl, *Working Partnership*, p. 138; C. Sykes, *Nancy: The Life of Lady Astor*, London, Collins, 1972, p. 305.

70 N. J. Weiss, *Farewell to the Party of Lincoln: Black Politics in the Age of FDR*, Princeton, Princeton University Press, 1983, pp. 20–1, 46; Baxter and Lansing, *Women and Politics*, p. 76, note that 'before 1940 only 12 per cent of the black population voted'; Higginson, 'In politics to stay', pp. 201, 206–12; M. K. Jennings, 'Women in party politics', in Tilly and Gurin (eds), *Women, Politics and Change*, p. 223; McKay, *American Politics and Society*, pp. 100–1; Terborg-Penn, 'Discontented black feminists', pp. 267, 275; L. R. Harlan, *Booker T. Washington: The Wizard of Tuskegee, 1901–1915*, New York, Oxford University Press, 1983, chapters 1 and 14; Neverdon-Morton, *African-American Women of the South*, p. 205; S. Ware, *Women in the New Deal*, Cambridge, MA, Harvard University Press, 1981, p. 72; M. Gustafson, *Women and the Republican Party, 1854–1924*, Urbana and Chicago, University of Illinois Press, 2001.

71 Chafe, *The American Woman*, pp. 27, 37; Pugh, *Women and the Women's Movement*, pp. 62–6, 140–1 and *passim*; Graves, *Labour Women*, p. 23 and *passim*; I. N. Gertzog, *Congressional Women: Their Recruitment, Treatment, and Behavior*, New York, Praeger, 1984, p. 6; Harrison, *Prudent Revolutionaries*, pp. 83, 129, 203; P. Thane, 'What difference did the vote make?', pp. 266–7; Gustafson, *Women and the Republican Party*.

72 Gertzog, *Congressional Women*, pp. 6, 35; Hollis, *Ladies Elect*, p. 478; Baxter and Lansing, *Women and Politics*, p. 137; Lemons, *The Woman Citizen*, pp. 73–81, 103–9; E. I. Perry, *Belle Moskowitz: Feminine Power in the Age of Alfred E. Smith*, New York, Oxford University Press, 1987, shows the constraints acknowledged even by a powerful political adviser.

73 Harrison, *Prudent Revolutionaries*, pp. 125, 145; and also by Harrison, 'Women in a men's house: the women MPs, 1919–1945', *Historical Journal*, vol. 29, no. 3, September 1986, pp. 623–54; Pugh, *Women and the Women's Movement*, pp. 56–61.

74 Harrison, *Prudent Revolutionaries*, pp. 200–4; Gertzog, *Congressional Women*, chapter 2; Law, *Suffrage and Power*, pp. 124, 167; Lemons, *The Woman Citizen*, pp. 104–5; material in Folders 229 and 230 in Box 10, Florence Luscomb Papers, SL; coverage of Minnie Fisher Cunningham in Folder 245, Box 8, Dorothy Kirchwey Brown Papers, SL.

75 Weiss, *Farewell to the Party of Lincoln*, pp. 81–2; Law, *Suffrage and Power*, p. 153. Harrison, *Prudent Revolutionaries*, p. 75, sees the WJCC as the likely inspiration for the CCWO; Pugh, *Women and the Women's Movement*, p. 70, sees the origins in NUWSS efforts in 1916 to unite suffrage groups.

76 The ten member organisations were: the League of Women Voters, the General Federation of Women's Clubs, the Women's Christian Temperance Union, the Parent–Teachers' Association, the National Federation of Business and Professional Women's Clubs, the National Consumers' League, the Association of Collegiate Alumnae (later the American Association of University Women), the National Council of Jewish Women, the National Women's Trade Union League and the American Home Economics Society: see Lemons, *The Woman Citizen*, pp. 55–6, 61–2.

77 Harrison, *Prudent Revolutionaries*, p. 75; Pugh, *Women and the Women's Movement*, pp. 70–1; Thane, 'What difference did the vote make?', p. 269.

78 Lemons, *The Woman Citizen*, pp. 56–7, 117f.; N. Hewitt, 'Politicizing domesticity: Anglo, Black and Latin women in Tampa's Progressive movements', p. 37, and C. Neverdon-Morton, 'The black struggle for equality in the South, 1898–1925', p. 57, and B. Sicherman, 'Working it out: gender, profession and reform in the career of Alice Hamilton, p. 139, in N. Frankel and N. S. Dye (eds), *Gender, Class, Race and Reform in the Progressive Era*, Lexington, University of Kentucky Press, 1991.

79 Pugh, *Women and the Women's Movement*, pp. 108–9, source of quotations; Strachey, *The Cause*, pp. 374f.; Law, *Suffrage and Power*, chapter 5; Graves, *Labour Women*, chapter 5; Thane, 'What difference did the vote make?', pp. 273–9; M. Andrews, *The Acceptable Face of Feminism: The Women's Institute as a Social Movement*, London, Lawrence and Wishart, 1997, especially chapter 5; C. Merz, *After the Vote: The Story of the National Union of Townswomen's Guilds in the Year of its Diamond Jubilee, 1929–1989*, Norwich, Adprint, 1988; C. Beaumont, 'Citizens not feminists: the boundary negotiated between citizenship and feminism by mainstream women's organisations in England, 1928–39', *Women's History Review*, vol. 9, no. 2, 2000, pp. 411–29; and C. Beaumont, 'The women's movement, politics and citizenship, 1918–1950s', in I. Zweniger-Bargielowska (ed.), *Women in Twentieth-Century Britain*, Marlow, Pearson Education, 2001, especially pp. 265–9.

80 Harrison, *Prudent Revolutionaries*, pp. 75f.; Harrison, 'Women in a men's house', pp. 624f., Lemons, *The Woman Citizen*, p. 58, chapter 5; Pugh, *Women and the Women's Movement*, pp. 114–16; Boris, 'The power of motherhood'; Gordon, *Heroes of Their Own Lives*, pp. 55–7; Scott, *The Southern Lady*, pp. 188–9; Clarke, *Hope and Glory*, pp. 119–20, 127, 137 (source of quotation); 'The struggle for child labor amendment as revealed by the Massachusetts referendum', pp. 7–8, Folder 199, Carton 9, Dorothy Kirchwey Brown Papers, SL; K. E. Nielson, *Un-American Womanhood: Antiradicalism, Antifeminism, and the First Red Scare*, Columbus, Ohio University Press, 2001.

81 See, for instance, J. L. Goodwin, 'An American experiment in paid motherhood: the implementation of mothers' pensions in early twentieth-century Chicago', *Gender and History*, vol. 4, 1992, pp. 323–42'; Michel, 'The limits of maternalism', pp. 290, 301 (source of quotation); M. Ladd-Taylor, 'My work came out of agony and grief': Mothers and the making of the Sheppard-Towner Act', in Koven (ed.), *Mothers of a New World*, pp. 331–4; Harley, 'Mary Church Terrell', pp. 312f. on the importance of national activities for black women; Belle Sherwin, President of the League of Women Voters, to Mrs Larue Brown, 25 July 1924, Folder 91, Dorothy Kirchwey Brown Papers, SL.

82 Neverdon-Morton, *Afro-American Women of the South*, pp. 174–5, 225–33; Terborg-Penn, 'Discontented black feminists', p. 271; J. D. Hall, *Revolt Against Chivalry: Jessie Daniel Ames and the Women's Campaign Against Lynching*, New York, Columbia University Press, 1979, pp. 62–5, 95f., 102–6, 181, 205; Gilmore, *Gender and Jim Crow*, pp. 177f.; Giddings, *When and Where I Enter*, pp. 155–8, 171–6; A. Fairclough, *Racial Democracy: The Civil Rights Struggle in Louisiana, 1915–1972*, Athens, University of Georgia Press, 1995, pp. 11–12; P. Dray, *At the Hands of Persons Unknown: The Lynching of Black America*, New York, The Modern Library, 2003, pp. 276–82.

83 Scott, *The Southern Lady*, p. 191; Dray, *At the Hands of Persons Unknown*, pp. 325–8, 355, 462, 499.

84 Neverdon-Morton, *Afro-American Women of the South*, pp. 225–6, source of quotation; Hall, *Revolt Against Chivalry*, p. 166.

85 Giddings, *When and Where I Enter*, p. 171; Hall, *Revolt Against Chivalry*, p. 167.

86 Hall, *Revolt Against Chivalry*, pp. 166, 206; Neverdon-Morton, *African-American Women of the South*, p. 226; Schecter, *Ida B. Wells-Barnett*; Dray, *At the Hands of Persons Unknown*, *passim*.

87 Bederman, *Manliness and Civilization*, chapters 1 and 2.

88 This paragraph and the preceding three have drawn on Hall, *Revolt Against Chivalry*, pp. 168f., 220–1, 225, 243, 255; and Dray, *At the Hands of Persons Unknown*, pp. 328–33 (quotation from p. 331). Dray also discusses lynching in the context of American anti-semitism and the rise of fascism: see pp. 319–20, 338.

89 Terborg-Penn, 'Discontented black feminists', p. 272.

90 Hall, *The Revolt Against Chivalry*, pp. 190, 221.

91 *Ibid.*, pp. 248f. on Ames's leadership style and views.

92 Stocks, *Eleanor Rathbone*, p. 116; Law, *Suffrage and Power*, pp. 161f.; Lady Margaret Rhondda to Doris Stevens, 9 July 1928, Folder 154, Stevens Unprocessed Papers, Personal Correspondence . . . Folders 123–68, Doris Stevens Papers, SL; and 'Why feminism lives', a pamphlet written by Vera Brittain for the Six Point Group, in Folder 1334, Alice Paul Papers, SL.

93 Lemons, *The Woman Citizen*, chapter 7; Cott, *The Grounding of Modern Feminism*, chapter 4.

94 Law, *Suffrage and Power*, p. 214, pp. 176–7, 214; Thane, 'What difference did the vote make?', p. 279.

95 Law, *Suffrage and* Power, pp. 207–8; J. Alberti, 'Keeping the candle burning: some British feminists between the wars', in Daley and Nolan (eds), *Suffrage and Beyond*, p. 297.

96 See, for instance, K. A. Yellis, 'Prosperity's child: some thoughts on the flapper', *American Quarterly*, vol. 21, Spring 1969, pp. 44–64; E. B. Freedman, 'The new woman: changing views of women in the 1920s', *Journal of American History*, vol. 64, 1974, pp. 372–93; A. J. Latham, *Posing a Threat: Flappers, Chorus Girls, and Other Brazen Performers of the American 1920s*, Middletown, CT, Wesleyan University Press, 2000.

97 L. Hellman, *An Unfinished Revolution*, London, Quartet Books, 1979 reprint of 1977 edition, pp. 32f.; E. Rathbone *et al.*, *Our Freedom and its Results, By Five Women*, London, Hogarth Press, 1936, p. 10.

98 Douglas, *Terrible Honesty*, p. 247.

99 C. Haste, *Rules of Desire: Sex in Britain, World War I to the Present*, London, Chatto and Windus, 1992, pp. 62; Alberti, 'Keeping the candle burning', pp. 300–1.

100 Cott, *The Grounding of Modern Feminism*, chapter 5; C. Simmons, 'Modern sexuality and the myth of Victorian repression', in B. Melosh (ed.), *Gender and American History Since 1890*, London and New York, Routledge, 1993, pp. 17–42; S. K. Kent's influential work, *Making Peace: The Reconstruction of Gender in Interwar Britain*, Princeton, NJ, Princeton University Press, 1993; L. A. Hall, 'Impotent ghosts from no man's land': flappers' boyfriends, or crypto-patriarchs? Men, sex and social change in 1920s Britain', *Social History*, vol. 21, no. 1, 1966, pp. 54–70.

101 Douglas, *Terrible Honesty*, pp. 97–8, 239f., 294–9, 328, 330, 344, 379–82, 408–14: the term Harlem Renaissance was coined by the New York *Herald Tribune*.

102 White, *Too Heavy a Load*, chapter 4; T. Martin, *Race First: The Ideological and Organizational Struggles of Marcus Garvey and the Universal Negro Improvement Association*, Westport, CT, Greenwood Press, 1976, pp. 23–5, 86 and *passim*; Lewis,

W. E. B. DuBois, *passim*; Neverdon-Morton, *Afro-American Women of the South*, pp. 233f.

103 Weiss, *Farewell to the Party of Lincoln*, *passim*; L. Reed, *Simple Decency and Common Sense: The Southern Conference Movement*, Bloomington and Indianapolis, Indiana University Press, 1991, especially chapters 1–4: Reed points out (pp. 72–3) that women were 'a large percentage of those who were unable to meet the poll-tax requirement, and women's organisations contributed to focusing national attention on the issue'; Ware, *Beyond Suffrage*, chapter 5.

104 Weiss, *Farewell to the Party of Lincoln*, chapters VI and VII; White, *Too Heavy a Load*, chapter 5; Giddings, *When and Where I Enter*, pp. 199–206; S. Ware, *Partner and I: Molly Dewson, Feminism and New Deal Politics*, New Haven, Yale University Press, 1987.

105 Giddings, *When and Where I Enter*, chapter XIII; Ware, *Holding Their Own*, pp. 92–3; Interview with Virginia Durr, pp. 41, 90–2, 94–6, Transcript of Oral History, 1974, Oral History Research Office, Columbia University, 1976, SL; R. Holt, *Mary McLeod Bethune: A Biography*, Garden City, New York, 1964; J. A. Hansen, *Mary McLeod Bethune and Black Women's Political Activism*, Columbia, University of Missouri Press, 2003.

106 'The courage to be', keynote address by Murray at a 1964 New England conference, pp. 6–8, Folder 1527, Box 88, Pauli Murray Papers, SL; and in Box 92, Folder 1598, 'Remembrance of Eleanor Roosevelt', 9/19/85, pp. 7–8, and 'Challenging Mrs. R', September 1983, pp. 22–3.

107 Hall, *Revolt Against Chivalry*, p. 166.

108 Weiss, *Farewell to the Party of Lincoln*, chapter III.

109 White, *Too Heavy a Load*, p. 150.

110 *Ibid.*

111 *Ibid.*, pp. 149, 158–9.

112 *Ibid.*, pp. 156–7.

113 See the grumbles against Mrs Roosevelt in the Doris Stevens Papers, SL.

114 White, *Too Heavy a Load*, p. 155; Terborg-Penn, 'Discontented black feminists', p. 276; G. Matthews, *The Rise of the Public Woman: Woman's Power and Woman's Place in the United States, 1630–1970*, New York, Oxford University Press, 1992, p. 278.

115 Weiss, *Farewell to the Party of Lincoln*, chapter IV; Plummer, *Rising Wind*, p. 137.

116 Harrison, 'Women in a men's house', pp. 623–4; Pugh, *Women and the Women's Movement*, pp. 57–8; S. Ware, *Holding Their Own: American Women in the 1930s*, Boston, G. K. Hall, 1982, pp. 95–6: compare her figures with those of Baxter and Lansing, *Women and Politics*, p. 136.

117 See, for instance, J. V. Gottlieb, *Feminine Fascism: Women in Britain's Fascist Movement, 1923–1945*, London and New York, I. B. Tauris, 2000, pp. 7, 164 and *passim*.

118 Baxter and Lansing, *Women and Politics*, p. 8 and *passim* on the way in which social reforms produce political change, not vice versa; S. Fraser and G. Gerstle (eds), *The Rise and Fall of the New Deal Order, 1930–1980*, Princeton, Princeton University Press, 1989, p. 193.

6 Feminism and class during the interwar years

1 Madame de Sevigné's aristocratic view of what was necessary to maintain the ancien regime, quoted in R. Sennett and J. Cobb, *The Hidden Injuries of Class*, New York, Vintage Books, 1973, originally published 1972, p. 247.

2 For a sensitive account of class relations between American women in the Progressive era, showing how they developed over time, see P. Murolo, *The Common Ground of Womanhood: Class, Gender and Working Girls' Clubs, 1884–1928*, Urbana and Chicago, University of Illinois Press, 1997, Conclusion and especially p. 151.

3 Cannadine, *Class in Britain*, pp. 15–17, 19–20; and see L. Davidoff, *Worlds Between: Historical Perspectives on Gender and Class*, Cambridge, Polity, 1995.

4 See, for instance, P. Fussell, *Class: A Guide Through the American Status System*, New York, Touchstone Books, Simon and Schuster, 1992, originally published 1983; R. Weiss, *The American Myth of Success: From Horatio Alger to Norman Vincent Peale*, New York, Basic Books, 1969; Sennett and Cobb, *The Hidden Injuries of Class*; B. Shafer (ed.), *Is America Different? A New Look at American Exceptionalism*, Oxford, Clarendon Press, 1991.

5 N. Kirk, *Labour and Society in Britain and the USA*, vol. 2, *Challenge and Accommodation, 1850–1939*, Aldershot, Scolar Press, 1994, pp. 57–8 and *passim*; and see McKibbin, *The Ideologies of Class*, chapter 1 and *passim*; the term class legislation 'became shorthand for legislation which classifies arbitrarily and unreasonably': see Baer, *The Chains of Protection*, p. 48.

6 R. Hofstadter, *The Age of Reform*, New York, Vintage Books, 1957, p. 308; G. Braybon and P. Summerfield, *Out of the Cage: Women's Experiences in Two World Wars*, London and New York, Pandora Press, 1987, p. 137.

7 Letter of Florence Luscomb to the editors of *Ramparts*, San Francisco, 23 February 1968, p. 3, in Folder 212, Florence Luscomb Papers, SL; and in *ibid*., Folder 214, Luscomb reported in the Sunday *Herald Traveller*, 15 November 1970, p. 6.

8 See Folder 3 of Mary Williams Dewson Papers, SL.

9 See Daniels, *Always a Sister*, p. 97.

10 See Box 2, Folder 2, National Women's Trade Union League of America Papers, SL, on anti-red attacks on women's organisations. The sub-title of the conservative (formerly anti-suffrage) journal, the *Woman Patriot*, was: 'Dedicated to the Defense of the Family and State Against Feminism and Socialism'.

11 Ware, *Beyond Suffrage*, chapters 1 and 2 on the factors that bound together the New Deal women's network.

12 Rheta Childe Dorr, a NWTUL member, quoted in N. S. Dye, 'Creating a feminist alliance: sisterhood and class conflict in the New York Women's Trade Union League, 1903–1914', in M. Cantor and B. Lurie (eds), *Class, Sex and the Woman Worker*, Westport, CT, Greenwood Press, 1977, p. 243; Lerda, 'We were no class at all', p. 122.

13 Bound volume about the meetings of the Consumers' League of Connecticut (Hartford), 1907, p. 76, Folder 7A, Consumers' League of Connecticut Papers, SL.

14 Mary Dreier's view of labour quoted by Theodore Roosevelt in a letter from him to her, 4 February 1913, Box 9, Folder 143, Mary Elizabeth Dreier Papers, SL.

15 See in *ibid*., Box 7, Folder 138, Mary Dreier to Helen Reid of the New York *Herald Tribune*, 2 May 1953.

16 Comments on Sue Shelton White by fellow New Dealer Nellie Tayloe Ross, in Folder of Personal Recollections, Sue Shelton White Papers, SL; and in *ibid*., Box 2, Folder 17, flier from Ethel M. Smith, Chairman, Committee on Protection of Women's Labor, National American Woman Suffrage Association.

17 Ware, *Beyond Suffrage*, Appendix B: the three women were Mary Anderson, Jo Coffin and Rose Schneiderman; Daniels, *Always a Sister*, on the association of unions and socialism; R. M. Jacoby, 'The Women's Trade Union League and American feminism', in Cantor and Lurie (eds), *Class, Sex and the Woman Worker*, p. 203.

18 The description of Rose Schneiderman, quoted in Daniels, *Aways a Sister*, p. 99.

19 'Summary on Minimum Wage Situation in States Other Than New York', 1936, Box 3, Folder 43, Elinore M. Herrick Papers, SL.

20 Maud Schwartz and Elizabeth Christman, 16 April 1926, to Belle Sherwin, 16 April 1926, Box 3, Folder 40, National Women's Trade Union League of America Papers, SL.

21 Anderson quoted in Ware, *Beyond Suffrage*, p. 25.

22 Pauline Newman to Rose Schneiderman, 26 July 1912, Box 5, Folder 77, Pauline Newman Papers, SL.

23 See, for instance, editorial for 'Labor', 31 May 1924, Box 3, Folder 41, National Women's Trade Union League Papers, SL; Becker, *The Origins of the Equal Rights Amendment*, pp. 213–14; R. Milkman (ed.), *Women, Work and Protest: A Century of U.S. Women's Labor History*, Boston and London, Routledge and Kegan Paul, 1985, p. 193; socialist feminist Meta Berger's unease with bourgeois feminists, quoted in S. M. Miller (ed.), *Flawed Liberation: Socialism and Feminism*, Westport, CT, Greenwood Press, 1981, pp. 117–18; and Jo Ann E. Argersinger, *Making the Amalgamated: Gender, Ethnicity, and Class in the Baltimore Clothing Industry, 1899–1939*, Baltimore, MD, Johns Hopkins University Press, 1999.

24 Stocks, *Eleanor Rathbone*, p. 107.

25 See Interview of 21 September 1976 of Brian Harrison with Margery Corbett Ashby, in *Tapes of Interviews on British Women's History in the Twentieth Century*, WL.

26 Interview with Miss Butler, in *ibid*.

27 Interview with Grace Roe, in *ibid*.

28 J. Alberti, *Beyond Suffrage: Feminists in War and Peace, 1914–28*, Basingstoke, Macmillan, 1989, p. 180; J. Alberti, 'British feminists and anti-fascism in the 1930s', in S. Oldfield (ed.), *This Working Day World: Women's Lives and Cultures, 1914–45*, London, Taylor and Francis, 1994, pp. 114–15; M. Joannou, *'Ladies, Please Don't Smash These Windows': Women's Writing, Feminist Consciousness and Social Change, 1918–38*, Oxford, Berg, 1995, chapter 1.

29 Swanwick, *I Have Been Young*, p. 125.

30 See, for instance, K. Israel, *Names and Stories: Emilia Dilke and Victorian Culture*, New York, Oxford University Press, 1999, pp. 191, 193.

31 Interview with Margery Corbett Ashby, *op. cit.*; and see McKibbin, *The Ideologies of Class*.

32 S. McIntyre, *A Proletarian Science: Marxism in Britain, 1917–1933*, Cambridge, Cambridge University Press, 1980, pp. 185–6; Miller (ed.), *Flawed Liberation*, p. 25; Kent, *Making Peace*, pp. 97 and *passim*, on feminist avoidance of class war rhetoric; D. Day, *The Long Loneliness of Dorothy Day*, New York, Image Books (Doubleday), 1959, p. 177, on the desire of an American radical to mitigate rather than increase class conflict.

33 M. L. Davies (ed.), *Life As We Have Known It: By Co-operative Working Women*, London, Virago, 1990 edition, first published 1931, p. 65; and Davies quoted in G. Scott, *Feminism and the Politics of Women: The Women's Co-operative Guild, 1880s to the Second World War*, London, UCL Press, p. 55.

34 H. Mitchell, *The Hard Way Up: The Autobiography of Hannah Mitchell, Suffragette and Rebel*, ed. G. Mitchell, London, 1984 edition, originally published 1968, pp. 190–1.

35 P. Thane, 'Women in the British Labour Party and the construction of state welfare, 1906–1939', in Koven and Michel (eds), *Mothers of a New World*, pp. 347–8.

36 B. D. Vernon, *Ellen Wilkinson*, London, Croom Helm, 1982, pp. 45, 64, 135, 137, 146–7; Harrison, *Prudent Revolutionaries*, pp. 141, 148 and *passim*.

37 Mitchell, *The Hard Way Up*, pp. 241–2; Graves, *Labour Women*, pp. 150, 164.

38 Alberti, *Beyond Suffrage*, p. 174.

39 Thane, 'Women in the British Labour Party', p. 346; McIntyre, *A Proletarian Science*, pp. 63–4, 94; Miller (ed.), *Flawed Feminism*, pp. 16, 50, 91–2; Graves, *Labour Women*, pp. 138f.

40 Miller (ed.), *Flawed Liberation*, p. 81; and see, for instance, M. Heinemann, 'The People's Front and the intellectuals', in J. Fyrth (ed.), *Britain, Fascism and the Popular Front*, London, Lawrence and Wishart, 1985, p. 183; R. Shaffer, 'Women and the Communist Party, USA, 1930–1940', *Socialist Review*, vol. 9, no. 1, January–February 1979, pp. 107–8.

41 Mitchell, *The Hard Way Up*, p. 179.

42 Shaffer, 'Women and the Communist Party', pp. 83–7; K. Weigand, *Red Feminism: American Communism and the Making of Women's Liberation*, Baltimore, MD, Johns Hopkins University Press, 2001.

43 See, for instance, Emma Goldman, *Living My Life*, London, Pluto Press, 1988, 2 vols., first published 1931, vol. 2, chapter LV, on such differences.

44 A. Wexler, *Emma Goldman: An Intimate Life*, London, Virago, 1984, pp. 95, 280; M. Forster, *Significant Sisters: The Grassroots of Active Feminism, 1839–1939*, Harmondsworth, Penguin, 1986, first published 1984, p. 314; C. F. Kessler, *Charlotte Perkins Gilman: Her Progress Toward Utopia With Selected Writings*, Syracuse, NY, Syracuse University Press, 1995, pp. 28–31; Goldman, *Living My Life*; B. W. Cook (ed.), *Crystal Eastman on Women and Revolution*, New York, Oxford University Press, 1978; P. S. Foner (ed.), *'Mother Jones' Speaks: Collected Speeches and Writings*, New York, Monad Press, 1983, chapters 3 and 4: on Lewis by M. J. Buhle, and Simon by G. and K. Kreuter, in Miller (ed.), *Flawed Liberation*; Harrison, *Prudent Revolutionaries*, chapter 5; Vernon, *Ellen Wilkinson*, pp. 48–9, 76, 82–3; J. Liddington, *The Life and Times of a Respectable Rebel: Selena Cooper, 1864–1946*, London, Virago, 1984; S. Bruley, 'The Communist party and the crisis in the cotton industry in England between the two world wars', *Women's History Review*, vol. 2, no. 1, 1993, pp. 83, 94; S. Rowbotham, *A New World for Women: Stella Browne – Socialist Feminist*, London, Pluto Press, 1977.

45 Foner (ed.), *'Mother Jones' Speaks*, p. 24, for a 1912 summary of 'her philosophy and her mission'.

46 R. Crossman (ed.), *The God That Failed*, New York, Bantam Books, 1965 edition, originally published 1950, pp. 9, 139, on Communist contempt for western intellectuals.

47 Miller (ed.), *Flawed Liberation*, p. 16; McIntyre, *A Proletarian Science*, p. 53.

48 Milkman (ed.), *Women, Work and Protest*, pp. 54–7; see also pp. 24–5, 45–6, 72, 80–1, 118–20, 194–5, 198, 200, 251–5; Vernon, *Ellen Wilkinson*, pp. 47–8, 53–7; Kirk, *Labour and Society in Britain and the USA*, volume 2, pp. 279–93.

49 Foner (ed.), *'Mother Jones' Speaks*, p. 366, for her last speech, in 1930.; and see E. J. Gorn, *Mother Jones: the Most Dangerous Woman in America*, New York, Hill and Wang, 2001, on this controversial figure.

50 See Kirk, *Labour and Society in Britain and the USA*, vol. 2, pp. 267–70.

51 See, for instance, K. E. McKenzie, *Comintern and World Revolution, 1928–1943: The Shaping of a Doctrine*, London and New York, Columbia University Press, 1964, pp. 152–6, 164–5, 284–5.

52 Gottlieb, *Feminine Fascism*, pp. 30 and *passim*.
53 C. R. Lubin and A Winslow, *Social Justice for Women: The International Labor Organization and Women*, Durham, NC, and London, Duke University Press, 1990, pp. 1–2.
54 R. M. Jacoby, *The British and American Women's Trade Union Leagues, 1890–1925: A Case Study of Feminism and Class*, Brooklyn, NY, Charlson Publishing, 1994.
55 Jacoby, *The British and American Women's Trade Union Leagues*, pp. 154–5, 160–1, 164; L. Middleton (ed.), *Women in the Labour Movement: The British Experience*, London, Croom Helm and Totowa, NJ, Rowman and Littlefield, 1977, p. 87.
56 Jacoby, *The British and American Women's Trade Union Leagues*, pp. 164–73, 177 (quotation from p. 170); Lubin and Winslow, *Social Justice for Women*, pp. 28–9, 35 (source of quotation). America rejoined IFTU in 1937.
57 Jacoby, *The British and American Women's Trade Union Leagues*, pp. 178–87 (quotation from p. 182).
58 Kirk, *Labour and Society in Britain and the USA*, vol. 2, pp. 307, 313 and *passim*.
59 Jacoby, *The British and American Women's Trade Union Leagues*, p. 174.
60 'Co-operation at the fountainhead', by M. L. Davies, *Life and Labour*, Chicago, September 1920, p. 53, Women's Co-operative Guild Papers, LSE.
61 Jacoby, *The British and American Women's Trade Union Leagues*, pp. 156, 158–60, 162–3.
62 *Ibid*., pp. 185–6.
63 On Bondfield see, for instance, Lubin and Winslow, *Social Justice for Women*, pp. 21, 29, 33–6.
64 *Ibid*., p. 38; Rupp, *Worlds of Women*, pp. 142, 214, 218.
65 'International Woman Suffrage Alliance. Resolutions as carried by the Congress, 1926', Box 51, League of Women Voters Records, Series II, LC; Chrystal Macmillan to Jane Norman Smith, 10 February 1934, and to members of the International committee of IWSA, 12 February 1929, Box 103, Folder 1352, Alice Paul Papers, SL; letter of 4 May 1935 to Mrs Lola Maverick Lloyd, Box 4, Folder 1365, in *ibid*.; Rupp, *Worlds of Women*, p. 145.
66 See, for instance, M. Bondfield, *A Life's Work*, London, Hutchinson, 1949; Becker, *The Origins of the Equal Rights Amendment*, chapter 5; 'World Woman's Party, Its Origins and Achievements, 1923–54', Box 102, Folder 1332, Alice Paul Papers, SL.
67 Lubin and Winslow, *Social Justice for Women*, pp. 38f.; 'The National Association of Women Lawyers at Geneva', 1938, Box 104, Folder 1376, Alice Paul Papers, SL; and see E. C. Lorenz, *Defining Global Justice: The History of U.S. International Labor Standards Policy*, Notre Dame, IL, University of Notre Dame Press, 2001.
68 McKenzie, *Comintern and World Revolution*, pp. 23–4.
69 Goldman, *Living My Life*, volume 2, p. 915.
70 McKenzie, *Comintern and World Revolution*, p. 294.
71 *Ibid*., pp. 237–8, 279–99.
72 DuBois, 'Woman suffrage and the Left', p. 43.
73 J. Braunthal, *History of the International, 1914–1943*, translated by J. Clark, London, Thomas Nelson and Sons, 2 volumes, volume 2, 1967, first published 1963, p. ix, chapter 11, pp. 471, 482–5 and *passim*.
74 *Ibid*., pp. 333–4, 339–40, 363–4.
75 Middleton (ed.), *Women in the Labour Movement*, pp. 89–91.
76 McKenzie, *Comintern and World Revolution*, pp. 65–6; Braunthal, *History of the International*, p. 334. The LSI likewise supported colonial freedom struggles.
77 McKenzie, *Comintern and World Revolution*, p. 241.

78 *Ibid.*, pp. 137–8, 160, 188, 199, 242–3.
79 McKenzie, *Comintern and World Revolution*, pp. 286–7.
80 Bush, *Imperialism, Race and Resistance*, pp. 44–5 and *passim*.
81 Bush, *Imperialism, Race and Resistance*, pp. 44–5, 163, 164–6; McKenzie, *Comintern and World Revolution*, p. 92.
82 'Co-operation as Applied to Domestic Work', talk by Catherine Webb, 1893 Annual Meeting of the Women's Co-operative Guild, Women's Co-operative Guild Papers, LSE; Scott, *Feminism and the Politics of Working Women*, p. 13; Black, *Social Feminism*, pp. 112–3. English and Welsh women worked together in the WCG; Scotland and Ireland had separate guilds.
83 See Davies (ed.), *Life As We Have Known It*, pp. xiii–xiv, 47, 53–4, 99; Scott, *Feminism and the Politics of Working Women*, chapter 1; Black, *Social Feminism*, pp. 116f.; Davies, 'Co-operation at the fountainhead', *op. cit.*, pp. 52–3; and, in Women's Co-operative Guild Papers, LSE, talk by Mrs Woodward, Birmingham, at the Annual Meeting of the WCG, 13–15 June 1993.
84 Davies (ed.), *Life As We Have Known It*, pp. xv, 107; N. Black, 'The mothers' International: The Women's Co-operative Guild and feminist perspectives', *Women's Studies International Forum*, vol. 7, no. 6, 1984, p. 471; Rupp, *Worlds of Women*, pp. 37, 41; interview by Brian Harrison with Margery Corbett Ashby, *op. cit.*; and, in Women's Co-operative Guild Papers, LSE: Davies, 'Co-operation at the fountainhead', pp. 50, 52; 'Suggested Resolution', 1927; Foreword to *The Woman With the Basket*, 1927, p. 5; Margaret Llewelyn Davies to the editor of 'Norges Kvinder', 1 February 1931; letter to the Association of Ukranian women, June 1934; 'Women and Co-operation', n.d., on the purpose of the ICWG; details of the Peace Pledge; 10 November 1921, press clipping on the importance of internationalism, and on correspondence to keep it going; 'Farewell words', 31 December 1921, by Margaret Llewelyn Davies and Lilian Harris; Black, *Social Feminism*, p. 151: and she has noted (p. 30) that the WCG was not hostile to middle-class women as such, even if their competing organisations aroused suspicion.
85 Davies, 'Co-operation at the fountainhead', *op. cit.*
86 Jeffreys-Jones, *Changing Differences*, pp. 38–9; D. Frank, *Purchasing Power: Consumer Organising, Gender and the Seattle Labor Movement, 1919–29*, New York, Cambridge University Press, 1994; Scott, *Feminism and the Politics of Working Women*, pp. 248–57, 258 (source of first quotation); Hannam and Hunt, *Socialist Women*, chapter 6 – second quotation from p. 147; Harrison, *Prudent Revolutionaries*, p. 60 on the difficulties involved in giving an effective institutional voice to British consumerism.
87 Report of Directors' Meeting, 15 October 1926, in Box 2, Folder 13, Consumers' League of Connecticut Papers, SL. But see L. R. Y. Storrs, *Civilizing Capitalism: The National Consumers' League, Women's Activism, and Labor Standards in the New Deal Era*, Chapel Hill, University of North Carolina Press, 2000.
88 Jeffreys-Jones, *Changing Differences*, pp. 47–9.
89 See, in the Women's Co-operative Guild Papers, LSE: 'A new basis for peace', article in *Foreign Affairs* for November 1920; Foreword to *The Woman With the Basket*; comments on the ICWG, pp. 128–9, in 'Special Education, Divorce and Independence'; and Margaret Llewelyn Davies quoted in *Westminster Gazette*, 31 December 1921. See also Scott, *Feminism and the Politics of Working Women*, pp. 203–12.
90 The Guild quoted in C. Miller, 'Geneva – the key to equality': inter-war feminists and the League of Nations', *Women's History Review*, vol. 3, no. 2, 1994, p. 232.

91 See, in Women's Co-operative Guild Papers, LSE: 'Special education', p. 128; letter to Davies from Emmy Freundlich of Austria, 4 October 1921.
92 Black, 'The mothers' international', p. 473; Black, *Social Feminism*, p. 122.
93 Scott, *Feminism and the Politics of Working Women*, pp. 213f.
94 See, in Women's Co-operative Guild Papers, LSE, Message of Margaret Llewelyn Davies and Lilian Harris; letter to Davies of 4/11/36.
95 Foreword to *The Woman With the Basket.*
96 Scott, *Feminism and the Politics of Working Women, passim.*
97 See Swanwick, *I Have Been Young*, pp. 385f.
98 Miller, 'Geneva – the key to equality'; and Miller, 'Lobbying the League', pp. iv, viii, 280f. and *passim*; also 'World Woman's Party', *op. cit.*
99 Circular of 11 September 1924, in Box 51, League of Women Voters Records, Series II, LC.
100 Mrs Corbett Ashby to members of IWSA's Committee for Like Conditions of Work for Men and Women, 28 May 1936, in Box 341, Series II, League of Women Voters Records, LC; and, in *ibid.*, Box 52, Series II, Call to the Tenth Congress of the International Woman Suffrage Alliance, Paris, 6 June 1926.
101 See, in *ibid.*, Box 51, letter to auxiliaries of 15 January 1926, from Julie Arenholt, of the Committee for Like Conditions of Work for Men and Women; Edith Abbott, 13 April 1926, Box 52, Series II, on the Committee's investigation. See also Rupp, *Worlds of Women*, pp. 143–4, source of quotation.
102 Resolution for Paris Congress, Legislation for Women in Industry, Proposed by National League of Women Voters, United States: Box 52, Series II, League of Women Voters Records, LC.
103 See Folder on Equal Rights Treaty. Formation of International, in Box 331, Equal Rights International Papers, WL.
104 'World Woman's Party', *op. cit.*; The Open Door Council, letter to members of the International Committee of IWSA from Chrystal Macmillan, 12 February 1929, Box 102, Folder 1335, Alice Paul Papers, SL; and in *ibid.*, Box 103, Folder 1351, extract from *Equal Rights* for 27 January 1934, on the ERI.
105 Reprinted in Box 102, Folder 1332, Alice Paul Papers, SL.
106 The Open Door International, circular letter of 19 December 1933, in Box 102, Folder 1348, Alice Paul Papers, SL.
107 Letter to Miss Ruth G. Williams, 3 April 1934, in Box 103, Folder 1360, Alice Paul Papers, SL; see Hannam and Hunt, *Socialist Women*, pp. 189f., on the post-First World War internationalism of British socialist women.
108 Margaret Bondfield, for instance, (see Bondfield, *A Life's Work*, pp. 175, 340) after her visit to the USA in 1919 did not return until 1938–9; see also Alice Paul to Dorothy Evans, 1 January 1934, and to Betty Gram Swing, 9 January 1934, Box 3, Folder 1350, Alice Paul Papers, SL.
109 The International Work of the Woman's Party, p. 1, Box 102, Folder 1332, Alice Paul Papers, SL.
110 *Ibid.*, p. 2.
111 The literature on birth control is large. The paragraphs that follow have drawn, especially, upon: J. Lewis, *The Politics of Motherhood: Child and Maternal Welfare in England, 1900–1939*, London, Croom Helm, 1980; L. Bland, *Banishing the Beast: English Feminism and Sexual Morality, 1885–1914*, Harmondsworth, Penguin, 1995; P. Fryer, *The Birth Controllers*, London, Secker and Warburg, 1965; R. A. Soloway, *Birth Control and the Population Question in England, 1877–1930*, Chapel Hill and

London, University of North Carolina Press, 1982; A. Leathard, *The Fight for Family Planning in Britain, 1921–74*, London, Macmillan, 1980, chapters 1–7; R. Ledbetter, *A History of the Malthusian League, 1877–1927*, Columbus, Ohio State University Press, 1976; J. Rose, *Marie Stopes and the Sexual Revolution*, London and Boston, Faber and Faber, 1992; M. Box (ed.), *The Trial of Marie Stopes*, London, Femina Books, 1967; M. Sanger, *My Fight for Birth Control*, London, Faber and Faber, 1932; D. Kennedy, *Birth Control in America: The Career of Margaret Sanger*, New Haven, CT., Yale University Press, 1970; E. Chesler, *Woman of Valor: Margaret Sanger and the Birth Control Movement in America*, New York, Simon and Schuster, 1992; J. Reed, *The Birth Control Movement in American Society: From Private Vice to Public Virtue*, Princeton, NJ, Princeton University Press, 1984; C. McCann, *Birth Control Politics in the United States, 1916–1945*, Ithaca, NY, Cornell University Press, 1994; L. Gordon, *Women's Body, Women's Right: A Social History of Birth Control in America*, Harmondsworth, Penguin, 1977, originally published 1976; F. Mort, *Dangerous Sexualities: Medico-Moral Politics in England Since 1830*, London, Routledge, 2000, second edition, originally published 1987; D. Gittins, *Fair Sex: Family Size and Structure, 1900–1939*, London, Hutchinson, University Library, 1982; Graves, *Labour Women*; Law, *Suffrage and Power*; Kent, *Making Peace*; S. Jeffreys, *The Spinster and Her Enemies: Feminism and Sexuality, 1880–1930*, London, Routledge, Pandora Press, 1987, originally published 1985; Alberti, *Beyond Suffrage*; D. J. Pivar, *Purity Crusade: Sexual Morality and Social Control, 1868–1900*, Westport, CT, Greenwood Press, 1973; A. Tone, *Devices and Desires: A History of Contraception in America*, New York, Hill and Wang, 2001.

112 McCann, *Birth Control Politics*, p. 101. See also J. F. Brodie, *Contraception and Abortion in Nineteenth-century America*, Ithaca, NY, Cornell University Press, 1994, chapters 6 and 7; and H. L. Horowitz, *Rereading Sex: Battles over Sexual Knowledge and Suppression in Nineteenth-century America*, New York, Knopf, 2002.

113 See, for instance, Gittins, *Fair Sex*, on distinctive working-class attitudes to contraception; Gordon, *Woman's Body*, chapter 7; McCann, *Birth Control Politics*, chapter 3.

114 See, for instance, Pivar, *Purity Crusade*, chapter 6; Mort, *Dangerous Sexualities*, pp. 92–3; Jeffreys, *The Spinster and Her Enemies*, chapter 1; Bland, *Banishing the Beast*, Part Two; Brodie, *Contraception and Abortion*, chapter 8.

115 See, for instance, Soloway, *Birth Control*, p. 298; Graves, *Labour Women*, pp. 81–4, 94; Kent, *Making Peace*, p. 130; Alberti, *Beyond Suffrage*, pp. 123–4; McCann, *Birth Control Politics*, pp. 55f., 130.

116 Sanger, *My Fight for Birth Control*, p. 181.

117 See McCann, *Birth Control Politics*, pp. 43–5; Kent, *Making Peace*, pp. 128–9; Jeffreys, *The Spinster and Her Enemies*, pp. 158–61.

118 See Rose, *Marie Stopes*; Kennedy, *Birth Control*.

119 Sanger, *My Fight for Birth Control*, p. 91.

120 Margaret Sanger to the Board of Directors, the American Birth Control League, 8 June 1928, Box 123, Margaret Sanger Papers, Sophia Smith Collection, Smith College, Northampton, Massachusetts.

121 See, for instance, Rose, *Marie Stopes*, pp. 144–5, 204–5; Gordon, *Woman's Body*, pp. 264, 288, 291, 293–9.

122 Rose, *Marie Stopes*, p. 134; Sanger, *My Fight for Birth Control*, p. 257.

123 Sanger, *My Fight for Birth Control*, pp. 27, 58, 71, 74; Rose, *Marie Stopes*, pp. 63–4, 80–2, 85.

124 Rose, *Marie Stopes*, pp. 90–2, 208–9; Sanger, *My Fight for Birth Control*, pp. 101–2, chapters xix–xxi; Ledbetter, *A History of the Malthusian League*, pp. 192–6, on its internationalism.

125 McCann, *Birth Control Politics*, pp. 177, 182; Gordon, *Woman's Right*, p. 324; Rose, *Marie Stopes*, p. 184; Sanger, *My Fight for Birth Control*, chapter xxv.

126 See Rose, *Marie Stopes*, pp. 135, 154.

127 Sanger, *My Fight for Birth Control*, p. 121.

128 Compare the works by Kennedy, Reed, Gordon and McCann with Rose, and R. Hall, *Marie Stopes*, London, Andre Deutsch, 1977.

129 Sanger, *My Fight for Birth Control*, pp. 58, 62, 102–3, 258, 262–3, 318.

130 Box (ed.), *The Trial of Marie Stopes*, pp. 129, 133.

131 Mort, *Dangerous Sexualities*, p. 163; Horowitz, *Rereading Sex*, pp. 37f., 312 (source of quotation), 316, 379, 427–8.

132 McCann, *Birth Control Politics*, p. 178; on the foolishness of American restrictive legislation following the Comstock Act of 1873, see Sanger to Mrs Joseph Wilshire, 25 October 1929, Box 37, Margaret Sanger Papers, Sophia Smith Collection; Sanger, *My Fight for Birth Control*, p. 265; Box (ed.), *The Trial of Marie Stopes*, p. 122; Brodie, *Contraception and Abortion*, pp. 281f.; Horowitz, *Rereading Sex*, chapters 16–19.

133 Box (ed.), *The Trial of Marie Stopes*, p. 122; Rose, *Marie Stopes*, p. 91.

134 See, in Lucile Lord-Heinstein Papers, SL: leaflet signed by Dorothy Bradford, and letter from Bradford to Lord-Heinstein, 9 June 1937, in Folder 3; President of Birth Control League of Massachusetts to Lord-Heinstein, 14 July 1937, and Cornelia Cannon to Lord-Heinstein, 24 July 1937, in Folder 4; and accounts of the struggle for birth control in Folder 13.

135 Cannon to Lord-Heinstein, *op. cit.*

136 See, for instance, McCann, *Birth Control Politics*, p. 42; Gordon, *Woman's Body*, p. 294.

137 See Lewis, Law and Alberti on Britain, Sanger and McCann on the United States.

138 McCann, *Birth Control Politics*, pp. 47, 52; Gordon, *Woman's Body*, pp. 315, 329–30, 334.

139 Thane, 'Women in the British Labour Party', p. 364; Graves, *Labour Women*, pp. 85–98: pp. 97–8 on the limited nature of the government concession.

140 Lewis, *The Politics of Motherhood*, p. 203.

141 Sanger, *My Fight for Birth Control*, p. 263.

142 Law, *Suffrage and Power*, p. 172.

143 *Ibid.*, p. 171.

144 Soloway, *Birth Control*, p. 299.

145 See Graves, *Labour Women*; Soloway, *Birth Control*, pp. 298–9; Gittins, *Fair Sex*, pp. 157–87.

146 See, for instance, Gordon, *Woman's Body*, pp. 330–1; McCann, *Birth Control Politics*, p. 147; B. Brookes, *Abortion in England, 1900–1967*, London, Croom Helm, 1988; Annual Report, Birth Control Clinical Research Bureau, 1930, p. 3, Folder 1348, Margaret Sanger Papers, Sophia Smith Collection.

147 McCann, *Birth Control Politics*, pp. 132f.

148 Shaffer, 'Women and the Communist Party', pp. 102–3.

149 See McCann, *Birth Control Politics*, pp. 175–6; Gordon, *Women's Body*, p. 330.

150 See Mort, *Dangerous Sexualities*, p. 159; Lewis, *The Politics of Motherhood*, p. 212 – but compare with Soloway, *Birth Control*, p. 315.

151 *Our Freedom and Its Results*, *op. cit*, p. 10 (source of first quotation); W. Holtby, *Women and a Changing Civilisation*, London, John Lane, The Bodley Head, 1934, pp. 69f., p. 82 source of quotation; Kessler-Harris, *Out to Work*, chapters 8 and 9; Kessler-Harris, *In Pursuit of Equity*.

152 See Bush, *Imperialism, Race and Resistance*, pp. 221–2; L. Tabili, *'We Ask for British Justice': Workers and Racial Difference in Late Imperial Britain*, Ithaca, NY, Cornell University Press, 1994.

153 Ethel M. Smith to Belle Sherwin, 10 May 1926, International Woman's Suffrage Alliance folder, Paris Congress 1926, Box 52, Series II, League of Women Voters Records, LC.

154 Beatrice Forbes-Robertson Hale in *The Woman Citizen*, July 1927, vol. xii, p. 38.

155 Frieda Schwenkmeyer, Amalgamated Clothing Workers of America, interviewed for the Oral History Project, *The Twentieth Century Trade Union Woman: Vehicle for Social Change*, SL; and W. Millikan, *Union against Unions: The Minneapolis Citizens Alliance and its Fight Against Organized Labor, 1903–1947*, St Paul, Minnesota Historical Society Press, 2001.

156 See Kirk, *Labour and Society*, vol. 2, pp. 267f. and 290f.; Florence Kelley to LaRue Brown, 1923, Box 8, Folder 239, Dorothy Kirchwey Brown Papers, SL; J. G. Rayback, *A History of American Labor*, New York, Free Press, 1966, pp. 294–5; Baer, *The Chains of Protection*, pp. 70f.; and Storrs, *Civilizing Capitalism*, on the struggle for labour standards.

157 Bolt, *The Women's Movements*, p. 261; Janiewski, *Sisterhood Denied*, pp. 83, 86, 154; Cott, 'Across the great divide', p. 163; Becker, *The Origins of the Equal Rights Amendment*, chapter 6; A. Kessler-Harris, 'Problems of coalition-building: women and trade unions in the 1920s', in Milkman (ed.), *Women, Work and Protest*, pp. 110–38.

158 Interview with Sara Barron, Amalgamated Clothing Workers of America, p. 53, first quotation, for the Oral History Project, *The Twentieth Century Trade Union Woman: Vehicle for Social Change*, University of Michigan, 1978, SL; and additionally, in this project, interview with Mary Callahan of the International Union of Electrical Workers, pp. 44–6; with Frieda Schwenkmeyer, *op. cit*, pp. 36, 61; with Beulah Compton of the Hotel and Restaurant Employees Union, p. 33; with Florence Luscomb of the WTUL, pp. 30, 32, 35; and with Ruth Wiencek of the Communication Workers of America, pp. 23, 26, 28–9, second quotation, 85. See also C. E. Ervin, Amalgamated Clothing Workers of America, to Doris Stevens, 16 July 1924, Folder 112, Doris Stevens Papers, SL.

159 Janiewski, *Sisterhood Denied*, p. 38.

160 Interviews with Beulah Compton, p. 33, and Freida Schwenkmeyer, p. 48, *op. cit.*, first quotation, SL; Elinore M. Herrick to Felix Frankfurter, 11 December 1937, Box 3, Folder 26, third quotation, Elinore M. Herrick Papers, SL.; M. Frederickson, '"I know which side I'm on": Southern women in the labor movement in the twentieth century', in Milkman (ed.), *Women, Work and Protest*, especially p. 159 (source of second quotation); and in *ibid.*, R. Terborg, 'Survival strategies among African-American women workers: a continuing process', p. 141; R. Halpern, 'Organized Labor, black workers, and the twentieth-century South: The emerging revision', in Stokes and Halpern (eds), *Race and Class*, p. 64: see also chapter 3 on 'Chicanas and Mexican immigrant families, 1920–1940: women's subordination and family exploitation', particularly p. 72; B. Nelson, *Divided We Stand: American Workers and the Struggle for Black Equality*, Princeton, NJ, Princeton University Press, 2002;

Janiewski, *Sisterhood Denied*, p. 175 and *passim*; Jones, 'The political implications of black and white women's work in the South', in Tilly and Gurin (eds), *Women, Politics, and Change*, pp. 120, 123; Ware, *Holding Their Own*, pp. 35–6, quoting Milkman and Kessler-Harris on female employment in the 1930s; see also M. Brattain, *The Politics of Whiteness: Race, Workers, and Culture in the Modern South*, Princeton, NJ, Princeton University Press, 2001.

161 S. Bruley, *Women in Britain Since 1900*, Basingstoke and London, Macmillan, 1999, pp. 60–8, 84; Graves, *Labour Women*, pp. 60–4, 141, 145–8; Kirk, *Labour and Society*, vol. 2, pp. 320–1: as Kirk points out, by 1924, the NUGW had become the vast National Union of General and Municipal Workers; Chafe, *The American Woman*, pp. 56–7, 108–9; S. Lewenhak, *Women and Trade Unions*, London, Ernest Benn, 1977, chapter 11; B. Drake, *Women in Trade Unions: An Outline History of Women in the British Trade Union Movement*, London, Labour Research Department, 1920, pp. 205–8; H. Srebrnik, 'Class, ethnicity, and gender intertwined: Jewish women and the east London rent strikes, 1935–1040', *Women's History Review* 1995, vol. 4, no. 4, pp. 283–99; Kessler-Harris, *Out to Work*; Kessler-Harris, *In Pursuit of Equity*; S. Boston, *Women Workers and the Trade Unions*, London, Davis-Poynter, 1980; Pedersen, *Family, Dependence and the Origins of the Welfare State*, pp. 208f., 299–300, quotation from p. 214: Pedersen points out that women unionists in the NFWW 'supported the majority trade union position' over women's war work (pp. 99–100), and that some married women unionists later opposed family allowances (p. 212).

162 Shaffer, 'Women and the Communist Party', especially pp. 75, 98–100, 103 (source of quotations); Fyrth (ed.), *Britain, Fascism and the Popular Front*, article by S. Bruley, 'Women against war and Fascism: Communism, feminism and the People's Front', pp. 140–1, 148–52; J. Stepan-Norris and M. Zeitlin, *Left Out: Reds and America's Industrial Unions*, Cambridge, Cambridge University Press, 2002; Bruley, 'Gender, class and party', pp. 83, 91–101; *We Are Many: Autobiography by Ella Bloor*, London, Lawrence and Wishart, 1941, pp. 229–30; and for NWP supprt for CIO activists, see Edith Houghton Hooker to Doris Stevens, 27 November 1937, Folder 122, Doris Stevens Unclassified Papers, Miscellaneous 'H' Correspondence, 1920–1949, Doris Stevens Papers, SL.

163 Ware, *Holding Their Own*, pp. 105–7; Bruley, 'Women against war and Fascism', pp. 142, 153; Kirk, *Labour and Society*, vol 2, p. 330; Bruley, *Women in Britain Since 1900*, pp. 65–6; Bloor, *We Are Many*, pp. 93 and 283; Shaffer, 'Women and the Communist Party', p. 103; Graves, *Labour Women*, pp. 204–8.

164 Ware, *Holding Their Own*, pp. 37–41; R. C. Lieberman, *Shifting the Color Line: Race and the American Welfare State*, Cambridge, MA, Harvard University Press, 1998; Storrs, *The National Consumers' League*; E. C. Green, *Before the New Deal: Social Welfare in the South, 1830–1930*, Athens, University of Georgia Press, 1999; J. M. Benowitz, *Days of Discontent: American Women and Right-wing Politics, 1933–1945*, De Kalb, Northern Illinois Press, 2002; S. Mettler, *Dividing Citizens: Gender and Federalism in New Deal Public Policy*, Ithaca, NY, Cornell University Press, 1998.

165 W. E. Leuchtenburg, *Franklin D. Roosevelt and the New Deal, 1932–1940*, New York, Harper Torchbooks, 1963, pp. 56–8, 261–3.

166 Graves, *Labour Women* (source of quotations), pp. 98, 149, 154–80, 164, 188–203 and *passim*; P. Thane, 'Women in the British Labour Party', pp. 362f.; H. Smith, 'Sex versus class: British feminists and the labour movement, 1919–1929', *Historian*,

November 1984, pp. 19–37; Pedersen, *Family, Dependence and the Origins of the Welfare State*, pp. 300f., 313; Hannam and Hunt, *Socialist Women*, pp. 21–3 and *passim*.

167 Chafe, *The American Woman*, pp. 57–61 (source of first quotation); Bruley, *Women in Britain Since 1900*, pp. 68–70; Kirk, *Labour and Society*, vol. 2, p. 294; Lewis, *The Politics of Motherhood*, chapter 6; Ware, *Holding Their Own*, pp. 27–9, 68f.; Graves, *Labour Women*, pp. 141f., 152 188 and *passim*, p. 142 source of fifth quotation; H. Smith, 'British feminism and the equal pay issue in the 1930s', *Women's History Review*, 1996, vol. 5, no. 1, pp. 97–110; B. Hobson, 'Feminist strategies and gendered discourses in welfare states: married women's right to work in the United States and Sweden', in Koven and Michel (eds), *Mothers of a New World*, pp. 396–429; Stocks, *Eleanor Rathbone*, pp. 113–18; Jane Norman Smith to Doris Stevens (source of fourth quotation), 13 November 1935, Folder 163, Personal Correspondence . . . Folders 123–68, Doris Stevens Papers, SL; P. Thane, 'Women in the British Labour Party', p. 368, source of third quotation; L. Gordon, source of second quotation, 'Black and white visions of welfare: women's welfare activism, 1890–1945', *Journal of American History*, vol. 78, no. 2, September 1991, pp. 559, 586–8; Feldstein, *Motherhood in Black and White*; Beaumont, 'Citizenship and feminism in England', pp. 422–3; Holtby, *Women and a Changing Civilisation*, pp. 93f.; Pedersen *Family, Dependence and the Origins of the Welfare State, passim*; Beaumont, 'Citizenship and feminism in England', pp. 422–3. During the 1930s the NWP finally gained support from some other women's organisations for its ERA stance: it was unlikely, therefore, to abandon it, especially when its international efforts for equal rights were gaining ground: see Foster, *The Women and the Warriors*, pp. 150–1.

168 'The struggle for Child Labor Amendment as revealed by the Massachusetts referendum', Box 7, Folder 199, Dorothy Kirchwey Brown Papers, SL.

169 P. Thane, 'What difference did the vote make? Women in public and private life in Britain since 1918', in *Historical Research*, vol. 76, no.192, May 2003, pp. 272, 274.

170 Thane, 'Women in the British Labour Party'; Graves, *Labour Women*, pp. 222, 223 (source of quotation).

171 Lady May Drummond-Hay to Doris Stevens, 23 July 1928, Folder 121, Doris Stevens Unclassified Papers, Miscellaneous 'H' Correspondence, Doris Stevens Papers, SL. And see C. Pateman, 'Equality, difference, subordination: the politics of motherhood and women's citizenship', in G. Bock and S. James (eds), *Beyond Equality and Difference: Citizenship, Feminist Politics and Female Subjectivity*, London and New York, Routledge, 1992, pp. 17–31.

7 The Second World War: a turning point for women?

1 See, in Alice Paul Papers, SL: Marion L. Kenney to Arthur A. Gaines, 9 January 1933, Box 102, Folder 1344; Resolution Adopted June 11, 1933, by the Women's Consultative Committee on Nationality . . . Geneva, Switzerland, Box 102, Folder 1345, second quotation; Chrystal Macmillan to Jane Norman Smith, 10 February 1934, Box 103, Folder 1352, first quotation; Lillian H. Kerr to Alice Paul, 25 October 1935, Box 104, Folder 1371; V. T. Perlman to Alice Paul, 19 November 1935, Box 104, Folder 1372; Sarah Pell to Alice Paul, 12 January 1934, Box 103, Folder 1351, third quotation; Holtby, *Women and a Changing Civilisation*, p. 190: Holtby also noted (p. 163) the 'additional impetus' to women's emancipation provided by nationalism in India, Egypt, Turkey and Arabia.

2 Gottlieb, *Feminine Fascism*, pp. 7–8, chapters 2–5 and *passim*; J. Alberti, 'British feminists and anti-fascism in the 1930s', in Oldfield (ed.), *This Working Day World*, pp. 111f.; Joannou, *'Ladies, Please Don't Smash These Windows'*, chapter 6.

3 Alberti, 'British feminists', pp. 118–21; Joannou, *'Ladies, Please Don't Smash These Windows'*, *passim*.

4 Leuchtenburg, *Franklin D. Roosevelt and the New Deal*, pp. 276–7; J. M. Burns, *Roosevelt: The Lion and the Fox*, New York, Harcourt, Brace and World, 1956, p. 385 (source of quotation); B. W. Cook, 'Eleanor Roosevelt and human rights: the battle for peace and planetary decency', in Crapol (ed.), *Women and American Foreign Policy*, p. 98.

5 D. Perkins, *The New Age of Franklin Roosevelt, 1932–1945*, Chicago, University of Chicago Press, 1964 edition (first published 1957), p. 132; J. Remak, '"Friends of the New Germany": the Bund and German–American relations', *Journal of Modern History*, 1937, vol. xxix, pp. 38–41.

6 Gottlieb, *Feminine Fascism*, p. 128.

7 See, for instance, the discussion in Alonso, *Peace as a Women's Issue*, pp. 141–4; and Foster, *The Women and the Warriors*, especially pp. 190–1.

8 Holtby, *Women and a Changing Civilisation*, p. 151; Mildred Olmsted to Gertrud Baer, 17 November 1938, giving Mrs Roosevelt's views, Records of the WILPF, American Section, Reel 70, Scholarly Resources Microfilm, SPC; Alonso, *Peace as a Women's Issue*, p. 140.

9 Shaffer, 'Women and the Communist Party', p. 101; Ware, *Holding Their Own*, pp. 130–1; Bloor, *We Are Many*, p. 283; Plummer, *Rising Wind*, pp. 64–6; Alberti, 'British feminists and anti-fascism', pp. 120–1; Joannou, *'Ladies, Please Don't Smash These Windows'*, p. 168; S. Bruley, 'Women against war and fascism: Communism, feminism and the People's Front', in J. Fyrth (ed.), *Britain and Fascism and the Popular Front*, London, Lawrence and Wishart, 1985, pp. 143–52; Bussey and Tims, *Pioneers for Peace*, pp. 141–3; Stocks, *Eleanor Rathbone*, pp. 240f.

10 Graves, *Labour Women*, p. 212.

11 Women's International League for Peace and Freedom, 1915–1938: A Venture in Internationalism, Maison Internationale, Geneva, 1938, p. 29, in Mary Nuttall WILPF files, Add.1, LSE; Bruley, 'Women against war and fascism', p. 152.

12 Alonso, *Peace as a Women's Issue*, p. 133 (source of quotation) and pp. 36f.; Young, *In the Public Interest*, pp. 128–9; Foster, *Women for all Seasons*, pp. 21–2. Popular Front activities also raised problems for activists in Britain – the conservative Duchess of Atholl, who was happy to collaborate with women colleagues and others on non-party issues, being condemned as a Communist when she criticised the government's non-intervention policy with regard to Spain: see Atholl, *Working Partnership*, 138, 223; also Liddington, *The Long Road to Greenham*; Ceadel, *Pacifism in Britain*, pp. 193f.

13 Moser, *Twisting the Lion's Tail*, chapters 1–6; P. Kennedy, *The Realities Behind Diplomacy: Background Influences on Britain's External Policy, 1865–1980*, London, Fontana, 1981, pp. 259–63 and *passim*; R. C. Self (ed.), *The Austen Chamberlain Diary Letters: The Correspondence of Sir Austen Chamberlain With His Sisters Hilda and Ida, 1916–1937*, Cambridge, Cambridge University Press for the Royal Historical Society, 1995, pp. 307, 313, 321 (source of quotation); C. Thorne, *Allies of a Kind: The United States, Britain and the War Against Japan, 1941–1945*, London, Hamish Hamilton, 1978, pp. 21–2, 592, 676, 679 and *passim*.

14 Bondfield, *A Life's Work*, p. 343.

15 A. Maude Royden Papers, WL: Box 221, American speeches; Sykes, *Nancy*, p. 455; Atholl, *Working Partnership*, chapter xxxiv; Bondfield, *A Life's Work*, pp. 342–3.
16 Randall, *Improper Bostonian*, p. 343.
17 Circular of 13 May 1938, signed by Helen Taft Manning (source of first quotation), Records of the American section of WILPF, Reel 70, SPC; Swanwick, *I Have Been Young*, p. 436 (source of second quotation); Bussey and Tims, *Pioneers for Peace*, chapters 13 and 14 (third quotation, p. 163, is from British WILPF activist, Barbara Duncan Harris).
18 E. Rathbone, *War Can Be Averted: The Achievability of Collective Security*, London, Gollancz, 1938, pp. 14–15, 134, 145, 154–6; Stocks, *Eleanor Rathbone*, chapters xiv–xv; Ceadel, *Pacifism in Britain*, pp. 157, 295–6, 315; Foster, *The Women and the Warriors*, pp. 257f.
19 V. Brittain, *England's Hour*, London, Macmillan, n.d. [1941?], pp. 47–8.
20 Membership figures were, however, complicated: thus, for example, in the United States the Followship of Reconciliation's membership increased after the passage of the Selective Service Act in September 1940 threatened young people with the draft, whereas the CCCW and WILPF struggled to survive; see Bussey and Tims, *Pioneers for Peace*, p. 173; Alonso, *Peace as a Women's Issue*, pp. 146, 152–3; Chatfield, *For Peace and Justice*, p. 327; Forster, *Women for all Seasons*, pp. 22f.; Ceadel, *Pacifism in Britain*, pp. 264, 294–7 and *passim* on the dificult choice for pacifists.
21 Chatfield, *For Peace and Justice*, pp. 332f.
22 N. Black, *Social Feminism*, Ithaca, NY, Cornell University Press, 1989, p. 149.
23 Holtby, *Women and a Changing Civilisation*, p. 164; Brittain, *England's Hour*, pp. xi, xii, 98, 100; see Jeffreys-Jones, *Changing Differences*, on 'peacetime pacifists'; Harrison, *Prudent Revolutionaries*, p. 90, for the quotation from Astor; and J. Hoff-Wilson, 'Conclusion: Of mice and men', in Crapol (ed.), *Women and American Foreign Policy*.
24 Ceadel, *Pacifism in Britain*, p. 233; S. M. Hartman, *The Home Front and Beyond: American Women in the 1940s*, Boston, Twayne, 1982, pp. 148–9; Alberti, *Beyond Suffrage*, pp. 210–17.
25 Jeffreys-Jones, *Changing Differences*, pp. 76, 89–90, 96–8.
26 Sykes, *Nancy*, p. 461.
27 Stocks, *Eleanor Rathbone*, p. 255; Harrison, *Prudent Revolutionaries*, on Wilkinson and Corbett Ashby; Jeffreys-Jones, *Changing Differences*, pp. 98–9; Williams, *Ladies of Influence*, pp. 113–15 on Atholl's fastidiousness and commitment to moral stands.
28 Jeffreys-Jones, *Changing Differences*, p. 98; Moser, *Twisting the Lion's Tail*, pp. 135, 138–40; Gottlieb, *Feminine Fascism*, pp. 236–7; Ceadel, *Pacifism in Britain*, pp. 281, 283.
29 Black, *Social Feminism*, p. 153 (source of quotation) on the WCG; Alonso, *Peace as a Women's Issue*, pp. 139–40; Mary Dingham to 'My dear friends', 1 May 1940, Folder 8, Mary A. Dingham Papers, SL; Record of Meeting, Thursday, 25 January 1940, National Conference Minutes, 1935–40, Folder 1, Committee on the Cause and Cure of War Papers, SL; Kathleen Innes, of the British WIL, to President Roosevelt, 4 October 1939, Records of the American section of WILPF, Reel 18, SPC.
30 Congresswoman Caroline O'Day to Mary Dreier, 4 November 1939, in which she still thinks American entry into the war 'will rest with the will of the people': Folder 129, Mary Elizabeth Dreier Papers, SL.
31 Letter of Charlotte Haldane, Corresponding Secretary of the Women's World

Congress for Peace and Liberty, 1 June 1939, Box 19, Committee on the Cause and Cure of War Papers, SL.

32 See Mary Dingham's letter of 3 September 1939, Folder 5, Mary A. Dingham Papers, SL.

33 Gertrud Baer to Heloise Brainerd, 15 August 1939, Reel 70, Records of the American section of WILPF, SPC.

34 'Issues Requiring Earnest Study and Immediate Action', in Box 14, Committee on the Cause and Cure of War Papers, SL; and, in *ibid.*, Meeting of the National Committee on the Cause and Cure of War, 25 January 1940, p. 4; and, in Folder 1, Minutes of Meeting, Wednesday, 24 January 1940, National Conference Minutes, 1935–40.

35 Letter of Mary Dingham, 1 May 1943, Folder 8, Mary E. Dingham Papers, SL.

36 Article in *St. Louis Post-Dispatch*, 5 March 1976, Folder 215, Florence Luscomb Papers, SL.

37 Young, *In the Public Interest*, pp. 135, 143; Massachusetts League of Women Voters, Program of Work, 1941–2, Box 5, Folder 148, Dorothy Kirchwey Brown Papers, SL.

38 'World Woman's Party', in Box 102, Folder 1332, Alice Paul Papers, SL.

39 Scott, *Feminism and the Politics of Working Women*, p. 221.

40 Bussey and Tims, *Pioneers for Peace*, chapters 15 and 16.

41 *Ibid.*, pp. 170–1.

42 Dorothy Detzer to Kathleen Innes, 26 December 1944, Reel 70, Records of the American section of WILPF, SPC.

43 Alonso, *Peace as a Women's Issue*, p. 143 (source of quotation); Mrs Catt to Mrs Corbett Ashby, 14 August 1942, Margery Corbett Ashby Papers, WL.

44 Minutes of Executive Committee Meeting, 24 March 1939, Committee on the Cause and Cure of War Papers, SL.

45 Dorothy Detzer to Barbara Duncan-Harris, 5 July 1944, Reel 79, Records of the American section of WILPF, SPC; and, in *ibid.*, Reel 70, letter from Dorothy Detzer to Mrs Duncan-Harris, 26 November 1941.

46 See Detzer's letter of 5 July 1944, cited in Note 45.

47 See Detzer's letter of 26 November 1941, cited in Note 45; and Mary Dingham to 'My dear Friends', cited in Note 29.

48 Jeannette Rankin in the United States and Vera Brittain in Britain are good examples of steadfast pacifists; in Britain there were some one thousand conscientious objectors (see Bruley, *Women in Britain Since 1900*, pp. 108–9).

49 Letter of 29 June 1941 from an officer of WILPF, in MICA 8, Margery Corbett Ashby Papers, WL; Jeffreys-Jones, *Changing Differences*, p. 95; Foster, *The Women and the Warriors*, p. 295. The support commonly shown by British women political leaders for anti-fascism prepared them to support Britain's entry into the Second World War, see Brabon and Summerfield, *Out of the Cage*, p. 151

50 Massachusetts LWV 1941–2 programme, cited in Note 37; and on the questionnaires, see Dorothy Detzer's letter to Barbara Duncan-Harris of 26 November 1941, cited in note 45; and letter of Emily Balch and Gertrud Baer to the National Sections, 30 September 1944, Reel 75, records of the American section of WILPF, SPC.

51 'Epilogue: To Our Jewish Fellow-Sufferers', in Box 39, papers of Emily Greene Balch, SPC; Wiesen Cook, 'Eleanor Roosevelt', p. 99, on the defeat of the Jewish Children's Refugee Bill.

52 'What causes peace', Folder 2, Mary A. Dingham Papers, SL.

53 Alonso, *Peace as a Women's Issue*, p. 148.

54 See on Japanese American Relocation, 1941–4, letter to WIL leaders of 31 January

1944, Box 47, Papers of Emily Greene Balch, SPC; also Foster, *The Women and the Warriors*, pp. 299–300; V. J. Matsumoto, 'Japanese American women during World War II', in M. B. Norton and R. M. Alexander (ed.), *Major Problems in American Women's History*, Lexington, MA, D. C. Heath, 1996, second edition (originally published 1987), p. 395; on Eleanor Roosevelt's ambivalent stand on Japanese civil liberties, see A. Black, *Casting Her Own Shadow: Eleanor Roosevelt and the Shaping of Postwar Liberalism*, New York, Columbia University Press, 1996, pp. 142f.

55 Alonso, *Peace as a Women's Issue*, pp. 146, 149–51: Alonso points out that hostile public opinion killed the proposal to draft women; Foster, *The Women and the Warriors*, pp. 303–4, 314–5; Bussey and Tims, *Pioneers for Peace*, p. 185; letter by Kathleen Innes to Detzer, 26 December 1944, cited in Note 42.

56 Stocks, *Eleanor Rathbone*, pp. 262–3, 277–8, 282–8, 300, 303–4. The British section of WILPF also petitioned the American president to relax the immigration laws and provide financial assistance for refugees: see resolution of 3 October 1939, Reel 18, Records of the American section of WILPF, SPC.

57 Bussey and Tims, *Pioneers for Peace*, p. 186.

58 'Copy of resolution adopted by the Executive Committee of the Women's International League for Peace and Freedom, British Section, at its meeting on 3rd October, 1939', and 'Pronouncement by the Executive Committee of the British Section of the Women's International League for Peace and Freedom, 55 Gower Street, London, W.C.1', both on Reel 18, Records of the American section of WILPF, SPC; S. Ambrose, *Rise to Globalism: American Foreign Policy Since 1938*, New York, Penguin, fifth edition, 1988, p. 25; M. A. Jones, *The Limits of Liberty: American History, 1607–1980*, Oxford and New York, Oxford University Press, 1991 edition, originally published 1983, p. 495.

59 'Women's International League for Peace and Freedom, 1915–1938: A Venture in Internationalism', p. 33, in Mary Nuttall WILPF files, WILPF Papers, LSE.

60 G. B. Tindall and D. E. Shi, *America: A Narrative History*, New York and London, Norton, 1993 edition, originally published 1984, pp. 816–7; Cordell Hull, 9 April 1944, speech reproduced in M. Jonas (ed.), *American Foreign Policy in the Twentieth Century*, New York, Thomas Y. Crowell, 1967, p. 111, source of quotation.

61 Eleanor Roosevelt to Mary Dreier, 25 August 1945, Folder 141, Mary Elizabeth Dreier Papers, SL; Black, *Casting Her Own Shadow*.

62 Tindall and Shi, *America*, p. 817; Jones, *The Limits of Liberty*, pp. 506, 514–5.

63 See WILPF Monthly News Sheet, reflections of Agatha Harrison, Add.3, WILPF Papers, LSE.

64 Bussey and Tims, *Pioneers for Peace*, p. 177.

65 'World Woman's Party', p. 3, Box 102, Folder 1332, Alice Paul Papers, SL; letter of Bertha Lutz, 29 July 1945, MICA C1–7, Margery Corbett Ashby Papers, WL.

66 Bertha Lutz to Margery Corbett Ashby, 25 July 1943, MICA C1–7, Margery Corbett Ashby Papers, WL.

67 Rupp, *Worlds of Women*, pp. 222–3; Bertha Lutz, 'Reminiscences of the San Francisco Conference that founded the United Nations', p. 3, MICA C1–7, Margery Corbett Ashby Papers, SL.

68 Lutz, 'Reminiscences of the San Francisco Conference', pp. 2–4.

69 Rupp, *Worlds of Women*, pp. 223–4, quotation from p. 224; 'World Woman's Party', p. 3.

70 Lutz, 'Reminiscences of the San Francisco conference', p. 5.

71 See letters in Doris Stevens Papers, SL; 'Inter American Commission of Women', Box 104, Folder 1378, Alice Paul Papers, SL; Becker, *The Origins of the Equal Rights Amendment*, pp. 184–5; Miller, *Latin American Feminism*, pp. 20–1.

72 Wiesen Cook, 'Eleanor Roosevelt', pp. 91f.; Black, *Casting Her Own Shadow*; Christine Bolt, 'Eleanor Roosevelt', in P. J. Parish (ed.), *Reader's Guide to American History*, London and Chicago, Fitzroy Dearborn, 1997, pp. 603–4.

73 Wiesen Cook, 'Eleanor Roosevelt', pp. 99–101, 113: quotations from p. 100; M. A. Glendon, *A World Made New: Eleanor Roosevelt and the Universal Declaration of Human Rights*, New York, Random House, 2001, especially on US caution about the declaration.

74 See Barbara Duncan-Harris to Dorothy Detzer, 25 January 1946, on the role of the Liaison Committee of Women's International Organisations, Reel 76, Records of the American section of WILPF, SPC.

75 D. Horowitz, *The Free World Colossus: A Critique of American Foreign Policy in the Cold War*, New York, Hill and Wang 1965, pp. 54, 61 (source of quotation).

76 Bussey and Tims, *Pioneers for Peace*, pp. 188–9.

77 Foster, *The Women and the Warriors*, p. 328.

78 See Dorothy Detzer to Barbara Duncan-Harris, 16 January 1946, Kathleen Innes to Detzer, February 1946, Detzer to Innes, 26 March 1946, Reel 75, Records of the American section of WILPF, SPC; and, in *ibid.*, Reel 76, letter of Edith L. Hayler to Detzer, 9 January 1946.

79 British weakness, in fact, forced the handing over of the Palestine problem to the United Nations in 1947: see Kennedy, *The Realities Behind Diplomacy*, pp. 364–5; also, Foster, *The Women and the Warriors*, pp. 328–9; H. Laville, *Cold War Women: The International Activities of American Women's Organisations*, Manchester, Manchester University Press, and New York, distributed by Palgrave Press, 2002.

80 This paragraph has drawn heavily on Williams, *Ladies of Influence*, pp. 159–77 (quotation from p. 171); see also Bruley, *Women in Britain Since 1900*, pp. 105–7; M. Stott, *Organisation Woman: The Story of the National Union of Townswomen's Guilds*, London, Heineman, 1978; C. Graves, *Women in Green: The Story of the Women's Voluntary Service*, London, Heineman, 1948; M. Morgan, 'The Women's Institute movement: the acceptable face of feminism?', in Oldfield (ed.), *This Working Day World*, quotation from p. 38.

81 K. Anderson, *Wartime Women: Sex Roles, Family Relations, and the Status of Women During World War II*, Westport, CT, Greenwood Press, 1981, pp. 87–90; S. M. Hartmann, *The Home Front and Beyond: American Women in the 1940s*, Boston, Twayne, 1982; D'Ann Campbell, *Women at War With America: Private Lives in a Patriotic Era*, Cambridge, MA, Harvard University Press, 1984; S. Gluck, *Rosie the Riveter: Women, the War and Social Change*, Boston, Twayne, 1987.

82 Chafe, *The American Woman*, chapters 6 and 8.

83 Anderson, *Wartime Women*, pp. 4–5; Braybon and Summerfield, *Out of the Cage*, p. 5.

84 Chafe, *The American Woman*, pp. 181–4.

85 P. Summerfield, 'Women and war in the twentieth century', chapter 12 in Purvis (ed.), *Women's History in Britain*, pp. 321, 324 (source of quotation) 325, 330: 'essential industries', Summerfield notes, 'included engineering, chemicals, vehicles, transport, the energy industries and shipbuilding'.

86 This paragraph has drawn on Brabon and Summerfield, *Out of the Cage*; Chafe, *The American Woman*; Kessler-Harris, *Out to Work*, chapter 10; Rosenberg, *Divided Lives*; Summerfield, 'Women and war'; Matthews, *The Rise of Public Woman*; Ander-

son, *Wartime Women*; Lubin and Winslow, *Social Justice for Women*, p. 64; and Jones, *Labor of Love, Labor of Sorrow*, pp. 239–40, 251; N. F. Gabin, 'Women defense workers in World War II: views on gender equality in Indiana', in K. P. O'Brien and L. H. Parsons (eds), *The Home Front: World War II and American Society*, Westport, CT, Greenwood Press, 1995, pp. 107–18; Gluck, *Rosie the Riveter*; M. Honey, *Creating Rosie the Riveter: Class, Gender and Propaganda During World War II*, Amherst, University of Massachusetts Press, 1984; Hartman, *The Home Front and Beyond*; P. Summerfield, *Women Workers in the Second World War: Production and Patriarchy in Conflict*, London, Croom Helm, 1984; N. C. Soldon (ed.), *The World of Women's Trade Unionism: Comparative Historical Essays*, Westport, CT, Greenwood Press, 1985, chapters 1 and 3.

87 Giddings, *When and Where I Enter*, pp. 237–8; Brittain, *The Politics of Whiteness.*

88 Chafe, *The American Woman*, pp. 142–3, quotation from p. 142.

89 Jones, *The Limits of Liberty*, p. 500; Bruley, *Women in Britain Since 1900*, p. 102.

90 M. F. Berry and J. Blassingame, *Long Memory: The Black Experience in America*, New York, Oxford University Press, 1982, p. 325.

91 See Anderson, *Wartime Women*; Kessler-Harris, *Out to Work*, pp. 295, 299; Summerfield, *Women Workers*; Hartmann, *The Home Front*; N. Gabin, 'Women and the United Automobile Workers' Union in the 1950s', in Milkman (ed.), *Women, Work and Protest*, p. 276 (source of quotation); Lewenhak, *Women and Trade Unions*, p. 257.

92 Braybon and Summerfield, *Out of the Cage*, pp. 197–8, 232; Summerfield, *Reconstructing Women's Lives*, pp. 165–7; Jones, *Labor of Love, Labor of Sorrow*, pp. 252–3.

93 Anderson, *Wartime Women*, pp. 34, 37; Giddings, *When and Where I Enter*, p. 237.

94 Bruley, *Women in Britain Since 1900*, pp. 96–7; Braybon and Summerfield, *Out of the Cage*, p. 250, p. 250; J. Sherman, '"The vice-admiral": Margaret Chase Smith and the investigation of congested areas in wartime', in O'Brien and Parsons (eds), *The Home Front*, pp. 128–9.

95 Williams, *Ladies of Influence*, pp. 166, 168; Hartmann, *Women's Organizations.*

96 Braybon and Summerfield, *Out of the Cage*, p. 163.

97 Summerfield, *Reconstructing Women's Lives*, pp. 182–5, on black West Indian ATS women.

98 Berry and Blassingame, *Long Memory*, pp. 324–5; and Reynolds, *Rich Relations*, p. 411 on the African American WACs.

99 B. Bousquet and C. Douglas, *West Indian Women at War: British Racism in World War II*, London, Lawrence and Wishart, 1991, chapters 8 and 9: quotation from p. 114.

100 Lubin and Winslow, *Justice for Women*, pp. 60f., quotations about the ILO from pp. 60–1 and 67; 'Women Labor Leaders Are Going to England in Good-Will Exchange With 4 From There', *New York Times*, 10 January 1945, Folder 8, Maida (Stewart) Springer Kemp Papers, SL; Y. Richards, *Maida Springer: PanAfricanist and International Labor Leader*, Pittsburgh, PA, University of Pittsburgh Press, 2000.

101 See, for instance, Clarke, *Hope and Glory*, pp. 207f.; O'Brien and Parsons (eds), *The Home-Front War*, pp. 4, 6, 157–9; L. J. Rupp, *Mobilizing Women for War: German and American Propaganda, 1939–1945*, Princeton, NJ, Princeton University Press, 1978.

102 See, for instance, R. M. Dalfiume, *Desegregation of the U.S. Armed Forces: Fighting on Two Fronts, 1939–1953*, Columbia, University of Missouri Press, 1969.

103 Berry and Blassingame, *Long Memory*, pp. 320–1.

104 P. F. Pfeffer, *A. Philip Randolph*, Baton Rouge, Louisiana University Press, 1990; M. E. Reed, *Seedtime for the Modern Civil Rights Movement: The President's Committee on Fair Employment Practice, 1941–1946*, Baton Rouge, Louisiana State University Press, 1991; D. Kryder, *Race and the American State during World War II*, New York, Cambridge University Press, 2000; R. M. Dalfiume, *Desegregation of the United States Armed Forces: Fighting on Two Fronts, 1939–1953*, Columbia, University of Missouri Press, 1969; S. M. Hartmann, 'Women's organizations during World War II: The interaction of class, race, and feminism', in M. Kelly (ed.), *Women's Being, Women's Place: Female Identity and Vocation in American History*, Boston, MA, G. K. Hall, 1979, pp. 313–33; Walter White of the NAACP, quoted in C. R. Koppes, 'Hollywood and the politics of representation: women, workers, and African Americans in World War II movies', in O'Brien and Parsons (eds), *The Home-Front War*, p. 27; Jones, *Labor of Love, Labor of Sorrow*, p. 262; Hartmann, *The Home Front and Beyond*, p. 148; White, *Too Heavy a Load*, pp. 150–1, 157–9, 172–5; P. Giddings, *In Search of Sisterhood: Delta Sigma Theta and the Challenge of the Black Sorority Movement*, New York, William Morrow, 1988.

105 Von Eschen, *Race Against Empire*, pp. 2–6, 16, 20, 53, 60, 73–4, 78–9 and *passim*; quotations from pp. 4, 5.

106 Plummer, *Rising Wind*, pp. 135–6.

107 *Ibid.*, pp. 130, 199–200; Von Eschen, *Race Against Empire*, pp. 78, 81–3.

108 Plummer, *Rising Wind*, pp. 131.

109 *Ibid.*, pp. 140, 200; Von Eschen, *Race Against Empire*, pp. 78, 81–3.

110 Plummer, *Rising Wind*, pp. 142–3.

111 Von Eschen, *Race Against Empire*, pp. 45–52, 81, 114; Plummer, *Rising Wind*, pp. 136, 142, 145; Bush, *Imperialism, Race and Resistance*, p. 225; article on her 1945 visit to Britain by Maida Springer Kent, p. 4, Folder 4, in Maida (Stewart) Springer Kemp Papers, SL; T. Borstelmann, *The Cold War and the Color Line: American Race Relations in the Global Arena*, Cambridge, MA, Harvard University Press, 2001; J. H. Meriwether, *Proudly We Can Be Africans: Black Americans and Africa, 1935–1961*, Chapel Hill, University of North Carolina Press, 2002.

112 Reynolds, *Rich Relations*, p. 218.

113 *Ibid.*, chapters 14 and 18; 1945 article by Maida Springer Kemp, *op. cit.*, on the subtle accommodations to the prejudices of white colleagues that she found in Britain; letter of Kathleen Innes of the British section of WILPF to John Carter of the League of Coloured Peoples, Add.2, WILPF Papers, LSE; G. A. Smith, *When Jim Crow Meets John Bull: Black American Soldiers in World War II Britain*, London, I. B. Taurus, 1987; Bush, *Imperialism, Race and Resistance*, p. 223; Bousquet and Douglas, *West Indian Women at War*, chapters 5–7.

114 Sherman, 'The Vice Admiral', p. 119, source of quotation; Bruley, *Women in Britain Since 1900*, p. 108; Hartmann, *The Home Front and Beyond*, pp. 150–1.

115 See Black, *Casting Her Own Shadow*, pp. 85f.

116 Ware, *Beyond Suffrage*, pp. 127–8.

117 *Ibid.*, p. 128.

118 Rosenberg, *Divided Lives*, p. 129; Matthews, *The Rise of Public Woman*, p. 220; and on the changing role of the Women's Bureau, see Kessler-Harris, *Out of Work*, pp. 305f., and Laughlin, *Women's Work*.

119 Sherman, 'The Vice Admiral', p. 127.

120 Ware, *Beyond Suffrage*, pp. 127–8; Hartmann, *The Home Front and Beyond*, p. 149.

121 Rosenberg, *Divided Lives*, p. 129.

122 Sherman, 'The Vice Admiral', pp. 120–30; Ware, *Beyond Suffrage*, pp. 129–30; P. Summerfield, 'Women and war in the twentieth century', in Purvis (ed.), *Women's History*, p. 53; J. Sherman, *No Place for a Woman: A Life of Senator Margaret Chase Smith*, New Brunswick, NJ, Rutgers University Press, 2000.

123 'Margaret Chase Smith: In Her Own Words', Margaret Chase Smith Oral History, pp. 47–50, 70–1, SL.

124 L. J. Rupp and V. Taylor, *Survival in the Doldrums: The American Women's Rights Movement, 1945 to the 1960s*, New York, Oxford University Press, 1987, pp. 25, 46–7, 62 (source of quotation); Hartmann, *The Home Front and Beyond*, pp. 130–3 and chapter 7: p. 123 is the source of the first quotation.

125 Rupp and Taylor, *Survival in the Doldrums*, chapter 3; quotation from p. 26.

126 Summerfield, 'Women and war', pp. 318–9; Bruley, *Women in Britain Since 1900*, pp. 95, 108, 119–20; Beaumont, 'The women's movement', pp. 270–2.

127 H. Smith, *War and Social Change: Britain in the Second World War*, Manchester, Manchester University Press, 1986, pp. 234–5; Pugh, *Women and the Women's Movement*, pp. 275–83; Beaumont, 'The women's movement', pp. 271, 273.

128 Summerfield, 'Women and war', pp. 398–9; Bruley, *Women in Britain Since 1900*, pp. 129–30; Stocks, *Eleanor Rathbone*, pp. 307–11; Pedersen, *Family, Dependence and the Origins of the Welfare State*, pp. 327–56, quotation from p. 350.

129 See Hartmann, *The Home Front and Beyond*, pp. 146–8; Pugh, *Women and the Women's Movement*, pp. 276–8 on tensions between working-class women and middle-class women's groups. The Standing Joint Committee of Working Women's Organisations, for example, declined to join the hundred women's groups supporting the Equal Pay Campaign. See also Rupp and Taylor, *Survival in the Doldrums*, pp. 75f.

130 See, for example, the work of Arthur Marwick and Harold Smith.

131 Brabon and Summerfield, *Out of the Cage*, pp. 2–5.

132 Summerfield, *Reconstructing Women's Lives*, p. 7 and *passim.*

133 R. J. Evans, *Comrades and Sisters: Feminism, Socialism and Pacifism in Europe, 1870–1945*, Brighton, Wheatsheaf Books, and New York, St Martin's Press, 1987, pp. 128, 149 and *passim.*

134 *History Notes: Women in Diplomacy: The FCO, 1782–1994*, London, Historical Branch, LRD, no. 6, May 1994, pp. 5, 8–9; the League of Women Voters in the United States epitomised the emphasis on civic, rather than gender, interests. See also R. D. Dean, *Imperial Brothrhood: Gender and the Making of Cold War Foreign Policy*, Amherst, University of Massachusetts Press, 2001, on its domination by elite white men.

8 The post-war women's movements

1 Pauli Murray on the role of women in the civil rights struggle, talk of 11 October 1962, pp. 4–5, Box 87, Folder 1522, Pauli Murray Papers, SL; A. Carter, *The Politics of Civil Rights*, London, Longman, 1988; League of Women Voters activities recorded in assorted folders, Dorothy Kirchwey Brown Papers, SL; and see Pugh, *Women and the Women's Movement*, second edition, chapter 10 and p. 312; Rupp and Taylor, *Surviving the Doldrums*, chapter 4; Young, *In the Public Interest*, pp. 173–4; E. G. Setch, 'The Women's Liberation Movement in Britain, 1969–1979: organisation, creativity and debate', University of London, PhD thesis, 2000, p. 20; R. Gatlin, *American Women since 1945*, Jackson, University of Mississippi Press, 1987; J. Lewis,

Women in Britain since 1945, Oxford, Blackwell, 1992; E. Wilson *Only Halfway to Paradise*, London, Tavistock, 1980.

2 F. Davis, *Moving the Mountain: The Women's Movement in America Since 1960*, 1991; M. L. Carden, *The New Feminist Movement*, New York, Russell Sage Foundation, 1974, Parts Three and Four; A. Coote and B. Campbell, *Sweet Freedom: The Struggle for Women's Liberation*, Oxford, Blackwell, 1987; Setch, 'The Women's Liberation Movement in Britain', Part II on Movement Creativity, and Part III on Movement Debate.

3 B. Bryan, D. Dadzie and S. Scafe, *The Heart of Race: Black Women's Lives in Britain*, London, Virago, 1985; J. Sudbury, *'Other Kinds of Dreams': Black Women's Organisations and the Politics of Transformation*, London and New York, Routledge, 1998; W. Webster, '"Race", ethnicity and national identity', in Zweiniger-Bergielowska (ed.), *Women in Twentieth-Century Britain*, chapter 19; W. Webster, *Imagining Home: Gender, 'Race', and National Identity 1945–64*, London, UCL Press, 1998.

4 See, for example, Hester Eisenstein, *Contemporary Feminist Thought*, London, Unwin Paperbacks, 1984, Second Impression; Carden, *The New Feminist Movement*, chapter 1; I. Whelehan, *Modern Feminist Thought: From the Second Wave to Post-Feminism*, Edinburgh, Edinburgh University Press, 1995; D. Bouchier, *Idealism and Revolution: New Ideologies of Liberation in Britain and the United States*, London, Edward Arnold, 1978; Kum-Kum Bhavnani (ed.), *Feminism and 'Race'*, Oxford Readings in Feminism, Oxford, Oxford University Press, 'Introduction' and p. 90; T. Lovell, *British Feminist Thought: A Reader*, Oxford, Basil Blackwell, 1990, especially Part III; G. G. Yates, *What Women Want: The Ideas of the Movement*, Cambridge, MA, Harvard University Press, 1975; R. D. Holden, 'The first New Left in Britain, 1956–1962', University of Wisconsin-Madison, PhD thesis, 1976, p. 261. J. Gelb, 'Social movement "success"', in Katzenstein and Mueller (eds), *The Women's Movements*, p. 271. As we have seen, the importance of the equality v difference debate is often exaggerated.

5 Coote and Campbell, *Sweet Freedom*, chapter 8; A. Snitow *et al.*, *Powers of Desire: The Politics of Sexuality*, New York, Monthly Review Press, 1983.

6 For an activist's view of the president's commissions for women, see interview with Emily Taylor, Council of Higher Education Office, Washington DC, 27 January 1982, Interviewer Lynn A. Bondfield, Emily Taylor Papers, SL; Rosenberg, *Divided Lives*, quotation from p. 216.

7 Bruley, *Women in Britain Since 1900*, pp. 158–9; Thane, 'Women in public and private', p. 278; Setch, 'The Women's Liberation Movement in Britain', chapters 1 and 7, and *passim*; E. Meehan, 'British feminism from the 1960s to the 1980s', in H. L. Smith (ed.), *British Feminism in the Twentieth Century*, Aldershot, 1990; H. L. Smith, 'The women's movement, politics and citizenship, 1960s–2000', in Zweiniger-Bargielowska (ed.), *Women in Twentieth-Century Britain*, chapter 18, quotation from p. 282; S. Rowbotham, *A Century of Women: The History of Women in Britain and the United States*, London, Viking, 1997, chapters 7 and 8.

8 See Coote and Campbell, *Sweet Freedom*; Setch, 'The Women's Liberation Movement in Britain', chapter 6; Bryan, Dadzie and Scarfe, *The Heart of Race*; Carden, *The New Feminist Movement*.

9 Folder; ERA, Box 22, Records of the National Council of Jewish Women, Group II, LC, especially news release of 22 September 1978 (source of quotation); 'The Equal Rights Amendment: Impact on Black America', issued by the NCNW, Box 92, Folder 1599, Pauli Murray Papers, SL; Florence Luscomb, May 1976, 'Action

Coalition for Equal Rights Amendment', Box 9, Folder 214, Florence Luscomb Papers, SL.

10 D. G. Matthews and J. S. DeHart, *Sex, Gender and the Politics of the ERA*, New York, Oxford University Press, 1990; Rupp and Taylor, *Survival in the Doldrums*, pp. 144f.; J. J. Mansbridge, *Why We Lost the ERA*, Chicago, Chicago University Press, 1986.

11 J. Radcliffe Richards, *The Sceptical Feminist: A Philosophical Enquiry*, Harmondsworth, Penguin, 1980, pp. 13–14 and *passim*.

12 Comment of 1975 feminist report on involvement in Mexico City conference, Box 138, Folder 2526, Pauli Murray Papers, SL; article on Florynce Kennedy, 18 October 1972, p. 6, Box 1, Florynce Kennedy Papers, SL.

13 Pauli Murray, 'Black Theology and Feminist Theology – A Comparative View', Box 87, Folder 1507, Pauli Murray Papers, SL. See also Murray's autobiography, *Pauli Murray: The Autobiography of a Black Activist, Feminist, Lawyer, Priest, and Poet*, Knoxville, University of Tennessee Press, 1987; and C. Taylor (ed.), *Black Religious Intellectuals*, New York and London, Routlege, 2002.

14 Pauli Murray to Mrs Clara Johnson, 8 September 1944, Box 87, Folder 1510, Pauli Murray Papers, SL.

15 Pauli Murray to editor of the *New York Times*, 9 March 1973, Box 87, Folder 1502, Pauli Murray Papers, SL.

16 'June 19, 1970. Statement of Dr Pauli Murray before the Special Committee on Education. In support of Section 805 of H. R. 16098', p. 5, Box 88, Folder 1540, Pauli Murray Papers, SL; and, in *ibid*., 'Jane Crow and the Law', 10 October 1969.

17 In Pauli Murray Papers: Memorandum to Mr Will Maslow from Murray, 7 February 1947, about the Japanese–American Citizen's League, Box 87, Folder 1512; 'The Brown Papers', National Institute for Women of Color, Box 92, Folder 1599; 'The Negro Woman in the Quest for Equality', Box 88, Folder 1528.

18 Rosenberg, *Divided Lives*, pp. 178–9.

19 In Pauli Murray Papers: 'Tribute to Mrs Rosa L. Parks', p. 16, Box 88, Folder 1530; Murray to Mr Oliver Jensen, Editor, American Heritage Publishing Co., 14 September 1971, Box 124, Folder 2226; note of 14 December 1983, Box 127, Folder 2317; 'Text of Address by Dr Pauli Murray at the Memorial Service for Dorothy Kenyon, 17 February 1972', Box 125, Folder 2269; Murray to John Fischer, *Harper's Magazine*, 9 August 1962; 'The Christian Woman's Responsibility for Human Rights', 14 May 1950, p. 10, Box 87, Folder 1516; and see, for instance, G. Murphy, '"Mr Roosevelt is guilty": Theodore Roosevelt and the crusade for constitutionalism, 1910–1912', *Journal of American Studies*, vol. 36, part 3, December 2002, pp. 445–6.

20 In Pauli Murray Papers: letter to the editor, *Washington Post*, 15 January 1977, Box 87, Folder 1502; 'A Feminist View of Nonviolence in the Resolution of Human Conflict', Box 87, Folder 1509; 'June 19, 1970, Statement of Dr Pauli Murray Before the Special Subcommittee on Education. In Support of Section 805 of H. R.16098', pp. 2, 4, 13, Box 88, Folder 1540; 'Response of Pauli Murray, Alumni Award, Harvard University Charter Day Dinner, 2 March 1970', pp. 2–3, Box 88, Folder 1540; 'American Law and the Black Community', 1972, Box 114, Folder 2052; letter of Murray, 28 September 1944, p. 2, Box 87, Folder 1510.

21 A. Barbrook and Christine Bolt, *Power and Protest in American Life*, Oxford, Martin Robertson, 1980, chapters 3–4; Christine Bolt, *American Indian Policy and American Reform: Case Studies of the Campaign to Assimilate the American Indians*, London, Allen and Unwin, 1987, pp. 268–9, chapter 12; L. Kurashige, *Japanese*

American Celebration and Conflict, Berkeley and Los Angeles, University of California Press, 2002.

22 A. N. Garcia, 'The development of Chicana feminist discourse, 1970–1980', in Ruiz and DuBois (eds), *Unequal Sisters*, pp. 538–40; Collins, *Black Feminist Thought*, p. 38 (source of quotation). I have mentioned some middle-class white coalitions (e.g. the WJCC and CCCW) on pp. 96–7 and the Standing Joint Committee of Industrial Women's Organizations on pp. 45, 55, 116 and 119; and see below, p. 251.

23 Bolt, *American Indian Policy*, p. 302; L. R. Wolfe and J. Tucker, 'Feminism lives: Building a multicultural women's movement in the United States', in Basu (ed.), *The Challenge of Local Feminisms*, p. 441; Florynce Kennedy, pp. 357–8, Box 1, Folder 1, Florynce Kennedy Papers, SL.

24 In Pauli Murray Papers, SL: 'June 19, 1970, Statement of Dr Pauli Murray Before the Special Subcommittee on Education. In Support of Section 805 of H. R. 16098', p. 8, Box 88, Folder 1540; 'New Vistas for Women of Tomorrow', 22 January 1950, p. 12, Box 87, Folder 1516.

25 See article, 'Black doubts in an age of white guilt', by S. Steele, *The Sunday Times*, 19 January 2003, News Review, p. 9.

26 F. P. Piven and R. A. Cloward, *Poor People's Movements: Why They Succeed: How They Fail*, New York, Pantheon Books, 1977, pp. 216–17: they acknowledge that black loyalty to the Democrats picked up again after 1960 (see p. 257).

27 Dr Julianne Malveaux, 'The Impact of Current Economic Trends on the Collective Consciousness of Black Women', p. 12, Box 92, Folder 1596, Pauli Murray Papers, SL; Florynce Kennedy Papers, SL, Box 1, Folder 1, p. 352; the attitudes of male radicals in the Students for Democratic Society resembled those complained of in the SNCC. Out of the large secondary literature, see especially B. Omalade, *The Rising Song of African-American Women*, New York, Routledge, 1997; B. Robnett, *'How Long, How Long'? African American Women in the Struggle for Civil Rights*, New York, Oxford University Press, 1997; V. Crawford, J. A. Rouse and B. Woods (eds), *Women in the Civil Rights Movement: Trailblazers and Torchbearers, 1941–1965*, New York, Carlson, 1990; S. Evans, *Personal Politics: The Roots of Women's Liberation in the Civil Rights Movement and the New Left*, New York, Knopf, 1980; P. Ling and S. Monteith (eds), *Gender in the Civil Rights Movement*, New York, Garland, 1999; K. Springer (ed.), *Still Lifting, Still Climbing: African American Women's Contemporary Activism*, New York, 1999; Caraway, *Segregated Sisterhood*, especially chapter 6; White, *Too Heavy a Load*, chapter 6; B. G. Sheftall, *Words of Fire: An Anthology of African-American Feminist Thought*, New York, New Press, distributed by W. W. Norton, 1995; W. Van Deburg, *Modern Black Nationalism*, New York, New York University Press, 1997; D. L. Schultz, *Jewish Women in the Civil Rights Movement*, New York, New York University Press, 2001, and letters in Box 22, Group II, Records of the National Council of Jewish Women, LC.

28 Elizabeth Anne Castle, 'Black and Native American Women's Activism in the Black Panther Party and the American Indian Movement', PhD Dissertation, University of Cambridge, 2000.

29 Garcia, 'The development of Chicana feminist discourse', quotation from p. 541.

30 See Bryan, Dadzie and Scafe, *Heart of the Race*, chapter 4, quotation from p. 176; Coote and Campbell, *Sweet Freedom*, pp. 28–31 and *passim*; A. Wilson, *Finding a Voice: Asian Women in Britain*, London, Virago, 1978; Collins, *Black Feminist Thought*, pp. 26–8, 39–41 and *passim*; H. S. Mirza (ed.), *Black British Feminism: A*

Reader, Routledge, London and New York, 1997, pp. 37 and *passim*: see especially the article by H. Carby; P. B. Rich, *Race and Empire in British Politics*, Cambridge, Cambridge University Press, 1986, pp. 198–9, 202; Wolfe and Tucker, 'Feminism Lives', p. 451; G. T. Nain, 'Black women, sexism and racism: Black or antiracist feminism', in M. Githens, P. Norris and J. Lovenduski (eds), *Different Roles, Different Voices: Women and Politics in the United States and Europe*, New York, HarperCollins, 1994, pp. 214f.; Setch, 'The Women's Liberation Movement in Britain', pp. 56, 59, 60–1, 83, 86; and Caraway, *Segregated Sisterhood*, p. 172f. on the difficulties inherent in seeking to create a 'multicultural politics of solidarity'.

31 Basu (ed.), *The Challenge of Local Feminisms*, pp. 3, 13, 18, 98 (source of quotation), 106, 319, 446; Lubin and Winslow, *Social Justice for Women*, p. 6; see also A. Winslow, *Women, Politics and the United Nations*, Westport, CT, Greenwood Press, 1995.

32 See material on the International Women's Year in Folder 222, Box 10, Florence Luscomb Papers, SL; and Jewish women's support for it in a news release of 17 October 1977 in Records of the National Council of Jewish Women, Group II, Box 22, LC.

33 Jeffreys-Jones, *Changing Differences*, pp. 104, 129, 161, chapter 8 and *passim*; P. J. Conover, 'Feminists and the gender gap', in Githens, Norris and Lovenduski (eds), *Different Roles, Different Voices*, pp. 51–60; E. Klein, 'The diffusion of consciousness in the United States and Western Europe', in Katzenstein and Mueller (eds), *The Jewish Women's Movements*, pp. 29–30.

34 Liddington, *The Long Road to Greenham*, pp. 172f.; Alonso, *Peace as a Women's Issue*, pp. 193f., 220, 226; *Twenty-Sixth International Congress of the Women's International League for Peace and Freedom: 80 Years and Beyond, Report*, Helsinki, Finland, 1995, p. 9, source of quotation; Coote and Campbell, *Sweet Freedom*, p. 49; L. R. Forcey, 'Women as peacemakers: contested terrain for feminist peace studies', *Peace and Change*, vol.16, no. 4, 1991; A. Harris and Y. King (eds), *Rocking the Ship of State: Towards a Feminist Peace Politics*, Boulder, CO, Westview Press, 1989; on Jewish women's opposition to militarism, and the Vietnam War, see material in Records of the National Council of Jewish Women, Group II, Box 23.

35 See J. M. Berry, *Lobbying for the People: The Political Behavior of Public Interest Groups*, Princeton, NJ, Princeton University Press, 1977, p. 176, who argues that WILPF had not 'become a source of information for congressional offices'; V. Amos and P. Parmar, 'Challenging imperial feminism', in Bhavnani (ed.), *Feminism and Race*, p. 29; Rupp and Taylor, *Survival in the Doldrums*, pp. 136f., on 'Communism, Anti-Communism, and the Co-optation of McCarthyism'.

36 Liddington, *The Long Road to Greenham*, pp. 207–9 (source of quotation), 212; see also S. Mathé (ed.), *L'Antiamericanisme: Anti-Americanism at Home and Abroad*, Aix-en-Provence, University of Provence, 2000.

37 Caine, *English Feminism*, pp. 253f.; Setch, 'The Women's Liberation Movement in Britain', pp. 13–14, 176, 241; A. Echols, *Daring to be Bad: Radical Feminism in America, 1967–1975*, Minneapolis, University of Minnesota Press, 1989.

38 See, for example, Camille Paglia, Catherine MacKinnon, Naomi Wolf and Kate Roiphe.

39 See folder on British-American Associates, Personal Papers, Six Point Group, 1961–78, Box 549, WL.

40 'Better View of Americans: East Bay Woman Corrects Some of Britain's Distorted Ideas', by Janet Henderson, 15 December 1966, Folder 102, Dorothy Kirchwey Brown Papers, SL; and in *ibid.*, 'British Learn Home Truths About Us', by Joan

McKinney, 15 December 1955; and information on the LWV's Overseas Education Fund in *ibid.*, Folder 103; Whately references in Six Point Papers, WL; and see documents in Mary Dingham Papers, SL.

41 In Maida Springer Kemp Papers, SL: 'Urban League Fellowship – Oxford, England, 1952–1953', 15 February 1954, p. 5, Folder 2 and 'Report of the Urban League on 1951–1952', Study Abroad, p. 20, Folder 2; Richards, *Maida Springer*; 'Women's Battle for Status', 12 February 1946, p. 9, Box 13, File 188, Elinore M. Herrick Papers, SL; and 'Memorandum for Secretary of State, the Honorable John Foster Dulles', Box 10, Folder 1320, Alice Paul Papers, SL; N. Ferguson, *Empire: How Britain Made the Modern World*, London, Penguin Books, 2003, p. 351; Folder on Foreign Policy, 1965–79, statement by Mrs Donald Brown, Records of the National Council of Jewish Women, Group II, Box 23, on the need for selective foreign assistance. And see Laville, *Cold War Women*, on the shift towards Americanisation.

42 Rich, *Race and Empire*, pp. 204, 207–9.

43 Bruley, *Women in Britain Since 1900*, p. 164 (second quotation); Soldon (ed.), *The World of Women's Trade Unions*, pp. 26–7; and on the United States see R. Milkman, 'Feminism and Labor since the 1970s', in Milkman (ed.), *Women, Work and Protest*, pp. 301f.; Lewenhak, *Women and Trade Union*, chapter 16; and J. J. Keneally, *Women and American Trade Unions*, St. Albans, VT, Eden Press Women's Publications, 1978, chapter 12; Florence Luscomb interviewed in *The Twentieth Century Trade Union Woman*, p. 35 (first quotation), SL.

44 M. Rose, 'Gender awareness among Chicanas and Mexicanas in the United Farm Workers of America', p. 480, in Norton and Alexander (eds), *Major Problems in American Women's History*; see also Matthews, *The Rise of the Public Woman*, pp. 232–3; V. Green, *Race on the Line*, Durham, NC, Duke University Press, 2001; X. Bao, *Holding Up More Than Half the Sky*, Urbana, University of Illinois Press, 2001.

45 Interview with Mary Callahan of the International Union of Electrical Workers, pp. 44–5, by Alice Hoffman, in *The Twentieth Century Trade Union Woman*, SL; other useful interviews include those with Catherine Conroy by Elizabeth Balanoff, pp. 65, 68 (second quotation); Mary Baker by Constance Myers; Ruth Weincek by Carol Bowie; Mary Baker by Constance Myers; and Antoinette Podojil by Lydia Kleiner p. 95 (third quotation); Coote and Campbell, *Sweet Freedom*, pp. 164, 173–4; R. Milkman (ed.), *Women, Work and Protest*, pp. 307–9.

46 Interview with Catherine Conroy by Elizabeth Balanoff, pp. 71, 82, SL; O. Banks, *The Politics of British Feminism*, Aldershot, Edward Elgar, 1993, p. 38.

47 Article by Milkman, 'Women workers, feminism and the labor movement since the 1960s', in Milkman (ed.), *Women, Work and Protest*, p. 311; and see D. A. Deslippi, *'Rights not Roses': Unions and the Rise of Working-class Feminism, 1945–80*, Urbana, University of Illinois Press, 2000, on shifting strategies by women and diverse union responses.

48 Milkman, 'Women workers', pp. 312–14.

49 *Ibid.*, pp. 314–5.

50 *Ibid.*, pp. 315–18.

51 Coote and Campbell, *Sweet Freedom*, pp. 137–8.

52 *Ibid.*, pp. 138–9.

53 *Ibid.*, pp. 156–9.

54 *Ibid.*, pp. 155, 157; Gelb, 'Social movement "success"', in Katzenstein and Mueller (eds), *The Women's Movements*, pp. 278–81.

55 Matthews, *Rise of the Public Woman*, p. 232; Bruley, *Women in Britain Since 1900*, p. 168; R. Terborg-Penn, 'Survival strategies among African-American women workers: A continuing process', in Milkman (ed.), *Women, Work and Protest*, pp. 172–5; Brittain, *The Politics of Whiteness.*

56 See Lubin and Winslow, *Social Justice for Women*, pp. 5–7, chapters 4–5.

57 See, particularly, the work of Sheila Rowbotham; and Eisenstein, *Contemporary Feminist Thought*, chapters 2 and 13, p. 132 (source of quotation); Pugh, *Women and the Women's Movement in Britain*, pp. 329–30.

58 Rosenberg, *Divided Lives*, pp. 222f.

59 Rupp and Taylor, *Survival in the Doldrums*, p. 158f.

9 Conclusion

1 Katherine Courtney to Miss Roelofs, 13 February 1931, Box 19, Committee on the Cause and Cure of War Papers, SL.

2 Miller, 'Lobbying the League', p. viii, notes that the peace lobby at the League remained united. I have referred (p. 245) to the work of the Joint Standing Committee of the Women's International Organisation and of the Liaison Committee of Women's International Organisations. And see chapter 8, note 22.

3 See the work of Joan Scott.

4 See, for instance, V. S. Peterson (ed.), *Gendered States: Feminist (Re) Visions of International Relations Theory*, Boulder, CO, and London, Lynne Reinner Publishers, 1992; R. Grant and K. Newland, *Gender and International Relations*, Milton Keynes, Open University Press, 1991; J. A. Tickner, *Gender in International Relations: Feminist Perspectives on Achieving Global Security*, New York, Columbia University Press, 1992. On the need for a transnational rather than international methodology, see Myall, 'Introduction'.

5 Black, 'The mother's international', pp. 474–5, touches on the debate over whether women's pacifism set them apart from men in a reactionary and unhelpful manner.

6 See, for instance, Bhavnani (ed.), *Feminism and 'Race'.*

7 Lady May Drummond-Hay to Doris Stevens, 23 July 1928, Folder 121, Miscellaneous 'H' Correspondence, Doris Stevens Unclassified Papers, Doris Stevens Papers, SL.

8 Lucy Burns to Doris Stevens, 18 November 1942, and 25 November 1957, in which she wishes Stevens tranquillity; explains her own aversion to 'racketing around the world' and to life with 'no center at all'; and remembers the early days of the NWP, implying that its early purity, like that of movements generally, had been lost: Doris Stevens Unclassified Papers, Folder 79, Doris Stevens Papers, SL.

9 Mrs Stephen Pell to the editor, *New York Times*, 20 December 1933, in Box 102, Folder 1348, Alice Paul Papers, SL.

Index